NICE GUY FINISHES FIRST:
THE
CLARKE WILLIAMS
STORY
AND THE BUILDING OF
TELECOMMUNICATIONS GIANT
CenturyLink®

Leo Honeycutt

The
LISBURN
PRESS

The Lisburn Press
www.TheLisburnPress.com

The
LISBURN
PRESS

THE LISBURN PRESS
3115 OLD FORGE DRIVE
BATON ROUGE, LOUISIANA 70808

NICE GUY FINISHES FIRST:
THE CLARKE WILLIAMS STORY
Copyright © 2014 by Leo Honeycutt

PUBLISHED IN THE UNITED STATES OF AMERICA

Visit our website at TheLisburnPress.com.

First edition published October 2014

Cover design by Sarah Powell
Text design by Kim Springfield
Editors – Patricia Stallman, Toni Lee
Author photo by Brian Pavlich

Library of Congress Cataloging-in-Publication Data is available.

ISBN: 978-0-578-14856-4

For information regarding special discounts for bulk purchases, please contact The Lisburn Press Special Sales at info@LisburnPress.com.

Printed in Canada

This book is printed on acid-free paper.

CLARKE WILLIAMS, MY FATHER

By Carolyn Williams Perry

I have been asked why I wanted my father's story written and retained Louisiana Literary Award winner Leo Honeycutt to write it. In going through pictures, letters, and newspaper articles, and in conducting interviews with those close to Mother and Daddy, I have not only relived precious memories, I have also realized the impact my parents had on my life and the lives of those with whom they came in contact. I wanted to preserve those memories for my family; however, I have come to believe that many people can appreciate the struggles and successes of a man who truly placed humility first and success second.

It was not my intent to create a history of Century Telephone Enterprises (CenturyLink), though the company played an integral part in the life of my father and my family. When Daddy began by buying Oak Ridge Telephone Company, all of the employees were family members. Today, the Century Link family comprises 47,000 people. It is my hope that in reading this book those employees will feel a sense of family, by relating both to my father's struggles building the company and to the principles he fostered.

I want to thank CenturyLink President Glen Post and Chairman of the Board Admiral Bill Owens for always including Daddy when talking about the principles upon which Century Link operates. Those were principles he lived, and I hope all who knew him will always remember those principles as his legacy. Both personally and professionally, he walked the walk.

If I could leave the reader with one thought it would be: "Good guys can finish first."

Carolyn Williams Perry

FROM THE AUTHOR

Riverbend, Baton Rouge
July 2014

The telephone was a mistake.

No, not in the sense that it consumes the lives of the younger generation or in the sense that in this day and age we might be too connected. The telephone was a mistake like so many inventions are. It was a byproduct of what Alexander Graham Bell had really intended to create which was an electric device to enable his deaf mother and deaf wife to hear. Bell went to his grave wealthy but disheartened that he failed in that purpose. He changed the world but those he loved never escaped the great silence.

Clarke McRae Williams is a fascinating story inside the fascinating story of telecommunications. In researching his life and industry, I had to go back to the germ from which sprang our indispensible cellphones today. You will find in these pages stories of eternal hope and how those with faith succeed. Clarke Williams, like Aleck Bell, could have given up on his dreams at any turn. His obstacles came frequently. His financials screamed bankruptcy for half his life.

But he didn't give up.

Mr. Williams was buoyed up by an undying faith in God, in himself and in his fellow man even in his darkest hours. He always put others first and proved scripture true that to be the greatest, a wise man chooses to be the least. That is the polar opposite of today's egomaniacal culture that praises the winner-take-all, self-made man. Clarke Williams proved business can be conducted fairly, honestly and inclusive of all parties, and that one can succeed by staying true to himself, his beliefs, his faith, and true to everyone else.

How did he have such enormous courage? Where did he get such an iron shield to deflect the slings and arrows and not retaliate when he was hurt? Dear friends turned on him as well as some family. But he kept going out of his way to befriend.

That's what this book is about. Doing it the right way, both in business and in life. I was curious about the environment that created such a person so I jumped back to his forebears and found a genealogical kinship to pioneer Daniel Boone. Nearly all of Clarke Williams' ancestors were trailblazers, unbowed by difficulty. In that age, there were no excuses. Mr. Williams adopted that attitude early.

This book has a dual purpose. The first half of the book chronicles the building of the man, Clarke McRae Williams. For family, friends and those interested, the Williams family genealogy is included as groundwork for all that came later. Life is a series of random turns until someone along the line organizes the effort, either by genius or divine guidance. Clarke Williams had the genius to listen to divine guidance in a world that delights in confusion.

The second half, starting with Chapter Six, takes a close look at how he masterminded the building of a great company. His success sprang from more than simple acquisitions. He mastered caring for others enough to consistently deny himself, a quality of such refinement as to elude most of us much of the time. I saw this for myself.

In a twist of irony, I met Clarke Williams three decades ago when I was a young television news reporter. I didn't know Century Telephone existed, but my wife Jackie and I spent two weeks on a church mission trip with Clarke and Mary Kathryn Williams in June 1984. I was filming a travelogue and documentary on a herd of teenage Christian singers performing across Europe. To justify the trip, I stopped in Britain to cover the 1984 London Economic Summit with President Ronald Reagan and British Prime Minister Margaret Thatcher. Though I had been in the Oval Office with President Reagan the year before, he avoided my questions most likely because I had the misfortune of standing next to Sam Donaldson of ABC News. Sam continually shouted at the president and the president continually ignored him. We all wanted to slap Sam.

Conversely, quiet Mr. Williams was so low key and unassuming, you hardly knew he was there. He helped carry my television gear without a word. His countenance was serene and giving and, aside from a few laughs, few words passed between us. My career path led me away from Monroe and I never saw Mr. Williams again but his spirit and compassion never left me.

A decade after his death in 2002, daughter Carolyn Perry felt the memory of her father's spirit and compassion slipping away. To her great credit, she took unprecedented and enormous action to capture her father's spirit for her children, their children and all of CenturyLink's over 40,000 employees and their families. Mrs. Perry wanted her father remembered in writing, not in some fanciful, sentimental, self-indulgent look back but in an attempt to capture that golden intangible for which he stood and translate that to anyone willing to listen. It is our hope that through this book, he will still teach.

I will be forever grateful to Carolyn and Harvey Perry for bringing me into this project. I am particularly grateful to Glen Post, president of CenturyLink, for taking precious time out of his tight schedule to help and encourage me along the way, as did directors former Congressman Dick Gephardt and Admiral Bill Owens; also, C. G. Melville, Calvin Czeschin, other board members, employees, and old friend John Jones for sharing so much. James H. "Jim" Brown of Lisburn Press always goes beyond the standard to carve out a quality book. Thanks also to many friends who offered quiet retreats: Tony and Annette Byrne, Arlin Dease, Bob Dean, and Gladys and Gloria Solomon. And as usual, thanks to English teacher Toni Lee for guiding my voice. Forty years later and she's still grading my papers. Also, veteran editor Patricia Stallman painstakingly proofed and offered invaluable advice.

Finally, I thank my parents, L. B. and Marie Honeycutt and sister Amanda, for the guidance that prepared me to write this book; and, of course, thanks to my wife Jackie who perseveres along with daughter Danielle and her husband Corey, and son Jarrod and his fiancé Ally. Now with granddaughter Evangeline, it starts all over except this time I have far greater perspective. I once had grandfathers, now I am one. That changes everything in ways you will understand when you get there. Smiles and giggles make the inevitable departure such sweet sorrow.

It is my sincere and fervent hope that you and I both will take the spirit of Clarke Williams with us from here on. We will be much better people, no doubt about it. He was always asked for his secret. Well, here it is.

FOREWORD

By GLEN F. Post, III
President & CEO, CenturyLink

It was my first opportunity to join Chairman and CEO, Clarke Williams, aboard the company's modest Beechcraft Queen Air turboprop. We were traveling to Hershey, Pennsylvania for the annual Convention of the United States Independent Telephone Association. Mr. Williams and I were joined by our wives, Mary Kathryn and Cynthia, and Executive Vice President R.L. Hargrove and his wife Lila.

I was thirty years old and newly appointed to the company's executive team. It was half a lifetime ago, but its memory seems so fresh.

As we initiated our approach to the airfield in Hershey, Mr. Williams (neither the manners instilled by my mother nor my respect for the man himself ever permitted me to address him as "Clarke") was quiet, watching through the window as the plane caught up to the shadow it had cast upon the runway. His countenance was relaxed and cordial; his manner graceful and humble.

Cynthia and I had climbed the steps of the plane earlier that day in Monroe, Louisiana with the same sense of quiet trepidation we felt when I had recently accepted Mr. Williams' invitation to join the executive team. Mr. Williams though welcomed us aboard and instinctively, effortlessly, labored to make Cynthia and I comfortable and to feel as if we belonged. He was a remarkable man, a man who lived by the values he bequeathed to his organization: Fairness, or the Golden Rule; Honesty and Integrity; Commitment to Excellence; Postive Attitude; Respect; Faith; Perseverance.

Upon our return to Monroe from Hershey, Cynthia and I reflected upon the trip. I told her, "I want to be like Mr. Williams one of these days." She smiled mischievously and replied, "I'm not sure that's possible!" Thirty years later, I'm still working to catch up to the shadow cast by this great man.

Clarke Williams was a man of vision, compassion, and wisdom. He touched the lives of many, and left a legacy of personal and professional success. He conducted business as he lived life, with integrity and generosity. His success established that compassion and faith have a place in the corporate world, and, indeed, are essential elements of "life and life abundant."

Clarke Williams was a man – he was a mentor – whom I'll never forget.

Glen

This book is dedicated to my Mother and Father, Mary Kathryn and Clarke Williams, and to each employee of CenturyLink who keeps their spirit of giving alive.

- Carolyn Williams Perry

CHAPTER 1

A loud click echoed through the cavernous stained-glass church. Hushed faces lined the pews, wall-to-wall, some mourners having flown in to Monroe, Louisiana, from far away, filling Parkview Baptist Church, quietly huddling as cars zoomed by on Forsythe Boulevard. When Babe Ruth played baseball mere feet away in Forsythe Park, Clarke McRae Williams' father sat in the stands. Now both his father and his son were gone.

Click. The funeral director shut the coffin lid on Clarke McRae Williams, Junior. Senior grimaced. Hundreds of eyes watched the aging founder of Century Telephone, Louisiana's version of AT&T and Alexander Graham Bell. Clarke McRae Williams, Senior, had turned seventy-five customers of Oak Ridge Telephone Company into three million in less than fifty years, leveraging billions in debt into innumerable acquisitions. He was a millionaire many times over, yet the money was, today, worthless.

The click punctuated a life that began forty-four years earlier when he raced to a Shreveport hospital with his young bride Mary Kathryn next to him. The birth of Clarke McRae Williams, Junior, was as clear as yesterday, flailing arms and legs and a good set of lungs. Sitting in the church, moments flickered through the father's mind, the baby's cries, tiny limbs, little legs running. Tickling, giggles, awed happiness on Christmas morning. The Boy Scout, the ball player, the playboy, the charmer, the Wall Street wunderkind, and the telecommunications giant. Clarke Junior had taken the baton and run with it, eclipsing his father's great success to catapult the family business into an industry leader.

Now the son's work was done, sound and fury gone like vapor on a cold morning. Perhaps if the son had known his life was half over at 22 in Vietnam, he might have taken a different path. The father considered, *Wouldn't we all want to know what's ahead?* Then, *It's probably fortunate that we don't know and leave the choreography to God.*

He remembered his son's anger when he had refused to pull the appropriate strings to keep Clarke Junior out of the Indochinese hell. The two clashed on discipline. As much as the father was a stickler for meticulous hard work and cautious humility, the son skewed just the opposite—boisterous, edgy, full-speed ahead. As different as they were, however, both Clarkes had vision. Clarke Junior had been right about the war and the insidious destructiveness it would bring to a proud America. Just as the son had feared, the psychological warfare that contaminated America paled in comparison to the actual disease he brought home.

Clarke Junior rose through the ranks in his father's business and arrived at the precise moment cellular appeared. He saw the potential long before almost everyone else did, including many at AT&T. The cellular shift was the real reason for Ma Bell's breakup, and that breakup opened the floodgates for Century Telephone. Clarke Junior barreled ahead into uncharted territory, fearless to grab all the licenses Century and its shareholders could afford and then some. Clarke Senior agonized over the sudden, dangerously risky move, but he had to admit it: Clarke Junior was right again.

Father and son had a history of going against the norm. Managers at Bell Telephone ridiculed a young Clarke Senior, insisting that his business model—buying up third-rate mom-and-pop telephone exchanges in rural areas, where a mile of wire reaped one customer—would not work. That's why the smart money stayed in cities. But Clarke Williams was a country boy at heart and his heart was with country people and country churches. He churned debt like taffy to make that model work and, with God's blessing, it did.

Then renegade visionary Clarke Junior took the foundation his father laid and springboarded the company into the stratosphere. Again, what should not have worked, did work.

Now on this bright May day, marred by death, what did work, froze temporarily. Everyone surrounding the father as he buried his son questioned God and such a cruel turn for such a righteous man. No parent should bury a child, but for a Godly man who had helped so many, the injustice was beyond cruel.

Clarke Williams sat on the pew as a real-life Job. If he ever questioned why God had thus rewarded his hard work and planning and doing the right thing, he never said it. He never even intimated it. He was wiser for his intense study of scripture, wiser for stringing miles of telephone wire until his hands bled, wiser for the faces of grateful country customers, wiser for the faces of men in suits who counted money, wiser for friends who became family and built alongside him, and ultimately wiser for those who betrayed him.

Wisdom was the only value a person could really accumulate. Moments in time are the only possession. He learned that early. On days of funerals, money, property, cars, houses, all the window-dressing of success washed away. Nothing was more important than being important to someone else. Nothing was more valuable than love, especially love earned in the fractured dysfunction called families.

Clarke blocked out his dying son's mad rages in those last days, recognizing the hurt pride and injustice of a body decimated in the cause of freedom. Both men had been dealt a bad hand on this one, but Clarke Senior knew from youth that for Godly men all hands ultimately win. Lasting happiness depended on reactions and on the ability to tell the difference between leading life or letting life whipsaw you. The world loves drama and that drama keeps Man agitated and that agitation robs his potential. Clarke thanked God in the presence of his dead son for allowing him the humility to remain quiet when others shouted. He had made a bright pathway for thousands of families as a result. Instead of Job, he was more like Moses splitting an ocean of impossibility.

In Clarke's hard-fought battle for wisdom, he had learned life's paradox: By being least, you become great; by being last, you become first. He was living proof.

That paradox started long before he did. The story of Clarke Williams' success began long before his first breath.

PART I
STARTING THE DREAM

CHAPTER 2

From the moment Alexander Graham Bell uttered, "Mr. Watson, come here. I want to see you," the world has never been the same. Voice communication flashed across copper wire, overtaking the telegraph in its golden age, never to look back. The world sped up and compressed. The decade after the Civil War, America was rebuilding and innovating, and speech pathologist Aleck Bell in Massachusetts was teaching and tinkering. He made that first telephone call on March 10, 1876, three days after he procured U.S. Patent number 174,465 from which every telephone on Earth derives.

But the Scotsman never intended to change anything at all. A third generation speech pathologist, Aleck Bell's goal was to amplify sound so that his deaf mother, Eliza Grace Bell, and his deaf wife, Mabel Hubbard Bell, could hear. His whole life he prayed, studied, and worked in the hope of a breakthrough so that Eliza and Mabel could join the rest of the family in sharing laughter and music. He found he could talk to both by placing his chin on their foreheads and speaking loudly. They could hear his words through bone resonance.

Aleck desperately wanted Mabel to hear the voices of their children. He longed for all deaf people to hear without reading lips, to hear birds chirping in the spring, the clip clop of horses' hooves on cobblestone, Beethoven's Fifth Symphony, the church choir. His speech professor father Dr. Alexander Melville Bell had immersed young Aleck in the study of sound waves, and the boy began to couple hundreds of ideas. From train windows, studying miles of shiny telegraph lines sagging up and down, he calculated how to convert human sound into electric impulses. Morse Code, a new form of human communication, was nothing more than the opening and closing an electric circuit. If staccato dots and dashes could streak along those wires, clicking handsets a hundred miles away, why couldn't he turn a human voice into electric impulses to resonate through a skull three feet away?

Growing up in Scotland, Bell read stories of U. S. President Abraham Lincoln's living in the Washington telegraph office during America's Civil War, anxious for news from the battlefield to help determine strategy. Communication was important, Bell saw, but speed was more important. As a teacher of deaf pupils, he lived daily with the frustration of his students' difficulty understanding him.

After Bell's two brothers died of tuberculosis, his parents, fearing respiratory ailments, moved to Canada in 1870. Bell, then 23, moved with them. Soon, he was hired to teach deaf instruction to Massachusetts teachers. Everywhere he landed, he continued to experiment in search of creating what he called an "acoustic telegraph."

A tinkerer all his life, Aleck invented a wheat-husking device when he was twelve, manipulated the vocal cords of the family dog to say, "How are you, grandma?" to the delight of neighbors, and, with his brother, made a lifelike talking head with working larynx and vocal cords. Bell studied the tuning fork experiments of German researcher Hermann von Helmholtz, as well as the works of philologist Alexander Ellis, from whom playwright George Bernard Shaw would derive Professor Henry Higgins in *Pygmalion*.

In Cambridge in 1871, having just turned 24, Bell focused his combined knowledge on experiments with electricity. After five years of work, he assembled a black and brass cylindrical concoction, first by stretching a membrane over the mouth of a cup, then turning the cup over and cutting a hole in the cup's bottom to form a mouthpiece. In the membrane, now on bottom, Bell placed a cork with a platinum needle.[1] That formed a diaphragm to vibrate sound waves. He then placed a second cup upright beneath the first, poured water into it, and eased the needle in the cork down into the water.

Into the water, he immersed a brass pipe, connecting it to a battery-electrified wire that ran to what he termed a solenoid-

---

[1] Alexander Graham Bell handwritten laboratory notes, March 10, 1876, page 40, United States Library of Congress Special Collections, http://lcweb2.loc.gov/cgi-bin/ampage

type "armature receiving device." He placed the receiving device, connected by the wire, in a closed-off adjoining room.

Completing the circuit, a wire ran from the delicate needle also to the electromagnetic armature in the adjoining room, where assistant Thomas Watson pressed his ear firmly against it. Watson pressed a hand tightly over the other ear, straining to hear a human voice vibrate the receiver. He waited to hear something, anything.

At last he heard Bell's tinny but distinct voice, *Mr. Watson, come here. I want to see you*, a deliberate instruction. Watson suppressed a shout. He flung open the door to Bell's room and joyously proclaimed, "You called?" Bell asked him to repeat the sentences exactly as he had heard them. Watson did so word for word.

The years of Bell's mother and wife living in silence were over, he hoped. He had just turned 29 the week before he made the world's first telephone call.

Half jesting in their brief celebration, Bell asked Watson, "Do you think people would actually pay to talk to each other?" They both shrugged. "Talk is cheap," they agreed, but even if Bell's resonance device failed to help deaf people hear, it would at least take audible voices wherever wire could be run, advancing telegraphy a huge leap forward. Western Union already had a vast copper wire network and now Bell had created an acoustic breakthrough.

Young Aleck Bell thought Western Union would be ecstatic, immediately offering to sell his patents to the company for $100,000. Western Union president William Orton laughed him out of the office, scoffing, "What use could this company make of an electric toy?" Orton ate those words within two years when he begged Bell to sell his patents for $2 million. Too late. Bell had started building out his own network. Eventually his company, American Telephone & Telegraph, would devour Western Union.

Bell sold the idea of a telephone network to his wealthy father-in-law and other investors, creating a sudden need to convert capital into copper. The Wall Street race was on. Seven decades later, Louisiana entrepreneur Clarke McRae Williams would duplicate Bell's capitalism, building out a niche that Bell's company left behind.

At the outset, trouble for Bell began immediately. The impractical water transmitter design was that of inventor Elisha Gray who filed for a patent the very same day as Bell, but weeks before Bell had an agent in Great Britain file his design there. The British Patent Office would issue patents only for discoveries not already patented elsewhere. Though Bell was considered first to make the design work, he and Gray would spend years in court fighting over patent rights.

Sixty days after he had called Watson, Bell substantially defused Gray's claim by unveiling a much-improved dry version of the transmitter at America's first World's Fair, the United States Centennial Exposition in Philadelphia. Alongside inventors of the Remington typewriter and Heinz ketchup, Bell and Watson dazzled thousands by demonstrating the device they named *the telephone*. In May 1876, the Exposition drew an estimated ten million visitors, among them agents of Britain's Queen Victoria. Within days, the Queen requested a private demonstration by a man she considered a British subject. The 29-year-old inventor nervously talked into his device, and Queen Victoria heard his crisp words on the receiver. Elated that a British inventor had made a scientific world breakthrough, Her Majesty told the press that the Scotsman's device was "most extraordinary." News streaked across Europe, but it would be many years before the novelty gained acceptance.[2]

In 1877, a young New Jersey inventor named Thomas Edison, older than Bell by only three weeks, perfected a much clearer carbon microphone that Bell immediately adopted. His company would use Edison's design in Bell telephones for the entire next century. Bell returned the favor by creating a multi-use wax disc for Edison's phonograph.

In the first decade, the convenience of voice communications became apparent with over 150,000 telephones in use in the United States. Each phone required its own wire,

---

[2] Ross, Stewart. *Alexander Graham Bell* (Scientists who Made History series). (New York: Raintree Steck-Vaughn Publishers, 2001. ISBN 0-7398-4415-6) pp 21-22.

however, and Bell noticed city streets gradually darken with thousands of telephone lines. He conceived of a way to use sunlight to transmit voice.

On June 21, 1880, Bell's Washington, D.C., assistant, Charles Sumner Tainter, captured a beam of sunlight on the roof of the Franklin School and transmitted his voice on the light beam to a parabolic receiver Bell held in his lab window 700 feet away. The ingenious invention became the world's first wireless telephone, nineteen years before the advent of radio and a century before cellular telephones. While Bell's photophone inspired fiber optics, his invention was impractical. It required sunny days and line-of-sight between transmitter and receiver.

Thomas Edison was creating an invention that could have helped Bell but it came too late. Edison perfected a 1,200-hour electric light bulb. Another twenty-five years of trial and error would pass before he arrived at virtually indestructible tungsten, too late for the photophone. Bell would go to his grave claiming the photophone—not the telephone—was his greatest achievement.

In a remarkable four years, from 1876 to 1880, Bell and Edison advanced the world's communications, electricity, lighting, and the permanent recording of sound beyond all centuries of such discoveries combined.

By 1917, four decades after Bell's first call, telephone wires finally etched southward into rural northeast Mississippi. In Iuka, the telephone fascinated young orphan William Clarke Williams, who would become the father of CenturyLink's Clarke McRae Williams. Both would be children of adversity.

Will Clarke Williams' great-grandfather Reuben Holman Boone, third cousin to Daniel Boone, received 160 acres of ceded Chickasaw land in Toshimingo County from President John Tyler in 1842.[3] Reuben's great-grandfather had been uncle to the famous explorer, and those stories later illuminated Will Clarke's imagination. Reuben Boone's 19-year-old daughter,

---

[3] United States Federal Land Grant document #11472, April 9, 1842, Old Tishomingo County, Mississippi, found at www.ancestry.com/tree/53140441/person/13664492623/media/3

Mary Leftwich "Polly" Boone, married Will Clarke's grandfather, Charles Wesley Williams, in June 1837. Civil engineer C.W. Williams surveyed the Chickasaw cessation,[4] became the first postmaster of Rienzi, Mississippi and a Mississippi legislator, and lost a fortune building the ill-fated *Mobile & Ohio Railroad* three months before the Civil War broke out.

C. W. was taught by Scottish surveyor James Brown who gave him the works of Sir Walter Scott, the world's first international English novelist. Scott's romantic themes of honor and chivalry weaved through his novel *Ivanhoe*, his biography of Napoleon Bonaparte, and his poem *Marmion* in which he coined the phrase, "Oh what a tangled web we weave when first we practice to deceive!" Thus, when C.W. and Polly Boone's last child was born in 1851, the boy was named Walter Scott Williams.

In 1877, Walter Scott Williams married Mary Jane "Molly" Barton, and on October 19, 1894, William Clarke Williams was born, the eighth of twelve children. Eight years later, his mother overheated in the kitchen and stepped out into a freezing wind to cool off. Walter warned her, "Molly, darling, you'll catch your death."[5]

Molly caught pneumonia and died three days later, leaving Walter to grieve himself to death. He died nine months to the day later, one week after Will's eighth birthday. In nine months, Will's happy, noisy house fell into dark silence, all warmth and stability gone. Relatives split up the six smaller children. Molly's widowed sister Harriet Barton Knowles sent her unmarried 26-year-old daughter Kitty Lou from Iuka to get two-year-old baby Charles with the instruction, "If you can't get the baby, bring the curly-headed little boy."[6] Kitty got curly-headed 8-year-old Will Clarke and carted him twenty miles east.

---

[4] Old Tishomingo County, Mississsippi, History: 1814-1894, specifically the "Mrs. Marvin Smitherman & Scott O. Fraser History"

[5] Mary Lee Williams Oglesby, "Let Not Ambition Mock their Useful Toil," a written account of family stories, date unknown, in the author's possession

[6] Ibid, page 1

The lonely boy cried in his upstairs bedroom, finding no comfort in learning that his dowager aunt's husband and son had both died in that room. "I cried myself to sleep for the first few months," Will Clarke Williams recounted decades later. "I was afraid and kept having toothaches. They loved me, but it was all so different."[7] The three formed a family, however, and his brothers and sisters stayed in touch. But the trauma never left him, nor did the meaning of family.

Will was surrounded by monuments and mystery. During the Civil War, quaint Iuka had the misfortune of being a major east-west link in Union supply lines. On September 19, 1862, 8,000 men clashed there, led by Union Generals Ulysses Grant, William Rosecrans, and Edward Ord against Confederate Generals Sterling Price, Henry Little, and Louis Hebert. A mysterious phenomenon happened. Grant and Ord had held their troops north of Iuka waiting to hear Rosecrans' cannon south of town, but a very stiff north wind blew in, pushing the sound of cannon blasts away. Grant and Ord never heard a thing. Their armies stood pat until a messenger rode up explaining that the battle was over, that 400 had been killed and a thousand wounded. Rumors that Grant was drunk fueled laughter among Iukan Confederates.

Both of Will's grandfathers were Confederate officers in the war, C.W. Williams a colonel and John Garth Barton, a Second Lieutenant in the Fifth Mississippi Regiment. All died before Will Clarke was born but their stories became family folklore. With Daniel Boone as an ancestor, community leaders, and Civil War heroes in the family, orphaned grandson William Clarke Williams lived with high expectations from the start..

He wasted no time embracing the future. Will attended school by day and by night kept Iuka's dim yellow lights burning from the five-year-old electric power plant. After graduating Tishomingo County High School in 1911, Will Clarke borrowed money to enroll in a business course but decided with a friend to first spend a few weeks hoboing across the country in boxcars.

---

[7] Ibid page 2

Dangling their legs from the open door of a moving boxcar, the two boys didn't notice as their train cut sharply onto a narrow bridge. The pants leg of Will Clarke's friend snagged the rail, jerking him out of the boxcar. As Will attempted to grab him, both fell onto the tracks and Will saw his friend decapitated. With his own leg badly broken, he watched the train puff away. Eventually, fellow hobos and trainmen nailed Will's leg back together and set it. For years, Iukans scoffed at Will's story until the local doctor bought an X-ray machine and challenged Will Clarke Williams to be the first X-ray in town. Will had been telling the truth. In fact, the doctor found one of the two crisscrossed nails working its way out and repaired the leg. For the rest of his life, Will hobbled on the stunted shorter leg.

The leg kept the Williams boy from jobs in farming or logging so after business school, at 20, he turned his sights on the town's newest technology company, Cumberland Telephone & Telegraph. Fate intervened a thousand miles west when a young Texas girl made an identical decision. The two independent decisions set in motion the dream that would become Century Telephone and CenturyLink.

Cumberland Telephone was Bell Telephone's licensee in Kentucky, Tennessee, Mississippi, and Louisiana, and the manager in Iuka, T. C. McRae, took a liking to the reliable and energetic Will Williams, saddling him with responsibility that included climbing poles with his bad leg. Since boot spikes were adjustable, Will Clarke found he could climb 40-foot creosote poles as well as the next guy. Understanding electricity, he learned quickly and liked the work.

As communication sped up, so did news, particularly after the sinking of *RMS Titanic*. As a Cumberland operator, Will began hearing news of two great wars raging in Europe, one at the hand of German Kaiser Wilhelm and the other by Russian Bolsheviks. President Woodrow Wilson resisted sending American troops for three years until a German submarine sank the *RMS Lusitania,* drowning 138 Americans. When Kaiser Wilhelm ignored Wilson's ultimatum to stop, on April 6, 1917, the United States declared war, calling up three million soldiers. Thousands of country boys, including Will Clarke Williams, jumped at the chance to get all-expense-paid trips to Europe. But when Will applied at the Iuka Draft Office on June 5, 1917, registrar B. L. Martin noted of blue-eyed, medium-build registrant #2805, "One leg short and stiff on account of break."[8] Will was rejected.

His friends donned sharp uniforms and doughboy helmets, delighting the girls before they shipped off to war. He buried himself at the telephone office, but in a town that celebrated the honored dead, people looked at him as if he were defective. He had to get away.

After the Civil War, most of his mother's folks, the Bartons, had scattered west. Will's grandfather, Lieutenant Barton, had straggled home after the war, finding Carpetbaggers protected by Union military occupation. Northern interests were determined to keep the South humble, proof to Lieutenant Barton that the war had been more about jealousy over the rapid buildup of Southern wealth. The lieutenant encouraged his children to blaze west, and when he died, Will's grandmother Kate Barton packed her treasured possessions, forsook memories in Missisippi, and traveled 800 rocky miles west to Coleman, Texas, where son Will Dixon Barton and his wife Katy settled. The family wound up moving farther into the frontier to newly-created Ozona, Texas, in Crockett County, named for Davy Crockett.

Grandmother Kate in Ozona didn't know in 1902 that her daughter Molly had died until a letter arrived days later. When Kate died five years after that, 13-year-old Will Clarke heard about his family in Ozona for the first time.

Rejected by the Army and missing the quick war, Will Clarke Williams headed west to the Bartons in Ozona. Dixon and Katy Barton were educated, full of new ideas, hope, and encouragement. Dixon kept the books for Ozona's largest department store, and his son Johnny worked as a clerk.

---

[8] World War I Selective Service System Draft Registration Cards, 1917-1918. Washington, D.C.: National Archives and Records Administration. M1509, 4,582 rolls, Mississippi, Tishomingo County, Draft Card W, image #161

Cumberland Telephone had no Texas exchanges, but the moment Will Clarke told of his experience with the Bell system, the mom-and-pop owners of Ozona Telephone Company hired him on the spot. Will did it all as operator and lineman, especially learning how an independent telephone operation can function without corporate hindrances.

He soon bunked in at the Cox Boarding House, run by Edward and Anna Cox with daughter Edelle and son Charles. One of the largest houses in Ozona, on a still-unnamed street, the Cox House boarded fifteen renters, professionals including the manager of up-and-coming Ryan Oil Company, Ozona National Bank accountants, a schoolteacher, a realtor, a tailor, an automobile machinist, painters, and carpenters. By the time census taker Mrs. A. P. Utterback polled those at the Cox House on Saturday, January 24, 1920, "Clark Williams" was listed as *Manager, Telephone Company.*[9]

At 25, Will Clarke Williams was his own man in his own town in his own apartment. He came and went without the advice he never asked for from the aunt and old maid. He worked all the time but learned Ozona history and that of Davy Crockett, whose legend paralleled cousin Daniel Boone. With another example of trailblazing, Will began to think, *Maybe that's what a man should do.* A Davy Crockett plaque shouted at him, *Be Sure You Are Right, Then Go Ahead.*

While Crockett was right in defending Texas, in reality he left behind six children in Tennessee. Between Crockett, Boone and the Civil War, Will saw that every trailblazing endeavor comes with a price for all involved. He also deciphered that Man is alone in the struggle but success has many friends.

Clarke, as he called himself by then, met another lost soul: a white fluffy unattached Spitz. He named the dog "Sweetie," and Clarke and Sweetie appeared all over town in the Ozona Telephone truck, greeting passersby with comical grins. Clarke got a kick out of it and Ozonans embraced the two.

---

[9] Fourteenth Census of the United States, 1920, *Justice Precinct 1, Crockett, Texas*, Roll *T625-1787*, Page *5A*, Enumeration District *24*, Image *1146*, Records of the Bureau of the Census, Record Group 29, National Archives, Washington, D.C.

To Clarke's north in Irion County, hot prairie winds in summer and icy sleet in winter whistled across twenty-six miles of new telephone wire stretching southwest from San Angelo to tiny Mertzon. San Angelo Telephone Company's new copper traced along new iron just laid for the *Kansas City, Mexico & Orient Railway*. For beautiful 15-year-old Willie Marie Hill in Mertzon, those exotic destinations gave hope that an outside world did indeed offer excitement. Any destination away from Irion's windmills and smelly sheep farms sounded good to her. Mertzon's only claim to fame was notorious outlaw Laura Bullion, the lone female in The Wild Bunch Gang headed by Robert Leroy Parker and Harry Alonzo Longabaugh, better known as Butch Cassidy and the Sundance Kid. Just before Willie Marie was born, Butch, Sundance, Laura, and the gang pulled off the Great Northern Train Robbery, the largest train heist in American history. Mertzon's population worried that Laura might return to knock over their bank and depot. Laura, Butch, and Sundance became the most hunted outlaws in history as Mertzon sat mortified

Amid similar folklore that cradled Will Clarke Williams, Marie was born in Sherwood, Texas, next door to grandfather Mark Benton, a former Confederate private in the 11th Missouri. Marie's Bentons and Will's Bartons had both left the South and migrated west after the war. But Marie's grandmother Celia Price Benton died during the move, leaving her husband Mark to homestead alone. Their daughter Dorah, Marie's mother, met courageous young stagecoach driver Andrew Cummings Hill. They married in 1894. Andy Hill whipped teams of horses back and forth across the dusty trail between Sherwood and San Angelo, willing at any minute to take a shotgun to highway robbers. Eventually he found himself racing his stagecoach alongside the iron horse, shamed by laughing engineers blowing their whistles and leaving him far behind. Andy had seen the future. According to family lore, Andy Hill made the last stagecoach run in Texas.[10]

The next year 55-year-old Mark Benton married twenty-years-younger Mary Elizabeth Thorpe who, after his death, became the ward of Andrew and Dorah until her death in 1937.[11] Andrew's mother, Lucinda Carlton Hill, also crammed into her son's household after Andy's father, 11th Texas Cavalry Sergeant Thomas David Hill, died near Dallas in 1906. Andrew vouched for his mother when she applied for Sergeant Hill's Confederate Pension in Irion County.[12]

When Marie was born, Sterling Price Benton, Dorah's brother and family prankster, begged Dorah to name her "Willie Minnie Dottie Arty Marie Hill" for the sheer comic value. Dorah refused. When Marie was nine, she and her classmates heard the faint clinking of sledgehammers driving iron spikes into crossties. KCM&O railroad director and San Angelo banker M. L. Mertz was fulfilling his promise to bring the railroad to Irion County. Marie's father left the stagecoach and joined the railroad. But the rails bypassed Sherwood a mile to the southwest where the new depot was christened *Mertzon.* When Old Engine #10 chugged into town belching black smoke and steam, Andy and Dorah were grateful for the steady job.

Half of Sherwood moved to Mertzon. Marie, along with her parents and sisters Mabel and Ada, oldest brother Marcus Lee, and brother Edgar piled into a rent house on Lake Street, surrounded by Andy's coworkers Thomas Edwards and Earnest Laird, along with KCM&O section chiefs Joe Smith and Newton Dawson. Mertzon's postmistress Emma Seals lived down the

---

[10] Mary Lee Williams Oglesby, "Let Not Ambition Mock their Useful Toil," a written account of family stories, date unknown, in the author's possession

[11] Texas State Library and Archives Commission; Austin, Texas; *Confederate Pension Applications, 1899-1975*; Collection #: *CPA16526*; Roll #: *105*; Roll Description: *Pension File Nos. 35469 to 35490, Application Years 1917 to 1918.*

[12] Texas State Library and Archives Commission; Austin, Texas; *Confederate Pension Applications, 1899-1975*; Collection #: *CPA19656*; Roll #: *300*; Roll Description: *Pension File Nos 19656 to 19680, Application Years 1899 to 1910.*

street. Andy's higher rent in Mertzon meant Dorah took in laundry to make extra money. Marie watched her mother tear up her knuckles scrubbing on washboards.

The Mexican Revolution slowed Andy and friends as they hammered *Kansas City, Mexico & Orient* rails past Mertzon. Mexican general Pancho Villa brazenly crossed the U.S. border and attacked Columbus, New Mexico, just west of El Paso. U.S. General John Pershing chased the banditos back across the border and for nine months. Though Pershing never caught Villa, he did capture wide admiration for leading the United States to victory in World War I.

As a sophomore at Irion County High School, Willie Marie Hill made the parallel decision of Will Clarke Williams in Iuka. She took a before-and-after-school job with San Angelo Telephone, heralded in 1903 by *The San Angelo Press* for its new switchboard capable of handling an astounding 850 calls. "The company now has 374 subscribers," the 1903 story continued, with a new operator assigned exclusively to long distance customers, "insuring more prompt service than when she had 100 local connections to look after."[13] Texas boasted 10,000 telephones because Colonel A. H. Belo, publisher of the *Galveston News* and *Dallas Morning News*, had met Alexander Graham Bell during his 1876 World's Fair demonstrations. Three years later, Belo installed the first telephone in Texas, connecting his home and Galveston office.

In 1917, San Angelo Telephone needed a bilingual operator in Mertzon for the English-Mexican community. Fifteen-year-old Marie Hill grew up with Mexican friends, learned their language, studied it, and became proficient in conversational Spanish. She landed the job. During the day at Irion High, Marie sported her trademark dark-haired Dutch boy, but at night she became a nameless, faceless voice at the end of a telephone line, an operator directing calls, connecting people, getting help, finding folks. She wasn't nameless for long. Soon she was a comforting voice to all of Mertzon.

---

[13] *The San Angelo Press*, San Angelo, Texas, August 26, 1903, front page

Exciting but not easy, her two-hour shift began at 6:00 a.m. connecting businessmen, shopkeepers, and salespeople trying to get a jump on the day. When she came back from school at 4:00 p.m., callers exchanged the day's news and businessmen settled up. She learned the rhythm of commerce, doing homework between buzzes until 10 o'clock at night.

Callers who did not have home telephones came to the Central Office to use enclosed booths. Marie soon learned who had money and who didn't, who had troubles and who didn't. Home phones cost one dollar a month while long distance was an extravagant five cents for three minutes. She tried not to eavesdrop on conversations in the same room when locals cried or yelled. After those calls, Marie avoided eye contact as she tallied up the per-minute charges.

San Angelo Telephone managers were quite pleased with the teenager. They could pay her peanuts and promote her bilinguistics as a leasing point to Spanish-speaking subscribers. Leasing phones was Bell's practice for a hundred years.

With no printed telephone directories, Marie wrote down the names of subscribers and each one's differing ring sequence. Each line often had a dozen subscribers. Each subscriber required a different ring sequence, such as two long rings and a short, or two short rings and a long, generated by the switchboard magneto which rang all the bells along the wire. Subscribers knew who was being phoned by the ring sequence. The appropriate subscriber would run to their two-foot-tall wooden-box phone on the wall. If the subscriber was really *up town*, she was using one of the new tabletop candlestick telephones, a black tube standing a foot tall with a fixed mouthpiece and removable ear horn hanging on a cradle switch.

Talkers seldom conversed long, tiptoeing toward wall phones straining into fixed mouthpieces or holding heavy metal candlestick receivers. In addition, callers could never be sure how many friends, or competitors, might be listening. If a conversation became particularly long-winded, neighbors expecting an important call or needing to make a call might go so far as to interrupt the talkers and ask for the line.

Powering phones was an issue, too. Most rural telephone exchanges used two Number 6 zinc-carbon batteries at both ends because batteries offered low-voltage direct current. Alternating current could electrocute customers. Also, in power outages, batteries would power voices over miles of wire. Switchboard magnetos provided short-burst AC current to ring phone bells and, in the early days, were wired separately to ringer systems. Heavy copper grounding wires ran into the ground to channel lightning strikes and to enable better electrical flow for clearer communication. In drought subscribers had to pour water around the ground wire to make a call. During storms, Marie pushed back from the switchboard, fearing a direct lightning strike.

When subscribers twenty miles from town wanted to make a call, they lifted the receiver off its cradle, opening the circuit, and whistled into the mouthpiece or thumped it until the switchboard operator heard a faint sound or buzzer or noticed a dim light above the subscriber's socket.

"Operator," teenager Marie would announce, confident and knowledgeable of practically everything in town. The distant subscriber would customarily ask, "Marie, please connect me with so-and-so." She would dutifully look down her list, plug the caller's wire into the line to be called, check the number of rings, and spin the magneto. Once the connection was made, Marie would disconnect from the conversation. When the callers had finished talking, the person calling would ring Marie back to inform her they were finished. She would unplug the line.

The tenth grader became a clearinghouse of messages as subscribers moved about town. Because she heard her share of business and gossip, residents sought her out for information. But she had a strong sense of propriety, learning early the value of confidentiality and well aware that a single complaint could cost her job.

Mertzon buzzed with cotton, wheat, and alfalfa farmers, sheep and cattle ranchers, merchants, and, in the fall, deer hunters, all congregating around the depot, continually calling for prices and shipping dates. Flatbed railroad cars offloaded lumber from back east while high plains wheat, cotton, cattle, and wool was loaded for points in both directions. Mertzon made national newspapers when cattle rancher A. M. Callison helped deliver a miniature 13-pound calf. *The Washington* [D.C.] *Herald* touted the birth as "the world's smallest calf."[14] Telephone communications made that news possible.

Marie was also first to know bad news, such as when lightning killed the brother of San Angelo Telephone Company manager Fred Green[15] and when Mertzon cowboy Jesse Seis on the J.D. Sugg Ranch was mysteriously shot.[16] Marie jumped on the case, excitedly making connections for Texas Ranger Captain Carrol Bates and Sheriff Frank Emerick calling area law enforcement, tracking leads, questioning townspeople, and tightening the noose around an escaping killer. She spoke to operators all the way to the Texas Rangers headquarters in Austin.

Mertzon's economy advanced again when cattleman Fayette Tankersley struck oil on his ranch a mile east. Spellman Oil Company's deep well test drilled down a whopping 200 feet before it tapped black gold. McReynolds Oil and Refining Company came in from Dallas to take over, and Irion County's oil boom began.[17] Mertzon telephones doubled and so did traffic.

Busy as she was, Marie fantasized about all the distant and mysterious places her wires led, wishing she could be there in person as quickly as her voice. Irion High School ended with the eleventh grade, which meant that she would graduate the following year at sixteen. She perturbed Mertzon's boys who often called just to talk but who soon learned Marie Hill did not mix business with pleasure. Her sights were much higher than Mertzon. She cultivated her voice, learning the power of clear communication and cultivated speech.

The Irion County School Board took note of Marie's good reputation and approved her taking the teacher's exam right out

---

[14] *The Washington Herald*, Washington, D.C., April 24, 1916, page 1
[15] *El Paso Herald*, El Paso, Texas, July 1, 1918, page 7
[16] Ibid, July 30, 1918, page 10
[17] *El Paso Herald*, El Paso, Texas, June 27, 1919, page 7

of high school, which she passed without a single college hour. At still just sixteen, she received her Texas teaching certificate and a classroom as the world changed yet again. She came of age just as the Women's Suffrage movement finally grasped women the right to vote, a half century after former slaves earned that right. Now Marie had a more powerful voice than any Hill woman ever had.

Her teaching assignment, however, landed her in a remote one-room schoolhouse in dinky Irion City. She left after one term and jumped at Mertzon's offer to teach English at Mertzon's Mexican elementary school. Living back home with family was good, but she joked to her parents that they were still running a hotel. Along with younger sisters Mabel, 17, Ada, 13, and brothers Lee, 25, and Edgar, 10, they had taken in Dorah's brother, 67-year-old Uncle Charles Benton, who brought with him Smith cousins Zula, 15, Hazel, 8, and Hal, 5. Eleven people crammed into the small clapboard house.[18]

Marie had to find her own place as the 1919-1920 school year ended. To supplement her meager schoolteacher salary, she asked her former telephone bosses for her old job, but with it filled, they instead offered her fulltime switchboard duties at Barnhart thirty miles southwest. She left education and returned to communications.

The November 1920 presidential election allowed ten million women to vote for the first time. They were a force, moving simultaneously to outlaw alcohol. Prohibition became law in October 1919 and would remain law for fourteen years, forcing flappers underground in the Roaring '20s. Speakeasies sprang up from Chicago to Mertzon. The Mob smuggled liquor in from Canada and Mexico. Killings, assassinations, and poisoned booze followed. That made no difference for God-fearing teetotalers like the Hills. Working on the railroad, Andy didn't have to look far to see the destructiveness of alcoholism.

In dusty little Barnhart, Marie's kind, helpful voice attracted friends. That voice crossed the border south, singing

---

[18] 1920 United States Census, Precinct 2 (Mertzon), Irion County, Texas, January 9, 1920, Sheet #2B, line 89 through 98, Family #47

along wires over Crockett County's dry gulches. That's where 25-year-old lineman and manager of Ozona Telephone Company, Will Clarke Williams, wiped sweat from his brow. Cleats dug into the pole, he rested a moment against the leather safety belt, drinking tepid water out of a canteen. He smelled the poles' aromatic creosote as tar bubbles blistered in the Texas sun. His sunburned neck, arms, and bum leg hurt while hat, clothes, and boots dripped with sweat. Will Clarke looped wires over thick green glass insulators and wondered why the magnified light didn't burn the wood.

Below him, Crockett County's grass prairies stretched forever, dotted with cattle, sheep, and sometimes whitetail deer. Farms turned purple and green with flowering alfalfa. In fall, patches turned white with cotton. Constant prairie winds kept his sweat cool but chafed every moving part of his body.

Will often listened to the singing wires as dry winds strummed across them like an invisible hand strumming a guitar. The wind's faint whistle mixed with a high oscillating crystalline sound, shimmering up and down the steel like violins in another world. Sometimes Clarke fancied he could hear the jumble of conversations passing through the wires. Sometimes, a whisper seemed to dance toward him.

Then Lineman Williams did hear someone, but the voice was much more than a whisper. A piece of his life's jigsaw puzzle clicked into place as he called Barnhart.

"Operator, this is lineman Clarke Williams of the Ozona Telephone Company; with whom am I speaking, please?" he asked into his portable, battery-powered telephone clipped to the line.

"With whom did you wish to speak, Mr. Williams?" came a velvety-clear lady's voice.

"I'm in Crockett County running wire and checking lines north, making sure Ozona-to-San Angelo telephone calls are good and clear."

"They're good and clear all right," the confident operator assured.

William Clarke Williams had spoken to hundreds of operators but a quality about this voice hooked him.

He ventured, "So you're not going to tell me your name?"

"What do you need it for, Mr. Williams?"

"Well, I'm new but I figure I'll be calling pretty often and I like to know with whom I'm speaking," he said with an educated air. He hastily added, "If that's all right."

"That's all right, Mr. Williams. The 'with whom' you're speaking to is Miss Hill. I'm Marie Hill, operator with San Angelo Telephone Company in Barnhart."

"Thank you, Miss Hill."

Intrigued, Will Clarke replayed the voice in his mind, clear as glass, playful, coy, aloof yet forceful and obviously single. Though he had no idea what she looked like, her voice affected him like no other. He began to manufacture reasons to call Barnhart: the lines, the weather, even the unfolding saga of fixing baseball's 1919 World Series. *Had cheapskate Chicago White Sox "take it or leave it" owner Charlie Comiskey starved his players into taking payoffs and throwing the Series to Cincinnati?* Marie had no idea and could care less, but she liked the attention. They laughed, joked, and shared personal stories until Clarke finally mustered the courage to ask her to dinner.

Marie accepted. She likewise had been captivated by his voice, that of an intelligent man who enjoyed his work and who, over the short course of their voice-only relationship, had been promoted to manager of the Ozona system. Even after that first call, Marie had leaned over to the other operator in Barnhart and proclaimed she loved Clarke Williams' voice.

"That's the man I'm going to marry," Marie stated confidently.[19] The friend just laughed. Love at first sound was unheard of. Soon, however, Ozona Telephone manager W. Clarke Williams knocked at the office. The moment he walked in, they knew each other. Neither was disappointed. He saw what had broken the hearts of local boys. Marie Hill was vivacious, outgoing, and full of optimism. Eager Clarke was captivated and within days of their first date, he asked her to

---

[19] Mary Lee Williams Oglesby, "Let Not Ambition Mock their Useful Toil," a written account of family stories, date unknown, in the author's possession, page 3

marry him. She refused. It was just too soon. "Besides," she would say years later, "I was having fun."[20] She remembered Dorah scrubbing clothes. Marriage was not appealing. Besides, Sweetie the Spitz did not like Marie's replacing her next to Clarke. Marie was a threat. But Sweetie warmed up, and the three soon made a complete and comical family.

Dangling from poles, Clarke kept talking to Marie, wooing her, the picture of her face held continually in his mind. He was smitten in a life-changing way. Clarke admired Marie's flapper-era independence but he despised it for keeping them apart. As fall turned winds cooler and cotton pickers shaved patches, Clarke proposed again, on the phone. She paused, but refused, busy at that moment summoning Mertzon's volunteer firemen to a cotton gin fire. Clarke realized she was waiting for him to develop. If he didn't climb quickly into more substantial means, she wouldn't see herself breaking free of West Texas poverty, at least not with him.

He searched for higher-paying jobs, calling old friends at Cumberland Telephone. Southern Bell-Cumberland had an opening in Monroe, Louisiana, in payroll. That was near management and that meant advancement. Not only did the position pay better than Ozona's backbreaking job, it was in an office. Clarke excitedly told Marie he had accepted and would she marry him?

Marie didn't answer.. She had been seeing another boy, unbeknownst to Clarke, and had been weighing her affections. Whether those ran hotter toward the other, no one ever knew. His first day to be in Monroe was Monday, September 27, 1920. Did she want to go?

The pause crushed him.

Bruised, William Clarke Williams left Ozona for Monroe, a bustling city of more than 30,000, the largest Will Clarke had ever called home. Monroe straddled picturesque Ouachita River with twin city West Monroe, the citizens of which were debating then whether to vote for annexation. Northeast Louisiana's metropolis offered everything: a huge and growing customer

---

[20] Ibid

base, friendly people, and civic minded leadership in progressive Mayor Arnold Bernstein. Monroe's natural gas field, touted as the largest in the world, provided cheap energy for carbon plants, oil refining, and paper mills. Monroe's economy was so promising that out-of-state investors, including W. L. Slayton of Ohio, bought nearly half of Monroe's $140,000 bond offering to build a new electric power plant.[21] Southern Bell would have trouble keeping up with the demand for telephones.

Just as Clarke moved to town, a late season hurricane blew inland at Morgan City and ripped northward, knocking out one hundred phones in Monroe. For days, all communications in south Louisiana, including Western Union, went silent. Travelers provided the only reports: extensive damage but little loss of life.

Southern Bell Manager O. H. Bynum sent Clarke back on the line repairing wires and resetting poles. He worked with crews around the clock, both to show gratitude and enthusiasm for Mr. Bynum and to keep his mind off Marie. Monroe people were good people, grateful for his efforts, but Monroe still didn't have Marie or anyone like her. The girls were pretty enough and friendly, but Will Clarke ran up considerable long distance charges to Barnhart, averaging twenty cents every three minutes.

Marie, meantime, held fast to a dream of seeing more of the world before settling down to have children. The Roaring Twenties posed new opportunities for women, beginning with putting Ohio Republican newspaperman Warren G. Harding into the White House with what the pundits called *the handsome vote*. Harding won also because Americans had grown suspicious of Woodrow Wilson's League of Nations to the point the U.S. Senate never ratified the Treaty of Versailles at the end of World War I. Norms of society across the world were changing.

The independence Clarke once found charming now fostered resentment. No arguments worked. Willie Marie Hill was evidently waiting for a better offer. He stopped calling. Christmas 1920 in Monroe offered warm people but cold, lonely

---

[21] *The Herald*, New Orleans, Louisiana, April 7, 1921, page 3

streets draped in tinsel under which decorated electric streetcars clanged. Nights were the worst: no one to go home to, no family around, and nothing besides work. He was orphaned again just like in Iuka.

As spring flowers burst into color, Clarke awoke on Sunday, March 20, 1921, his eyes wide open, his mind made up. He had been in Monroe half a year and still no Marie. Barnhart could in no way, shape, or form compete with Monroe, and Marie needed to see that. Coming for an unchaperoned visit was out of the question, which left one choice. Will Clarke gave himself and Marie an ultimatum. That spring Sunday morning he woke up the clerk at Monroe's Western Union office at the foot of the Desiard Street Bridge and wrote out one simple telegram aimed at Mertzon, Texas.

Six hundred miles west, Mertzon was sleeping on a Sunday morning. The Hill women got up early, bottlenecking at the bathroom and clanging pots in the kitchen. Andrew had kindling fires going in both fireplace and stove. Dorah, Marie, Mabel, and Ada switched between jobs of bathing, washing clothes, and cooking breakfast for eleven. On Sundays, Marie helped her mother brown a pot roast or cut up chicken for dinner. Smells of wood smoke, biscuits, bacon, and coffee got the boys up. Sundays were always a family time that included the luxury of breakfast, an unhurried Sunday dinner, and sermons of hope and redemption at Mertzon Baptist Church.

Marie grew up steeped in Christianity. Its messages of love, restraint, and tolerance had helped her avoid the moral traps that ended the dreams of friends. Prohibition had caused wholesale hypocrisy with a backlash of lasciviousness for girls who had lost boyfriends, husbands, and brothers in the Great War. The flapper generation relished and feared the briefness of life. Christian beliefs, however, tempered Marie who saw the need for integrity in both herself and country.

A knock came at the Hills' door.

A young box-hatted messenger stood there next to his bicycle.

"Telegram from Western Union!" He was smiling so, obviously, the message he had transcribed couldn't be bad.

"Hope I'm not too early with this new Daylight Savings Time. Why can't the government just leave things alone?"

"Who's it for?" Marie asked.

Rechecking the addressee, he announced, "Telegram for Miss Marie Hill."

No telegram had ever arrived at the noisy Hill household on Lake Street. Andrew looked up from his paper. Drying their hands, Dorah, Mabel, and Ada walked up to the door. Marie stepped forward in the now crowded front room. Cousins Zula and Hazel joined them. Brother Edgar was keeping Hal occupied. Everyone stopped breathing as Marie ripped open the envelope and unfolded the message.

MEET ME IN FORT WORTH. NOW OR NEVER.
WILLIAM CLARKE WILLIAMS.

Marie read the telegram again and again, a smile breaking across her face and tears welling up. Clarke would no longer take *no* for an answer. *Now or never.*

Dorah looked over Marie's shoulder as the girls crowded around to read the message. Marie looked dead at her father.

"Papa," Marie began confidently, "will you go with me to Fort Worth tomorrow?"

"Whatever for?"

"I'm going to meet Clarke and we're going to get married."

"Oh, no you're not!" her leathery railroad father replied, emphatically crushing the paper.

His 19-year-old daughter looked at him, wiping tears but too happy to be denied, while Dorah read the telegram and hugged her child.

"Well, then," Marie told her father, "I'll go by myself."

Seeing he was outnumbered, Andrew Hill reluctantly softened with a "Humpf!" and then, "All right, I guess I'll go with you."

The next morning, Monday, March 21, 1921, all the Hill girls stood around the Mertzon depot crying, laughing, and crying, happy for Marie but sad they couldn't afford a wedding or even witness a civil ceremony. Andrew and Dorah would have been hard-pressed to afford the smallest wedding in Mertzon let alone some affair in Fort Worth, but her daddy escorted her just the same. Andrew bought Marie's ticket at the employee discount while he, the KCM&O employee, rode for free. Dorah hugged her oldest for a long time, not knowing when or if she would ever see her again this side of heaven. Monroe, Louisiana, might as well have been on the far side of the Earth. The whistle blew, the locomotive's giant iron wheels spun and caught, and the waving, crying Hill family slowly grew smaller. When Marie's eyes could see her mother no more through her tears, she dabbed them and thought of all that Dorah had told her in the last days about being a wife and a mother. Marie had never considered how demanding the best job in the world might prove, but she had finally come to the realization that good-hearted, good-souled Clarke was worth it. She knew that even before she saw him. He was the first man who had wanted her as a partner, not as a servant. In short, he needed her, and there was no better human feeling than to be needed.

Marie and Andrew chugged into Fort Worth past smelly cow yards, slowing at the depot, where Clarke met them, all smiles and in his suit. Marie on the platform was a vision to Clarke, an answer to prayer. As for Andrew, Clarke noticed that despite himself, his soon-to-be father-in-law looked pleased after all.

The trio walked seven blocks west from the depot to the columned Greek Revival edifice of the First Methodist Church at Seventh and Taylor Streets. Marie was Baptist and Will Clarke was Methodist, but she agreed to marry in the Methodist church nearest the depot. They would sort out later which faith to follow.

Methodist minister Reverend P. F. Culvert, on duty that Monday, married the young couple from opposite ends of the railroad, wishing them *Godspeed* as they left to catch the *Vicksburg, Shreveport & Pacific Railroad* to Monroe. When the time came for crusty old Andrew to part with his daughter, he too held her for a while, and Marie noticed tears streaming down his weathered sunburned face. She had never seen her burly stagecoach-railroad father cry. Marie was his first-born baby girl.

"I'll be fine, daddy, don't worry. I'll see you soon."

With hardly a word in reply, railroad man Andrew Hill climbed aboard the *Kansas City, Mexico & Orient Railway* and steamed toward home. Watching his train disappear into the hubbub of Fort Worth, Marie wished she had remembered to tell him that she would call home often, since Clarke's job provided both a home phone and reduced long distance rates.

Marie and Clarke turned fresh faces toward an exciting new life together, alone in a strange land but together. Clarke had rented a house in less-expensive West Monroe. He would walk across the Desiard Street Bridge to work. Their home truly would be their home, since neither had family around. Will Clarke had no parents and Marie had no in-laws. Unless one of his brothers or sisters came calling, there was no one to meet and impress.

Times were promising and that's why Southern Bell was hiring. But not all was idyllic. The couple stepped off the train into a firestorm of controversy, one led by a rabblerousing young lawyer and Railroad Commissioner named Huey Pierce Long.

CHAPTER 3

No one including Alexander Graham Bell envisioned the scope and magnitude of the telephone's impact. He created American Telephone & Telegraph but quickly realized one company could not singlehandedly string millions of miles of cable and, at the same time, build thousands of switchboards and millions of telephones quickly enough to meet growing demand. With his patents running out in eighteen years and most of that time in court, Bell offered hundreds of entrepreneurs the chance to buy licensed franchises of Bell service and equipment. With no standardization, the size and service of each exchange varied widely.

On January 30, 1894, Bell's original two patents expired and 6,000 new independent telephone carriers sprang up overnight. Bell's *Western Electric* faced unprecedented rivalry from equipment start-ups Stromberg-Carlson in 1894 and the Kellogg Switchboard & Supply Company in 1897. Fifty years later, Stromberg-Carlson would be key in the creation of Century Telephone and, thus, CenturyLink.

Amassing two million subscribers in ten years, independent carriers shot past Bell Telephone's 1.3 million subscribers. By 1903 independents claimed over 6,000 exchanges to Bell's fifteen hundred.[22] Bell profits fell. Each city became a battleground, as independents fought fiercely over the same subscribers, promising one-upsmanship in service. A 1902 newspaper advertisement announced, "Residence phones on party lines *of not more than four on a line* at $1 per month will give perfect service...on full metallic circuit [with] long distance service."[23] While individual ideas and techniques made some systems better than others, competition prevented standardization. Rarely did competing exchanges carry each other's telephone calls as they battled for the same subscribers.

---

[22] "Bell and the early independents" by A. Billings; *Telephone Engineer and Management*, March 15, 1985, pp 87-89.
[23] *The Wichita Daily Eagle* (Wichita, Kansas), January 8, 1902, page 6

In cities, businesses had to subscribe to multiple phone systems and list all their telephone numbers in advertisements. Solvency was an issue as well. Smaller exchanges were continually listed in newspapers for delinquent taxes, which signaled no money for improvements. In Louisiana, offenders included Castor Telephone Company in Bienville Parish with 35 subscribers and Verda Telephone in Grant Parish with 38 phones. The disarray led to poor service, costly duplication, thousands of unhappy customers, and, eventually, government intervention.

In 1907, retired visionary Bell Telephone president Theodore Newton Vail returned to salvage AT&T. He believed an effective telephone system had to offer standard equipment and service and that AT&T should be that system. He began buying out Bell licensees and independents, streamlining them into a powerful technological network under central corporate leadership. But when Vail bought rival Western Union, the one giant that could give AT&T real competition, federal regulators filed an anti-trust lawsuit. They threatened to nationalize the entire Bell System and indeed would make good on that threat during wartime from 1918 to August 1919.

Just in time to head off a government takeover, in 1913 Vail took his campaign of "One Policy, One System, Universal Service" directly to Capitol Hill, showing definitively how a government-sanctioned monopoly could better serve telephone customers while galvanizing America's telecommunications system. For the sanction, he agreed to sell off Western Union. The argument worked.

In what became known as the Kingsbury Commitment, named for lead AT&T Vice President Nathan Kingsbury, Vail agreed not just to divest AT&T of Western Union but also to provide long distance service to most independent exchanges and to make only the acquisitions that the Interstate Commerce Commission sanctioned. The Kingsbury offer made regulators appear authoritative but in effect allowed AT&T to consolidate massive control over very profitable urban areas as well as the lucrative long distance market.

Bell profits soared, strengthening infrastructure and customer services as well as making AT&T the largest corporation in the world. Competitors and politicians wasted no time crying foul, swinging public opinion like a pendulum. Many accused AT&T of transitioning from streamliner to steamroller in rate cases.

In Louisiana, Southern Bell Telephone ran headlong into a brick wall called the Louisiana Railroad Commission. The three-man commission, later the Public Service Commission, handled all rate cases in the state. Commissioner Huey Pierce Long, the young quick-thinking 27-year-old lawyer from backwoods Winnfield—nobody could explain his genius— brilliantly handled cases all the way to the United States Supreme Court. Long had two goals: to be governor of Louisiana and then president of the United States. Feeding that ambition, he made a name for himself by not rubber-stamping rate hikes. At the time, Bell-licensee Cumberland Telephone was merging into Southern Bell based in Atlanta, Georgia.

When America entered the Great War in 1918, Postmaster General Albert Sidney Burleson convinced President Woodrow Wilson to let him take over both the Bell system and Western Union for the duration of the war. Burleson had advocated as early as 1913 for nationalization of the country's communications. With unlimited wartime powers, Wilson and Burleson overrode state rate commissions to grant a 12-percent rate hike for Bell Telephone. Wartime shortages skyrocketed costs, and with government inefficiency, the 12 percent evaporated at once, pushing telephone systems back to the brink of insolvency. To recoup losses, just as President Wilson relinquished control in August 1919, his agencies granted AT&T, thus Bell and Cumberland, a hike that threatened to double long distance rates.

In Louisiana, Huey Long accused Cumberland of manipulating the wartime loophole to shove through a hike of "about 100 percent on long distance calls in Louisiana."[24] He

---

[24] Huey Pierce Long statement, Louisiana Railroad Commission, January 21, 1919, as quoted in *The Colfax Chronicle*, Colfax, Louisiana, January 25, 1919, page 2

filed an injunction that a Baton Rouge court granted and the Louisiana Supreme Court overturned. Cumberland-Southern Bell convinced the other two commissioners of the need and long distance rates doubled.

When publicly-traded AT&T published astronomical profits and salaries, people were outraged. The AT&T board of directors had authorized $90 million in new stock to 151,000 shareholders who already held nearly half a billion dollars' worth. Those figures to the working man made rate increases insulting.

To AT&T's consternation, Henry Ford at the same time very publicly announced a 31 percent price *reduction* in Ford cars, stating, "Now is the time to call a halt to war methods, war prices, and war greeds."[25] He became a hero in papers worldwide. Indeed, the Monroe, Louisiana, Chamber of Commerce took the opportunity to solicit Ford to build an assembly plant in Monroe powered by locally abundant cheap natural gas. Monroe already had a refinery producing three million gallons of gasoline a year retailing at 22 cents a gallon.[26] Ford explored the idea and toyed with financing pipelines to transport the gas northward, but he built his Louisiana plant in New Orleans to take advantage of shipping.

Ford's price reductions made AT&T look greedy and insensitive. Because of AT&T's executive salaries and its raising $90 million in stock, telephone workers began to unionize. In 1919, they struck Southern Bell in Atlanta, claiming certain employees had been fired because of union activities. Though government inspectors found no evidence, that didn't prevent disruption of service along Southern Bell's lines. *The New Orleans Herald,* in which Cumberland-Southern Bell was a significant advertiser, editorialized, "There is an old saying that corporations are without a soul, cold-blooded and all business, but it is shown that the telephone company is an exception to the rule. ...The Bell and Cumberland Companies have been exceedingly liberal to their employees...giving so many benefits of life and accident insurance, sick and disability

---

[25] *The Monroe News-Star*, September 25, 1920, page 2
[26] *The Monroe News-Star*, February 15, 1921, front page

benefits, pensions and making provisions for the family after death, etc. that other companies employing the same labor have found it very difficult to secure employees."[27]

Between attempts to thwart rate hikes by the Huey Longs in various states and strikers sabotaging service, the president of Southern Bell-Cumberland, J. Epps Brown, wrote a series of six paid columns to go in Southern newspapers in late 1920 assuring subscribers that "the interests of the public, the telephone company and its employees are identical."[28] Brown's six public pleadings attempted to stem the tide of Huey's rantings and, with the new advertising dollars, to stem harsh editorials in newspapers. If one state's commission denied an increase, the rest would fall like dominoes. Brown danced along the line between showing losses to get rate hikes while AT&T showed profits to hike stock prices.

In Louisiana, from 1915 to the first half of 1920, Southern Bell-Cumberland installed a net average annual gain of 2,103 telephones. But in 1919, the year after the Great War, Brown said installations shot up 600 percent to 13,850 telephones, overloading switchboards and forcing the hasty construction of thousands of miles of new wire. Cumberland Telephone in Louisiana recorded 1,771,467 toll phone calls in 1915, but by 1920 the company handled that many calls in just the first five months. Once telephones transitioned from fad to fixture, everyone wanted one immediately. Brown begged for patience, "Needed facilities are never paid for out of the earnings of the company, and the employees are never paid out of the capital of the company. ...[We know] the service now is not adequate to meet the unprecedented demand."[29]

Brown explained the war shut off raw materials. As demands for telephones quadrupled, manufacturing except for war materials practically stopped. "Platinum in switchboards

---

[27] *The Herald*, New Orleans, Louisiana, June 19, 1919, page 2

[28] J. Epps Brown, "The Facts of the Telephone Situation in Louisiana #1," *The Era-Leader*, Franklinton, Louisiana, September 23, 1920, page 5

[29] J. Epps Brown, "The Facts of the Telephone Situation in Louisiana #2," *The Era-Leader*, Franklinton, Louisiana, September 30, 1920, page 5

came from Russia," Brown explained, "silk for insulating wires from Japan, diamonds for [extruding] fine copper switchboard wires from Europe, and old manila rope for making paper insulation for cables from the wharves of the world. These foreign sources of raw materials were eliminated during the European War and are now far below normal."[30] The United States government, Brown said, also ordered AT&T to ship millions of dollars' worth of wartime telephone equipment to France "that was never returned."

Brown wrote that "...strikes and embargoes...are also prime factors in the present shortage in telephone materials and facilities."[31] Prices had skyrocketed and left Southern Bell Louisiana, said Brown, with a net operating loss of $40,562.38 in 1919, chopping return on investment to a paltry 5.59 percent. "You could not conduct your business without our business," he insisted. "Our business cannot continue to serve your business unless these figures are speedily changed. No one could. The U. S. Government tried it and failed."[32]

In Brown's fifth installment, "The Solution," he goaded Louisianans to invest in Southern Bell's $3 million capital expansion because, "Can you expect strangers to invest their money in a business located in Louisiana in which the people of Louisiana will not invest their money? ...To have telephone service you must either invest your own money or permit such a profit...as will induce strangers to invest their money in the state of Louisiana to serve you."[33]

In his final plea, "What the Company Asks,"[34] Brown reiterated Bell should make a "fair and just profit" to attract investors, to build facilities, to improve service, to meet new demand, all to satisfy a public who wanted, in his estimation,

---

[30] J. Epps Brown, "The Facts of the Telephone Situation in Louisiana #3," *The Era-Leader*, Franklinton, Louisiana, October 7, 1920, page 3
[31] ibid
[32] J. Epps Brown, "#4 The Company's Meager Profit," *Era-Leader*, Franklinton, Louisiana, Oct. 14, 1920, page 3
[33] J. Epps Brown, "#5 The Solution of the Problem," *Madison Journal*, Tallulah, Louisiana, Oct. 16, 1920, page 3
[34] J. Epps Brown, "#6 What the Company Asks," *Colfax Chronicle*, Colfax, Louisiana, Oct. 23, 1920, page 6

someone else to pay the freight. Finally, with every company fighting for post-war expansion capital, he stated, "To reproduce the Company's plant at today's prices…would cost 80 percent more…."[35]

The Louisiana Railroad Commission did not deny Southern Bell-Cumberland's 25 percent rate hike request but did push the decision from December 1920 into 1921. Telephone managers fanned out across Louisiana speaking to civic groups. Southeast Louisiana manager C. A. Stair addressed a special meeting called by the Bogalusa Chamber of Commerce of which Louisiana newspapers reported, "The chamber passed resolutions unanimously recommending to the Railroad Commission that the proposed increase in rates be allowed."[36] Managers A. D. Robinson of Tensas Parish and A. P. Baird of Alexandria spoke, too, but with less success. The reporting of such appearances had the effect of polarizing civic groups over rate issues.

In the rate fight, everything and everyone connected to the telephone business became news. When a peeping-Tom frightened Arcadia, Louisiana, night operator Daisy Marshall at 1:00 a.m. on September 6, 1921, *The Bienville Democrat* headlined the story.[37] The assailant got away. Newspapers started reporting sicknesses and vacations of operators.

Western Union then hurt all rates cases by defying a U.S. Senate mandate to deny a British cable from landing in Miami. Congress was retaliating against post-war Britain, France, and other allies who were trying to cut U.S. companies out of a share of Germany's lucrative cable systems. Western Union rebelliously connected to the British cable in Cuba. "The State Department can tear up the cables from Havana to Miami if it wants to," Western Union president Newcomb Carlton warned the Senate Interstate Commerce Committee, "but we propose to

---

[35] ibid

[36] *The Rice Belt Journal*, Welsh, Cameron Parish, LA, and *The Madison Journal*, Tallulah, Louisiana, December 25, 1920, pages 5 and 1 respectively

[37] *The Bienville Democrat*, Arcadia, LA, September 8, 1921, page 7

go ahead and will be ready to send messages within a short time."[38] Carlton's bold comments made his company and the other communications giant, Bell, appear defiant, too big, and too powerful. Bell Telephone's rate hike requests became all but laughable.

Southern Bell-Cumberland reduced its request to 20 percent. Two Railroad Commissioners granted the increase in February 1921. Huey Long still voted against it, writing in his dissent:

> "The Cumberland admits that 99 percent of its stock is owned by the Bell and that 100 percent of the Bell stock is owned by American Telephone & Telegraph Company, and the latter concern owns the stock of a great majority of the telephone companies of the nation, which, when all combined, are sometimes almost called a monopoly. AT&T owns 97 percent of Western Electric [which] supplies Cumberland with equipment [for which it pays] 4½ percent of Louisiana gross revenues to AT&T.... A mere corporate fiction prevents calling all these concerns one and the same company and there is no reason why this fiction should not be swept aside... It is not proper to impose an added burden upon a public struggling under recent economic reverses..."[39]

Reaction was swift, angry, and polarizing. In Long's district, an Arcadia assembly vowed to fight the increase.[40] In Colfax in central Louisiana, the mayor and aldermen called the hike "unwarranted, unjust and unfair" in light of falling

---

[38] *The Madison Journal*, Tallulah, LA, December 25, 1920, front page
[39] Huey Long dissent, February 26, 1921, 23rd Annual Report of the Louisiana Railroad Commission, pp 29-31, found in the Harvard Law Library, Cambridge, Massachusetts.
[40] *The Bienville Democrat*, Arcadia (Bienville Parish), Louisiana, March 10, 1921, front page

commodity prices and the country's "depressed and chaotic" financial condition.[41] *The New Orleans Herald*, however, reported that the hike should have "no opposition on the part of reasonable thinking people."[42]

The Alexandria, Louisiana, Chamber of Commerce publicly advised "holding up payment of telephone bills until after March 16" while it decided how to stop the hike. A statewide conference there elected a delegate from each of Louisiana's eight congressional districts to protest as one body before the Railroad Commission. The statewide delegation promised "a fight to the finish," with one resolution "advising the users of telephones not to pay the increased rates."[43]

Into this fight, the *Vicksburg, Shreveport & Pacific Railroad* carried Clarke and Marie Williams. With *The Monroe News-Star* headlining, *MONROE WILL BE IN PHONE FIGHT TO STOP RAISES IN LOCAL RATES*, city officials entered a heated public fight with Clarke's company. On the newlyweds' first full day in Louisiana, March 22, 1921, at Louisiana's gothic State Capitol in Baton Rouge, two railroad commissioners were accosted by hundreds of protestors while Huey Long basked in the glow of having voted against the increase. When the two commissioners thwarted Long's request to rehear the issue, one of the anti-hike delegates, W. F. Brown of St. Landry Parish, punched Commission Chairman Shelby Taylor twice in the face.[44]

Louisiana was not alone. In Bloomfield, Nebraska, 700 telephone subscribers struck against a 22 percent rate hike by disconnecting themselves from the Bell grid "until such time as

---

[41] *The Colfax Chronicle*, Colfax (Grant Parish), Louisiana, March 12, 1921, page 2

[42] *The Herald*, New Orleans, Louisiana, March 10, 1921, page 2

[43] *The Colfax Chronicle*, Colfax (Grant Parish), Louisiana, March 19, 1921, front page

[44] *The Bienville Democrat*, Arcadia (Bienville Parish), Louisiana, March 24, 1921, page 2

the company would agree to restore the old rate."[45] A phone electrician advised the 700 they could loosen two screws on their receivers, pull out the wire and disconnect en masse. "Everybody did it," reported newspapers nationwide. Citing 1921 farm commodity prices dropping by one-third to one-half, the Nebraskans felt the telephone companies "ought to be willing to lose money for a time when everybody else is doing so." Telephone managers reminded them that they were restricted to what were deemed *normal profits,* when farmers enjoyed wartime price hikes.

Newspaper publishers were only too happy to stir the controversy against what might overtake them as preeminent news sources. Inventors and investors worked hard to find a way around Bell and Western Union. In sleepy Kemp's Bend, Mississippi, thirty-five miles up the Mississippi River from Vidalia, Louisiana, the Kemp Bend Shipping Company boasted a new wireless telephone as its way to keep contact with steamboats and dredgers, a system independent of Bell Telephone. "We would like to see an amateur radio station installed in Vidalia," opined *Concordia Sentinel* editor Percy Rountree, Senior, "[to] be able to get messages elsewhere with dispatch."[46]

Under immense pressure, Louisiana's Railroad Commission had no choice but to rehear the rate increase and to suspend part of it. Adding drama, Huey Long was arrested for criminal libel after accusing Governor John Parker of dispensing patronage to Standard Oil Company. Baton Rouge Judge H. F. Brunot, unconvinced by Governor Parker, found Huey guilty of a technicality, suspended his sentence, and fined him one dollar. Huey left the courtroom smiling, having defied the powerful.

W. Clarke Williams was only too happy to work buried in Southern Bell's accounting department. He had a front row seat to watch how his manager, O. H. Bynum, stared down hostile crowds, defending the phone company while calming hysteria.

---

[45] *The Colfax Chronicle*, Colfax (Grant Parish), Louisiana, May 14, 1921, front page

[46] *The Concordia Sentinel*, Vidalia (Concordia Parish), Louisiana, March 26, 1921, page 4

Bynum still failed to stave off the Monroe Chamber's decision to join other chambers in vocally fighting the rate increase.

Finally, civic organizations pushed the telephone company and the Railroad Commission to evaluate each city and hamlet case by case to judge whether increases were necessary. Bynum termed such a task impossible in time, money, and application. Will Clarke saw that, depending on whether you were the company or subscriber, the company or employee, everyone had different ideas of what constituted "fair and just" rates as well as "fair and just" wages. People, like Mr. Bynum, who survived the slings and arrows, did so because they were flexible and could bend to help others, even when accommodation was not in their economic interest. Together Clarke and Marie's solid character and church upbringing enabled them to navigate all those issues by keeping in mind one simple, ancient rule: *Do unto others as you would have them do unto you.*

This message they instilled in their three children born within five years. Two months after Clarke and Marie had married, the yellow rose of Mertzon announced she was pregnant. Two weeks after her 20th birthday, on Monday, February 6, 1922, Willie Marie Hill Williams found herself having contractions at Monroe's St. Francis Sanitarium, northeast Louisiana's largest hospital, administered by the Catholic Church in a Protestant area. With Dorah and sisters 600 miles away, Marie would be the first in her family to give birth in a hospital. Dr. Armand G. McHenry and nurse Henrietta Johnson at 2:30 in the afternoon delivered a healthy nine-pound baby boy, all arms and legs and a good set of lungs.

Will Clarke was beside himself. His firstborn was a son. He finally had a family of his own, one to which he would always belong. As he looked at the perfect child, the 27-year-old father realized how quickly everything had changed. He thanked God for answering prayer. The previous February he had been alone in Monroe, heartbroken, sullen, lovesick, and in many ways rudderless. In twelve quick months, now he had both Marie and a family. Likewise, Marie relished how far she had come from connecting calls in dusty little Barnhart, Texas.

She did miss Dorah, though. Now she was a mother with a child, and a husband who loved both of them desperately.

Marie insisted they call their son *Clarke* after his father. Will Clarke added *McRae* as a middle name in remembrance of his first boss, T. C. McRae, the kindly manager of Cumberland Telephone's Iuka office. Mr. Bynum insisted he take the little family home in his automobile. Neither Marie nor Clarke could be expected to walk the mile home carrying a newborn, blankets, diapers, and bottles. Buying a car then became top priority on Clarke's agenda but new ones cost about $400, depending on whether a built-in starter was included. He had seen many hand-cranks bruise or break arms when the cylinder compression kicked back. Also, with an average 13 miles per gallon, gasoline at 22 cents a gallon meant a 10-gallon fill-up every other week or an extra $4.40 a month.

Since horses and buggies still used streets and roadways, horseshoe nails kept expensive car tires flat. Monroe Police also had gone to fining drivers for excessive speed, for illegally passing streetcars, and for spraying gravel that broke store windows. For all the hassle, Will Clarke would have kept walking, but Clarke McRae changed that. The young father weighed these concerns at midnight as he walked the floor with a son trying his best to wake the neighbors. All he could do was trust God to see them through. At least when *his* son cried at night, his father and mother heard him.

Six months after Clarke McRae's birth, Alexander Graham Bell died at his estate in Nova Scotia. By his bedside sat his wife Mabel, still deaf, the reason for the invention that changed the world and made them rich. Bell despaired that he had failed in giving Mabel the gift of hearing. As Aleck and Mabel watched the moonrise at 2:00 a.m., Mabel whispered to him, "Don't leave me." Bell traced the sign for *no* on her palm, then died peacefully in their bed.

The news gave Will Clarke and Marie pause, not just because the telephone business was their chosen career but because the timing of births and deaths was significant to them. Early in courting, Will realized that Marie Hill had entered the world the week his mother left it. That week to him had become mystical, as if God were choreographing across time and across the distance from Iuka to Mertzon. Will Clarke believed in destiny, and the eerie coincidence was partly why he would not take *no* for an answer, a stance which Marie perceived as confidence and, thus, she cast her lot with the limping Mississippi boy. Bell's death coinciding with their son's birth seemed to Will Clarke more than just coincidence, it was fate.

Southern Bell became more of a punching bag when it finally completed 70 miles of long distance copper between Monroe and El Dorado, Arkansas. Old Bastrop native D. M. Clower, a former Confederate telegraph operator, sneered in *The Monroe News-Star* about the time it took. The 86-year-old veteran claimed that after the fall of Vicksburg, he tore down 40 miles of the Monroe telegraph line while dodging Yankee bullets, then strung telegraph wire in weeks from Shreveport all the way to Houston to connect Confederate Generals Kirby Smith and John Magruder.[47] He questioned why Southern Bell needed 40 years to string telephone wire a mere 70 miles.

Everyone still wanted telephones. Mr. Bynum bumped up Will's salary to help him provide better for his family and buy a car. In a year, Clarke and Marie had saved enough for a down payment on a black Ford coupe with horsehair seats, a tall affair atop spindly wheels. In Clarke McRae's Baby Book, Marie recorded that his first trip was a ride in the Ford on the road going to Shreveport. They didn't linger there because, as Prohibition continued, federal revenuers were continually smashing illegal stills west of town and engaging moonshiners in gun battles. With seedy bars closed and drunks off the streets, the young Williamses were glad that their son wouldn't grow up with the ravages of liquor as they had.

But north Louisiana during Prohibition didn't insulate them from other violence and threats. With a national resurgence of the Ku Klux Klan into the 1920s, Monroe Klansmen boldly dared in *The Monroe News-Star*:

---

[47] *The Monroe News-Star*, August 17, 1921, front page

"The Klan's purpose is to inculcate the sacred principles and noble ideals of chivalry, the development of character, the protection of home and the chastity of womanhood, the exemplification of a pure patriotism, the preservation of American ideals and the maintenance of white supremacy. ...No man is wanted in the order who hasn't manhood enough to assume a real oath...or cannot swear an unqualified allegiance to the government of the United States of America, its flag and its Constitution."[48]

Familiar with Klan activities in Mississippi, Will Clarke found irony that General Nathan Bedford Forrest had started the Klan to fight Union protected land-grabbing speculators but that now the Klan wanted "unqualified allegiance" to the same government. Most saw through the talk of patriotism to what the KKK was really about: intimidating blacks, Jews, and Catholics. Newspapers reported race riots in Richland and Caldwell Parishes, and lynchings in Oklahoma, Mississippi, and rural areas. To Will Clarke, the KKK was regaining too much prominence in his adopted town.

Monroe Rabbi Dr. H. A. Merfield pleaded to the Monroe Rotary Fellowship Committee to shun the divisiveness of the "Invisible Empire of this reconstruction period which has appropriated to one class all the claims to pure Americanism which those left outside dare to protest."[49] Taking the opposite view, First Baptist Church pastor Frank Tripp argued publically that the law-and-order and moral precepts of the KKK were good and deserved support. In a twist of irony, as the Klan gave to the underprivileged while denouncing blacks, white Monroe bowed at the death of former slave Felix McCleo. Respected by both black and white, McCleo had been elected and reelected Justice of the Peace and Constable since 1868, a major feat in

---

[48] *The Monroe News-Star*, November 10, 1920, page 4
[49] *The Monroe News-Star*, October 14, 1921, front page

the racial divide. McCleo's memorialization gave Will Clarke and Marie hope for their adopted city

Southern Bell-Cumberland lost its rate hike battle on January 15, 1923. Huey Long, now chairman of the Railroad Commission, convinced new Commissioner Francis Williams to outvote former chairman Shelby Taylor. They rolled back the 1922 rate increases by as much as 70 percent. This meant Will Clarke and other accountants had to split a $440,000 refund among hundreds of Louisiana customers while reducing residential phone rates to $2.45 a month in Monroe. Long insisted Southern Bell pay the $440,000 in the form of refund checks and not by bill reductions. After two years of hard fighting, the soon-to-be Louisiana Kingfish wanted customers to see the money he was returning to them. He knew every time they picked up the phone, they'd think of Huey Long. Southern Bell unwittingly was funding Huey's campaign for governor.

Monroe suspended all political and racial polarization when springtime came and brought baseball with it. Forsythe Park, north of downtown, lovely and tree-lined, was the site of the ballpark and where the young Williamses picnicked with Clarke McRae. There, in a fluke of history, Will Clarke watched the legendary Babe Ruth. The homerun-hitting Great Bambino came to Monroe in the spring of 1923 after Monroe's Chamber begged the New York Yankees and Brooklyn Dodgers to stop there on a Southern promotional tour. For 75 percent of gross receipts and a guarantee of $250, American League business manager E. G. Barrows agreed to a Yankees-Dodgers exhibition game in little Monroe, a town of only 13,000.[50]

Stepping off the train from Vicksburg, Babe Ruth told the *News-Star*, "It's all bunk about my having lost confidence in myself."[51] The Sultan of Swat was in a slump during the 1922 season after he had rocked the baseball world in 1920, cracking a solo record 54 home runs, only 10 fewer than the entire Philadelphia Phillies championship team that year. In 1921, the

---

[50] *The Monroe News-Star*, December 16, 1922, front page
[51] *The Monroe News-Star*, April 5, 1923, front page

southpaw batter and pitcher hit 59 homers. The 6'2", 215-pound pudgy Babe from Baltimore was loved, worshipped, and envied as America's highest-paid athlete at a stratospheric $52,000 a year. The Curtiss Candy Company capitalized on his fame, producing a candy bar named the *Baby Ruth* but by denying any connection to Ruth, they didn't pay him royalties. By 1923, Babe Ruth was attracting over a million fans to Yankee Stadium. Whole families stampeded baseball parks wherever he played. In Detroit, he knocked one homer 575 feet, the length of nearly two football fields, a record yet unbroken. But in the '22 season, the Great Bambino sat in the dugout with injuries, leading to speculation he might have been a flash-in-the-pan. Sportswriters who punned that the Yankees were "Ruthless" propagated news of the Babe's apparent loss of confidence.

"Those fellows up there are liable to say anything," Babe Ruth said wearily to *The News-Star*. "The truth of the thing is I'm just feeling fine and as fit as a fiddle, and if I don't break the old record, it will not be because I have lost confidence in myself. We'll beat the Giants at the World Series if they are our opponents again. We have the best baseball club in both leagues and we'll prove it this season."[52]

Heavy rains drenched Monroe the night before, yet on steamy Thursday, April 5, 1923, a whopping 3,571 tickets were sold, more than one-fourth of the whole city. Ticketed and unticketed waded through mud, packed stands, stood on every inch, and climbed trees to witness history's greatest baseball teams face off in Forsythe Park. Mayor Arnold Bernstein threw out the first pitch to Yankees centerfielder Whitey Witt.

"I'll do my best to knock a homerun this afternoon," Ruth offered *The News-Star,* and in practice, he knocked three over the fence. Dodger spitball pitcher Burleigh Grimes walked him in the first inning, put two others on base, and Babe Ruth scored the second run. At the top of the seventh inning, the Babe singled to left, scoring second-baseman Mike McNally before rounding for home plate himself. Then the most exciting play of the game came at the bottom of the frame. With bases loaded

---

[52] Ibid

and two outs, the Bambino came back to the plate. If he were going to hit a homer, this would be the time. The crowd rose to its feet, hoping for a rare, record-book grand slam, something to tell their grandchildren. Four thousand stood motionless and hushed, hardly breathing in the thick, steamy air.

Sweating, Dodger relief pitcher Leo Dickerman had allowed five hits in the seventh. Now he faced Babe Ruth a second time in the same inning. Ruth wiped his brow, his leftie bat cocked high. Dickerson fired the first ball past him. "Strike one!" shouted "Umps" McGowan. Runners off their bases taunted Dickerman. Ruth stared at him. Dickerman fired again, and again the ball sailed past the Sultan. Ruth still seemed confident. "C'mon, Babe!" someone shouted. Dickerman sifted the dirt and wiped his hands on his pants. Lanky legs and arms wound up and Dickerman fired his patented curveball. The Great Bambino swung at the white blur but the ball pulverized the glove. Ruth looked at "Umps" McGowan. McGowan signaled "out." Monroe groaned mournfully and sat down, sad for the Great Bambino. He had struck out.

In the two-and-a-half hour game, though Ruth hit only once out of four at-bats, his three runs led the Yankees to a 9-to-4 victory over the Dodgers. Monroe and Will Clarke had witnessed a once-in-a-lifetime game. He jumped on a streetcar to get back to the phone office on South Grand.

Later that summer, President Warren G. Harding, the first elected by women, died suddenly at 57. Mrs. Harding's refusal to allow an autopsy fueled speculation he was poisoned, and rumors doubled when the First Lady had all the president's papers, official and unofficial, burned at the White House and at their home in Ohio. Vice President Calvin Coolidge took over and the Roaring Twenties took off. Telephones sped up speculation on Wall Street until sixteen percent of Americans were gambling their savings in stocks. Brokerage houses loaned speculators 90 percent of stock purchases, building a shaky house of cards.

For Will Clarke in Monroe, the rate reduction and rebate doubled his work and created a boon for Cumberland Telephone.

Linemen couldn't install telephones fast enough. *Wherever your thought goes, your voice may go,* boasted Cumberland's ads. *Your telephone is the latch to open for you any door in the land.*[53] Of Louisiana's 7,000 installations in 1923, Monroe accounted for 2,036.[54] Southern Bell-Cumberland crowed of its $1.7 million investment in Louisiana, 3,800 new poles, 50 railcar loads of cable, nine carloads of copper wire.[55] Records were broken every day as Louisiana operators connected 264,376,000 local calls and 3,074,750 long distance calls. Considering Monroe's huge natural gas field, Southern Bell's statisticians in Atlanta projected that Monroe and West Monroe would grow from 18,000 in 1924 to 48,000 by 1944. With the national economy turning red hot, Southern Bell-Cumberland planned a $20 million investment over five years. Profits, pay, and prices jumped. Cars ranged from $590 for a Ford on the "Ford Weekly Purchase Plan" to $2,190 for the top Nash. The Dow Jones Industrials climbed at breakneck speed. Southern Bell moved O. H. Bynum up and J. W. Warren in as manager of the Monroe office.

At home in West Monroe, Clarke McRae took his first steps at 15 months. Four years after his birth, nearly to the day, February 11, 1926, his sister Kittie Marie Williams was born, and the year after, sister Mary Lee was born on December 8, 1927. Marie anxiously carried her third child as the Ouachita River rose to touch the Desiard Street Bridge. Called the Great Flood of 1927, the Mississippi River overflowed its banks fifty miles wide and 100 miles long from Vicksburg nearly to Monroe. When not keeping fragile phone lines out of the water, Will Clarke joined his neighbors piling sandbags along the Ouachita. Five-year-old Clarke McRae helped with his baby sisters, doing his part to keep the family safe just blocks from an angry, dark river. He watched men desperately sandbagging, tripling the levee in size.

The threat receded by late 1927, just as Marie came to term. Meantime, to get away from crying sisters, Clarke and his

---

[53] *The Monroe News-Star*, July 21, 1924, page 4
[54] *The Monroe News-Star*, January, 15, 1924, page 4
[55] *The Monroe News-Star*, January, 22, 1924, page 5

buddies explored Natchitoches Street. The steam whistles of paddlewheelers summoned them to the levee top, where they watched the brown sandbags of 1927 eventually turn green with grass and slowly form an irregular levee obscuring the river. The whistle of the Vicksburg, Shreveport & Texas Railroad reverberated from the geometric iron bridge just upriver. When bridge tenders rotated the center spans of both bridges to allow steamboats to pass, the boys stood in awe of the marvels of modern science.

Each time the wind blew out of the southwest, a stink filled the air from the new Brown Paper Mill, the first American mill producing high-tensile-strength brown paper for grocery bags and paperboard. The process of grinding Louisiana's pine trees into chips and digesting wood pulp thin enough to roll into paper created an odor that gave the boys many a joking opportunity.

Politics began smelling too, as evangelical Huey Pierce Long, the old Railroad Commissioner who beat Southern Bell, won the state's highest office in early 1928 as Louisiana's 40th governor. Because Long increasingly characterized Bell Telephone as an evil monopoly, his victory put the company in jeopardy. Clarke McRae overheard adults debating Long's "steal from the rich and give to the poor" philosophy. Long's face looked out from every newspaper; his preacher's cadence rang from every radio. Will Clarke privately appreciated the governor's radical idea of free school textbooks.

Those books came in handy in the fall of 1928, when Clarke walked with neighborhood friends to the new two-story brick West Monroe Grammar School at 700 Natchitoches Street. He and his friends would listen for the rickety Ford open-air school bus to put-put by, bringing in the country kids from down near the paper mill. Mr. Billy Eyre, the driver, would toot his rubber horn. Eyre kept his right headlight aimed ahead and his left aimed down to see potholes better at night and on dark, stormy days. The boys laughed at the bus that looked as if it were winking.

In 1929, new signs went up changing the school name to Crosley Elementary in honor of the family who gave the land.

But with pumpkins out at Halloween, Clarke and his buddies noticed an ominous shift in grownups' moods. People stood in lines at banks. Something had crashed up north and no one laughed anymore. The sound of excited radio announcers wafted from open windows. Clarke heard his father talk gloomily to his mother about tough times for telephone companies, for bankers, for farmers, for everyone.

Governor Huey Long ranted that the rich on Wall Street had thrown the world into economic chaos. He and others targeted millionaires Bernard Baruch, J. P. Morgan, John D. Rockefeller, and Joseph Kennedy. Will Clarke didn't like living at the whims of others and certainly not at the whim of nefarious Wall Street. He had worked too hard all his life to be maimed by the greed and mistakes of others. The October crash forced a decision: he'd had enough, in the same way he resolved that Sunday to telegraph Marie, *NOW OR NEVER*. Will had to find a way to take fate in his own hands.

Through the 1920s at Monroe Bell, Will Clarke had befriended many rural folks who had switchboards in their homes. Though most barely met expenses, they provided decent service for neighbors who in turn provided steady income. Clarke particularly liked the charm of a small community in Morehouse Parish named Oak Ridge, a quiet town in cotton country. Oak Ridge looked like a postcard, its stately oaks cooling wide green lawns with patchwork shadows, presiding over white clapboard houses with verandahs, and picturesque churches with steeples, and a downtown business strip of red bricks and commerce. Oak Ridge Telephone Company was owned and operated by Earle and Hulda Hogan. They served 72 reliable customers, sometimes 75.

Will Clarke and Marie had managed to retrieve their meager savings as bank closures threatened. Ten months after the crash, 744 banks had failed, ten times the yearly average, creating more panic. People stopped buying, plants shut down, and by 1932, thirteen million Americans were thrown out of work. The next year would be catastrophic, with 9,000 banks failing, turning savings of $140 million into dust.

Just ahead of the hysteria, Will Clarke and Marie grabbed their money, sensing the greater risk lay in doing nothing. Will knew cash money in hand when banks failed made their money more valuable. With prices also falling in the panic, the cash doubled in value again. And with costs cheaper in small towns, Clarke saw the opportunity to maximize what little money they had by moving to Oak Ridge.

Telephones were all he and Marie knew, and the Hogans, finding themselves caught as the panic unfolded, agreed to sell out lock, stock, and barrel. The price: $500. Looking out from the family Ford, 8-year-old Clarke McRae took in the picturesque town, a little stung at leaving his friends in West Monroe. He would also have to adapt from being a city boy to a country boy and he was old enough to know that country boys liked to scrap. As they pulled up to the Hogan's small telephone building, Clarke McRae saw a boy about his age, Earle Junior, and his eleven-year-old sister Grace.

> Earl Hogan, Jr.: "The first time I saw the Williamses, they drove up in a black two-seater Ford right across from our phone building. Clarke Jr. was the first to get out, the oldest of the three children who got out of the car that day. He was about my age and we became good friends even though I was a year older and a grade ahead of him in school. We lived in a small town. Everybody knew everybody. In those days, there was a sign going into town that said 350 people lived here. In 1930, I was going into the Third grade so Clarke was going into the Second grade and we became good, lifelong friends."[56]

Clarke and Marie were proud but nervous owning their very own telephone exchange. They were one mistake away from bankruptcy at a time when bankruptcies and foreclosures were

---

[56] Earl Hogan interview, Oak Ridge, Louisiana, September 25, 2012

just beginning. Because phones were a luxury, Oak Ridge Telephone was a big gamble. Receivables most assuredly would slow and subscribers might skip payments. Clarke and Marie were betting that the old cotton money that had survived the Civil War had long since stabilized both the community's assets and those of the local bank. Old money meant that land and equipment were paid for, profits were larger, and cash pooled in a conservative bank. That made Oak Ridge, in Clarke's estimation, the perfect place to ride out the storm. When the economy turned around, Clarke felt the Railroad/Public Service Commission would have to allow higher rates.

Purposely insulated in the quiet town while the rest of world crumbled, Will Clarke and Marie knew they were in a precarious position but they trusted God to see them through. They taught their children the same trust, and Clarke McRae, Kittie, and Mary Lee saw their parents live that trust. "Many things in life are completely unpredictable," their father would preach, "some unfair, but all worth it. Keep your faith. Remember who you are."

After long careers working for others, Clarke and Marie now depended only on themselves. No one else's whims would threaten their livelihoods. They would keep customers happy while cultivating new ones. There was no way to know anything with certainty in 1930 except that the Roaring '20s were over. As the Crash, bank failures, and the Great Depression squeezed men's souls, the Williams' new venture could fall either way.

Clarke McRae saw it all.

CHAPTER 4

"USE IT UP, WEAR IT OUT. MAKE IT DO OR DO WITHOUT."
                                WILLIAM CLARKE WILLIAMS

*"TIMES WERE PRETTY TIGHT. AS SOON AS I WAS OUT OF SCHOOL, I HAD
TO GO COLLECTING. MANY OF THEM WOULD SAY, 'HEY, BOY! GIVE ME A
CHECK. I'LL SIGN IT FOR YOU.' SO I'D WRITE THE CHECK OUT FOR
THEM AND THEY'D SIGN IT FOR ME."*
                                CLARKE MCRAE WILLIAMS

*"WE LEARNED A LOT ABOUT HUMAN NATURE. SOME PEOPLE WHO WERE
VERY NICE IN PERSON COULD BE VERY RUDE OVER THE TELEPHONE."*
                                MARY LEE WILLIAMS OGLESBY

The five Williamses moved from West Monroe to Oak Ridge in April 1930, slipping between late census takers in West Monroe and early ones in Oak Ridge, but there is no doubt the town welcomed the young family promising better phone service. In the town's politeness, Will Clarke discerned something else, almost as a warning. With extensive experience in Southern culture, versed as he was in Mississippi's post-Civil War resistance, he knew that Oak Ridge's genteel façade beguiled an iron will to protect its own. A couple of generations of Oak Ridgans were experienced in how to spot outside threats, especially those seeking to part them from their money.

Will Clarke guessed right that Oak Ridge's cushion of old cotton fortunes had delayed and minimized the effects of the 1929 Crash. Remote from metropolitan Monroe and all other towns, Oak Ridge was an oasis, standing as a lone sentinel of antebellum prosperity after the Civil War, too far off the beaten path for troops or carpetbaggers. The rest of Louisiana, however, wrestled with carpetbag-military governments for the twelve years called *Reconstruction.*

The planter class held firmly to traditions of chivalry and honor mixed with agrarian science. The well educated and well traveled of Oak Ridge enjoyed a continuance of the aristocratic Southern pastimes of music, art, literature, and an unending social season. Teachers from across the nation were drawn to the town, Clarence Austin from Alabama, Lucille Stewart from

Mississippi, Evylen Bates from Arkansas, and local husband-and-wife educators Samuel and Willie B. Lucky. Native educator Effie Carter took note of the unusual politeness, ethic, and intelligence of the phone company's only son, Clarke McRae Williams. She mentioned his qualities to her husband, Joe Sidney Carter, who years later would act on Mrs. Carter's glowing assessment. He spied the Williams boy offering help to everyone, especially on the switchboard now in the Williams' front parlor.

> Clarke McRae Williams: "We did not have a directory as such. How anyone knew their number, I don't know, but it didn't make any difference because nobody used a number anyway. Each jack had a number, such as '2-6.' *Number 1* was the Hogan line and that was part of the agreement that my father made with Mr. Hogan when he sold the company to my father, that Number 1 would be his number from then on. That worked all right until we upgraded to a dial system. We had a hard time working that out, which we were not able to do."[57]

Clarke McRae Williams grew up unique in a unique town, one of very high standards. The hamlet boasted three accomplished physicians, bachelor Dr. W. A. Russell and parish physician Dr. Charles Hope, both of Mississippi, and Dr. Ben Barham, whose family's vast cotton acreage had funded an extensive education to give Oak Ridge a hometown doctor. During the 1930s, young Dr. Paul Herron became the fourth. Filling their prescriptions, Patrick Henry Wade mixed compounds at Wade's Drug Store, also a magnet for town youth, huddling around the only soda fountain. Menfolk gathered at Dave Perriot's antiseptic-smelling, mirrored barbershop, scrapping over politics, news, and farming techniques, negotiating land and jobs, complaining about young people, and

---

[57] Clarke Williams, Sr. interview, *KNOE Special Report* with Jamie Patrick, KNOE TV8 News, ©1992 Noe Enterprises, Inc.

still talking about lightning striking Will McDuffie back in the summer of '26. They particularly debated property lines, a crazy angular mismatch of old Spanish land grants that tormented surveyors.

Canvassing for Southern Bell, Will Clarke found Oak Ridge in a world of its own, exhibiting the telltale signs of old prosperity: Nearly every rooted family maintained a staff of house servants—cooks, maids, and gardeners, many of them descendants of former family slaves. The gentry lived in homes to which they had given names, "Forest Grove," "Oak Hall," "Sunnyside," "Norman's Retreat," "Hope Hall," "Como Plantation," "The Elders," "The Fluker," and whimsical camps, "Breezy Bend" and "Wrecker's Roost." It was almost as if the Civil War had never happened.

If the destructiveness of war had not rattled Oak Ridge, neither would the Great Depression. While most of the South's poor noticed no change, the wealthy pretended there was none. The war and aftermath fostered skepticism because to Oak Ridgans it had been about domination and the wholesale theft of land and cotton. They had kept their guards up ever since. Merchants could spot a shyster coming a mile away, so by the 1930s, dry goods stores and grocers operated healthy, brisk businesses. John Sawyer, Frank Files, Earl Barham, and May and Ellie Traylor, who had sharp eyes for good credit, managed tall storefronts clustered on Oak Street. James Shaw served as town butcher. George Files kept Oak Ridge Power & Light going.

Railroad Agent Marion Bardin kept an eye on traffic in and out. Old Will Whithorne, born in 1860, along with Frank Montgomery kept the oldest of Oak Ridge's three cotton gins ginning at capacity. Oak Ridge cotton farmers accounted for the lion's share of Morehouse Parish's 20,000 annual bales. The surrounding sea of white meant cotton was still king, and the king kept his white gold in tiny Bank of Oak Ridge, another key factor in Will Clarke's decision to move from the city. Oak Ridge's diminutive brick bank may have been a closet compared to Monroe's ten-story limestone Ouachita National Bank, but Will Clarke suspected its simple façade veiled great assets, enough to retain three fulltime cashiers, Lucille Huffman, Henry Wofford, and Edward Folse. In the *Morehouse Enterprise*, Bank of Oak Ridge boasted $336,000 in post-Crash capitalization.[58] There had never been a run on the Bank of Oak Ridge mainly because when President Franklin D. Roosevelt closed banks temporarily, Oak Ridge's bank merely operated out of the back door and commerce continued.

Productive and powerful families underpinned the town. The extensive Barham family built an empire of cotton plantations, mercantile ventures, banks, and land in Oak Ridge, and of political forces in both Baton Rouge and Washington. Postmaster Eugene Barham streamlined operations with Jonathan and Myrtle Barham as husband-and-wife carriers and was first to know many trends and secrets. To keep the peace, Oak Ridge depended on longtime Marshal John Morris along with local Deputy Sheriff Fred Blakemore.

As he grew, Clarke McRae saw that businesses in a small town stayed in business only by treating people right. Everybody knew everybody from the moment they were born. He also noticed that because of the town's high level of education, people embraced new technology. Leaders were ecstatic when industrialists built a high-employment carbon plant on Monroe's gigantic natural gas field, the largest in the United States.

Oil and gas exploration fueled an unprecedented economic boom that converged with the reign of Governor Huey Long. The governor leveraged severance windfalls into state bonds, and as the Depression deepened, put thousands of Louisianans to work extending the state's paltry 311 miles of paved road to over 2,000. Long beat his chest everywhere, electric rants reverberating off buildings, first in Monroe, then in Bastrop, impressing young Clarke McRae as well as annoying him. Boisterous and crude, yes, but no one could argue that Long didn't keep promises. He was employing one-tenth of all the road workers in America, providing near full employment in the Depression. Next door to Frank and Hulda Hogan, who started

---

[58] *Morehouse Twice-a-Week Enterprise*, April 14, 1930, page 3

Oak Ridge Telephone, Sam Inghram's Boarding House stayed full with a dozen highway workmen and cooks. Their paychecks from Baton Rouge added to the brisk local economy at a time when relatives in other states were starving.

At Oak Ridge Telephone, Marie was not terribly excited when Will Clarke began hauling relays, wires, cabinets, and an old switchboard into their parlor. Like most mom-and-pop phone companies, though, home was Central Office. The Hogans had kept the business in a separate one-room building that was not part of the sale. To Will Clarke, the building was too far away and too small for Marie to work and keep up with three children. The Hogans had kept two operators, each working 12-hour shifts, six days a week with no phone service on Sunday. Will Clarke knew that Sundays were the one day that working people could leisurely use the telephone.

With the switchboard in their home, the Williams family added Sunday service, closing only from 10:00 a.m. to 3:00 p.m. for church and Sunday dinner. Marie had her hands full getting three children ready for church while connecting phone calls, but the work would prove worth it, Will thought, as he watched phone subscriptions jump in nearby Bastrop from 260 to over 700. The month they moved to Oak Ridge, Bastrop's Southern Bell switched on a $75,000 *Western Electric* upgrade. Will felt sure that with that many subscribers a few miles away, toll calls to Oak Ridge Telephone would jump. The world was connecting everywhere and every way possible. Just south of Oak Ridge, the ballyhooed transcontinental U.S. Highway 80 finally linked the east and west coasts when officials opened a colossal $7 million bridge at Vicksburg.

Just as the Williamses had moved to Monroe amid controversy, once they arrived in Oak Ridge, Congress proposed using Morehouse Parish's flat Prairie Jefferson –Oak Ridge– as a spillway for redirecting floodwaters from the Mississippi River. The 1927 Flood had backed up only one foot into Oak Ridge, but if the Jadwin Plan passed, another flood would wipe the town off the map. Their first summer there, 1930, Will Clarke and Clarke McRae in a crowd of townsfolk watched black cars and serious men blow in one afternoon to decide if they disliked Oak Ridge enough to submerge the town and 73,000 cultivated acres under 10 feet of water. Judge J. T. Shell pleaded, "We wanted you to see our lands and our homes…hope you have found us good, loyal citizens of the United States. Our case is in your hands. We hope for judgment that this splendid section of Morehouse Parish, Louisiana, over which you are passing today, is not the proper place to 'spill' the headwaters of old man River."[59] His words fell on deaf ears. Jadwin passed.

What saved Oak Ridge from the 1937 flood was the Corps of Engineers straightening out the Mississippi River. The Corps cut out 170 miles of bends between Memphis and Vicksburg, lowering flood heights by five feet.

More threatening than a flood, a scarlet fever epidemic broke out. Eight-year-old Clarke McRae and 2-year-old Mary Lee caught the dreaded disease, a child killer in the 1930s causing chills, nausea, and red, peeling cheeks. Dr. Barham prescribed new sulfur drugs, long before antibiotics and penicillin were perfected in the 1940s. Marie nursed her children for a week while juggling the switchboard with the help of 4-year-old Kittie.

Young Clarke couldn't wait to get outside where his father drove a truck and climbed poles. Inside, all the mechanical gizmos fascinated him, too. He took a keen interest in watching his parents cobble together a phone system, relay by relay. He could tell, however, that his father was having difficulty. Will had been behind a desk for ten years and now in his mid-30s was back shinnying up 40-foot poles, running or untangling wire. Clarke McRae saw the trouble with his father's bad leg, heard the groans and grunts; the boy offered to help, but, no, he was too young and too short. Clarke insisted his handicap was no different from his father's and he soon got his chance.

> Mary Lee Williams Oglesby, sister: "Clarke McRae began his telephone career by uncrossing lines tangled by the wind. I don't know in what order he took on more difficult roles such as

---

[59] *Morehouse Enterprise*, July 24, 1930, front page

climbing poles and installing or repairing telephones, but he took his turn –as we all did– 'working the board,' answering the calls that came in on the switchboard, and trying to collect the monthly bills."[60]

"We dreaded facing certain men because we knew they would put us off with some excuse. We learned a lot about human nature. Some people who were very nice in person could be very rude over the telephone."[61]

A quick learner, Clarke mastered the switchboard in no time, a confident voice helping adults. When townsfolk realized they were talking to an eight-year-old but intelligent operator, people laughed about it yet developed a healthy respect. Clarke McRae was wise beyond years. When he rode up on his bicycle to hand-deliver 72 phone bills, they admired him even more. He quickly put faces to voices, enjoying the panache of representing the telephone company and his technologically advanced family. All this on a bicycle.

Clarke McRae soon noticed something odd: In West Monroe, bike-riding boys filled the streets but in Oak Ridge he was the only one. Farm boys rode horses, dreaming of bikes and mechanical wizardry you didn't have to feed and clean up after. Clarke became conscious of envious eyes.

Earl Hogan, Jr.: "The only thing I worried about was Clarke had a bicycle. Nobody else had one. Eventually I got a bicycle. A boy about a mile west had a bicycle in the garage but never rode it so Dad bought it, cleaned it up and I got a bicycle.

"Clarke used his. He was a leader in town. He was looked at as an industrious guy. He got on

---

[60] Mary Lee Williams Oglesby, "Your Chairman Remembered," a paper in possession of niece Carolyn Williams Perry, circa 1980

[61] Mary Lee Williams Oglesby handwritten letter in possession of niece Carolyn Williams Perry, October 1987, page 4

that bicycle and collected for the seventy-two stations (phones) in those days. When you call on seventy-two homes, everybody gets to know you."[62]

Townspeople quickly warmed up to Clarke, impressed that someone so young displayed such a consistent ethic of helpfulness, hard work, and cheerfulness. Humble to a fault, he looked for ways to help others. Early Christmases were bleak and he felt the strain his parents were under, so young Clarke took charge.

Mary Lee Williams Oglesby: "One of my dearest memories of those years is that one Christmas, still in the Depression, Santa Claus brought Kittie and me each a doll. Mama's gift to us was clothes she had made and crocheted for the dolls. Clarke McRae –we always called him that– gave us each a beautiful little cedar chest to hold the clothes. I was awed by that gift. I didn't know how much it cost but I knew he'd worked long hours and spent his money on us. I wasn't able then to properly express my appreciation. In later years I did tell him what that gift meant to me."[63]

Clarke understood poverty. When he stood on a front porch with the monthly bill and the family couldn't pay, their fondness for Clarke translated into vegetables, baked goods, preserves, meat, eggs, milk, or butter. He would graciously accept with no hint of haughtiness. Though times were hard and his family needed money more than most, through Clarke's example the Williamses quickly became known as Good People.

---

[62] Earl Hogan, Jr., video interview, September 25, 2012, Oak Ridge, Louisiana

[63] Mary Lee Williams Oglesby, "Your Chairman Remembered," a paper in possession of niece Carolyn Williams Perry, circa 1980

Clarke McRae Williams: "Times were pretty tight in the mid-1930s and we needed the money as soon as we could get it. From the very first day of every month as soon as I was out of school, I had to go collecting. But I had a lot of good relationships with the people in Oak Ridge. They were always real nice to me. Many of them would say, 'Hey, boy! Give me a check. I'll sign it for you.' So I'd write the check out for them and they'd sign it for me."[64]

The young businessman grew up considering everyone a friend without knowing just how idyllic Oak Ridge was. He developed many friendships, even a certain awe that he conducted business with friends' parents. Boys looked up to Clarke McRae and had fun at his house, partly because Clarke's home became a menagerie.

Mary Lee Williams Oglesby: "Daddy couldn't pass an abandoned animal. He was always bringing something home. One dog he rescued he named Sailor, after a Monroe wrestler who had bowlegs like the dog. Daddy said Sailor was the only dog he had ever seen that ran *from* a rabbit. Clarke McRae had a dog named Jack we all loved and Jack was with us a long time. When Jack was dying, Clarke McRae and his friends formed a circle around Jack as he died. It was very sad and I felt so sorry for Clarke McRae's grief."[65]

Tragedies come with the territory but the prodigious Williams kids knew before most that sadness only heightened

---

[64] Clarke Williams, Sr. interview, *KNOE Special Report* with Jamie Patrick, KNOE TV8 News, ©1992 Noe Enterprises, Inc.
[65] Mary Lee Williams Oglesby handwritten letter in possession of niece Carolyn Williams Perry, October 1987, page 9

laughter. The kids found ways to entertain themselves and every other child in Oak Ridge.

> Mary Lee Williams Oglesby: "We played games mostly in our yard that appealed to every age. One was called 'Statue' where a 'thrower' would swing you around, then let go and how ever you fell, you'd have to 'freeze' like a statue. We played 'Red Rover,' too, and of course made mud pies. As sundown approached in the long summer evenings, we'd chase fireflies and watch for the first star. Then we'd say, *Starlight, Star bright, First star I see tonight.* Then we'd make a wish and to 'seal' it, you then had to find another star and look at it before you saw the first one again. We also made wishes on loads of hay and on white mules or horses. When you saw a white mule or horse, you licked your right thumb, touched your left palm with the thumb, then stamped it with your closed right fist. It took 100 horses to make a wish come true but only one load of hay."[66]

Intricate wish-giving protocols may have created their own truth, but for adults Will and Marie, wishing on any number of stars, horses, or haystacks did not solve oppressive money worries. No number of white horses in hayfields under starlit skies could seem to make Oak Ridge Telephone profitable. To feed the family Will and Marie planted an extensive home garden. Clarke learned from his parents how to plant, when to plant, and what to plant. He learned nature's law of seedtime and harvest, of delayed gratification, of nurturing a project, of multiplied rewards, and of the joy of harvest. In addition, responsible Clarke also kept up with the family cow, Brownie, and learned to milk and separate the cream to make butter. The city boy had become a farmer.

---

[66] Mary Lee Williams Oglesby handwritten letter in possession of niece Carolyn Williams Perry, October 1987, page 11

As much as he liked gardening, he despised mowing. He sweated and grunted for hours across the huge Williams yard pushing a heavy cast iron cylinder mower. If summer rains delayed him much more than a week, mowing thick grass would take twice as long in the hot sun. When done, Clarke then had to clean the mower and file the curved blades back to point. Sometimes the ordeal took the whole day nearly every Saturday in the summer, cramping his social life.

Lawns were big in Oak Ridge, the site of garden parties and dances for any and all occasions. Nearly all Oak Ridge families hosted young people at their homes each weekend, spreading white linen over outside tables on which they mounded barbeque, hamburgers, steaks, pork and beans, potato salad, and iced-down Coca-Colas and Pepsis, lemonade, and punch. While Clarke knew older folks' parties involved spirits, he also heard muffled whispers of rampant alcoholism among the landed gentry. That was some of Oak Ridge's best gossiping, tales of how plantations were lost or ruined because the owner's children, soft and lazy, fell to drink. Southern towns reeked of such lore. Observant Clarke knew poison when he saw it and he stayed away from it.

Garden parties also hosted games, Chinese checkers, gin rummy, pin-the-tale-on-the-donkey, charades, and dominoes, and a game called "42." Since gambling-style poker and most card games were disapproved, "42" enabled groups of four to play a card game without cards by "catching tricks," using dominoes to score points. In afternoons and sometimes at night under Tiki torches, Clarke and his friends would play for hours. Chores for the boys included taking turns hand cranking ice cream churns, but it was all worth it when fresh ice cream topped warm apple pie, peach cobbler, chocolate cake, pecan pie, or any of an array of sweets over which hostesses competed for superiority.

> Mary Lee Williams Oglesby: "He had a lot of friends and they had good times. Sometimes they would gather in our front room and play records on the Gramophone, the kind you had to crank. I

remember one time Clarke had a crush on a girl who had visited from Georgia. After she left, he played 'Georgia on My Mind' until he wore the record out."[67]

While fundamental Protestant north Louisiana frowned on dancing, graceful Oak Ridge never stopped. "Oak Hall" often rocked to midnight with young people swirling across hardwood floors to small juke bands, a record player, or sometimes a radio catching signals from New Orleans or Chicago, pulling big band clarinets and saxophones out of the sky. For those hours, the youngsters dreamed of living anywhere but Oak Ridge.

Clarke began taking Catherine Barham to the socials.

Catherine Barham: "Clarke did not dance but it was not because of his heart [he had a rapid heartbeat], it was because he was real Slew-footed. He didn't dance but he ran the record player and enjoyed that. The PTA bought a record player and people from Rayville and all the towns around would come to the dances, usually Friday or Saturday nights. Schools had cakewalks. They entertained the town. We even had movies from the theatre in Rayville in the schoolhouse until they decided they might set it on fire. We had minstrels, talent shows, cakewalks, and Easter parades for the children. Everybody included all ages because if they didn't we wouldn't have enough people to have a party. We went swimming on Sunday in the river and in the lake and went to people's houses. Mrs. Norman and Mrs. Hogan were the kind that when you went to their houses you played games like musical chairs. We had wiener roasts almost every Friday night, had banana pudding, homemade ice cream, peach ice cream, and

---

[67] Ibid

watermelon. You could put the watermelon in water and cool it. And we had all kinds of vegetables. Everybody shared tomatoes, sweet potatoes, and apples. But you had to have all kinds of fans in the summer because you couldn't stay inside in the house. We had sprinklers in the yard, little round ones, that sprayed water all the time. Sand piles, tire swings, all that sort of stuff is how we played."[68]

When Clarke McRae was 13, on a crisp January day he heard an unusual noise skyward as an airplane tossed and tumbled in loops and figure-eights. The impromptu air show attracted Oak Ridgans to an adjacent field where the shiny single-engine plane landed on grass. George W. Files and Erle M. Barham got out. Young Barham explained he'd just completed pilot training at the Parks School of Aviation in St. Louis and had thus become Oak Ridge's first licensed pilot. In celebration, Barham took the bravest of souls for introductory airplane rides. Barham grabbed shy, meek Clarke McRae and in one minute the 13-year-old watched the ground drop away beneath them. Oak Ridge's towering steeples now looked like toys, corrugated fields ran to the horizon, barren trees looked like dandelions. The telephone and power poles he sweated to climb were no more than toothpicks. He couldn't see the wires but he knew they were there. Problems seemed small from up high. Work seemed less strenuous or important. Flying was liberating.

Writing that day for the *Morehouse Enterprise*, correspondent Nettie Traylor recorded, "Mr. Barham's flying with many breathtaking stunts was the admiration of all who witnessed his ability to be numbered among the bird-men of the nation."[69] Clarke vowed that as soon as he could, he would become Oak Ridge's second licensed pilot.

---

[68] Catherine Barham interview, Oak Ridge, Louisiana, August 13, 2013
[69] Nettie Traylor, "Oak Ridge News," *Morehouse Enterprise*, January 10, 1935, page 3

Come Sunday, though, the Reverends Morris Wynne of Oak Ridge Baptist and Alton Lawson of Oak Ridge Methodist sermonized about the first hangings in thirty-five years that unsettled Morehouse Parish and particularly Oak Ridge Deputy Sheriff Fred Blakemore. Blakemore watched Joe Winn and Bo Webb, African-Americans, dangle at the end of hangman's nooses for killing an elderly white man. The gang leader who planned the murder got away.

The tragedy confirmed the Biblical truth that the wages of sin is death, no escaping that. Even if you got away from man, God would be waiting. Pastor Wynne reiterated to Clarke McRae, his family, and the congregation that life would always be a continual battleground between good and evil. Satan had a silver tongue that convinced many to fall on their own swords.

Clarke began to put together the concept that good, disciplined decisions produced good, productive lives. Bad, selfish decisions created strife, heartbreak, disappointment, and sadness, but in the moment, the people who made those bad decisions never saw them as bad. Even a reasonable person could fool himself. Young Clarke consciously pieced the jigsaw together as he sat listening two-thirds of the way back in the dark proscenium of Oak Ridge Baptist Church. He could always tell when Reverend Wynne challenged everyone's souls because the carved mahogany pews would creak under uneasy shifting. Nothing proved success better than longevity, so the church and the Word that existed long before him and would exist long after him was worth listening to: A Messiah named Jesus promised to save Man from evil. It didn't take long for Clarke McRae to see that what Man really needed saving from was himself.

As Clarke McRae grew into manhood, he saw life's paradox that to be a success, one needed to focus less on his own ambition and more on others. Since no one could ever have all the information with which to make perfect decisions, he had to rely on a higher power to navigate the unknown. The basis of success, the key to living one's life, was called *faith*.

Guided by loving parents, embraced by a community, and immersed in the wisdom of scripture, Clarke McRae found that he needed faith in every decision and that faith in people was paramount. That involved trust, a troublesome problem for Man, the lack of which caused wars. To make sense of it all, Clarke McRae never questioned God but rather embraced Him. He sensed this acceptance would lead him to trustworthy people in whom he could believe and with whom he could build.

> Mary Lee Williams Oglesby: "Clarke considered it his duty to keep Kittie and me on the straight and narrow. When we failed in his sight to do right, he would bend our little fingers until we agreed to mend our ways. But he was good to us. One time a travelling show came to town and it so scared Kittie and me that we couldn't go to sleep unless he was sitting by our bed. It took several nights of his protection before we could go to sleep without his presence."[70]

His sisters looked up to and trusted him because he took his job as Big Brother seriously. With Will Clarke gone most of the day, Clarke McRae assumed leadership and responsibility for the house. The respect and reliance of his sisters matured the boy who saw his decisions growing important to them. While the brother enjoyed his sisters' admiration, he felt the growing responsibility and scrutiny. Clarke carried himself as an adult, and everybody in town noticed it. Ultimately, everyone held him to a higher standard. Hungry for knowledge on how to be a leader, Clarke became a voracious reader and scholar of history. He realized that the Williams' loving household did not resemble the world outside, and he wanted to protect his sisters from a world of unforgiving mistakes.

Both Deputy Blakemore and Oak Ridge remembered those hangings. Winn and Webb had easily confessed and actually thanked law enforcement, all white, for its courteous treatment. When given a chance for final words as they stood at the gallows, neither so much as blamed the escaped mastermind.

---

[70] Mary Lee Williams Oglesby, "Your Chairman Remembered," a paper in possession of niece Carolyn Williams Perry, circa 1980

Clarke McRae saw it as a tragic story of one unguarded, dark temptation turned fatal for both victim and perpetrators. A smart man developed a sixth sense for such traps because a smart man "leaned not unto his own understanding."[71] He relied on faith, a concept that came unusually easy to Clarke.

Cotton planters relied on Oak Ridge Telephone Company to complete their early morning calls to check market prices at cotton exchanges in Memphis and New Orleans. Marie and teenager Lillian Fitch worked each line to track down the named receiver no matter how far away. A certain Oak Ridge cotton planter called in one morning, frantic to find a cotton buyer whom he had met a few days before while the buyer was passing through Oak Ridge. All the planter could remember was the man had only one arm. He couldn't remember the buyer's name or where he lived. Marie shifted into detective role, calling town after town, talking with numerous operators and cotton buyers she had come to know. Finally, someone remembered the man, his name, and where he lived. After hours of costly connections in and out of Louisiana, Marie tracked down her customer's buyer in Memphis, Tennessee.[72] To make the connection for the Oak Ridge planter, Marie spun the magneto on her switchboard to ring up the operator in Monroe, the nearest large station, who in turn rang up either Little Rock, Arkansas, or Jackson, Mississippi, whose operator then rang up the operator in Memphis who connected to the one-armed man's office. With phone cords plugged in on four different switchboards hundreds of miles apart, Marie once more spun the magneto, which rang the telephone in the buyer's Memphis office. When he answered and Marie spoke into the headset, "Long distance calling," the buyer identified himself in the hollow sound of four hundred miles of wire and she told the Oak Ridge planter, "Go ahead." Her subscriber was impressed. Each operator had started a large-face alarm clock, noted the length of the call, and charged appropriately for the use of their section of telephone line. At a

---

[71] Proverbs 3:5

[72] "A Review of the Life of a Telephone Pioneer, Clarke McRae Williams, Sr.," writer unknown, published for private use circa 1980, in possession of Annette Williams Carroll, page 3

dime a minute in days when dimes were hard to come by, long distance calls were very expensive but were modern miracles of convenience. The very idea of talking to somebody hundreds of miles away was still a thing of wonder.

With no printed telephone directory, Marie again jotted down names, phone numbers, addresses, children's names, others in the household, temporary boarders, in-laws, aging grandparents, and relatives down on their luck. She again had to remember tricky ring patterns for subscribers on party lines. Marie was again the clearinghouse for people's movements about town, expected to know when people were gone, where they had gone, and sometimes why.

One day an inquisitive neighbor of Miss Emma Barham tried repeatedly to call Miss Emma but to no avail. Lillian and Marie reported that Miss Emma obviously was not home. The caller gave up. Two hours later, Miss Emma called Central to ask who had called her. "I heard the phone ringing," Miss Emma explained, "but I was working in my flower garden and did not want to come in right then to answer the telephone. Who called me? Would you ring them please?"[73] Everyone in town had peculiar idiosyncrasies that Marie and Lillian filed away for future missed calls.

At rare times when Marie and Lillian were preoccupied, Clarke McRae, Kittie Marie, and Mary Lee manned the switchboard, threatened within an inch of their lives never to repeat anything they heard. Privacy, Marie insisted, was absolutely crucial. One afternoon, a town busybody called the Williams kids repeatedly, catching each one individually as she fished for information about an event. Clarke McRae, Kittie Marie, and Mary Lee each denied knowing anything. Exasperated, the lady exclaimed, "You are the know-nothingess children I have ever seen!"[74]

Answering calls in the middle of the night became a problem, too, waking everyone in the house. When Marie had worked nights in Mertzon as a 15-year-old, losing sleep didn't bother her, but as she neared 30 with three children, sleep was

---

[73] Ibid, page 4
[74] Ibid, page 5

precious. Since they could not afford round-the-clock operators, she and Will Clarke alternated night shifts.

Will Clarke relished being his own boss, but the phone system just did not pay the bills. He would have to find paying jobs in addition to maintaining lines and phones. Expansion was out of the question. Banks were not interested in loaning money to the still-unproved fledgling telephone industry.

With no hope of a loan or investors, Will Clarke drove gasoline trucks for a local oil distributor, harvested cotton, ginned, anything to earn a few extra dollars. When W. D. Stewart, manager of the Oak Ridge Service Station, moved his family up the road to Lake Providence, Will Clarke took over the station, partnering with cousin W. F. Hubbard and Weldon Fitch. Though fixing flats, changing oil, and pumping gasoline was no easier than climbing poles, the cash flow was healthier.

While slow economies turned others grim, Will Clarke stayed positive, knowing others didn't have his advantage of an orphaned childhood or a friend beheaded by a boxcar. Will had to look no farther than his own children to remember how fortunate he was. People noticed his unsinkable personality. Clarke McRae noticed, too, his father's perpetual lightheartedness. He laughed at his father's constant mantra, *"Use it up, wear it out. Make it do or do without."* That translated to Clarke McRae, Kittie, and Mary Lee that self-reliance and resourcefulness were requirements, not options. Clarke McRae and his sisters were expected to figure out how to keep something working instead of waiting for someone else to fix it. Whether by design or default, Will's admonitions accelerated their growth.

As Clarke grew older, he could see his father thinking ahead, anticipating, generating income, hoping and praying the long drawn-out Depression would pass. No one ever knew how long dire times would last, but waiting for perfect conditions, their father said, was merely a façade for procrastination and laziness.

Oak Ridge did not completely shield the Williams family as the Great Depression worsened. When the New York Stock Exchange collapsed in October 1929, with sixteen percent of the nation in the market, investors' margin accounts held more borrowed money than all the money physically in circulation. The Crash wiped out $30 billion, shuttered half of America's industries, and idled thirteen million Americans by 1932. In Minneapolis, desperate mobs smashed grocery stores, grabbing food before a hundred policemen stopped them. In Michigan, 3,000 unemployed Ford autoworkers stormed their closed factory, engaging police in a gunfight. Four workers were killed. In New York, the Bank of the United States failed, losing $200 million of depositors' money, the largest bank failure up to that time. By 1933, half of America's 25,000 banks had closed. Over $140 billion vanished.

Ill-timed, 20,000 World War I veterans descended on Congress demanding, after 15 years, their bonus pay. The vets camped around the White House and Capitol. Though they had saved the world from German domination, police tried to remove them. Two veterans were killed. President Hoover ordered federal troops to clear the grounds. Young General Douglas MacArthur led the cleanup. Senators killed the Bonus Bill.

In November 1932, New York Governor Franklin Delano Roosevelt, previously defeated in a bid for vice-president, enjoyed a landslide victory over President Hoover. FDR closed all banks for four days, infusing money into the system, announcing, "The only thing we have to fear is fear itself." By April 1933, though 75 percent of the banks had reopened, depositors' losses were staggering. People began stuffing what little cash they had into mattresses or burying it in the backyard.

> Carolyn Williams Perry: "The federal government insisted that Bank of Oak Ridge close. The front was closed but unofficially they still did business out of the back door."[75]

Depression misery descended on America. Under pressure from distilling moguls such as Joseph P. Kennedy, Congress ended Prohibition. Police jailed bootleg gangster Al Capone not

---

[75] Carolyn Williams Perry email, December 21, 2013

for murder but for tax evasion. Terrorizing the South, Dallas lovers Bonnie Elizabeth Parker and Clyde Chestnut Barrow became folk heroes by stealing from bankers what depositors had already lost.

A trend far more insidious, however, alarmed Oak Ridge's educated and well-read citizenry. Boisterous bumpkin Governor Huey Pierce Long was pushing beyond telephone rate fights toward outright socialism. When he became governor in 1928, he smashed the old bourgeoisie dictatorship controlled from New Orleans and set up his own fiefdom. The next year's stock market crash had played right into Huey's I-told-you-so hands. The disenfranchised rallied around him blaming the greedy rich. Tilting the world still closer to madness, an equally charismatic crude little man across the Atlantic was proliferating anti-Semitism and German superiority. Adolf Hitler grabbed control of the Nationalist Party, the Nazis, and galvanized a very industrious nation into an unprecedented war machine that began gobbling up blocks of Europe.

In the economic chaos, Will and Marie watched anarchy manifest in Bonnie and Clyde and a governor who ascended to the United States Senate but continued to run Louisiana. Huey Long hit his stride just as the Depression gave him a platform and national radio gave him a conduit. Many in Oak Ridge tuned in to hear Long's evangelical cadence, to hear cornpone jokes, stories, and political rants, riveting for sheer entertainment value alone. But the depth of his message, his passionate explanations as to why the few rich grew richer while millions grew desperate, grew an army of listeners. Thousands across the United States joined Long's "Share the Wealth" societies. An avalanche of mail forced the Senate to give Long a second office with more staffers. The movement shook Washington.

After Long helped Roosevelt win the presidency, the new president froze out his rival. Since FDR could not ignore the Louisiana juggernaut, he undercut Long's momentum by liberalizing the New Deal. FDR invented Social Security to appease Long followers. Long threw down the gauntlet. In August 1935, he announced he would challenge Roosevelt in the 1936 presidential election. Debates in political Oak Ridge clashed between a favorite son ascending to the world's highest office and the specter of his turning the United States toward socialism.

Will Clarke remained cautious, well remembering old Southern arrogance judging him in Iuka. Those rich had taught the orphan well, and now he watched as the Redneck Robin Hood began leveling the playing field, for personal ambition, yes, but also for everyone else. It took courage to take a whack at the powerful. The loudmouth who rose up just three parishes away in Winnfield was now within reach of the White House.

Like Huey, though in their own way, Bonnie and Clyde took the war to the rich. Clyde Barrow figured out that he, Bonnie, and the gang could rob banks near state lines and flee into adjoining states. He capitalized on the knowledge that lawmen were powerless outside their jurisdictions and notoriously uncooperative with each other. The two became folk heroes because many saw their crimes as no different from the banking establishment's stealing depositors' savings in the Crash and retreating under the protection of law. Life savings vanished, but no one went to jail.

When Bonnie and Clyde began claiming victims in shootouts, their run was over. Three parishes west of Oak Ridge, on Wednesday May 23, 1934, on a lonely pine woods stretch of Louisiana Highway 154 near Gibsland, four Texas and two Louisiana lawmen joined hands in organizing an ambush. They recruited the father of a Barrow gang member to fake car trouble on the roadside. Just after 9:00 a.m., Clyde Barrow slowed his Ford V8 at the breakdown, realized the decoy, and slammed the accelerator. Ambushers opened fire, pumping 130 rounds into the car and the couple. The Ford coasted 50 yards into a ditch, as lifeless as its occupants. Before a coroner could get there, souvenir seekers clipped locks of Bonnie's bloody hair, and one tried to cut off Clyde's trigger finger. Hundreds scoured for bullet casings, glass, and car parts.

The Dallas Herald sold a record half-million copies as the bodies returned home. Twenty thousand turned out for Bonnie's funeral. Notorious gangsters Pretty Boy Floyd and John Dillinger defiantly sent flowers when they should have noticed a shift in the wind. Police had come together to make Bonnie and Clyde their first coordinated success right down to using two-way radios to synchronize the ambush. Two months later, young Bureau of Investigations agent J. Edgar Hoover organized a similar ambush that killed Dillinger. Three months after that, Ohio lawmen ambushed and killed Pretty Boy Floyd. The next month, Illinois police ambushed and killed Lester "Baby Face Nelson" Gillis. Within a year, Hoover convinced Congress to create the Federal Bureau of Investigation.

When 13-year-old Clarke McRae assembled the headlines, he sensed that both gangsters and demagogues were symptoms of the same evil that sprang from hunger, hate, envy, and malice. He was not surprised as Senator Huey Long, who capitalized on the same forces, could no more escape fate than had Bonnie and Clyde.

Some were jubilant, some remorseful, but most were shocked on the night of September 8, 1935, when soft-spoken, bespectacled 28-year-old Dr. Carl Weiss reportedly shot two bullets into Senator Long's right abdomen. Trigger-happy bodyguards executed the physician in a hail of 62 shots. Long died two days later and in two more days over 100,000 pilgrimaged to his funeral. The same newsreel cameras that had carried Long's announcement for president only three weeks earlier now showed the world its latest martyr. Clarke McRae heard vehement debates that Long was a dictator and Long was a savior, but in the end, Long was dead. Had mild-mannered Dr. Weiss gone mad? Or did unseen and sinister forces indeed rule the world?

Clarke McRae read Wade's Drug Store newspapers cover-to-cover, incredulous that world shock waves Bonnie and Clyde and Huey Long rippled from Louisiana. In the depths of the Depression, their deaths were deeply personal and for the same reasons. They had the guts to call out the powerful and they had been silenced. Newsboys shouted from street corners while radio announcers shouted from the heavens, all while Hitler and Mussolini shouted across Europe. From capitals to street corners, peace was unraveling.

UAW riots at Ford and General Motors increased. In Chicago, ten Republic Steel workers were killed when a company picnic turned violent. For introspective teenager Clarke McRae, stately Oak Ridge contrasted sharply with the tempest falling around them. He realized that while death might neutralize bigger-than-life personalities, the needs of people they had championed never changed.

He was used to his parents' desperation, the short money, the tight budgets, and the ever-present wolf. But he also watched Will and Marie refuse to give up. The teachings of the man from Galilee seemed to offer a rock-solid reference in a world gone mad. Jesus was a man who worried not one whit about Earthly wealth and, in fact, left a resounding message that wealth only masqueraded as happiness. Clarke didn't have to stand on many post-bellum porches to observe that those families who gave money the greatest importance wound up the saddest. They worried when they had money, when they lost money, when the world threatened to take their money, and when the world remained eerily silent, and they passed that anxiety on.

The Williamses, as hungry as everyone else, chose instead to have faith, and that was amazing to their son. While his mother worried, his father kept a sense of humor, laughing away at the tough times he'd seen. Will Clarke passed on to his children the knowledge that all anyone truly possessed was faith. Faith allowed one to shift focus off his problems, help others with theirs, and solve both. In a world jumping from one calamity to another, Clarke learned to anticipate cycles, not to fear them.

From the pulpit and elsewhere, the young man learned that all answers resided in scripture. The Holy Bible became his constant companion and not just on Sundays at Oak Ridge Baptist Church. Coming of age in Man's worst economic time, Clarke found within those covers the secrets of human nature, eternal reference points unchanged since Adam and Eve. Because most did not actually read the Bible, he began to see patterns others couldn't see, revelations that seemed to surprise everyone but him. Clarke McRae saw that the temptation to be selfish usually triggered a downfall. He saw that reactions to obstacles made the difference. That's why Christ taught, encouraged, accepted, and revealed but ultimately left each person to make his own choice. Salvation was not a series of laws; it was about growth, about living at a higher level, about parceling out one's life to as many others as possible because the combined effect of friendships was limitless. At a time when boys were learning to blur right and wrong, Clarke focused more sharply.

In the Bonnie and Clyde killing summer of 1934, John Dillinger paid for his sins on a July Sunday. Two Sundays later, on August fifth, Reverend Morris Wynne stood waist deep in Oak Ridge Baptist's baptismal pool gripping the arm and back of Clarke McRae Williams. Will Clarke and Marie proudly watched their son's public decision to die to self, well knowing a strong belief might be all the defense he would have. Disappointments, challenges, and setbacks sucked the life out of most. Cold to his waist in front of a crowd, Clarke McRae felt Reverend Wynne's grip tighten then plunge him below the surface. All sound ceased except for muffled underwater tones as Pastor Wynne continued addressing the dry audience. The loss of air and sudden disconnection was not lost on Clarke. Next time it would be permanent. Air and sunshine became rare and precious. Time became a tool.

Up out of the water, Clarke gasped for air. His parents smiled while his sisters worried about being plunged underwater. He shouldered the responsibility as a rite to manhood. Friends might leave him but he resolved to befriend anyway. Others might see his baptism as ritual but Clarke saw it as the beginning. If the disciplined precepts of Christianity created purpose out of chaos, he was ready for the discernment he expected from God. Leaving the baptistery, the past life dripping away, he felt liberated and older and excited for the next step.

God still didn't write a blank check. As Clarke helped his father weekends and after school, Will explained how he needed to find new subscribers and encourage long distance tolls, and how he'd heard Oak Grove Telephone Company 40 miles north might be for sale.

Clarke McRae Williams: "My father had always been interested in expanding. When I was in high school, he investigated buying Oak Grove Telephone. It was a possibility we explored thoroughly. Unfortunately, the property was unattainable for us because it just required so much more financing than we were able to put together. He also explored the possibility of installing a system between Oak Ridge and Monroe [but] lending institutions considered the telephone industry risky."[76]

To help with family finances, Clarke McRae worked after school at Wade's Drug Store with druggist Patrick Henry Wade. Eager Clarke learned about drugs, chemicals, compounding, pharmacology, but mostly about human nature in serving the public. He was clerk, carrier, and chief bottle washer when friends showed up at the soda fountain.

Catherine Barham: "Clarke knew exactly how long it took to chill a Coke and have ice form on the inside when you opened it. If he didn't do it just right, he had complaints from his customers when he took that icy Coke out to their car. He made milkshakes we called 'buzzes.' He made three dollars a day, I think. They had little marble-topped tables and chairs but we didn't sit around and talk. We got what we wanted and left because our druggist was kind of high strung. Mr. Wade believed in destiny, that this world was coming to an end and he didn't joke about it either. He was well read, from a family in an antebellum home in Port Gibson, Mississippi, and he knew his medicine. If a doctor prescribed two medicines together that he did not think were

---

[76] *A Review of the Life of a Telephone Pioneer*, Century Telephone in-house publication in possession of Carolyn Williams Perry, circa 1980, page 11

good for you, he'd tell you and he'd tell the doctor."[77]

Mary Lee Williams Oglesby: "Clarke McRae would make frozen cokes and cherry phosphates for Kittie and me. Down one side of the store were counters of cosmetics and gifts. We could spend long hours choosing gifts if we had a quarter, which was rare. For Mother's Day we always got a small bottle of 'Evening in Paris.' It was only a quarter and the Coty perfumes were fifty cents. 'Evening in Paris' came in a tiny blue bottle with a silk tassel. I expect all of Oak Ridge enjoyed the aroma of 'Evening in Paris' after the second Sunday in May. I'm sure we taxed Clarke's patience when Kittie and I shopped."[78]

Earl Hogan, Jr.: "People from out of town would come to the drug store because Clarke would take goods out to the car. I worked in a meat market and didn't get to meet people. Clarke was straightforward and popular, just a nice guy. That's the only reason he had dreams of a big telephone company and could make them come true."[79]

Catherine Barham: "We'd spend his three dollars on Saturday nights. After he got off work and would ask his mother, we'd drive a carload to Monroe to get a hamburger. We didn't have any hamburgers in Oak Ridge. And in the summer time it was so hot. That was the only way we could cool off."[80]

---

[77] Catherine Barham interview, Oak Ridge, Louisiana, August 13, 2013
[78] Mary Lee Williams Oglesby, "Your Chairman Remembered," a paper in possession of niece Carolyn Williams Perry, circa 1980
[79] Earl Hogan, Jr. interview, Oak Ridge, Louisiana, September 25, 2012
[80] Catherine Barham interview, Oak Ridge, Louisiana, August 13, 2013

High schools in 1939 graduated students in the eleventh grade and in Clarke's senior year, a front page story in the *Morehouse Enterprise* caught the 17-year-old's eye. One of Morehouse Parish's claims to fame, coffee baron William Reily, who grew a corner store in Bastrop into a coffee empire in New Orleans, was celebrating his 80th birthday. His unpretentious estate "Kalorama" overlooked nearby Collinston. Showered with kudos statewide starting in the *Times-Picayune*, Reily told reporters, "I've found the Golden Rule to be the best philosophy of life and…after more than three-quarters of a century of life, I have reached the conclusion that the only happiness one derives from life is the happiness he gives to others."[81]

Oak Ridge had its share of business drama, rumors, fights, and feuds, so Clarke found it refreshing that a millionaire from Morehouse Parish confirmed what Clarke had hoped, that a man could succeed in the world by being kind and humble, perhaps even soft-spoken. Reily obviously had helped many people along the way and they had returned the favor, making him a fortune in the process. Clarke read Reily's words again: *The only happiness one derives from life is the happiness he gives to others.*

In contrast, that very week English teacher Mrs. Helen Kovac fascinated Clarke and fellow seniors with William Shakespeare's *The Tragedy of Macbeth*, the quintessential essay on reckless ambition. Clarke read and discussed how a brave Scottish general fell victim to flattery, then to his wife's manipulations to commit murder to become king. The deed done, Macbeth and Lady Macbeth both descended into madness, paranoid that a friend might kill them next. Mrs. Kovac took the whole senior class, all five students, to Louisiana Tech to see thespians James Hendrickson and Claire Bruce play Macbeth and Lady Macbeth. *Double, double, toil and trouble* stuck with Clarke. Temptation forced choices. Easy at first, evil soon becomes very heavy. Not all ends justified the means, and pride was the biggest trap of all.

---

[81] *Morehouse Enterprise*, March 9, 1939, front page

So taken with Shakespeare, Clarke acted out "A Lover of Nature" at his Junior-Senior Banquet. With Hope Hall swathed in red and white streamers, and roses and tables under a canopy of Maypole ribbons, little sister Mary Lee danced for Queen Jacqueline Greer who reigned as Queen of the May Pole. Gold-crusted menus announced a royal course of the Queen's favorite culinary delicacy, barbeque chicken.

The rite of passage ushered in graduation at Oak Ridge High on Tuesday evening, May 23. Salutatorian Clarke McRae Williams addressed the Class of '39. Arthur Carroll, best friend since third grade, had edged one point ahead to serve as valedictorian. Jacqueline Greer recited the class poem and Jack Norman the class history, and Douglas Wathen prophesied the five graduates' futures. Theme for graduation: "The Rosy Pathway," ironic for children of the Depression. After hearty applause for his speech, Clarke announced the Class's merry "Will and Testament," then turned somber as Professor S. G. Lucky conferred on him the American Legion award.

Graduation week filled with receptions, ice cream socials, and fortunetelling at the Norman family's "Wreckers Roost" and culminated with the typical Oak Ridge over-the-top thematic five-course dinner at the A. B. Carroll's. The "Carroll-Greer Roundup" provided a western sendoff of campfire motifs, saddles, Indian blankets, ranch hardware, and menus on stretched cowhide. Acting in hat, jeans, and boots, Cowboy Clarke galloped in as "Dude of the Ranch," the *Morehouse Enterprise* reporting, "Clarke Williams scored a hit."[82]

Most of Clarke's friends a grade ahead, including Catherine Barham, had finished their first year at Louisiana Tech. Will and Marie did not have the money to send Clarke to college, but as salutatorian he received a partial scholarship to the Northeast Center of Louisiana State University in Monroe. Best friend Arthur Carroll left for the real LSU in Baton Rouge.

Little changed that summer. Clarke still climbed poles, untangled lines and concocted buzzes at the soda fountain. Late summer, most of his friends fled Oak Ridge in a cloud of dust.

---

[82] *Morehouse Enterprise*, June 1, 1939, front page

Clarke watched them, still mulling how he could pay for college. Room and board was out of the question. Then he polled Jack Norman, Reese Baker, Douglas Wathen, and Jacqueline Greer about an idea.

> Mary Lee Williams Oglesby: "He had a head for business early on. He convinced Daddy to buy a 1941 Plymouth, figuring he could drive to Northeast Center [now University of Louisiana at Monroe] and pay for the car by charging other students to ride. That deal worked, but Daddy squelched another big idea. Clarke read in a magazine he could get rich raising and selling bullfrogs. All you had to do was dig a pond in the yard and get a few bullfrogs, which of course were sold by the people in the ad. He worked on Daddy for weeks, but in the end his powers of persuasion failed him. The answer was NO. Who knows what success he might have obtained in the bullfrog business if Daddy had only agreed?"[83]

Clarke dwelled continually on new innovations and specifically on how to make Oak Ridge Telephone profitable. Oak Ridge was not growing, looking pretty much as it had a hundred years earlier, but Clarke, haunted by the ever-present strife in Will and Marie, knew he had to find an answer. He had watched his father jump from job to job, telephone operator, lineman, installer, bookkeeper, payroll specialist, gas station manager, gas truck driver, cotton baler, anything and everything to scrape together enough money to support five people. The son and the town admired his father's backbreaking work –Will Clarke would never be accused of laziness– but an observant Clarke wondered if it profited a man to be a jack of all trades and master of none. He looked around at the wealthy in Oak Ridge. Most were cotton planters but they were very good

---

[83] Mary Lee Williams Oglesby, "Your Chairman Remembered," a paper in possession of niece Carolyn Williams Perry, circa 1980

cotton planters, focusing on one science: improving each year in planting, nurturing, and harvesting cotton. Cotton was all they had talked about and studied for a century. Theirs were the homes of columns and verandahs, house servants and new automobiles. They hired people to do the hard work, people like his father.

The observant high school graduate determined that whatever he found his life's vocation to be, he would attack it with single-mindedness heretofore unknown in his family.

In September, Clarke McRae began his shuttle service, and Catherine Barham left Louisiana Tech to join friends being chauffeured to Monroe.

> Catherine Barham: "He took me down to this business school, BMI, in Monroe and then he went back to school. Clarke went to the Northeast Center of LSU for two years. That's the only education that I know of that he got in college. I went to Louisiana Tech, I went to Louisiana College, I went to the business school BMI in the Bernhardt Building in downtown Monroe. Clarke drove a car with students to Monroe and they paid him and that's how he got to go to school. And we had flats. Clarke could change a tire in about five minutes. He did it many a morning driving us kids to school."[84]

Clarke calmly accepted the reality that he would encounter flats along every journey. He learned to expect interruptions, and he learned that, with friends, even flats could be fun. He enjoyed his first profitable venture and enjoyed his success, realizing right off the bat that helping others first gave him the goal he desired. The carload of friends, all helping each other, became his first team. That was the answer, leveraging the help of many. While the world applauded the self-made man, he liked people too much to go it alone. That's exactly what Will Clarke

---

[84] Catherine Barham interview, Oak Ridge, Louisiana, August 13, 2013

had done and it had gotten him nowhere. In fact, in the new year 1940 Will's latest job was in construction in Alexandria, a hundred miles from family. This meant Clarke, in addition to his college studies, had to keep the telephone infrastructure going by himself.

Clarke asked himself if making a living was worth leaving your family, if money was worth doing that, or if money was worth anything at all. That summer offered another example. A Morehouse Parish landmark, Davenport Plantation –built down the road in Mer Rouge in 1860 at the height of antebellum opulence– burned to the ground in a midnight blaze. Leon Davenport, son of the builder, grabbed only a ledger before flames engulfed home, portraits, art and antiques. Wiring was deemed the culprit. Less than half was insured but, as the area's founding family with Abraham Morehouse and Baron de Bastrop of Spain, the Davenports' historic museum-quality contents were irreplaceable. Reading the details, Clarke thought the Davenports lucky to have escaped with their lives and how, in less than two hours, a century of ancestry and heirlooms vanished into the night. The struggling Williams family now had the better home.

If Clarke learned anything, it was that a sense of humor kept heartaches bearable. He often reminded himself and those around him of the scripture, "Be of good cheer." When times seemed darkest, he reveled in practical jokes.

> Mary Lee Williams Oglesby: "Clarke was having a Halloween party and before the guests arrived he dressed as a ghost and stationed himself way back in the back lot. Mama sent me to ask him something and, when I found him standing still, he didn't answer me. I repeated the question and he just made a movement. I ran back to the house in terror."[85]

---

[85] Mary Lee Williams Oglesby, "Your Chairman Remembered," a paper in possession of niece Carolyn Williams Perry, circa 1980

> Catherine Barham: "He could tell the same story two times and it would be just as funny the next time as it was the first time."[86]

While older folks scoffed at picture shows, Clarke McRae, Catherine Barham, Kittie, Mary Lee, and all their friends enjoyed the occasional lighthearted fare of a Judy Garland-Mickey Rooney film. The Technicolor sweep of *Gone with the Wind* in 1940 reminded them of Oak Ridge's fabled opulence. Girls dreamed of Clark Gable but Clarke McRae saw that one character accepted defeat while the other profited from it. The steadfast survived. Hollywood dispensed inspiration the same way old man Wade bottled pills, yet even erudite producers could not have guessed how timely those lessons would soon prove.

Americans climbed out of the Great Depression to war clouds over Europe. Hardly into Clarke's first year in college, President Roosevelt instituted the draft, calling up seventeen million men to register for the service. Louisiana became a hotbed of activity with war games at Camps Polk, Beauregard, Livingston, Claiborne, and Barksdale and hundreds more facilities across the country. In west central Louisiana, 400,000 soldiers massed under the direction of Major General George Patton, specifically testing conventional forces against armored divisions. Colonel Dwight Eisenhower, Lieutenant Colonel Omar Bradley, Generals George C. Marshall and Matthew Ridgeway, and Second Lieutenant Henry Kissinger installed themselves at the Bentley Hotel in Alexandria. Despite news blackouts, word spread that something big was afoot. America was gearing up for war. Clarke studied harder than ever, cramming in as many classes as he could afford, including a summer session.

His relationship with Catherine Barham grew. Catherine prided herself as Oak Ridge's no-nonsense, outspoken Scarlett O'Hara, which Clarke found refreshing in a sea of shrinking violets. Prior to the fall 1940 semester, Clarke accompanied

---

[86] Catherine Barham interview, Oak Ridge, Louisiana, August 13, 2013

Catherine, her mother, and Mrs. T. E. and Theodore Barham on a business trip to Jackson, Mississippi. A few nights later, he took Catherine to the Moonlight Dance at Oak Hall where an aluminum-wrapped silver moon and glittering stars hung down amid red and blue lights.

> Catherine Barham: "I don't know whether you would call it sweet or not, but we were as close as brothers and sisters. I had three brothers but I didn't go to the ballgames with them because they always had the boys in our car. We had two cars and Clarke drove our car a lot. He was a good driver. I could almost tell you what Clarke was thinking before he ever said anything. I just knew what kind of person he was."
>
> *Leo Honeycutt to Catherine Barham: "If he had asked you to marry him, would you have said yes?"*
>
> CB: "No. He didn't have any money when I knew him!"[87]

Protective big brother Clarke, for the Moonlight Dance, triple-dated with little sisters Kittie and Mary Lee and their dates William Whithorne and Sidney Fitch. One year later, Clarke would be a pallbearer at William's funeral. Fallen power lines electrocuted Whithorne as he tried to rescue an injured man from an accident.

The tragedy made Clarke extra cautious as he helped uncross telephone lines from power lines tangled when a powerful hurricane ripped from the coast through northeast Louisiana in late September 1940. Standing atop poles looking down zigzagged lines on cockeyed poles made another impression on the college boy. He never wanted to see that again. Storms would always sock Oak Ridge Telephone's thin profit.

For Thanksgiving 1940, Clarke chauffeured and fixed flats on an ancestral trip to Mertzon, Texas, driving mother and sisters

---

[87] Ibid

out to see grandparents Andy and Dorah Hill. Except for paved stretches of new U.S. Highway 80, all roads were gravel, dirt, and mud. At Christmas, he, Catherine, Kittie, and other Oak Ridge Baptist youth delighted parents with a stage play called *The Star*. But 1940 ended in a pall, as Adolf Hitler steamrolled across Europe. The social Epworth League threw a Depression Party with devotees wearing old clothes "and every facility to chase the gloom away and forget the hard times."[88]

After New Years 1941, Clarke drove his father back to work in Alexandria, taking time to circle the palatial Bentley Hotel. The reports were true. Army uniforms, military vehicles, and brass were swarming like bees. He told everyone that weekend, as he and Catherine provided entertainment for the Oak Ridge High senior class "Ice Carnival" at Oak Lawn Hall. He'd brought a friend home, too, John Hooks of Rayville, who sobered up conversations with hometown boys about the coming war. They stood discussing Hitler in fake snow covering white ice caves and beneath icicles and rainbow lights depicting the Aurora Borealis.

Clarke graduated Northeast Junior College in two years, and by summer 1941 wanted to learn to fly in the Army Air Corps, reading aloud to Will and Marie newspaper accounts of Louisiana boys becoming pilots. Uncle Sam turned Monroe's airport into Selman Field, pouring acres of concrete for rows of bright yellow T-6 training aircraft. Delta Airlines that spring had moved their corporate operations from Monroe to Atlanta leaving substantial hangars and tarmac. Young flyers came from all over the United States. Fourth of July cookouts swelled with seas of green coats, blue jackets, khakis, brass, and army boots. Clarke's friends came in: Weldon Fitch from the Marine Corps in San Diego, Billy Wasson from West Point, and Andy Wofford from the Coast Guard Academy in Connecticut.

Record summer deluges drove the Williams men mad chasing down "hums" in their lines. Soaked and miserable, college graduate Clarke could not believe Southern Bell was spending $51,000,000, to expand 3,913 miles of long distance

---

[88] *Morehouse Enterprise*, January 13, 1941

lines for "defense and industrial needs." $51,000,000! To Clarke, that signaled that the telephone giant saw increased business in the future. In the first half of 1941, long distance calls blew past records at four million but Oak Ridge Telephone still couldn't pay its bills. That didn't make sense, as the fourteen cotton gins of Morehouse Parish had cranked up to full capacity that fall as the surrounding industry employed hundreds. Oak Ridge's three gins, owned by R. E. Barham, J. S. Rolfe, and banker J. W. Broadnax, filled the air with the nutty smell of burning cotton chafe, the annual change of seasons that, this time, signaled to Clarke that it was time to go. The final straw hit October 29 when tornadoes knocked down lines yet again, killing 13 across the state line in Arkansas.

Clarke accepted Arthur Carroll's invitation to bunk in with him the rest of the year at Louisiana State University in big city Baton Rouge where they joined 46,000 fans –a hundred times the size of Oak Ridge– for Tiger football games. Clarke had never seen such pageantry and such screaming as LSU lost a heartbreaker to archrival Ole Miss by one point. He'd also never seen Louisiana's Ole War Skule buzzing with war drills nor the drunken revelry of kids free of their parents. Clarke thanked God he felt no need to indulge. He pitied the drinkers for the troubles they were drowning and those they were creating. Now in Baton Rouge, with Marie and the girls in Texas, his father in Alexandria, and Lillian Fitch on the switchboard, Clarke felt homesick.

Winding down toward Christmas break, Clarke and Arthur had just finished lunch on the first Sunday in December when people began yelling. The eerie, stereophonic sound of several radios in houses and cars turning up at once announced, *JAPANESE WARPLANES HAVE ATTACKED PEARL HARBOR, HAWAII. HEAVY CASULTIES REPORTED. MUCH OF THE U.S. FLEET DAMAGED.* Everyone gulped.

In Oak Ridge, Will and Marie were back home for the weekend entertaining the S. J. Daigles from West Monroe when a couple knocked on the door. They pleaded with Marie to open the switchboard so they could call their son at a faraway military camp.

"Haven't you heard? They're bombing Pearl Harbor."

Marie's heart froze. The war was here. Clarke was not. Her son was the perfect age for military service. Will's radio crackled alive with panicked news from a place foreign to Oak Ridge, so far away it was still morning there. Hawaii sounded tropical but it was home to the entire United States Pacific Fleet. Radio newsmen breathlessly reported that all ships had been in harbor when Japan attacked the United States in peace time.

> *The Japanese attack upon Pearl Harbor naturally would mean war...Japanese envoys now at the State Department emphasize the gravity of the situation...word has just arrived of a second wave of attacks both at Pearl Harbor and now at our naval bases in Manila....*

Miles apart, Will, Marie, the Daigles, Clarke, and Arthur froze as the death toll topped 2,000 Americans...sons, fathers, husbands, wives, girlfriends, and sisters. President Roosevelt angrily declared war on Japan. America's youth flocked to recruiting offices. Old men shook their heads that world war was starting again just 20 years after the Kaiser had been whipped. Now Germany was back at it, this time with Japan. Marie cried for Clarke.

Clarke McRae saw it as an adventure. He couldn't see how anyone could be surprised with 400,000 troops massed in Louisiana, and he was ready to defend the land of his birth and opportunity. Conversations changed dramatically. Baton Rouge boys all but forgot LSU football's 4-4 season. The time had come for real fighting.

But just as Iuka's draft board dismissed Will 25 years earlier because of his game leg, the Oak Ridge draft board denied Clarke McRae as well. They insisted he stay behind as the only male child to carry on the Williams name and because a medical examination revealed an elevated heart rate.

Marie's tears would prove insufficient. Clarke felt keenly his obligation to community and nation and that meant only one choice. It was true that it was Clarke's bad luck that, just as he arrived at manhood, three angry men in Germany, Japan, and Italy would force life-and-death decisions for smalltown men everywhere. But the student of scripture and history Clarke McRae knew at 19 that if he failed to face death now, he could never hope to face life.

He read a letter by Private Harold Shipman of Bastrop published by his mother in the *Morehouse Enterprise* of the sea change in thought of Clarke's generation. From Camp Sam Houston, Private Shipman wrote that night of the Pearl Harbor attack:

> *I wish you could have seen something that happened this afternoon in my barracks. There were about 50 boys sitting around on bunks listening to the news broadcast. A band started playing 'Stars and Stripes Forever,' and there wasn't a boy in the room that didn't get onto his feet and stand at attention until the music was over. If they had heard it a few days ago, before this trouble broke out, they probably would not have moved off their bunks. Love to all of you, Harold.*

Clarke McRae Williams had to be part of it. He volunteered.

CHAPTER 5

"HERE'S THE LATEST... THE JAPANESE HAVE ATTACKED PEARL HARBOR, THE UNITED STATES NAVAL BASE IN THE HAWAIIAN ISLANDS. THIS MEANS WAR IS UNDERWAY BETWEEN JAPAN AND THE UNITED STATES."
> -H. V. KALTENBORN, NBC NEWS RADIO ANNOUNCER
> 97 MINUTES AFTER THE ATTACK

"HOSTILITIES EXIST. THERE IS NO BLINKING AT THE FACT THAT OUR PEOPLE, OUR TERRITORY, AND OUR INTERESTS ARE IN GRAVE DANGER. WITH CONFIDENCE IN OUR ARMED FORCES, WITH THE UNBOUNDING DETERMINATION OF OUR PEOPLE, WE WILL GAIN THE INEVITABLE TRIUMPH -- SO HELP US GOD."
> -PRESIDENT FRANKLIN D. ROOSEVELT
> DECLARING WAR ON JAPAN, DECEMBER 8, 1941

"THAT'S WHAT THIS ARMY NEEDS –A LITTLE OF MY ADVICE."
> FLIGHT ENGINEER SGT. CLARKE MCRAE WILLIAMS
> 3RD AIR FORCE, DREW FIELD, TAMPA, FLORIDA

Bells chimed Oak Ridge awake on crisp December Sundays, mingling with fragrances of fireplaces, fried chicken, baked pies, and fresh cut cedar trees. Lazy holidays crept like slow clocks as red embers crackled. Stores were shut tight. If God rested one day in seven, Oak Ridgans reckoned there was a good reason.

But the town woke that Sunday, December 7, never to sleep again. Clarke came home to the news of Oak Ridge's first Pearl Harbor casualty, Walter Savage, nephew of Dr. J. W. Darby. His death, wrote newspaperwoman Nettie Traylor, "will not go unavenged."[89]

Indeed, American deaths were avenged thirteen days later on December 20, 1941, and by a Louisianan. U. S. Army Air Force Colonel Claire Chennault grew up in the small Louisiana towns of Gilbert and Waterproof south of Oak Ridge. He rose to fame by leading his squadron of P-40 Warhawk attack planes, called the "Flying Tigers," in the first aerial dogfight in China over Kunming. The Tigers zipped the Warhawks through ten

---

[89] Nettie Traylor, *Morehouse Enterprise*, December 18, 1941, page 4

Japanese Zeros, destroying four and routing the rest back to Tokyo. Newspapers, magazines, and newsreels heralded Colonel Chennault across the world, renewing Chinese resolve and galvanizing Americans.

Nineteen-year-old Clarke McRae Williams was certainly galvanized, not so much by the exploits of the Flying Tigers as by Colonel Chennault's hailing from Louisiana just miles down the road in Gilbert. Between Savage and Chennault, the war indeed hit home in a personal way, as if the two were members of his family. Hundreds of area men in Clarke's generation had the same idea. They flocked to recruiting offices all wanting to be pilots.

For Christmas, Clarke's grandparents drove in from west Texas with Marie's sister Mabel and niece Evelyn. War tension was palpable and everyone grabbed Clarke McRae to advise him. But his mind was made up. He would join and become a pilot.

Talk of war subdued all parties. Somber and melancholy, one featured two violinists and a pianist playing "Ave Maria." Mrs. Jack Abraugh, Mrs. C. E. Gay, and Miss Beatrice Smith also performed Liszt's elegant but poignant "Leiberstraume" and Brahm's old world "Hungarian Dance Number V." The hushed crowd, awed by such an inspired performance in quiet Oak Ridge, brooded over the coming sacrifice. Governor Sam Jones appointed rationing boards to restrict drivers to four gallons of gasoline a week and the entire state to 2,833 tires for all of January. Will Clarke was lucky to get ten miles a gallon and 10,000 miles on tires on gravel roads. The bright spot was a sharp increase in telephone business as Bastrop callers averaged a record 1,000 calls an hour, which kept all the Williamses on the switchboard. Marie was grateful to keep her mind busy.

New Years 1942, when Clarke McRae announced he was joining the Army Air Corps, the Corry family invited all his friends to their new home for a congratulatory dinner. Concerned that his 90-beats-a-minute heart rate would disqualify him, Clarke decided to pay for private pilot training, hoping the Army would let him fly if he were already licensed.

He and friend Jack Barham enrolled at Dixie Aircraft School in Shreveport, then moved to the U. S. Navy training airport in Grand Prairie, Texas. There, instead of runways, the Navy designed two hexagon-shaped mats 1,500 feet in diameter to give trainers plenty of room.

In April, Marie, Will, the Gibbs, and Catherine Barham dropped by the airfield on U. S. Highway 80 en route to Mertzon. Clarke was happy to see them, impressed Cat Barham would come that far, but they stayed only two hours before his next class.

On April 18, the trainees cheered as Lieutenant Colonel Jimmy Doolittle eclipsed Chennault by leading a squadron of sixteen B-25 medium bombers on a daring raid over Tokyo. Few military targets were destroyed but Japanese civilians were shocked that the Pacific no longer protected them. Sixty-nine out of Doolittle's 80 raiders survived to fly again, convincing Clarke McRae that survival odds were greatest in the air. Chennault hadn't lost a single Flying Tiger. Doolittle's Raid boosted recruiting and shook Japanese military leaders who then erred by calling their aircraft carriers home from the Indian Ocean. When the Japanese fleet attacked Midway Island en route, the U. S. Navy sank four of their carriers.

Clarke returned from Texas in June in time to help his father win the mayor's race. Will Clarke succeeded Mayor John McClernon, joking he was the only one of Oak Ridge's air raid wardens who wanted it. Ninety-seven local men registered for the service that month, eighty-seven of whom were black. Clarke deferred registration when he heard about and landed a job at General Motors Aircraft parts manufacturing plant in Memphis. Clarke's team built plastic bombardier noses for B-25 medium bombers, the planes Doolittle used. He worked his way to seventy cents an hour and moved upstairs into Mrs. Montgomery's boarding house at 1154 Monroe Street. He often reclined on the front porch with her and daughter Elizabeth. *I sure like it here*, he wrote home. *They are so nice to me.*

Clarke McRae minimized bouts of homesickness with prolific letter writing. He wrote "Dearest All…" to his parents, grandparents, sisters, cousins, and friends who reciprocated and sometimes sent cakes and other baked goods. He also wrote to a host of girlfriends including Dot, Libby, Virginia Ann Bridgers, Earline, and of course Cat Barham, writing to his parents,

> *Something tells me that I wasn't cut out for this romance business, although I enjoy it while it's not too serious.*

Clarke exchanged letters with "podnah" Arthur Carroll, nicknamed *Pod*. Arthur nicknamed Clarke *Deacon* for his straight and narrow ways. Pod loved to shock, writing on June 12,

> *I'll just be dang if I'm going to mail this letter to you 'til I hear from you, unless I gets real tenderhearted and thinks about you up there all by yo'self and don't know nobody. Ain't a single thing happened since you left [except] Dr. Maddry has done messed in his hip drawers.*

Dr. Maddry threw a large barbeque without inviting a number of prominent neighbors,

> *...and Miss Emma Barham is strictly raising sand. You know messing with Oak Ridge society is really one heckuva job! Doc ought to have had better sense....Better stop or it'll cost me more than one stamp and I know darn well I ain't going to spend over 3 cents on you.*

Clarke sensed a little envy for his working in Memphis at an aircraft plant while Arthur was stuck at his father's store and gas company. He missed the old boy's boisterous attacks on the English language and if Pod ever joined up –and he did eventually pass exams– Clarke feared what a drill sergeant might do to him.

One thing Pod never seemed to worry about, though, was money. Deacon Clarke envied him there because Clarke existed in Memphis on $1.75 a day. He shipped every other paycheck home to be invested in war bonds. In August, he applied for the draft; that is, Mrs. Montgomery stood in line with his application while Clarke worked at the plant. He desperately hoped his pilot training and B-25 expertise would land him in the cockpit.

In September, Clarke volunteered and the Army Air Corps accepted. The *Morehouse Enterprise* put his picture on the front page in full dress uniform. He shipped out from Memphis with twenty-four buddies crammed onto a trainload of recruits bound for Nashville to swear in at Camp Forrest. He became Private Clarke McRae Williams, U.S. Army Serial #14-156-147.

We were the only ones that could laugh and joke around. Some of the other boys were ready to cry.

He was ready to cry after passing the physical but failing to qualify for pilot training because of his rapid heartbeat. The Army also made good on his only-son status to keep him stateside. Deeply disappointed, he boarded the train to Fort Oglethorpe, Georgia, on the Tennessee line.

After administering I.Q. and mechanical aptitude tests, the Army loaded him with Government Issue boots, summer and winter uniforms, field jacket, dress coat, overcoat, raincoat, socks, underwear, mess kit, razor and blades, brush, toothbrush, and two duffle bags.

When I threw those two bags on my shoulder, I thought I was taking ole Brownie a sack of meal, they were so heavy. Don't worry about me. I'm having a big time.

Lillian Fitch's brother Sidney shipped off to Australia where he read a letter to his mother on international shortwave radio. Clarke tuned in. *I like it here very much*, came the familiar voice, oscillating ghostlike as in a dream, *but it sure would be good to be back home.*[90] Mrs. Fitch didn't hear the broadcast but received postcards from listeners in California and a transcription from South Louisiana shortwave hobbyist A. J. Bergeron. Clarke thought it unfair he was stateside for being an only son while all three Fitch sons, Sidney, Francis, and Weldon, were scattered in harm's way across the world.

Clarke longed to join them but after inoculations, written tests, and interviews at Oglethorpe's Company D, the brass stamped him "stateside." He was, however, eligible for Officer Training School. Disappointed again, just after chow, Company D lined up before drill sergeants for a jog.

> *I sure didn't want to do that. A corporal came up at that time and wanted 3 volunteers to go to the bakery. My two buddies and I nearly ran to him so they took us to the camp bakery –to cut the darn grass.*

Private Williams suffered boot camp in St. Petersburg, Florida, staying in the posh seaside Vinoy Hotel, before shipping off to the 308th Technical School Squadron at Keesler Field in Biloxi, Mississippi, grousing to his West Texas grandparents,

> *Hot weather! We have had a lot of drilling the last few days with gas masks... a lot of fun. We sure look like a circus with our masks on.*

Concerned more about their health, he asked Andy and Dorah to consider moving to Oak Ridge where Will and Marie fought the battle of telephones. Even as calling doubled, they stuck at seventy-five customers while Bastrop's Southern Bell zoomed past 1,000, "a 100 percent increase from 1935," claimed local Manager W. T. Terrell in the *Enterprise*. "A thousand telephones in a town of 6,000 is said by telephone officials to be an unusually high percentage [indicating] progressiveness and

---

[90] *Morehouse Enterprise*, "Oak Ridge Boy Writes Home from Australia," September 24, 1942, page 6

financial integrity of residents."[91] Will couldn't understand it except that his farmers and families either did not need or want phones. He had first miscalculated the depth of the Depression and then how set Oak Ridge was in old ways. He prayed that younger people would embrace telephones the way their parents took to automobiles. Until then, Will had to keep finding oddjobs to subsidize the phone system for everyone else.

Will landed a job at Northeast Louisiana Power Cooperative in Oak Grove, an hour north, resigned as mayor, and turned over house and phone company to Marie's sister Mabel "Gibbo" Gibbs. On Sunday October 4, 1942, Will, Marie, and Mary Lee pulled away, leaving Kittie in Oak Ridge to finish her senior year. Kittie enjoyed being editor of Oak Ridge High's school paper, *Chatterbox*, and when Nettie Traylor resigned as local correspondent to the *Morehouse Enterprise*, Kittie took over the Thursday column. She also led the local war effort, "Collect Scrap to Slap the Jap," amassing unused metal from car bodies to ice boxes and even the old school bell. Kittie headlined, "From bells to bullets."[92]

In Oak Grove, Will and Marie started over and as soon as she became an operator at Oak Grove Telephone, Clarke called. Afterward, he wrote his grandparents.

> *She said she liked her job and that they were doing fine. She said it didn't worry her to run the switchboard because she didn't have to worry whether a telephone line was down or not as she did in Oak Ridge. I know her hours are not as long as they were in Oak Ridge.*

Biloxi's coastal dunes were cold at daybreak, hot by afternoon, and always humid. Many got sick. Clarke kept colds at bay with Vick's Salve. He stayed upbeat listening to Keesler's Army Air Corps marching band. He embraced

---

[91] *Morehouse Enterprise*, "Bastrop has 1,000 phones, Largest Number in History," March 4, 1943, page 1
[92] Kittie Williams*, Morehouse Enterprise*, "Oak Ridge News," October 29, 1942, page 6

integration as African-American soldiers, later called the *Tuskegee Airmen*, began arriving.

News trickled in from home that one of Clarke's schoolmates, standout athlete and pilot Pat Meeks, was killed in action. Wounded on a mission over Europe, Meeks heroically piloted back to England before his plane crashed. In the Pacific, another friend, Annapolis graduate Lieutenant Eugene Barham floated five hours after the *USS Lafayette* sank during the Battle of Guadalcanal. New Orleans-made Higgins boats scooped up the Americans who won the Island. Barham later explained to Bastrop Kiwanans, "The Japs mostly are good fighters and brave but a little stupid. Once given instructions they follow through without altering plans" and would rather commit suicide than be taken prisoner.[93] Casualties happened stateside too. In Monroe, seven airmen from Selman Field died when their B-25 bomber crashed into Lafourche swamp.

Working on B-class bombers, Clarke mulled over what might have caused the Monroe crash. Engine failure? Stall? He still wanted to fly and knew someday he would, but his career so far had put him everywhere but the cockpit. He began sending cartoon postcards depicting two poetic GIs sweating over an engine.

We poke and pry,
We cannot fly,
Our life is not romantic;
But in our way
We'll have our say
And drive der Feuhrer frantic.

Sensing his disappointment, the family circled him with prayer and showered him with goodies. He laughed at a national survey that said what most GI's wanted, 79.4 percent, was cigarettes. Clarke McRae smoked with buddies but not enough to use all his ration cards, so he boxed up cartons and sent those to Will. Marie and Will sent him a small radio. *Don't see how*

---

[93] *Morehouse Enterprise*, "Oak Ridge Naval Officer tells of Sea Battle," February 11, 1943, page 6

I ever got along without that little rascal, he wrote of overnight watches enlivened by big bands and Lux Theatre on WWL radio in New Orleans and KWKH in Shreveport. He wrote that he had to wake up *the fellows that are flying, going on K.P., and the rest going to work.* He watched yellow T-6 trainers and Piper tail-draggers take off into the morning sun, reminding himself that God had something better for him. He envisioned how beautiful the coastline and Gulf must be from up there.

While the New Testament Bible came in seventeenth in the GI survey, Clarke placed it first, always carving out time to read. No longer in the safe cocoon of Oak Ridge, he was tempted like everyone else but avoided honky-tonks. He chuckled at those imbibers who paid a high price Sunday and Monday mornings. Staying healthy and clear-headed was far more enjoyable.

At Thanksgiving, lonesome for home 200 miles north, he called. Marie told him Kittie brought home friend Gloria Carroll for Christmas, then described the turkey, dressing, and sweets. Clarke salivated, writing to his grandparents,

> *I sure wish I could eat one meal of those hot biscuits, Texas beans and onions, coffee, and five or six of those pies! It would sure do me a world of good.*

His commander, Sergeant Moore, surprised Clarke with a short furlough home. In Oak Grove, Private Williams did not find the Oak Ridge Christmases of old. His folks lived in an unfamiliar house in an unfamiliar town three times the size of Oak Ridge. Still, Oak Grove was charming with a courthouse square aglow in Christmas lights and train horns and bells peeling from the busy yellow depot west of town. Will toured him around the power office, watching for whether Clarke intended to return now that the Army had significantly widened his options. Clarke's work now was far more glamorous than climbing poles.

The fun birthday of unconventional, outspoken Bessie Catherine Barham on December 23 proved the bright spot of his visit. She turned 21 and as a gift to herself, immediately joined the Women's Auxiliary Army Corps. "Although Oak Ridge boasts a number of fighting men," Kittie wrote in her column, "Miss Barham is the first young lady to join our forces."[94] WAAC Cat Barham took her oath on January 4 and shipped out to Fort Des Moines, Iowa, then to Fort Riley, Kansas.

The Army would soon get an earful, he laughed, but that laugh hurt his mouth. Back on base, Clarke's Army dentist informed him he had a mouthful of bad teeth.

> *I'm going back in a couple of nights so he can tear in again. He's a real trailblazer and I don't mean maybe. He's just like General Sherman– he burns everything in his way. I'm going to take a fire extinguisher when I go.*

Running in sand dunes amplified the pain. Clarke described to home folks that as soon as his lieutenant ordered the platoon to double time under full backpacks through the sand, the officer shouted, "Gas!" Everyone fumbled with clumsy GI-issue gas masks.

> *I was so out of breath that I couldn't get enough air through the darn thing. I just politely opened one side and got a heap of air. If it had really been gas I'd have to wait until later to tell you about it.*

The exhaustion of drills, classes, night watches, and dental work combined to give Clarke a serious cold. *Old Vick's Salve is catching the dickens,* he wrote, but it wasn't enough. He landed in the infirmary for two weeks.

> *They took a heap more of my blood. I think they drained one arm empty and then they drained the other.*

---

[94] Kittie Williams, *Morehouse Enterprise*, "Oak Ridge News," January 14, 1943, page 6

More worrisome, the doctor diagnosed possible hyperthyroidism. As he pondered the new malady, a full brass general resembling old bank president Mr. Brodnax walked in, asking if anyone had any complaints. Clarke wanted to ask for help to get into pilot training, but being in the infirmary was hardly an assurance of ability or health.

Clarke recuperated just as a winter blast turned beaches to ice and instructors to madmen, forcing simulated war conditions of repairing aircraft outdoors overnight.

> *I was so dang cold I could hardly move. At 5:00 a.m. we just had to quit and go in the tent by the plane. There we huddled up and started some singing that the Ink Spots couldn't beat.*

For chow, Clarke's squadron filled their mess kits and moved into a closed dining tent heated by a roaring fire.

> *Some dang city-Yankee got an armful of green wet pine needles and threw it on the fire. I got enough smoke in my eyes and lungs to cure a hundred hogs...had to get out of there as cold as it was. If the Army doesn't hire the Boy Scouts to take care of us, I fear we'll never make it.*

Kittie reported in the *Enterprise* that local men were building a "plane-spotter's watch tower" twenty-five feet high in case Jap or Nazi planes attacked Oak Ridge. Will installed an emergency telephone up top while below they built a Red Cross sewing room. Kittie ennobled the tower as the community's "spirit of American cooperation."[95]

Late March 1943, the Army shipped Clarke to the Lockheed-Vega defense plant in Burbank, California. Buddies teased him as they railroaded through Williams, Arizona. First, he was awed by the majestic scenery, then by Hollywood.

---

[95] Kittie Williams, *Morehouse Enterprise*, "Oak Ridge News," March 25, 1943, page 5

Really beautiful country, a lot like West Texas.
[In Hollywood] *My eyes had so much to see that*
they jumped around like jumping beans. There's
Graumanns Theatre where all the movie stars put
their handprints, footprints, signatures, etc. Bob
Hope stuck his nose by his signature and by the
impression wrote, 'This is my nose.'

Bob Hope, Bing Crosby, Ginny Simms, and Cecil B. DeMille performed a free show at the Lux Theatre for servicemen. Clarke and Don Domain got tickets four rows from the stage. They were the last of Clarke's original Memphis group of twenty-four.

Bob, Bing and Ginny look like they do in Movies.
Bob and Bing are strictly two good comics, they
cut up all during the program. Bing had on a
pair of rust red pants, a dark blue shirt and a
green sport coat. Bob Hope made remarks about
that all night. We really had a time. Cecil
[DeMille] told me he wasn't any relation to Newt
V. [DeMille, a friend].

China's First Lady Madame Chaing Kai-shek attended the show, passing right by Clarke and Don. *She's nearly beautiful!*
I think I'll look the ole girl up if I ever hit China (I hope I don't
hit there, tho).

At the Hollywood Palladium, he and Don found Benny Goodman and his band playing "Why Don't You Do Right?" one of Clarke's favorites.

It has the verse 'Get out of here and get me some
money.' Well, his singer sang that one and it sure
was killing! You can't imagine how nice and
friendly the people are here. They all have a
smile for us. We can't afford to flag a car for a
ride – they'd have wrecks trying to stop for us. All

*we do is stand near a curb and along comes a
ride.*

At Lockheed-Vega, the Army Air Corps promoted Clarke
to Corporal: *That means $16 more each month and that's not
chicken feed, that's clear profit.*   Inside vast hangars, brass
entrusted Corporal Williams and his mechanics to inspect, clean,
and repair the United States' largest wartime airplane, the B-17
Flying Fortress. At 74 feet long with a 104-foot wingspan and
weighing eighteen tons, the behemoth could take off fifteen tons
heavier with men and armament. Clarke's crew labored around
the clock in a land of giants, dwarfed by four Wright R-1820-97
turbo-charged radial engines called *Cyclones,* each taller than a
man. Clarke knew the B-17 inside out.

> *It takes five men just to take off and replace one
> wheel. The Air Corps is strictly particular about
> them being ready to go at any time.*

Even with sleep loss, he, Don, and all of Squadron G from
Barracks 26 ran cross-country at dawn rain or shine.

> *Every time, ole Doman catches hold of my fatigue
> pockets and I have to tow him. I believe if a Jap
> got after him he'd sit down and rest awhile. It
> takes an hour for him to wake up enough to know
> what it's all about. I had to put his shoes on
> practically. He reminded me of how I use to
> wake up every winter morning with you all
> prodding me along.*

Clarke rolled Don out early one Sunday to travel forty-eight
miles east to Santa Ana where Pod Carroll was stationed. For
four hours, the two hitchhiked through Los Angeles, riding *in
several new station wagons, a new Buick coupe, and several
others.* The boys ate oranges as they thumbed through a grove.
They sure were good.

Clarke wrote to Pod's parents that Arthur found them by sheer luck.

> *A large formation came marching by and I heard, 'Hey, Buddy!' It sure sounded like music to my ears. When the formation was dismissed we went into his barracks and talked like a couple of women at a get-together. You can't imagine how glad I was to see the ole rascal. He really looked fine, seems to have gained a little weight also. There are some fine fellows in his barracks and as the usual case with him, he's very popular with all of them. You can bet that he will get along fine anywhere he goes...so don't worry about him.*

Clarke wrote something different to his parents, that Arthur's base was dismal.

> *...the sorriest looking hole I've ever seen. Keesler was a beauty compared to it... Ole Pod looks well and seems okay. He has a bunch of buddies already. They cut his hair very short, like when he was a freshman at L.S.U. It was like old times for us to be together again.*

He was proud little sister Kittie was setting records selling war bonds. Clarke smiled with news she had dressed up as Columbia and narrated the Victory Bond Selling Concert to a full Oak Ridge High auditorium. Norwood Knight portrayed Uncle Sam and every student took part. Oak Ridge's $37,000 in bonds helped Louisiana exceed $6 million in bond sales, matching that of larger states.

> *I feel pretty old having a sister graduating from school. She seems to really enjoy being a senior. I'm really proud that she made valedictorian.*

Corporal Williams graduated, too, in a formal ceremony at Lockheed-Vega, but his scroll had secret reassignment orders. Disheartened at leaving Tinseltown, Clarke wrote a code to his parents hoping his destination was so exotic, it was classified.

> *Suppose we let Sailor be Australia, Midge – China, Betty – England, Spot – Africa, and Blackie – Ireland. Also the first letter of each paragraph may spell the place when you put them together. Do you understand that OK?*

He needn't have bothered. The 396th Bombardier Group chugged by train up the entire Pacific coast to Washington State. Brand new Moses Lake Army Air Base in central Washington housed the 482nd Fighter Squadron. Twin-engine, twin-tailed P-38 Lightning fighters sprinted overhead, but Clarke's lumbering B-17s soon arrived. The P-38s were beautiful, swift as falcons. German pilots called them "fork-tailed devils."

> *It's just a shade cool up here. The wind has been blowing like it's from Texas, really brings dust with it. Combat flight crews will receive their training here in B-17s. We will be here to take care of the planes, which is supposed to be quite a job because new pilots are said to be quite rough on planes while learning. Rumors are we'll be here from six months til the duration.*
> *I sure did appreciate the money, Daddy. It made my last two bucks look a lot bigger.*

The money meant a lot not because it tided him over but because he knew his parents had little to spare and were sacrificing for him. Clarke would pay back every dime, which meant the Good Lord had to return him home safely.

Corporal Williams excelled at office work, thankful for high school typing class.

When I saw we were going to dig rocks, shovel coal, etc. today, I politely high-tailed it for a nice typing job in the orderly room, typing for the adjutant and supply officer.

[Of the base's two barbers] *One is worse than* [Oak Ridge barber] *Mr. Perrit so we really don't have but one. I'll have to tie my hair up with string before long.*

Discouraged by the inefficiency and crudeness he witnessed in three assembly plants and at four bases, Clarke urged cousin Evelyn not to go back to defense work.

I've seen enough of that in Memphis and Burbank to change my mind from what I once thought. I wouldn't want Kittie or Mary Lee in a plant and I sure don't want Evelyn in one either. I don't mean to sound unpatriotic—I just know what it's like. The financial end is not what the general public thinks it is either.

Working long hours, Clarke began experiencing sharp pains in his right side. Medics drove him twenty-three miles to Soap Lake Hospital near Ephrata, Washington, where doctors treated a mild case of appendicitis without operating. They forgot about the patient. One gave him a pass to go into tiny Soap Lake to get a haircut.

The barber told me all the news from 1899 up until the present. According to him, he's making more money than he can use. Soap Lake is large with steam baths all around. The water tastes worse than Mineral Wells [Texas] water and has the same effect.

After ten days, Corporal Williams became restless in his unexpected furlough and asked for sleeping tablets one night.

When the ward boy came back with them, he asked me what my name was. When I told him, he said I'd been discharged on the hospital record seven days ago.

Corporal Williams left the hospital amid a great commotion of doctors and ambulances. Another B-17 had crashed into a mountain seven miles away. Despite their efforts, doctors lost all thirteen crewmen. Clarke wondered again why the Air Corps would train pilots in mountainous terrain. Questions were piling up.

Cranking the powerful Cyclones from the pilot's seat of a B-17 and firing them with the four throttles became the only aspect he enjoyed. He could tell by listening whether an engine was synchronized with the others. As the cockpit shook and rattled under full brakes, the Fortress bucking to take off into a starlit heaven, Corporal Williams wanted to release the brakes and soar like an eagle into the sunrise. The Army could have had a great pilot if it hadn't been so picky. If his heart was the problem, that didn't stop the Army from making him run hundreds of cross-country miles.

Clarke grew disenchanted with the Army's hurry-up-and-wait inspections.

We worked all Friday night and when we got off Saturday morning, we had to put our uniforms on and march out on the ramp at 7:30 a.m. We stood out there until 10:45, and were we one unhappy bunch! I started dozing while we were at 'Parade Rest' and dang near jumped out of ranks when the band blared out on 'This is the Army, Mr. Jones.' When I woke up good, I agreed with the band. You can't imagine how we despise those pointless, foolish inspections... standing at attention for unusual lengths of time. [One day] was pretty hot and 3 boys fell out. This place is getting rotten.

> *One of these days I'm going to get full of that ole*
> *evil hate and blow up right in front of the*
> *Colonel.*

Being promoted to crew chief barely lifted his spirits until the brass gave him his own shiny new B-17 named *Hilo Hattie*. With two assistants, Corporal Williams kept the green behemoth in shape from nose to tail.

> *We had a surprise inspection by a colonel and a*
> *captain. Since I was the crew chief I had to*
> *follow them as they inspected my ship and note*
> *any corrections. When they finished they were*
> *practically speechless. They had not found one*
> *thing wrong with it and the captain said,*
> *'Corporal, you've got a mighty fine ship here.'*
> *They were both swell guys and they stood around*
> *talking with us for some time. We like fellows like*
> *that but they're few and far between.*
> *The only fun about this* [overnight watch] *job is*
> *at five in the morning when I go thru the barracks*
> *blowing a whistle all the way thru and maybe*
> *ducking a big G.I. shoe. I sure do feel for the*
> *guys in tents when they have to get up and dress*
> *in the cold. It reminds me of those 3 or 4 times*
> *that I jumped up real early in the morning and*
> *built the fire in the fireplace.*

From Catherine Barham's letters, he realized he wasn't the only one disillusioned. She was struggling, too. Both were too intelligent to be in a rigid army.

> *I'm beginning to feel sorry for Cat now that she*
> *is strictly down on the WAACs. You can strictly*
> *be miserable in the army if you let it get you*
> *down.*

Corporal Williams kept his dreams alive even if he never left the ground.

> *Night before last one of our ships had a flat about three miles out from the ramp. We took another tire and wheel for it and our line chief taxied it back in. I helped him in the co-pilot's seat part of the time and for the rest of the time rode in the bombardier nose. Those big babies sure do ride easy. While I was in the co-pilot's seat I sure would love to have given that baby full throttle and taken off for home. I guess we'd have had to bail out over home though—there's no place large enough to land.*

Clarke did jump out of the bombardier hatch one night on the tarmac and peeled skin off fingers on both hands. On the bright side, he scribbled,

> *All my buddies sure look over Kittie's and Mary Lee's pictures. They said they were glad to know where the Looks went in the family!*

Clarke was gratified to get Kittie's graduation invitation but wondered where she'd sleep at the Oak Grove house since grandparents Dorah and Andy Hill had moved in. Clarke wrote them all at Box 275, Oak Grove, Louisiana, USA.

> *I had my pictures of you out today and looked you over—sure will be glad to come home.*

The girls were having a ball in Oak Grove. Their favorite film that summer was *Casablanca* with Humphrey Bogart and Ingrid Bergman, a personal love story set against the world's fight for freedom. Clarke saw it, too, on base, and noted a man often had to sacrifice for the greater good. As for romance, he frequently wrote Virginia Ann Bridgers of San Antonio. From Baldwin College in Virginia, she answered his letters but not much more. Clarke had Marie send his picture in uniform to her but the coolness remained. He wrote his folks of sightseeing trips in Washington's mountain splendor where he met many "glamor girls," he said, working at apple canneries. He compared notes with a "cute" girl at a soda fountain about the work but found she had better war stories than Clarke ever would.

> *She was at Pearl Harbor when it was attacked.*
> *What about the depot agent's daughter in Oak*
> *Ridge? How does she look?*

The cute soda fountain girl had the best of war stories to tell her children and grandchildren. Pod Carroll, the Barham boys, and many friends from Morehouse Parish had stories, too, but Clarke had nothing. He couldn't even fly. He steeled himself with resolve, though, that he would never lose faith in himself or America. All the good nations of the world had to triumph if for no other reason than Clarke McRae Williams had to return to Oak Ridge and make the telephone company a success. That became a central theme in his letters.

> *Tell me about Oak Ridge telephone and how it's*
> *coming along. I've got to keep up with my*
> *company!*

Corporal Williams did have war stories but they were limited to water fights in the showers that soaked clothes, shaving kits, shoes, socks, hats, helmets, everything.

> *Our line chief (a master sergeant) was right in*
> *the middle of the fight with us. He's sure a swell*
> *fellow. Rank doesn't mean a thing in our*
> *squadron. We call each other by name instead of*
> *'Corporal or Sergeant.' As for saluting and such*
> *stuff, we very seldom salute a 2nd lieutenant. We*
> *salute from Captains on up tho! All the Looies*

[lieutenants] *at Keesler would go AWOL if they were here. They were crazy about salutes there.*

Top brass either noticed a lack of protocol or screened Clarke's letter because within days, headquarters issued a stern warning that everyone would salute ranking brass or face court-martial.

Don't think for a minute they're joking. A few guys have been 'busted.' We are all fed up with this place's rules and regulations. At times we feel like telling them to take our stripes and choke on 'em.

The Army issued each soldier a mimeographed order commanding him to salute. Crew Chief Williams chuckled. Not getting their due was bothering upper level hacks and they were disguising pettiness as respect.

The only time I get a shade unhappy is when we have to stand review once every two weeks. I really get the brass bars and leaves told then—to myself however!

Respectful all his life, Clarke understood the necessity of organization but hated arrogance. He despised both the waste he saw of resources, energy, men, work effort, and material and the mandates that stifled creativity and promoted dissention. Brass somewhere feared an underling might be smarter and some routinely stole credit for success. Clarke understood respect in fighting situations, but in remote Washington State he felt many were taking self-importance to an extreme. He was, however, grateful to the Army for its inadvertent lessons. No one taught petty pecking order in school and only through observation from the bottom up could anyone discern the personalities of true leadership.

As Clarke was writing a report one day in *Hilo Hattie*'s radio room, he heard a sudden racket *sounding like someone throwing tin cans and beating them with a hammer.* The firing mechanism of a neighboring B-17 belly machine gun had jammed firing off twenty-seven bullets. One blew a hole in *Hattie*'s tail just feet from Clarke. Outside he saw three men wounded, one fatally. Both survivors had legs amputated. *I still shudder when I think about it,* he confided to family. The long hours and overnights were getting to him.

> *Don't let any of my letters worry you all if I seem disgusted. Sometimes I get a bit unhappy because I can't depend on some of the good rumors we hear, but after a good night's sleep, I'm O.K.*

The Army rewarded Corporal Williams for controlling his disenchantment by promoting him to Buck Sergeant on his one-year anniversary, *drawing $78 a month –not bad!* Out of the blue, orders sent Sergeant Williams and crew back south for immediate departure. In minutes, they were packed and hurtling away from Mt. Shasta crossing the whole country to Tampa, Florida. At Drew Field, he joined the United States Army 3rd Air Force and his dream finally came true. Clarke got to fly.

> *Last night was perfect for flying, the moon was out pretty and we were low enough to see scenery. I was lucky to ride co-pilot most of the way over and back* [to Mobile, Alabama]. *Bilotta, the pilot, let me fly for better than an hour. At night you fly by instruments, so when I turned it over to him I'd done a hard day's work. You have to work eyes, hands, feet and ears to the limit.*

One of his assigned planes had just crashed in the Gulf and the crew floated all night on life rafts. Another B-17 struck a tree while landing. *Only the Good Lord saved that crew,* he wrote.

Through Christmas 1943 into spring 1944, Sergeant Williams excelled as crew chief but still pined for Europe or the

Pacific. With that possibility all but gone, he turned his attention to plotting a course for when the war ended.

> *I sure would like to go over your territory with you, Daddy. We'll have to do that when I come home. I knew that you had to drive a lot, but I didn't realize that you had put that many miles on behind the wheel.*

During the war, the Army joined with states in beginning to require driver's licenses. Farmers went ballistic and everyone feared the written exam. Louisiana Governor Jimmie Davis, famous for singing "You Are My Sunshine," passed the state's first law requiring licenses and received Louisiana Driver's License #0001, which he used for over seventy years.

Uproar over licensing dominated Oak Grove conversations on Clarke's quick furlough in late April 1944. A carload of family picked him up at Selman Field, which buzzed like a beehive with yellow trainers. Marie, Will, Kittie, Mary Lee, and Evelyn gave Sergeant Williams a hero's welcome. They pelted him with questions but he only gave highlights of fun and beaches, embarrassed he'd been kept from real fighting.

A month later, the United States, Great Britain, and Canada mounted the largest sea invasion in the history of mankind. On June 6, what became D-Day, five thousand ships and 13,000 aircraft rapidly deployed 160,000 soldiers on and behind fifty miles of French coastline. "We will accept nothing less than full victory," Supreme Allied Commander General Dwight D. Eisenhower told his troops. Overwhelming numbers crushed the Nazis, driving them into retreat and turning the war. The price was 9,000 killed or wounded Allied soldiers whose blood stained the surf. A hundred thousand more marched on Berlin. Everyone at Drew Field became antsy to fight.

> [Line chief] *Seibert came back from furlough and said a woman wanted to know why he wasn't across like her boy who's been in the army only*

ten months. Instead of telling them why, he told
them he was too old and no good.

Few would ever understand the stigma felt by stateside crews, especially with a boy fighting on foreign soil. Pod Carroll, Allen, Hootie, and other Oak Ridge friends in the middle of the action sent letters full of drama. Letters from Pod to Clarke described heroics as well as enviable seven-day furloughs in France and England. It was too much for Clarke. He snapped and began scolding homefolks for not writing, especially his parents, wondering if they were embarrassed because their son was not "over there."

I'm glad to see you both got back on the ball and
have decided to write your only son…
Well I finally heard from you…
…and you talk about me not writing!

Jokes evaporated from his letters and he began censoring himself, tearing off the bottom of one letter because it *was some more of my complaining about this outfit so I decided it wasn't pleasant reading.*

Her son's exasperation disturbed Marie. After hearing horrific details of D-Day, Marie began having vivid, emotional dreams of Clarke McRae, enough that she related them to her son. Like all mothers, Marie would worry until Clarke came home for good.

From the dreams you had, Mama, I must have
been starting an army of my own to be run the
way I like it. That's what this army needs—a
little of my advice.

News of D-Day buzzed everywhere. As soon as Kittie finished spring 1944 finals at L.S.U., she and cousin Mabel Gibbs jumped in a car on Sunday June 11 and boldly drove to Tampa to help relieve Clarke's homesickness. Their favorite sergeant was ecstatic. He introduced his girlfriend Betty and his roommate, Staff Sergeant Lawrence B. "Tiny" Terwilliger. Tiny was smitten with Kittie and heartbroken when they soon left.

Clarke's seaside romance with Betty flourished through the summer of 1944 to the point he wrote his parents for permission to bring her home.

> *Betty and I went to the beach last Sunday and had a fine time. The water was clearer than I've ever seen it with not a bit of seaweed. I might add that we're getting rather serious, in fact I'd like to bring her home so you can meet her.*

Clarke grew concerned when little sister and sweet sixteen Mary Lee had a tonsillectomy at the end of March, then an appendicitis attack and surgery in June. Clarke was home for the first surgery but couldn't get another furlough until Thanksgiving. Remarkably, he was granted two weeks, November 23 through December 7. He was overjoyed until Betty stopped him. Her plans did not include meeting his family.

Heartbroken, Clarke pepped up a little when Tiny insisted he spend Thanksgiving in Oak Grove with the Williamses and, of course, with Kittie. They caught a plane to Selman Field, still swarming with army aircraft, and again the Williams clan showered the returning warriors with hugs and kisses. Tiny glowed in the presence of Kittie. Slightly envious, Clarke smiled, happy for his sister and good friend.

In Oak Grove, a houseful of friends and family awaited them. Clarke was shocked to see Mary Lee still thin from two surgeries. She wrapped spindly arms around his neck while he cracked every joke he'd ever heard to make her laugh. Suddenly, his eye caught, laughing across the room, a dark-haired beauty with a captivating smile. The girl was a friend of Kittie and Mary Lee's and her name was Mary Lee, too, but Lee was her last name. Mary Kathryn Lee was the daughter of Oak Grove's hardworking, entrepreneurial, and successful George Leroy Lee and wife Ola Mae. "Roy" Lee had run third in the last election for tax assessor. Clarke wasted no time striking up conversation. Miss Mary Kathryn was a student at Louisiana Tech, a leader in the Baptist Young Women's Association, and frequently hosted many large Y.W.A. groups in her home. She was young and accomplished and visibly impressed with a staff sergeant in uniform.

Clarke sensed something more in Mary Kathryn. She was self-assured and comfortable, and her sense of humor mirrored his own. For the first time in a long time Clarke really felt at home. It didn't matter that it was Oak Grove instead of Oak Ridge. In the blink of an eye, Mary Kathryn became his most important reason to come home.

As Will's electric crews crossed multi-colored lights over streets, the glittering holiday dream became a dream come true for Clarke. God had delivered the helpmate for whom he had prayed. He and Mary Kathryn became inseparable. When he traveled south to Oak Ridge to check on the telephone company, she went with him. She lingered through his quick but boring audit of the books, discussing the business with his aunt, uncle, and favorite cousin Evelyn. Mary Kathryn watched Sergeant Williams inspect switchboard relays and wiring, and studiously gauge the proximity of telephone lines to tree limbs as they drove the roads.

All in all, Oak Ridge Telephone looked okay but, in his heart, Clarke McRae knew it was as obsolete as a buggy whip. Marie added to his worry by telling him that subscribers of Oak Grove Telephone, owned by a man in Chicago, were near mutiny because of bad service. Phones died or hummed with the slightest rain. Clarke realized the disparity was not coming from his exposure to the Army's advanced technology; rather, country folk were just fed up. He had to come home quickly and would have to borrow money to overhaul Oak Ridge Telephone Company before he had a mutiny on his own hands. Exactly how he would do that, he didn't have a clue, but he did have faith.

With turkey and dressing and Grandma Dorah's famous fried pies gone, Sergeants Williams and Terwilliger tore themselves away as Christmas was beginning. No parting for Clarke had ever been such sweet sorrow as when he touched

Mary Kathryn's face and kissed her before climbing aboard a flying hunk of green metal. He saw nothing but her face as he rose into the clouds, chuckling to Tiny that that's exactly where their heads were. Clarke looked down through white puffs at a green checkerboard of pastures and barren cotton fields below. He would marry the divine Miss Lee when he came home.

At Drew Field, morale worsened when most were denied leave for Christmas 1944. A particularly unpopular officer made things worse, demanding rigid adherence to protocol and enforcing a crackdown. Clarke described him as sadistic.

> [He's] *some half-cracked Major that should be in Hitler's Gestapo. He has a mania for busting a man in rank. (I'd like to bust him in the teeth.) I passed right by him day before yesterday without saluting because I didn't notice him. He was too busy spouting off to a couple of lieutenants to bother me, tho.*

Clarke's exceptional line chief, a man named Bills, blew his top. In a group of five, Bills hit a staff sergeant over the head with a quart bottle.

> *He's scheduled to stand a court-martial. They'll probably be awful rough on him. The other four are scared sick and Bills even worse. We're nearly having open rebellion.*

A bright spot came unexpectedly when Mary Kathryn sent an 8 x 10 portrait and other pictures. Clarke proudly showed his roommates.

> *My buddies wonder what a good looking girl like her sees in a beat up ole soldier like me. I didn't tell them that sometimes I wonder myself.*

With Kittie back at L.S.U., the two Marys became fast friends. The girls spent most of their time at the Williamses in case Clarke called. Dainty but adventurous, Mary Kathryn often volunteered to help Mary Lee in the chicken coop to chase down, kill, and clean chickens. Will and Marie were impressed as was Clarke. He wrote to Granddad Andy of the girls' chicken hunts, *Papa, did you give 'em a little lecture in Mexican?*

Mary Kathryn's affection proved genuine in a torrent of letters to Drew Field. Those letters brought a new and unusual joy amid nonsensical army make-work. Clarke lightened up. He had something to fight for and work toward and the face that looked back at him from the picture was worth all of it.

News lightened up, too, as Allied forces triumphed from Europe to the Pacific. Starting in February 1945, U. S. Marines successfully raised Old Glory over Iwo Jima, Manila and the Philippines while American B-29s firebombed Tokyo and other cities. In Europe, on worldwide radio, General Eisenhower demanded Germany surrender as Yanks and Brits crossed the Rhine River toward Berlin while Russians closed in from the east. Adolf Hitler went berserk, screaming at his military leaders, calling them treacherous incompetents. He ordered his successor, Reich Marshal Hermann Goring, stripped of rank and Reichsfuhrer Heinrich Himmler shot for attempting to surrender.

Across the ocean just as victory came within his grasp, President Roosevelt died unexpectedly in Warm Springs, Georgia, on April 12. The refined, eloquent New Yorker gave way to rural Missourian Harry "The-Buck Stops-Here" Truman. The plainspoken haberdasher became Thirty-third President of the United States. Two weeks later on April 28, fascist dictator Benito Mussolini donned a woman's dress and attempted to escape Italy with his mistress but was exposed, stripped, and shot. An atheist, he had shouted many times before Catholic audiences for God to strike him dead. As his body swung upside down in Milan, thousands stoned and spat on it, believing he had fulfilled his own arrogant prophecy.

Hiding in a bunker the next day, Adolf Hitler married his companion Eva Braun. They honeymooned in hell, committing suicide the following day. Germany unconditionally surrendered one week later and the Third Reich dissolved forever.

Missing all history-making events, Sergeant Williams fought the battle of military incompetence. Commanders demanded more inspections.

> *We know the war is progressing in our favor. As we get closer to victory the more unnecessary work they'll order done on these ships. There'll come a day when we'll have to polish the things.*

As celebrations enveloped Europe but none in Tampa, sentimental Clarke remembered Mother's Day. *Wish I could be with you, Love, Clarke,* said Marie's card attached to a bouquet of flowers from Robinson Flowers in Bastrop. The telegrammed flowers were a rare indulgence for Clarke who kept close reins on finances. He and roommate Corporal Taylor scouted Tampa's shipyards for extra work. Clarke couldn't rest until he paid back his parents.

> *I still haven't forgotten the money you both have given me and I sure appreciate it because I know you should have used it on yourselves. I won't forget it although I'm slow about returning it.*

Clarke adamantly knew he would not make a career of the military as Pod Carroll hinted he might. He had to lead an army in Oak Ridge, starting with marrying his Oak Grove girl.

> *Now when Mary Kathryn and I finally get married, she can listen to all the radio programs such as 'Dr. Malone,' etc. she cares to during the week, but on Saturday night I'm going to listen to Prince Albert's Grand Ole Opry.*
> *...Mary Kathryn called me again and her voice was sweeter 'n honey to me!*

Practical Clarke opted for prodigious love letters instead of long distance charges. He made clear his intentions to marry her as soon as he returned. He repeated those intentions after Mary

Kathryn was shaken when an unfaithful soldier broke a friend's heart.

> *Mary Kathryn, you'll never have any cause to be jealous because I love you so much, I'll never give you reason to believe there could ever be anyone but you. With you by my side and your love to always keep me happy, I know we will always get over any obstacle and live good lives together. So many forget God, but we must never ever let Him down, Darling.*

Clarke sustained a belief that the only glue of relationships was the ever-present love of the Father, a love carried out by humans attuned less to their needs than to the needs of those around them. In a world of spiritual warfare, he put in writing his intention never to forget the eternal relationship, a tall order for anyone, especially a young man starting out and needing acceptance. Indeed, with no end in sight at Drew Field, Clarke confidently wrote Mary Kathryn on July 15, 1945, that he did not want to stop her from having fun and to date others if she wanted to.

> *Compare me to them and make sure there is no one else for you except me. I love you more than life itself and you should love me the same way. I'll do everything in my power to keep our love from breaking up because, Mary Kathryn, you are so much a part of me that, without you, I would never be the same again.*

He splurged on February 14, 1946, telegramming *Happy Valentine's Day from Your Civilian Sweetheart*, knowing the impression a courier's delivery would make. The telegram was an echo of the one his father had sent to his mother 25 years before, but Clarke McRae delivered no ultimatums. The formal teletype lettering under the *Western Union* banner was enough impression for Mary Kathryn and her girlfriends. Mary Kathryn Lee had her knight in shining armor.

Clarke fought serious doubts as to exactly how shiny that armor was. With hardly a dime to his name, he grew more concerned how a broken down telephone company would support them when it had never supported anyone. He confided to her that making it was going to be *"a long and hard job."* Clarke was still bothered that the main reasons he had lost girls like Betty and Cat Barham was his lack of money and few prospects. Love may be blind, but Clarke was not foolish enough to think that money didn't matter to an upper middle class girl. Even middle class in Oak Ridge would be difficult without cotton land or an oil well.

Sergeant Williams dove into the latest communications research in both military and civilian worlds. He knew Bell laboratories couldn't keep breakthroughs secret for long as they jockeyed for defense contracts. Bell's two major competitors, Stromberg-Carlson and Kellogg Switchboard & Supply Company, devised ways around Bell patents and made improvements. Clarke turned his focus off military affairs at Drew Field and solicited prices, credit information, and installation techniques from both companies. He continually scanned scientific journals in the library, writing to his father:

> *I'm sending Kellogg's letter that I got today. Daddy, what is our CMP* [Civilian Metal Production] *allotment for cable? Write and tell me how much we can order because I want to get all the stuff I need and have it waiting in Oak Ridge for me.*

Weeks later:
> *I'm sending Stromberg-Carlson prices in separate envelopes. You choose between Kellogg and Stromberg-Carlson, Daddy. We don't want that $700 stuff!*

More than ever, Clarke felt pressure to bank all the money he could. He and Corporal Taylor got on with other G.I.s at the shipyards, working days on base and nights off base. Though he wrote whimsically, *I've sure enjoyed working out there—seeing how the other half of the world lives,* his focus was not on the good life, but instead on amassing capital for Oak Ridge Telephone. While he understood others spending every dime to party away stress, Clarke's discipline and unwavering commitment to Christian beliefs actually made reaching his goals easier, as nothing could tempt him from them. Investing made sense to him. Just as he had talked Will into the new Plymouth, he went halves with Taylor on a used Ford so they could quit hitchhiking and get to work on time.

Saving like a miser, investing in war bonds, tithing at church while eating crumbs, Clarke McRae shoved all value to the future. Family was his only indulgence, delighting in shipping home small gifts. Watches, rings, bracelets, hats, cigarettes, candy, clothes, and even car parts. *Mama,* he joked, *the cigarettes in with your ring and Mary Lee's watch don't go to you. I thought I might mention!* Homefolks returned the favor. Will packed up a car jack and tire pump because neither came with the boys' old Ford.

The ladies shipped Sergeant Williams home-cooked cakes, pies, cookies, jams, and Grandma Dorah's famous fried pies. As soon as he cracked open the boxes, sweet smells permeated the barracks and friends came running. They devoured everything like piranha. When Sergeant Tiny drove up to see Kittie, he brought back a carload of cakes and Dorah's fried pies. The feast lasted days and covered several letters.

Sergeant Williams also shared much more. He maintained *deacon* status by sharing his faith with the few who asked. Sundays found Clarke, Taylor, Tiny, roommate Clymer, and others piled into the Ford headed for church. They didn't care if they were branded a little naïve and goody-goody. Whatever Sergeant Clarke Williams had, they wanted. He stood like a beacon as the most genuine, compassionate, fun loving, and loyal man they had ever known. Their sergeant operated at a higher level in everything.

Learning spiritual power couldn't have come sooner.

With Hitler and Mussolini dead, sense returned to Europe but Japan held out.   Free of "Il Duce," Italy turned on the Imperial Japanese Empire and declared war.   Two days later, on July 16, 1945, a top-secret U. S. battalion assembled in the high desert of Alamogordo, New Mexico. A button was pressed and Albert Einstein's theory of chain reactions in the Sun became reality on Earth. A white hot flash followed by the world's first nuclear mushroom cloud culminated America's top-secret Manhattan Project.   Einstein had won the race against his students in Germany. He immediately regretted it.

So did Japanese Emperor Hirohito. The imperial leader refused to acknowledge the Axis was dead. He refused to see the devastation of Allied firebombings of Tokyo. He refused all demands to surrender.   Thus, on August 6 a Boeing B-29 Superfortress, named *Enola Gay* for the commander's mother, from 30,000 feet dropped the world's first wartime atomic bomb on Hiroshima, Japan.   In a 4.7 square mile area, the blast vaporized 75,000 people.   Hirohito still refused.   Three days later, a silver-plated B-29 Superfortress named *Bockscar* dropped a second 20-kiloton atomic bomb, killing 35,000 more. Hirohito surrendered. Abruptly, World War II ended.

Four days later, Kittie and Evelyn returned to Tampa, arriving by train to celebrate with Clarke. He dutifully wired his mother.

> *KITTIE AND EVELYN ARRIVED ON TIME.*
> *UNABLE TO CALL DUE TO DELAYS. SAM*
> [Williams] *AND TINY VERY HAPPY. I MISS*
> *MARY EVELYN* [meant KATHRYN].   *WILL*
> *CALL AUNT MBEL TUES NITE*
> *LOTS OF LOVE= CLARKE.*

As quickly as the girls arrived, as quickly they vanished. Their brief celebration in the sand was a memory almost before it started, so much blurred Clarke's mind, desperate for release. They vicariously joined celebrations around the world through movie newsreels.   As Kittie and Evelyn's train disappeared,

Staff Sergeant Williams grew even more determined to get home. He joined everyone in hounding Army brass for dates to muster out but no one was leaving. Army time ground excruciatingly slow. Training in B-17s tapered off and soon the giants sat in huge green lines bordering runways.

Some of the so-called *crates* made routine cross-country training missions and at daybreak on Tuesday, September 18, Sergeant Williams hopped aboard a Fortress headed to Barksdale Air Field near Shreveport. With Mary Kathryn only an hour east at Louisiana Tech, Clarke called her and his parents to meet him in Ruston. When he landed, he commandeered an Army vehicle at Barksdale. Everyone met up at lunchtime for a joyous but short reunion. Clarke's plane and crew had to return to Drew Field by sundown and Sergeant Williams had no intention of going AWOL *after* the war.

Hardly an hour had passed when tearful goodbyes stained his khaki shirt. He sped back to Barksdale; then the four Cyclone engines cranked loudly, spitting blue-black oil smoke, and soon the clouds were beneath them. Another quick trip, almost dreamlike.

Newspapers full of victorious Yanks coming home to tickertape parades, commendations, speeches, and medals starkly reminded those at Drew they had missed everything. Sullenly, everyone stayed on base, drilling, marching, pulling K.P., cleaning-up, tuning engines, and doing what the Army was best at: senseless work. The waste dragged through fall, past Halloween, past Thanksgiving and many neared mutiny when they couldn't leave to go home for Christmas.

Out of the blue, little sister Mary Lee shocked everyone when she married friend William Wasson at Oak Ridge Methodist Church the Sunday before Christmas. Over the phone, Clarke's mother described Mary Lee in a suit of holiday green in a sea of red poinsettias, holly, red berries, ferns, and twenty-eight candles hastily put up after the morning service. Reverend G. H. Corry never left the pulpit. A short wedding trip and Mary Lee reported back to L. S. U. and Billy to Texas A. & M. Clarke never guessed that the youngest would become the first to marry.

New Year's 1946 finally brought orders: Go home. Ecstatic soldiers hoisted Clarke in a wave of celebrations but he waved off the barhopping. His happiness came from thanking God that he could go home in one piece. He helped file discharge papers for others, but to Sergeant Williams' frustration, top brass ordered the Third Army Air Corps 170 miles north to Camp Blanding on circular Kingsley Lake near Starke, Florida. Twenty-five miles south of the Georgia line in scrubby pines and swamp, Camp Blanding boasted that it was Florida's fourth largest city with 10,000 buildings where 800,000 soldiers had trained. It was a zoo. Clarke had to laugh. The Army had crisscrossed him from Tennessee to Biloxi to Hollywood to the Great Northwest to Tampa, now to muster him out in the middle of a Florida swamp. Par for the course.

Smack between Lincoln's Birthday and Valentine's Day, Staff Sergeant Clarke McRae Williams, Serial #14-156-147, finally headed the line for honorable discharges. Along with release papers, the officer clerk shoved an award in his hand.

FOR MERITORIOUS SERVICE
The commanding General Army Air Forces
Extends the gratitude of the
United States Army Air Forces to
S/Sgt Clarke M Williams
Whose wholehearted and sincere services
contributed to the successful prosecution of
World War II against those who sought to
subjugate the civilized world.
Signed: Capt. James Y. Watson and
General H. A. Arnold, Commanding General

Clarke read the typed form with a smile. Army sincerity was underwhelming. He folded up the award and put it away, sobering up at the thought of thousands who would never go home. The Army had taught him a lot, mostly how not to treat people.

Civilian Clarke McRae Williams walked outside in the Florida sun, still in G.I. khakis, and boarded a bus for the westbound train to Oak Grove. His long strange odyssey that began in 1942 finally ended three years, five months, and two days later.

He dreaded sharing war stories with Pod and others who'd seen action.

Clarke relished returning to the war of wires, poles, customers, wind, rain, and ice. Difficult it may be, he thought, but he would regain control of his fate. Nothing would ever be more valuable than the freedom for which he had just fought.

CHAPTER 6

"I BROUGHT MARY KATHRYN HOME TO A SMALL HOUSE WITH A
SWITCHBOARD IN IT AND THAT WAS OAK RIDGE TELEPHONE
WHICH DIDN'T SEEM LIKE VERY MUCH TO A NEW BRIDE."
                                    CLARKE MCRAE WILLIAMS

"WE'RE SORRY, CLARKE, BUT MR. BRODNAX DIDN'T LEAVE
ANYTHING IN WRITING ABOUT YOUR LOAN. WE'LL HAVE TO
DECLINE GIVING YOU THE MONEY."
     BANK OF OAK RIDGE BOARD OF DIRECTORS, SUMMER 1947

"I'M GOING TO TIE YOUR HANDS BEHIND YOUR BACK. I'M
GOING TO TAKE A MORTGAGE ON EVERYTHING YOU HAVE. AND,
MIND YOU, I DON'T WANT TO RUN THE TELEPHONE BUSINESS. I
JUST WANT YOU TO PAY THE THING OFF."
       JOE SIDNEY CARTER, CENTURYLINK'S FIRST INVESTOR,
                    UPON MAKING HIS FIRST LOAN, JULY 1947

Army life behind him, duffle bag on the floor, civilian
Clarke McRae Williams seized control again of his destiny. The
three-year hiatus from reality felt like a lifetime, but now reality
was back: Nobody had made Oak Ridge Telephone profitable
while he was gone. Wires, switchboard, and phones had three
years' more wear with virtually no maintenance.

Clarke had begun preparations for the next phase of his life
on his last furlough when he asked Mr. George Leroy "Roy" Lee
face-to-face for the hand of his daughter. The potential father-
in-law liked the Williams boy, knew he would come knocking
as soon as the war was over, and knew his daughter loved the
sergeant, but the businessman in Roy Lee remained skeptical of
Oak Ridge Telephone. In the sixteen years the Williamses ran
the operation, the phone system had never supported one family,
much less two. Another economic pressure he feared for Oak
Ridge and Oak Grove was how the war had spoiled America's
youngest generation with a taste of the big world. To Roy, that
meant young people would flee to the cities and leave small
towns to die. Oak Ridge at best would stagnate.

Clarke explained earnestly his plans for growing the
operation, very unlike his father's strategy, though Clarke was
careful not to find fault. Banks had continually rejected Will

Clarke's appeals for capital because loan committees saw telephones as a fad, the first nonessential to go the moment an economy hiccupped. Clarke McRae saw telephones becoming essential but through better service.

He saw that the only way to compete with juggernaut Bell Telephone was with technology, specifically the new automated dial-up service he had seen in cities. Automation meant the subscriber merely dialed a telephone number and electric relays did the rest fast and efficiently. No more sometimes embarrassing interaction among caller, operator, and answering party. Further, deeply personal telephone conversations had never been private. A dial-up system, however, ensured total privacy, except on outlying party lines; the new, complete privacy in town would double traffic. Everyone had stories and wanted to tell them and Clarke knew privacy would establish the telephone as essential once and for all. Telephones would become the biggest conveyor of news and secrets since the printing press.

For Oak Ridge Telephone, automation meant cutting costs with less need for 24-hour operators. Clarke McRae and Mary Kathryn could field long distance calls while relays did all the rest. Reduced payroll left more money for improvements. At the rate Bastrop, Monroe, and other surrounding towns were installing telephones, Oak Ridge was a sure bet for increased long distance charges for the calls crossing their lines. Roy Lee seriously questioned Clarke McRae, who fielded every concern.

The father looked into the earnest eyes of his future son-in-law: They were eager, determined, and alive with the energy of youth. The older man could see that Uncle Sam's Army had forged Clarke McRae into a leader by teaching him what leadership was and was not, a rare gift worth a thousand college degrees. Roy Lee had no choice but to hand over a father's most prized possession. Strictly because of Clarke McRae Williams' character, though with misgivings, Mary Kathryn's parents consented to the marriage.

Mary Kathryn still chirped of how creatively her beau had proposed. They were in the Williams car, Clarke said he had a headache and would she get the aspirin tin out of the glove box? She pulled it out.

"Would you get me a couple?" he asked.

When she opened the tin, a shiny gold ring sparkled. A note was attached and, unfolding it, she read, *"Would you take a headache for life?"*

"Yes!" she cried, grabbing Clarke around the neck and kissing him. "Yes, yes! I will!"

Everyone laughed and girls cried over the story of Mary Kathryn's good fortune. She immediately dragged Clarke to every Lee clan family function.

> Bill Newton, family member and a later employee: "The first time I met Clarke, I was seven years old. Mary Kathryn brought him out and introduced him to mother and dad and told us they were going to get married. Clarke was in a uniform. I was impressed with that uniform. When he talked to everybody, he got their attention. He had a lot to do with how I turned out. He just had something about him that was very special and that was Clarke always was more concerned about everybody else."[96]

As the betrothed made rounds, some privately reminded Mary Kathryn that the Williamses were not West Carroll people. Their people were from towns in Texas and Mississippi nobody ever heard of. Mary Kathryn blinked them away, reminding the whisperers that Marie and Will had served people graciously and efficiently in Oak Grove for four years. As far as knowing the Williamses' past, there was nothing to know. For the skeptics, however, Sergeant Williams would have to prove worthy of Miss Lee.

The summer of 1946 also appeared not the greatest time to start a family. Front page photographs of nuclear mushroom clouds in the South Pacific heralded a new, modern, and frightening era. Military scientists were testing the effects of the

---

[96] Bill Newton interview, Ash Flat, Arkansas, October 23, 2012

new warfare on naval forces but, more importantly, they were flexing victorious American muscle to discourage the Bolsheviks. Morehouse sailors Ernest C. Doss and Charles P. Fancher took part in the tests at Bikini Atoll, making the doomsday machine too real for homefolks.

How to contain the nuclear threat forced creation of the United Nations. Many world leaders blamed the failure of Woodrow Wilson's League of Nations as having allowed Adolf Hitler's rise to power, and they blamed the League's failure on the United States having never joined their own League. Now, since the United States was first to use nuclear warfare, America had to join the United Nations to contain its own threat.

On the bright side, while 1945 ended badly for Louisiana business, L.S.U.'s Bureau of Business Research reported in the *Enterprise*, "It is clear for both state and national indexes that the fall in business activity which began after the close of the Pacific war was checked in December 1945."[97] Clarke hoped every banker in Louisiana read that report because farm economies, he hoped, were coming back. From 1944 to 1945, crop values in Louisiana plummeted by half from $215 million down to $127 million even though America's war machine continued at full tilt through summer 1945.[98] Cotton in Oak Ridge particularly suffered from ill-timed rains. Science, however, was bringing promise.

The greatest breakthrough with a direct impact on Oak Ridge was a compound that ended the boll weevil's 30-year reign of terror on cotton. The insecticide was Dichlorodiphenyltrichloroethane, too much for farmers to say so they called it simply *DDT*. During the war, DDT all but eradicated malaria and typhus from Europe to India. Swiss scientist Paul Mueller won the Nobel Prize for his work. When Clarke came home, Emmett Barham, Gerald McLendon, and Reese Baker formed the Oak Ridge mosquito abatement crew, liberally spraying DDT around every home and building.

While DDT directly helped Oak Ridge's economy, Southern Bell tightened up competition for Clarke. Bell won

---

[97] *Morehouse Enterprise*, January 24, 1946, Sec 2, p 2
[98] Ibid, Sec 2, p 8

rate increases and extended telephone lines by 26 miles "and 380 poles," covering two-thirds of Morehouse Parish with service independent phone companies couldn't match. North of Clarke, Bonita community's phone system crashed for weeks when owner Victor Watts' home burned. If Clarke didn't act soon, Oak Ridge subscribers might join Oak Grove in clamoring for a Bell takeover.

Through towering mushroom clouds, bad economies, and the decline of mom-and-pop phone operations, Clarke McRae steadied himself in scripture. "Fear not," he continually read, and, "There would be wars and rumors of wars," all of which was to say, *Don't waste time worrying about threats you can't control because most will never happen.* Besides, a Christian did not live in a spirit of fear and was not paralyzed by imaginings. As he had seen in the Army, laziness often used bad headlines and the threat of death as excuses. A Christian put his trust in God who was Time itself and in a savoir named *Jesus* who promised ultimate perfection. Clarke McRae decided early to let them handle the big issues and was always awed at how God resolved everything. Anything could turn positive, anything at any time.

Clarke felt a Christian couldn't waste time. He must be about the Lord's work in super-modern 1946. The war had wiped out sixty-five million people, which proved Man was powerless against great evil because evil always sneaked in by appearing good. Discernment was key and that alone was reason enough to place his faith and trust above. His number one job as husband and father was to guide his family spiritually. Everything else would fall into place. If his family went up in a flash, it would meet the next world prepared and joyous. In short, this Williams family couldn't lose.

With firm resolve, at 2:00 p.m. on the hot summer Sunday of July 21, 1946, Clarke McRae Williams walked in front of the humid sanctuary of Oak Grove's First Baptist Church with Mary Kathryn's pastor, Reverend J. D. Cheatham. Best man Benjamin Wade grinned at him, his choice after weeks of agonizing over Pod Carroll, Tiny Terwilliger, Earl Hogan, and his father. Ben Wade's family had been good to Clarke in the pharmacy, where the groom had enjoyed many philosophical discussions. Ben was a true confidant and a true representative; the other friends agreed he was Clarke's "best man."

The celebratory wedding of Roy Lee's daughter couldn't have come at a worse possible time financially as his grocery and other businesses suffered post-war contractions. Mary Kathryn sensed the difficulty, and, without asking her father, announced she preferred a simple afternoon wedding with no attendants. She and her parents had attended a number of military weddings, big nighttime affairs with sharp young men in uniforms lined up to the right and delicate attendants lined up to the left, ablaze in enough candlelight to worry a fire department. Showoffs tailored their dresses out of the finest silks and satins and then added orchids, with receptions flowing in punch, food, and a towering wedding cake. Mary Kathryn sighed as she and Ola Mae did the best they could.

Two hours after the morning service, pianist Dilsie Hamilton began the wedding march. Thin curtains fluttered lazily in the warm breeze as hand fans flickered across the sanctuary. In the same economical way Mary Lee had married, Clarke and Mary Kathryn prevailed on Pastor Cheatham to squeeze them in while everyone was still in town after church. White tapers on tall candelabras burned valiantly against sunlight and breeze. Tall pedestal vases held sprays of gladiolas, ferns, and palm branches. Beads of sweat ran down Clarke's ribs. As Dilsie began Richard Wagner's "Here Comes the Bride," little ring-bearer Tom Sawyer, Jr., tentatively made his way down the aisle holding a satin pillow with two shiny gold rings. Behind him, flower girls Kathryn Rae Tyson and Mary Alice Thomas gingerly tossed rose petals. Mary Kathryn's best friend, Maid of Honor Betty Jo McBride, glided toward the altar in a white dress adorned with a huge vibrant red corsage. Finally, as Mary Kathryn turned the corner on the arm of her beefy, sweating father, Clarke beheld a vision unlike any he'd ever seen. She floated toward him like an angel dressed in a delicate, flowing gown of aqua blue. She carried on her arm a bouquet of salmon-pink gladioli. Pure joy radiated from her face in the smile with which he had fallen in love. Clarke felt deep gratitude for such an undeserved blessing and quietly thanked God for such tender mercy.

As Dilsie played the piano, Kitty Buckles thoughtfully sang "I Love You Truly." Mary Kathryn had so enjoyed her singing at Louisiana Tech that Kitty drove three hours from Shreveport to sing at the wedding. With the exchange of vows and rings, Kitty sang "Because," after which the young couple bowed their heads in prayer and all was done. Reverend Cheatham pronounced Clarke McRae and Mary Kathryn man and wife. From the audience, watching them kiss were Captain Arthur B. Carroll, who, to Clarke's amusement, had unexpectedly stayed in the Army, and Cat Barham, who, also to Clarke's amusement, had not. Cat was stoic. As of that day, the youth she had shared with Clarke came to an end.

Clarke whisked Mary Kathryn away to honeymoon on Florida's white beaches. As they left town, driving down Oak Grove's main street, Mayor and Fiske Theatre owner Donald Fiske waved from a ladder as he lettered the marquee. *The Bells of St. Mary,* starring Bing Crosby and Ingrid Bergman, would start tomorrow.

While the couple honeymooned, Aunt Mabel, Uncle Charlie, and Cousin Evelyn moved out of the Williams home where they had switched calls for four years. Mabel and Evelyn prepared the old home for the new bride. As for Clarke, if the Army hadn't snuffed out his dreams, nothing would. Military service had shown him that anyone could be forced into service but that lasting success came mostly through enlisting the willing help of others. Every opportunity had to prove good for everyone. And timing was key, which meant he had to be prepared for opportunity.

Clarke went to see Bank of Oak Ridge founder and president Joseph W. Brodnax. Mr. Brodnax had organized the bank in 1910, then served as president for thirty-seven years. He had also contributed to his community as the longest-serving president of the Morehouse Parish Police Jury. Clarke grew up with Mister Joe's soft-spoken and humble example, a man quietly tenacious, whether discussing hard-topping roads or securing depositors' money from loss or theft. Brodnax had survived the Crash of 1929, bank closures, and the Great Depression and was overjoyed at the creation of the Federal Deposit Insurance Corporation. As FDR spoke the FDIC into being with *"The only thing we have to fear is fear itself,"* depositors at last found protection from cyclical panics, losses, and bank robbers.

Robbers in fact attempted to test the FDIC by breaking into the Bank of Oak Ridge the month after Clarke and Mary Kathryn married but were foiled by security. The regal 80-year-old banker was still laughing about it two months later when the 24-year-old owner of Oak Ridge Independent Telephone Company sat down in front of him. Clarke noticed a credenza absent of family photographs. Mr. Brodnax and his wife Minnie were childless. Brodnax instead channeled his energies full time into bank and civic duties. While Mr. Brodnax had never thought much of phones –he considered long conversations a waste of time– the banker had observed the great potential of the Williams boy. Clarke surmised that the kindly old man probably had wanted a son and thus mentored many a farmer and businessman. The two warmed to each other, both men humble, accessible, and open to all points of view. They were gentlemen at two opposites, one ending a career, the other starting. With no hesitation, the bank president granted Clarke nearly $4,000 for the dialup system. They shook hands. Clarke couldn't wait to call Kellogg Switchboard with his very first order.

Will Clarke was proud of his son. Clarke McRae got a loan from the same bank and banker who had turned him down, and Will had been mayor of Oak Ridge. How had a 24-year-old done it? Clarke insisted he got what he wanted in the strangest way, by not demanding anything at all.

> Clarke McRae Williams: "My daddy was aggressive but he happened to live in a period when money was very difficult to get. The telephone industry was considered risky by

lending institutions and funds for expansion were not available."[99]

Fresh from honeymooning in Florida, when Clarke carried Mary Kathryn over the threshold of their new old home, she could scarcely believe her good fortune –until she walked into the front room. There sat the hulking piece of worn wooden furniture called "the switchboard." That and two phone booths took up most of the living area. Their home was a public building.

> Clarke McRae Williams: "I brought Mary Kathryn home to a small house with a switchboard in it, and that was Oak Ridge Telephone, which didn't seem like very much to a new bride."[100]

Mary Kathryn did not complain. She rolled up her sleeves and became Oak Ridge's newest operator. When she married Clarke, her in-laws signed Oak Ridge Telephone over to them, but while outwardly the gift seemed generous, Mary Kathryn quickly saw Oak Ridge Telephone was more of an albatross. Will and Marie hoped their son could bring home what he had learned using Army technology.

What he came home to was a wreck, worse than when he left. William Clarke Williams started life in simplicity and stayed there, attacking problems with more brawn than brains. Seldom did he buy precut, smooth telephone poles; instead he hewed saplings. Trolling the roads, Clarke found wires strewn everywhere, through trees, across fence posts, just above the ground across hills and hollows, and between buildings, all barely enough to keep the system functional. What kept the

---

[99] *A Review of the Life of a Telephone Pioneer*, Century Telephone in-house publication in possession of Carolyn Williams Perry, circa 1980, page 11
[100] *A Review of the Life of a Telephone Pioneer*, Century Telephone in-house publication in possession of Carolyn Williams Perry, circa 1980, page 7

whole phone system from grounding out were small white porcelain insulators every place Will could nail them.

> Clarke McRae Williams: "My father would cut
> trees, not a big tree, but one with about an eight-
> inch diameter or so and would trim it up and go
> dig a deep hole. We had some posthole diggers
> with handles about seven feet long and he would
> dig the hole and sit the tree in there. Then you'd
> get a porcelain insulator and a nail to separate the
> line from the tree."[101]

Clarke sighed deeply at the rigging, a little overwhelmed. It was all his, all his to own and all his to work. He had to replace the entire network or run himself to death repairing breaks. While waiting for the new dialup system, he shipped in reels of wire, rented a mule from a local farmer, and began laying new wire by himself, one pole at a time. He first shouldered the harness, drove the mule, unharnessed and pulled wire over his shoulder while scaling the pole.

> Mary Kathryn Williams: "Clarke got out with a
> mule and strung lines up and down the highway
> and built new lines out in the country because the
> old ones were laying on fence posts and in trees.
> When a big wind came up, the tree limbs would
> knock them together and put the line out. We've
> gone out many times at 2:00 o'clock in the
> morning to straighten out some lines so people
> would have service. He did everything. He
> pulled wire over his shoulder, he climbed poles.
> I can't tell you how many poles he may have
> climbed in his life. The poles were not as high as
> the Louisiana Power & Light poles but they
> always seemed insurmountable to me. He never

---

[101] *Louisiana Lifetimes*, December 9, 1996, Television production of Century Telephone, Inc.

minded any kind of work. He was always happy."[102]

Clarke McRae Williams: "In the original magneto telephone system, which merely meant it was a one-wire telephone system, the very oldest that we had, children would call for their grandparents and they all had little nicknames for them. For example, the Files girls—all three since married—their grandfather was Postmaster Eugene Barham in Oak Ridge. Well, when their mother Sadie got on to them pretty heavy, they'd come to the telephone crying and they'd ring that ringer and either my wife would answer the telephone or I'd answer the switchboard and we'd say, 'Number please.' No one ever gave us a number but we always said, 'Number please' anyway because that was just the standard greeting like when you pick up the telephone and say, 'Hello.' Well, on other end of the line we'd hear this voice say, and they'd be crying and sobbing, and they'd say, 'Give me Papa!' So we knew they were looking for Mr. Eugene so we'd ring the post office for them."[103]

Young Clarke *was* the phone company, and since he promised better service, there was no better advertising than for subscribers to drive past Clarke and his mule. Friends stopped to offer help or water, but others fogged past Clarke in a cloud of dust. At home, he saved Mary Kathryn steps by rigging a buzzer she could hear anywhere in the house. Except for the switchboard and booths, Mary Kathryn's house lacked furniture and some essential appliances. Friends came to the rescue, first, with a late July outdoor tea in Oak Grove hosted by Lee family friends Mrs. W. T. Everett, Mrs. Russell Stroud, and Mrs. H. M.

---

[102] Ibid
[103] Clarke Williams, Sr. interview, *KNOE Special Report* with Jamie Patrick, KNOE TV8 News, ©1992 Noe Enterprises, Inc.

Thomas. Guests sweltered not in the house but under shade trees in hopes of catching a dusk breeze but July ended exceptionally hot and breezeless. Yellow flames stood perfectly still in candelabras, gold against a red sunset, as Maid of Honor Betty Jo McBride served cold watermelon punch from a hollowed-out watermelon. Martha Ann Stacy and Johnnie Redell played selections on a piano rolled into the open air.

Few were listening, though. The thirty-five ladies pelted Marie with questions about whether Oak Grove Telephone would stay in business. That week, a heated public meeting ended with Louisiana Public Service Commissioners ordering owners of Oak Grove Telephone "to improve local service '2,000 percent' in a reasonable length of time or the company would be cited for contempt and a heavy fine imposed."[104] Owners argued that only five of Oak Grove's 300 customers properly "rung off" by telling operators they were finished, which unnecessarily kept lines tied up. Will Clarke thanked his lucky stars because only a few years before he had almost bought Oak Grove's exchange.

In Oak Ridge, Catherine Barham was first to fete the new bride. On Thursday morning August 1, 1946, Cat hosted a "cola hour" to make introductions. Clarke McRae's former employer, the Patrick Henry Wades, also hosted a tea for Mary Kathryn, adorning tables with sprays of pink roses. Friends Mary Ann and June Castleman drove in from Oak Grove. The merger of the Williams and the Lees was also the merger of the two Oaks, Ridge and Grove. Days later Clarke drove Mary Kathryn to Booneville, Mississippi, specifically to show her off and to tour the Williams ancestral grounds. Clarke McRae filled in the blanks about her father-in-law's long journey to Louisiana.

Mary Kathryn juggled being an operator with learning her way around the kitchen. Determined to surprise Clarke with her first sumptuous Southern fried chicken, the young bride reluctantly bought a live chicken and tried to remember how Mary Lee had rung necks a year earlier in the chicken coop. Gathering her nerve, she clutched the bird and began pulling its

---

[104] *West Carroll Gazette*, August 1, 1946, front page

head. The hapless bird squawked loud enough that Clarke came flying out the back door.

"What are you doing!" he yelled. "Give me that chicken. I can't stand to see it suffer." She managed to cut up and fry the chicken to a savory crisp, but her neck-wringing days were over. Either Clarke would do the wringing or she'd buy fryers.

Chickens aside, marriage turned out better than Clarke thought possible. Central to their relationship, Mary Kathryn lovingly embraced her husband's faith, joining all aspects of Oak Ridge Baptist Church, while Clarke proudly displayed the beauty and intelligence of his bride. The two became quick favorites, organizing a Sunday school group of young Oak Ridge married couples into the "Winsome Class" for those starting out. Among them were Evelyn Gibbs and her husband Sam Williams, no relation to Clarke, and Roy Norman and his wife. Cat Barham tagged along as a single.

Many weekends, the young couple burned 40 miles of gravel visiting their parents in Oak Grove, or the parents visited them in Oak Ridge. Roy, Will, and Clarke discussed the phone and its future. Marie, Ola Mae Lee, and Mary Kathryn discussed grandchildren. Sometimes Clarke and Mary Kathryn joined Will and Marie in the ten-hour round-trip journey to Baton Rouge to see Kittie and Mary Lee at L.S.U. With Mary Lee and Clarke married, Kittie became serious about a boy at L.S.U. named Charles Shaw.

During the week, Clarke struggled with Oak Ridge Telephone, buying copper and steel wiring as post-war prices came down grudgingly. Southern Bell suffered likewise, except that it could publicly mount a rate hike case before Louisiana's Public Service Commission. Bell lawyers complained that expenses had escalated 117 percent over pre-war prices. Clarke read Bell's blitz of advertisements, one headed with the picture of a quizzical young woman with the caption, *"What have Telephone Earnings got to do with me?"* The ad explained, *"Earnings have declined rapidly. They are not only the lowest in history, they are dangerously low."*[105] They couldn't be that "dangerously low," Clarke thought. Large corner ads in

---

[105] *Morehouse Enterprise*, January 30, 1947, p3

newspapers didn't come cheaply. Clarke privately hoped Mr. Brodnax didn't see the ads. If gigantic Southern Bell struggled to make a profit while GI subscribers clamored for telephones, how was Oak Ridge Telephone making it?

In truth, Clarke's only increase in revenues came not from $1.75-a-month subscribers but from increasing long distance traffic. That proved a two-edged sword, as more people made pleasure calls at all hours, even past midnight. Clarke's solution, one with which Mary Kathryn was not happy, was moving the switchboard into their bedroom. At a buzz, he could turn over in bed, connect the lines and go back to sleep, unless the drunk and depressed were looking for a sympathetic ear.

Mary Kathryn endured sleep interruptions for a short time before putting her foot down. Clarke moved the switchboard back, reworked schedules, and alternated operators across night shifts. Since he and Mary Kathryn took shifts, often Clarke worked 24-hour days, grabbing catnaps whenever he could. Now he was face-to-face with what his father had encountered, the reality that higher local call volume did not translate to higher revenues, only more work to maintain the system.

Clarke caught wind at that time that his parents were struggling in Oak Grove. The same outrage toward bad service from Oak Grove Telephone had spilled over to complaints about Oak Grove Power & Water and the Rural Electric Association. Oak Grove citizens weren't happy that utility owner F. A. O'Neill was a Chicago city slicker who cared little about Oak Grove. Will Clarke tried his best to keep everyone happy, but Oak Grove aldermen forced O'Neill to submit a rate reduction plan. O'Neill responded in early 1947 by selling out to Louisiana Power & Light, which combined the utility with its gas distribution interests and moved new managers to West Carroll Parish. They scrutinized Will Clarke Williams with his gimp leg. At 52 years old, Williams did not appear a viable lineman much longer. That, combined with Marie's exasperation at Oak Grove Telephone, and good son Clarke McRae could see his parents might soon be jobless.

As Clarke promised dialup magic, Oak Ridge Junior High teacher Mrs. J. C. Rolfe asked him to explain to her seventh- and eighth-graders what *dialup* meant and the need for telephone courtesy. At 25, though Clarke didn't seem much older than the kids, he was billed as "Manager of Oak Ridge Independent Telephone Company." Wednesday morning February 26, 1947, Manager Williams enlightened fresh faces with how they should ask an operator to place a call. Since their parents were still using old black battery-powered candlestick phones and some grandparents still had wooden box wall-mount magneto phones, the kids marveled at Clarke's modern squat-cradle phone with a never-before-seen whiteface dial. One finger rotated the dial. Mouthpiece and earpiece combined in the same futuristic handheld receiver they could simply hold to their heads. No more holding the heavy candlestick clunker in one hand and earphone in the other and having to click the cradle to get an operator's attention. In fact, they wouldn't need the operator at all. The Oak Ridge dialup would be only the second in the whole state. All the youngsters had to do was merely dial numbers to connect directly with a friend across town. Now they could exchange homework and secrets without fear of being overheard. Young Mr. Williams was offering them the freedom of grownups.

Enterprise correspondent Annie Reese sat listening with keen interest. She wrote, "We are glad to hear the good news that dial telephones are coming in. Clarke is expecting the dial telephones in July and every one who wants one may have it."[106]

The next day, the same students crowded into pretty Miss Mary Kathryn's front parlor while she explained the switchboard and duties of an operator. "We can handle about fourteen people at a time," Mary Kathryn clarified. "That's seven pairs of calls going on at the same time." Clarke smiled. His beautiful newlywed wife had learned everyone's telephone numbers, rings, and occupations in less than half a year. Twelve months before, she had been a 16-year-old student at Louisiana Tech, turning seventeen on March third just as Clarke mustered out. In a few days now, she would turn 18. Their worlds had completely changed in a single year and now, as a veteran operator, she fascinated a roomful of pre-teens, taking calls,

---

[106] *Morehouse Enterprise*, March 6, 1947, p 7

crisscrossing wires, and talking to others miles away. It was all so incredibly modern and fantastic. From that very parlor, beautiful Mrs. Williams could connect them to anyone anywhere in the world. They listened intently as she called long distance operators to connect a man in Oak Ridge with another person all the way over in Monroe. That people could talk to someone else several miles away and never leave their house was truly miraculous. 1947 was a wondrous time.

They learned a week later that technology could also be misused when, for a second time in seven months, thieves tried to crack the Bank of Oak Ridge, this time using an acetylene torch to cut through the window bars and the vault's outer door. But when they burned into Mr. Brodnax's booby-trapped inner vault, tear gas blasted their eyes. As the bank alarm clanged to life, panicked and choking robbers made off with only a pearl-handled pistol from the guard's desk and a secretary's kitty containing 90 cents. They left behind a few hundred dollars' worth of acetylene equipment. A few weeks later, police in Roanoke, Virginia, arrested Breard Burks, the mastermind, for disturbing the peace. When they found the FBI wanted Burks for going AWOL, he begged for leniency by ratting out his three Oak Ridge accomplices. Agents announced that Oak Ridge was the first attempted bank robbery in U.S. history perpetrated by an "all-negro" gang.

After shaking hands with Mr. Brodnax and boasting how Oak Ridge phones would be second to none, Clarke sweated when Kellogg Supply didn't produce. He had initiated negotiations in mid-1945, but only after Mr. Brodnax's loan promise did work begin. For eight more months, post-war strikes hampered raw materials deliveries, delayed jobs, and paralyzed transportation. Teamster president Jimmy Hoffa reorganized longshoremen and autoworker leadership back to pre-war levels. He wrestled with managements into the 1950s, using violent tactics not restrained until John and Robert Kennedy headed a Senate investigation that tied Hoffa to the Mafia.

For most of 1947, Kellogg engineers wired and soldered through Hoffa's disruptions. Finally in July, two years after initiating the order, Clarke's state-of-the-art equipment arrived by Missouri Pacific freight at the Oak Ridge Depot. The black steam-shrouded engine blew the whistle and by the time Clarke got there, depot agent Marion Bardin had the paperwork ready for the half-dozen crates.

"Uh oh," said Mr. Bardin.

"What's wrong?" asked Clarke.

"This is COD. Plus delivery charges have to be paid before I can let you have it. I'll need a cashier's check for $3,500 plus a $150 delivery charge. That comes to $3,650."

"I'll be right back. Let me run over to the bank," Clarke said enthusiastically. But as he crossed the street and touched the front door of Bank of Oak Ridge, he froze with a sudden sickening. Mr. Brodnax was dead. His death had been so sudden last New Years Eve that it went completely unnoticed by Clarke and Mary Kathryn, in Oak Grove for the holidays. Mister Joe's death and private home funeral passed in less than 48 hours attended by only his wife Minnie, three sisters, and a brother. No one delivered public eulogies for his presidency of both bank and police jury, and no packed church celebrated an accomplished life. Mysteriously, Brodnax bypassed his local Baptist membership and requested that Reverend J. H. Hooks of Rayville's First Baptist Church officiate, along with Oak Ridge Methodist minister S. T. Emmanuel.

Clarke and Mary Kathryn, meanwhile, were miles north celebrating Kittie's Christmas Day engagement to Charles Shaw. Clarke started the New Year diving back into dialup preparations and hounding Kellogg Supply, confident of Mr. Brodnax's handshake back in the fall.

Suddenly it was July, the equipment was at the depot, and Clarke broke into a sweat hoping Mister Joe had written something down or told someone of their agreement. He nervously explained to lifelong bank cashier Lucille Huffman, who slipped into the office of Brodnax's successor, Robert E. Barham. She returned unhappy.

"Clarke," she began, "I'm sorry but nobody here knows anything about a loan for you or the phone company. Mr. Brodnax didn't say anything to any of us about an agreement with you. And he didn't leave anything in writing. I'm sorry."

Shocked, Clarke pleaded, "But the new equipment is across the street at the depot right now."

Miss Huffman thought a moment. "Clarke, we know you and your family. Let me see if we can get a majority of the board together to discuss the loan."

Clarke breathed a sigh of relief, waiting two hours more at the depot before Lucille Huffman frowned again after the emergency meeting.

"We're sorry, Clarke," she said, "but the board decided that, times being what they are, and since Mr. Brodnax didn't leave anything in writing about your loan, we'll have to decline giving you the money."

Times being what they are meant Southern Bell had made such a public case to the PSC for losing money that no one on the board could see how Oak Ridge Telephone could service a loan. Truthfully, Clarke didn't know himself, but dialup was his only hope.

Clarke steadied himself out in the heat. He could hardly breathe. He had served his country diligently for three-and-a-half years at the expense of Oak Ridge Telephone and now board members, his customers, rejected him. Quarterly public reports showed Bank of Oak Ridge with a record over-one-million dollars in assets and yet its board couldn't loan $3,650 to a man they had known all his life.

Embarrassed, Clarke would be the laughingstock all over town when Missouri Pacific returned the cargo. Slinking toward home, questions haunted him: *Why had he boasted? Why had he made promises? Why had he tried to be a big shot?* He'd stubbed his toe every step of the way, too poor to go to a big college, too frail to fly for the Army, too preoccupied to notice Mr. Brodnax had died and too late to make other arrangements. Utter failure at every turn. Now he had a wife, one he plucked from her home and put into a town of strangers, some of whom blamed Clarke as too good for a local girl. *Well now, look a here, the braggadocios boy who did not fight in Europe but stayed safely stateside was proving a little big for his breeches.* He had even bragged in the Bastrop newspaper how his technology would surpass gigantic Bell's. Now, David had been stomped by Goliath. Only a favored few in Oak Ridge made $4,000 a year, and they weren't chopping cotton or climbing poles. No one he knew had that kind of money.

> Clarke McRae Williams: "That was the blackest day of my life, the first real disappointment in the company. In fact, I remember walking back from town with my eyes focused on that train depot. I was so despondent I didn't know what in the world to do."[107]

Clarke stopped his thoughts and began to pray. Like a sunbeam through storm clouds, Oak Ridge cotton planter and entrepreneur Joe Sidney Carter appeared out of nowhere and pulled alongside him. Mister Joe Sidney had a reputation for thinking differently, smiling as he was from a dusty, self-modified Chevrolet pickup. Though townspeople considered him eccentric, no one could argue with his success. Before the war, Clarke briefly drove the school bus, and saw Mister Joe Sidney most mornings. Carter had often exchanged tips in the Williams garden with Will and Marie. Many years earlier, when Clarke had been a young boy of 8 riding his bicycle to collect telephone payments, Mr. Joe's wife had pointed out to her husband the boy's strong work ethic and decency.

"Clarke?" inquired Mr. Carter bluntly, "I understand you got a problem."

Clarke knew Oak Ridge was a small town but he didn't know news traveled *that* fast. Lucille must have called him as soon as the loan committee disbanded.

"I sure do, Mr. Joe."

"Well, I know a little bit about it," Mr. Carter admitted. "I take a nap every day about two o'clock and am up about 3:00. Why don't you come by and see me then?"

Clarke agreed and Joe Sidney drove on. *What just happened? Was Mr. Joe offering to loan $4,000 for untested*

---

[107] *A Review of the Life of a Telephone Pioneer*, Century Telephone in-house publication in possession of Carolyn Williams Perry, circa 1980, pp 8-9

equipment, sight-unseen, to a 25-year-old? Clarke grinned from ear to ear. He evidently had done something right because not only had Mister Joe heard of his plight, the old man had wasted no time coming to Clarke's rescue. The prayer had been answered so quickly, it scared him.

Now God needed to work a miracle in Oak Ridge Telephone's financials. Clarke nervously spent two hours running thin figures and, at 2:55, walked to the Carter house. Sweat stained his notes. He was sure Mr. Bardin at the depot wondered where he was.

Joe Sidney Carter spared the boy a tense monologue of numbers that probably didn't work anyway. He got straight to the point. "Clarke, I don't know anything about the telephone business because I'm just a planter but I think it must be all right. If you want to take a chance, I'll let you have the money."

Clarke flushed red, grinning unabashed. He thanked God.

"But," Carter continued, a finger in the air, "I'm going to tie your hands behind your back. I'm going to take a mortgage on everything you have, everything. And, mind you, I don't want to run the telephone business. I just want you to pay the thing off."[108]

Clarke froze a little. A mortgage on everything, the business, his house, truck, switchboard, and a hundred new dialing telephones. Pressure mounted to make Oak Ridge Telephone do what it had never done before: pay for itself *and* support a family.

"Thank you, Mr. Joe," he replied, vigorously shaking the older man's hand. "You won't regret it, I promise you."

"Make it work and neither one of us will regret it," Joe said shortly.

Make it work. The phrase stuck in his throat. Clarke was certain Mister Joe knew Oak Ridge Telephone's tenuous position, especially with Bell shouting that the telephone business was unprofitable. The Hogans hadn't made it work; Will and Marie hadn't made it work; and Aunt Mabel and Evelyn hadn't made it work. Now Staff Sergeant Clarke McRae

---

[108] Ibid, p 9

Williams, fresh from existing as a tiny cog in a big inefficient machine, *had* to make it work. He *was* the machine now, and on his shoulders alone rested success and failure.

He shook it off. God always provided a way even if that way was seldom easy. This time, the very fact Joe Sidney Carter pulled alongside him out of the clear blue was the way. He paused a minute, stopping cold on the street. Joe Sidney knew the score that Oak Ridge Telephone was virtually unprofitable and yet he invested anyway. The reason came to Clarke and he was warmed and humbled by it. Joe Sidney was not investing in Oak Ridge Telephone, *he was investing in Clarke McRae Williams*.

Clarke looked up to a sky that in two short hours had gone from black to a beautiful deep blue. With a full heart, he thanked his living God.

At the depot, Marion Bardin smiled as he accepted the cashier's check, relieved for the earnest Williams boy. He asked him what *dialup* meant and Clarke happily explained. Bardin signed up on the spot. At the office, Clarke called Bell installation engineer J. D. Hudson. Installation was only the beginning of many problems.

> Clarke McRae Williams: "I found out that just because it was automatic didn't mean it would work by itself. It had to have technicians. I was able to find friends in Monroe –J. D. Hudson and other Bell workers– who came and helped me repair the switchboard when it would malfunction."[109]
>
> "I grew up when it was just two wires and, if one broke, you could fix it. But these dialup switchboards had relays and diagrams that were very complex and a little beyond me."[110]

---

[109] *Louisiana Lifetimes*, December 9, 1996, Television production of Century Telephone, Inc.
[110] Clarke Williams, Sr. interview, *Louisiana Legends with Gus Weill*, © 1999 Louisiana Television Education Authority

Friends came out of the woodwork to help him and he wondered why. Clarke McRae gleaned certain motivations from scripture and one was character. He refused to claim superior intelligence because he certainly hadn't done anything to prove that. It hit him with a shock that everyone in town had been watching him his whole life, on his bike collecting bills, in Wade's Drug Store running prescriptions to cars, diligently helping his father, driving others to college, standing at weddings, cheerfully helping others, fighting in Uncle Sam's Army, fixing phones, untangling wires, and using a mule to string more. All of these actions added up to explain the two Joes, Brodnax and Carter. Clarke thanked God for His guidance in youth because, until that moment, he had not realized that a man's reputation was critical long before a young man even knew he had one.

Clarke McRae knew keeping a pure heart would get him into heaven, but he hadn't expected dividends so soon. He pondered why we make so many crucial decisions in youth when we are least capable of making them, except that God perhaps has injected Man with irony as a teacher. Scriptures were clear about not *leaning unto one's own understanding* and Joe Sidney Carter's rescue was beyond understanding.

Clarke McRae mulled these issues as he, J. D. Hudson, and others pieced together a dialup system more intricate than Clarke had imagined. Life just passed too quickly for a person to live long enough to figure it all out. That meant that his devotion from youth to studying centuries of collective wisdom in the Bible, as silly and square as that appeared to friends, had been correct after all. It had provided him a solid foundation.

Joe Sidney Carter took Clarke under his wing because there was no one else to do it, because he had invested his money in Clarke, and because he determined that Clarke was a young man smart enough to know what he did not know, especially about money. Joe Sidney assessed that local dial-up was not enough, that the quickest source of revenue growth was long distance. That paid by the mile and by the minute. As people minded long distance premiums less, statistics showed those calls increasing.

Impatient in a smart way, Joe Sidney suggested that Clarke go all-out to improve Oak Ridge Telephone by automating long distance service.

"But, Mr. Joe, do you realize that would cost about $10,000?" Clarke asked.

"You need it," Mr. Carter said matter-of-factly. "I'll loan it. Let's do it."

Clarke McRae couldn't believe his good fortune. He called Kellogg, sent the money ahead this time, and within weeks he was installing North Louisiana's very first combination local and long distance automated dial-up service. A mere eight weeks after his darkest hour in July, Clarke was astounded that his greatest dreams were already exceeded. *The Morehouse Enterprise* took notice on September 9, 1947.

OAK RIDGE EXCHANGE GETS NEW EQUIPMENT

THE SECOND INDEPENDENT DIAL TELEPHONE SYSTEM IN LOUISIANA AND THE ONLY ONE IN NORTH LOUISIANA WILL SOON BE IN OPERATION AT OAK RIDGE, C. M. WILLIAMS, OWNER OF THE OAK RIDGE TELEPHONE COMPANY ANNOUNCED.

ALREADY IN PARTIAL OPERATION, THE SYSTEM WILL BE COMPLETELY AUTOMATIC WHEN EQUIPMENT IS OBTAINED TO PROVIDE DIRECT LONG DISTANCE SERVICE TO MONROE. WILLIAMS SAID THAT WHEN INSTALLATION OF ADDITIONAL EQUIPMENT IS COMPLETED THE DIAL SYSTEM WILL BE SECOND TO NONE IN THE STATE.

WILLIAMS PLACED HIS ORDER FOR NEW EQUIPMENT BEFORE THE END OF THE WAR AND WAS FORTUNATE IN SECURING A PRIORITY. STRIKES, HOWEVER, DELAYED DELIVERY, BUT THE NEW EXCHANGE EQUIPMENT HAS BEEN ASSEMBLED AND INSTALLED AND ALL BUT LONG DISTANCE EQUIPMENT IS IN SERVICE.

APPROXIMATELY $10,000 HAS BEEN
SPENT ON NEW EQUIPMENT TO MAKE OAK RIDGE
EXCHANGE ONE OF THE MOST MODERN AND
EFFICIENT IN THE STATE.[111]

Mary Kathryn proudly clipped several copies of the front-page story and mailed them to family and friends. Clarke had leveraged Oak Ridge Telephone into a public relations home run. His young bride began to ascribe to her husband's belief that anything was possible in the spirit. Most people procrastinated because they had to see proof first. By definition, faith meant you could not see proof, and out of Clarke's faith had come reality, had come his knowing that the *how* would present itself because he was prepared spiritually. Ten days later, that spiritual strength was put to a gigantic test.

With dialup installation almost complete and Clarke and Mary Kathryn mortgaged to the hilt, the most powerful hurricane in over thirty years tore across Louisiana on Friday September 19, 1947. The Category Five storm, fourth in 1947's active hurricane season, packed winds of 155 miles per hour as it hit Florida. Covering half the Gulf of Mexico, the tempest made a direct hit on New Orleans still churning 110 miles an hour. The number of storms prompted meteorologists at the United States Weather Bureau to name the storm "Hurricane George," the first named hurricane in history. George flooded New Orleans, ripped Baton Rouge with 100-mile-an-hour winds, and aimed for Shreveport, tearing a path 60 miles wide.

George grudgingly gave up, gusting 60 miles an hour into Morehouse Parish, knocking down trees and power lines and making spaghetti of phone wire. An ancient oak one block from Clarke and Mary Kathryn fell across 13,000-volt transmission lines in a spectacular blue fireball. Lights flickered to black. Clarke sighed in the darkness. Falling power lines melted phone wire beyond recognition.

When some customers realized they were still connected and battery-powered phones still worked, the switchboard lit up.

---

[111] *Morehouse Enterprise*, September 9, 1947, front page

Mary Kathryn and Clarke turned their parlor into a candlelit sanctuary, connecting emergency long distance calls while Clarke prayed the shingles didn't blow away. He kept buckets ready to catch drips over his new system.

Overwhelmed in the gale, Clarke stopped. Worry was a waste of energy. He knew the Father had brought him this far not to destroy but to build, and he knew this because the plan was tracking nowhere close to what Clarke originally had envisioned. Events were unfolding along some absurd, miraculous plan over which he apparently had no control.

In the howling wind and beating rain he remembered how a preacher had once said storms were the constant. "Expect them," he'd said. "Souls are either in a storm, entering a storm, or coming out of a storm," and in life's storms, a Christian's job remained the same, losing oneself in the aid of others. As George roared overhead, Clarke and Mary Kathryn were busy alleviating fears, calming those out there alone in the dark, frightened, sitting in dim rooms lit by a pale candle, children clinging tighter at each thunderclap. They needed hope and Mary Kathryn was there with her wonderfully reassuring voice. The storm will pass, she would say, "All will be okay."

As the Kellogg automation clattered beautifully, Clarke regretted a little that callers would soon miss his bride's caring voice. He felt honored to be this close to her and smiled when she occasionally winked from under the headset. In the golden glow of candlelight, her face was even more of a vision. If he begrudged anything, it was the phone's continual interruption of their intimacy. The switchboard needed to come out.

In the storm, Southern Bell in Bastrop broke all records as local calls zoomed from 15,000 to 23,000 and long distance from 500 to 700. Oak Ridge Telephone reaped some of those rewards, relatives checking on loved ones, farmers checking damage. By the direction from which calls were not coming, Clarke could tell where lines were down. Mary Kathryn reported which lines hummed as word came that water had knocked out hundreds of phones in Bastrop. Many country neighbors stayed on party lines, needing assurance. Some braved lashing rains to tell Clarke lines were down. Mostly, they just wanted to talk. Clarke had the telephone to thank for that. Before phones, people rode out gales alone, getting closer to God in case the night was their last.

Mary Kathryn put on a pot of coffee as the Williams parlor filled with customers and lawmen. The Williams abode became the town's communications center as skies turned from dense black to purple to gray. The sun eventually peeked through the cracks, symbolizing to Clarke that Light is always there even when hidden.

Out in the debris, Clarke thanked God that most of his lines had withstood the tornadic winds. What repairs were needed, townsfolk pitched in to help.

> Gerald McLendon: "I worked with Clarke a lot shooting trouble. When the lines would go out, we'd get a bamboo fishing pole and ride up and down the road until you found where the lines were crossed. Then we'd take the fishing pole and uncross the wires and get the service back on. These lines were usually on saplings that had been cut out of the woods and stuck in the ground so any time you had a high wind or rainstorm usually you'd have trouble with the lines."[112]

Louisiana Power & Light linemen worked days restoring power, rehanging some telephone lines out of respect for Clarke and his LP&L father. Clarke's company was back in full operation within days. When a few folks groused at Clarke to deduct the outage time from their phone bills, Joe Sidney Carter stepped in. Nobody bothered Clarke again.

The unusually active storm season of 1947 included unusual ice storms that winter. Freezing weather seemed particularly bone chilling forty feet up in the air. Lashed about by winds and sleet, Clarke kept a bottle of tepid Coca-Cola in his pocket, a rewarding burn that defrosted him. The truck's heater struggled to keep up with the cold. He could barely feel

---

[112] *Louisiana Lifetimes*, December 9, 1996, Television production of Century Telephone, Inc.

hands, feet, nose, and ears, and muttered to himself that such solo work would turn him into an old man just as it had Will.

He hated being trapped, unable to afford help, but complaining would do no good. Farmers broke their backs seven days a week during planting and harvest, but phones never slept. Then, one Wednesday, Clarke and his hardworking friends were incredulous to find the Bank of Oak Ridge locked up. They learned that Act 306 of the 1946 Louisiana Legislature allowed state banks to close all day Wednesday as a "Day of Public Rest." Bank of Oak Ridge announced it would close Saturday, Sunday, and Wednesday during the summer. Clarke still stung a little from the bank's rejection and thought that if ever given the opportunity, he would open that bank to everyone more, not less. Joe Sidney Carter had elevated him with the bank's committees, but not everyone had an advocate.

Gratified with the new system's efficiency, Clarke and Joe Sidney discussed the vast opportunity in streamlining hundreds of Mom-and-Pop telephone exchanges with automated dialups. Out of the blue, Clarke's friend Leland Lockridge, traveling with the American Red Cross, returned home and made a beeline for Clarke. Leland had just driven through the piney woods hamlet of Marion, Louisiana, up near Arkansas where citizens were in a stir because their phone system was for sale. With no offers, they were forming a citizens' cooperative to run it. "You can imagine how that'll work," Leland laughed, "a bunch of hicks running a phone system. Can you imagine the bickering? That's probably why the family's selling it."

Clarke knew he was right. Farmer cooperatives were notorious for infighting, and Marion was too small for Bell. A light went off. He could kill four birds with one stone: buy the phone company and more than double the size of Oak Ridge Telephone, upgrade and expand to help customers, make a place for his parents, and perhaps make his business just large enough to qualify for an anticipated government loan program.

"How will you handle a phone company over in Union Parish?" Joe Sidney asked.

"Daddy probably is about to lose his job in Oak Grove," Clarke explained, "and he and mother can move there to oversee day-to-day operations." What he needed was $5,000 to buy the exchange. When Clarke and Joe Sidney arrived to meet with owner S. F. Richardson, a group of citizens was waiting for them. The subscribers were not happy, doubly so when they discovered they were dealing with a lanky 25-year-old boy. Suspiciously, they sat down and pelted Clarke with questions. They noticed his calloused hands.

Clarke quietly listened to their concerns and told them he would install dialup. When S. F. Richardson asked $4,000 for the company, Joe Sidney winked at him, and on a handshake, Marion Telephone with ninety stations was his.

Will and Marie praised God when Clarke and Mary Kathryn called. Marie was weary of Oak Grove's angry callers and mad at owners who wouldn't fix the system despite Public Service Commission orders. Will walked a tightrope between pleasing LP&L up the chain and helping customers down the wire. They jumped at the chance to move to Marion, welcomed by veteran office manager Etta Stripling, who became indispensible.

> Clarke McRae Williams: "Etta, before we formed Century, was my right and left hand, both legs and sometimes my thinking cap. She was marvelous."[113]

Mary Kathryn's parents left Oak Grove at the same time, moving to Baton Rouge, where Roy Lee pursued real estate. Roy was very proud of Clarke's first leveraged acquisition and proud he was helping his parents. Clarke was smart about it, too, streamlining technologically with a system he could repeat anywhere. His son-in-law didn't just dream, he took action and did so fearlessly. Roy knew that Clarke was religious, perhaps a little more than his liking, but no one could argue when a man's faith actually worked. He sensed Clarke was being guided to some greater purpose because he was the unlikeliest of entrepreneurs. In him was no pride, boastfulness, or guile.

---

[113] *A Review of the Life of a Telephone Pioneer*, Century Telephone in-house publication in possession of Carolyn Williams Perry, circa 1980, p 10

Mr. Richardson liked Clarke, too, and pointed him to the tiny exchange at Choudrant, Louisiana, a few miles west of West Monroe. While wire strung through the piney hills serviced only a handful of phones, Clarke anticipated that an expansion of nearby Brown Paper Mill might soon give steady incomes to more workers and loggers. Clarke and Joe Sidney closed the deal in less than a week, and if Clarke proved right about an influx of workers, he'd install his third dialup system.

> Clarke McRae Williams: "With Marion and Oak Ridge together, I began to have enough of a nucleus that I could begin borrowing money from a government source through the Department of Agriculture. Up until then, I was too small in numbers to get a loan."[114]

In 1949, Congress amended the Rural Electrification Act, enabling small rural exchange owners to obtain long-term, low-interest loans. Clarke qualified for little but loans meant he could convert enthusiasm into growth and growth into momentum. Joe Sidney, after financing the dialup and two acquisitions, had had enough financial exposure. He had seen businesses expand too quickly, then fail if a recession hit, so when Clarke told him the Plain Dealing, Louisiana, system was for sale, he wasn't interested. At three hundred subscribers, Plain Dealing was twice the size of Oak Ridge and Marion combined.

Clarke turned to his father-in-law. Roy Lee said that no great rewards came without risk and that life was a risk. Clarke and Mary Kathryn drove to Baton Rouge in their 1942 Plymouth. Will and Marie had owned the car and sold it to a friend for $200 and a few bushels of corn, but when the friend defaulted, Will gave the car to Clarke and Mary Kathryn. A side window was missing and a piece of cardboard flapped over it to Baton Rouge and back. In the shadow of Louisiana's 30-story miniature Empire State Building capitol, Roy Lee asked Clarke how he logistically planned to run a phone system "on the other

---

[114] Clarke Williams, Sr. interview, *KNOE Special Report* with Jamie Patrick, KNOE TV8 News, ©1992 Noe Enterprises, Inc.

side of the state." Plain Dealing sat above Shreveport on the Texas line.

"Mary Kathryn and I would have to go there, with Daddy and Mother at Marion and Aunt Mabel back in Oak Ridge."

"If we can make the deal, I'll buy the exchange in Plain Dealing and you and Mary Kathryn can get it up and running," Roy agreed. But when the two set out for a meeting with the owner and Clarke headed for his 1942 Plymouth, Roy balked.

"Let's go in my car," said Roy, indicating Clarke's broken window, "because I'm planning to buy that telephone company on credit. Anyone who sees your car isn't going to sell us anything. They're going to figure if you can't afford to buy a window for your car, how are you going to afford to buy anything else?"

Pulling into Plain Dealing, the two found the town eerily quiet. The telephone office was closed. A funeral procession had stopped commerce, and when Clarke and Roy asked who had died, the answer shocked them. It was the very man they had come to see.

> Clarke McRae Williams: "When we arrived, we were quite embarrassed. We didn't know what to do. They were looking for us and we were looking for them. Finally, we got word to the man's son."[115]

Clarke detected a pattern. Wild obstacles and setbacks seemed to plague every move. Bank president Brodnax died leaving Clarke holding the bag; Hurricane George blew in just as his dialup went online; and Marion subscribers scoffed at his youth.

"Clarke," Roy offered his disheartened son-in-law, "this is all part of the deal. Obstacles teach you and make you better. You've overcome everything this far and I'm mighty proud of you. Let's check into a hotel and try to see the family tomorrow."

---

[115] *A Review of the Life of a Telephone Pioneer*, Century Telephone in-house publication in possession of Carolyn Williams Perry, circa 1980, p 14

The next day, they found that the deceased owner's son had little desire to continue the telephone business or to manage it. Clarke had tossed all night, fearing he would appear unscrupulous and opportunistic. With great humility, he recounted his conversation with the son's father and ended with, "Now, if you have any reservations whatsoever and you don't want to sell or this is not a good deal for you, then I wouldn't do it. If you say yes, everybody stays on. Nobody is fired."

Roy raised an eyebrow but told the son, "Maybe we should offer a proposal later."

In the car, Roy told Clarke, "We'll write him a letter that we want to buy the company on credit. We'll offer a hundred dollars down and a hundred dollars a month."

Clarke shook his head in disbelief. "Man, we'll never buy a company like that."

"Maybe not. But we might."

Still skeptical, Clarke dutifully wrote the letter. A week later came the reply: "Thank you. We accept your offer."

Roy Lee winked. The student had a lot to learn. In April 1948, Roy and Ola Mae moved to Plain Dealing. Clarke once again handed the Williams house keys to Aunt Mabel and to grandparents Andy and Dorah Hill, who were moving in, too. Clarke and Mary Kathryn moved in with Roy and Ola Mae. Quarters were cramped but the arrangement worked.

Now Clarke and Roy were not just in-laws, they were business partners. Roy knew partnerships seldom worked and within a family could be disastrous. But Clarke was different. The thought never entered Clarke's mind that he might be working harder than everyone else. Roy could see that. Work was what drove him.

Roy closed the deal on September 22, 1948, with $100 down and $100 a month for 100 months at no interest. He paid $10,000 for the company or $33 per subscriber, compared to Marion where Clarke and Joe Sidney paid $44 per subscriber. The sellers benefited with monthly income and, if Roy defaulted, they would get the business back.

Out in the field, however, nothing was plain about Plain Dealing. The former owner had complicated everything by refusing to carry telephone lines farther than the city limits. Private landowners began buying their own wire and splicing into the phone system, creating a hazardous patchwork of naked wires on leaning poles. Clarke saw what had driven the former owner to his grave.

> Clarke McRae Williams: "He didn't want to service them because they were poor lines. You couldn't talk over them and people wouldn't pay him to go out and construct new lines, so he just cut them all off."[116]

Partly in retaliation and partly because it was good business, a grocery store installed a single telephone line from Plain Dealing to Shreveport and advertised it as a free long distance service. Customers flocked in, shopping while they waited to call, saving the Plain Dealing Telephone charge of forty cents a minute.

> Clarke McRae Williams: "There we were right down the street at the telephone company trying to put lines into rural and residential areas and, yet, all of our toll business was going out through the grocery store."[117]

The district's gruff Public Service Commissioner then demanded Clarke and Roy Lee do what the previous owner never did.

> Clarke McRae Williams: "I was somewhat afraid of him. He came charging into the office and said

---

[116] *A Review of the Life of a Telephone Pioneer*, Century Telephone in-house publication in possession of Carolyn Williams Perry, circa 1980, p 15
[117] *A Review of the Life of a Telephone Pioneer*, Century Telephone in-house publication in possession of Carolyn Williams Perry, circa 1980, p 15

he would see that rural people received telephone service."[118]

Roy Lee turned the commissioner's demand into an opportunity, firing back, "If you want these people to have telephone service, you better get that free line out of the grocery store. They offer a free line to Shreveport to get customers in and it is hurting our toll revenue. We will attempt to put lines in the rural areas if you will get that telephone out of the store."[119]

The commissioner yanked out the store's free line and demanded that Roy and Clarke launch a massive overhaul of the system. Revenue from increased long distance calls was a pittance compared to the cost of steel telephone lines. Clarke and Roy did not have the money to expand while maintenance costs on all four exchanges were escalating. With no funds, no promise of funds, no borrowing ability, no bank lines of credit, and no benefactors, Clarke and Roy had boxed themselves into a corner.

Clarke again found himself at a dead end with no way out. He dropped to his knees, as he often did, and asked for guidance. The idea came quickly. He would ask his subscribers for the money. In Oak Ridge, Marion, and Choudrant, Clarke drove the roads, visiting the ten people on each of his party lines. One by one, he explained the truth about system financials and the complete lack of money for improvements. The PSC might raise telephone rates but that would be long in coming, too late to help build the system. Clarke mustered the nerve and asked each person, rather than his pushing for a large rate increase customers would be stuck with permanently, would they lend him $300? He would deduct their bills until $300 in service had been reached. He was asking them to pay forward more than a year's worth of telephone service. Many went white. Most in rural areas barely saw $300 in cash in a year.

Most of the families scraped together $300 and gave it to the earnest young man. Shiny new wire soon draped from new

---

[118] *A Review of the Life of a Telephone Pioneer*, Century Telephone in-house publication in possession of Carolyn Williams Perry, circa 1980, p 15
[119] Ibid, page 16

poles into the countryside. With wide financial backing, Clarke persuaded a bank to lend him enough money to finish the project.

Now it was Roy Lee's turn to be astounded. For Plain Dealing Telephone, Roy modified his son-in-law's system, telling his banker, "I have to string wire into rural areas. If I can get twenty-five or thirty people out there to sign a note, you can take those notes, let me have the money, and as they pay me for telephone rental, I'll pay you back everything." Roy persuaded nearly sixty to sign notes ranging from $200 to $300 each.

Clarke was a hero but a tired one. He burned the roadways between Oak Ridge, Marion, and Plain Dealing while dreaming up new forms of financing. He hoped PSC commissioners would appreciate his costly efforts and grant rate increases. Bell Telephone continually placed ads in newspapers either touting telephone service as a small fraction of a family's budget or with outright pleas for increases.

Something else dawned on Clarke. Plain Dealing's former owner was indicative of the plight facing the whole industry: a desperately aging infrastructure with owners aging as well. The choice for the mom-and-pops was to dive into debt or sell out, and if their children had no interest, they sold. That excited Clarke. With the age of most systems between 25- and 50-years-old, a flood of exchanges might soon form a buyers' market.

To see those opportunities emerge, Clarke joined civic groups, church groups, and social groups, and happily accepted membership into a professional group called The Telephone Pioneers of the United States. At 27, Clarke was among the youngest of the "Pioneers." His same winning personality on the job translated into good relations with both colleagues and competitors in The Telephone Pioneers and word about him spread.

Conventioneers hooted at Clarke's cornball humor and compared industry horror stories. But they hushed and leaned in when Clarke described his rare dialup system, something most of Bell had yet to install. At some conventions, Bell management scoffed at Clarke's business model, "We string a mile of wire and get a hundred customers. You string a mile and get one. That won't work." Clarke would politely listen, and sometimes turn red, but he never engaged them, giving a simple, "We'll see," or if pushed, "Tell you what. What say you tend to your business and I'll tend to mine." The Bell boys walked away admitting they were just employees while Clarke was the owner of four systems.

Back in Plain Dealing, the team of father- and son-in-law had picked up the pieces of a previously bitter fight and managed to get customers to give *them* money. From up on poles, Clarke made it a point to wave at subscribers as they passed, gratified they were now his investors. He dared not obsess about being in so much debt. Halfway as a joke, he even hired a crusty old lady who became a notorious operator.

> Clarke McRae Williams: "She used to be a dispatch operator for a cab service during the war. She was a tough girl. She had a heart of gold but she was pretty tough and she connected a call one night between an old boy and girl, neither of whom should've been talking to each other. In the conversation, he said, 'I'll bet old Annabelle's listening.' And Annabelle was listening and she said, 'That's not so!' The story was all over town the next week and everybody was saying, 'That's not so!' She could have gone in on the key to see if they were talking and if she'd just been quiet, they'd have never known whether she was on the line or not, but it got her goat when they said, 'I'll bet old Annabelle's listening.'"[120]

The Lees and Williamses often traded off switchboard duty at night.

> Clarke McRae Williams: "In Plain Dealing, when we operated the switchboard at night, we'd

---

[120] Clarke Williams, Sr. interview, *KNOE Special Report* with Jamie Patrick, KNOE TV8 News, ©1992 Noe Enterprises, Inc.

just turn the bed right next to the switchboard. I could prop up on my elbow, answer the switchboard, ring the number and then go back to sleep. Sometimes I'd leave folks connected all night. That was the way we operated and we considered it to be normal."[121]

Mary Kathryn was less than thrilled with the switchboard back in their bedroom. During the day, as Clarke traveled the roads with linemen, Mary Kathryn fought the battle of bills, glitches, and complaints. The loss of sleep from interruptions began taking its toll. Though she charmed most complainers, the occasional malcontent made her day miserable. She was glad Ola Mae was handy but she began to feel nauseous just after New Year 1949 with a flu that would not go away.

Ola Mae's expression suddenly changed from concern to a smile.

"You're in the family way," she cried.

After her doctor confirmed the pregnancy, Mary Kathryn leapt into Clarke's arms. He was euphoric on the one hand and terrified on the other, grateful to be a father and challenged to be a provider.

Sometime in September when his child was born, he would start a long journey full of triumphs and tragedy. It would be the same unspeakable journey in which most fathers learn just how inadequate they are.

---

[121] *A Review of the Life of a Telephone Pioneer*, Century Telephone in-house publication in possession of Carolyn Williams Perry, circa 1980, p 15

PART II
THE FAMILY

CHAPTER 7

"EVERY TIME WE HAD A CHILD, CLARKE HAD TO GO OUT AND GET ANOTHER JOB. AT ONE TIME HE WAS GOING TO WORK AT 4:00 A.M. AS AN ELECTRICIAN. HE'D COME HOME ABOUT 2 IN THE AFTERNOON AND CLEAR UP TELEPHONE TROUBLE. AT NIGHT, HE WOULD GO TO ONE OF THE GINS AND KEEP BOOKS. HE WORKED REALLY HARD ALL HIS LIFE."
MARY KATHRYN WILLIAMS

"I WAS COMPLIMENTED BY THE FACT THAT I WAS ABLE TO GET ALL THESE JOBS AND HAD GREAT RELATIONSHIPS WITH ALL OF THEM. BUT WE DIDN'T HAVE ENOUGH MONEY TO PAY THE OPERATORS AND LIVE AND IT JUST TOOK EXTRA JOBS TO GET IT. THAT WAS THE REASON I HAD TO EXPAND IN ORDER TO GET ENOUGH BUSINESS THAT WE COULD HAVE A LIVING."
CLARKE MCRAE WILLIAMS

Saturday September 10, 1949, dawned bright in Plain Dealing. Mary Kathryn nudged her husband. "We need to go" was all she said. Clarke jumped up and dressed in a flash. They had a half-hour drive ahead of them to Shreveport and anything could happen in a half hour. Clarke had been packed for a week. He had kept the gas tank in their car full. For weeks, swinging from poles, he kept calling the office to check on her. Now the time had come.

Ola Mae jumped into the car with them and the three barreled down narrow Louisiana Highway 3 to northwest Louisiana's premiere Doctors' Hospital. Clarke and Mary Kathryn had considered large Charity Hospital, the legacy of Huey Long, for its low-cost medical service, but it stayed full of long lines and hard luck stories. Just that week Shreveport officials broke ground on a third hospital, a $6 million facility as ultra-modern as its name was ancient, Confederate Memorial. Surplus Confederate Veterans Pension funds, accumulated as the men in gray died, floated construction bonds for the hospital.

As Mary Kathryn's contractions grew closer, Clarke bore down on the accelerator. Though Ola Mae said not a word, Clarke caught her in the mirror grimacing at the speed. He backed off. He hadn't been this nervous stalling B-25s in check flights.

He wheeled into the emergency entrance where a nurse took Mary Kathryn and Ola Mae to delivery while Clarke scribbled through papers. Then he joined the other new fathers in a smoke-filled waiting room. He could hardly breathe. Would he have a son or a daughter? Friends had speculated the baby was a girl by the way Mary Kathryn carried it, but he couldn't tell if they were joking. Whatever God sent him was fine. He just prayed for healthy lungs, legs, and arms.

Each time the delivery room door swung open, all the men stood up, and Clarke could hear the cacophony of many an upset newborn. It hit him he was going to take that noise home. He wondered if he had been a fussy baby for Marie and Will. But mostly he wondered if he had a boy or a girl. Either way he couldn't lose. If he had a boy, he had a pal and coworker. If he had a girl, she'd be as beautiful as Mary Kathryn. He thanked God for his good fortune, and he thanked God he didn't smoke.

Finally, a nurse in starched white knocked the door aside and called his name. She was smiling. Into his arms she placed a tiny bundle swaddled in a soft cotton blanket.

"Congratulations, Mr. Williams," she said. "You've got a boy. Seven pounds, six ounces." Ola Mae was beside herself with the widest smile he'd ever seen.

"How's she doing?" he asked her.

"Just fine, Clarke. She's fine. Congratulations."

He could scarcely believe it. He was a father. He had a son. Clarke McRae Williams, Junior, looked back at him with tiny blue eyes set in a wrinkled face. He was the most beautiful thing Clarke had seen since he first laid eyes on Mary Kathryn. The miracle of life continued in a world of trouble and hope.

"Everything works?" he asked.

"Oh, yeah," the nurse said rewrapping Clarke Junior. "Got a great set of lungs."

The small clapboard house they shared with his in-laws grew even smaller, and smaller still when Clarke's mother and cousin Evelyn Gibbs Williams and her children came in the following weekend. Excitement and love filled the house, a welcomed distraction for Clarke. *The tie that binds*, he thought: The joy in Marie's face alone, as a new grandmother, said it all.

She also brought news that Earl and Bobbie Hogan, best friends now living in Ruston, had had a son, too, David Earl, born only five days before Clarke Junior.

Clarke envied Earl and Bobbie for living much closer to home, but as the phone family reached out, Plain Dealing reached back. Subscribers in and out of the city limits liked Clarke because he did what he promised and he worked harder than any of his part-time hires. Clarke McRae took the hardest jobs, whether up on a pole or down in the mud.

Beyond grunt work, young Clarke continually studied young technology with fascination and with fear of being left behind. He had read in the Army about an evolution of radio with pictures, and by 1948, in Dallas, Texas, licensees of a new technology called *television* were among the very first to beam video signals. In Plain Dealing 200 miles east, Clarke watched with his wealthier customers as faint black and white images flickered on a glass tube. Voices faded in and out. On a screen the size of a frying pan, the phosphorescent glass showed not a movie but real people talking and moving in Dallas that very second. Clarke marveled at the giant leap from talking to someone hundreds of miles away to the imminent possibility of seeing that person. Modern 1949 was a remarkable time to be alive, even if everyone felt overwhelmed by the rapidly changing technology. As "TV" antennas sprouted from houses, Clarke saw communications soon going wireless. Everyone in the future would pack their own personal phones like small versions of the Army's walkie-talkies.

Walkie-talkie phones couldn't come too soon for all the sweat and toil up on poles. Always the optimist, he talked excitedly about the future to customers and coworkers but, mostly, Clarke just liked people, asking about their families, their hopes, dreams, and desires. He impressed by remembering their names, their spouses' names, their children's names, what grade, which school, and even whether they had been sick. Clarke amazingly never forgot such details.

When working crews, Clarke was uncomfortable with the title "boss." He didn't want a position above anyone. In the Army, he had noticed that men who wanted to be bosses cut themselves off from genuine communication, thus losing valuable time and information. Clarke liked listening to everyone, because competing ideas often saved many steps. After hearing everyone out, he gently nudged workmen toward what he thought was the best solution.

At first, linemen and office help thought Clarke Williams, fun and kid-like, was just too good to be true. He was a churchgoing man who seemed to live the creed. He never cursed, never complained, never raised his voice, never put anyone down. In fact, he never discussed politics or how the system was geared against the little guy or how politicians were crooks or how taxes were unfair or how mean people could be or how the rich exploited the poor. Those themes bombarded the public every day in headlines and gossip. Indeed, at the dawn of the 1950s, oil and gas interests made hollow threats to leave Louisiana over severance taxes, purposely rattling the state's economic foundation.

Clarke chuckled when worried businessmen snagged him and the crew alongside the road, voicing dire consequences should Esso Standard Oil and wildcatters pull out. "They can't take the oil with them," Clarke replied calmly, "so they won't leave; they just want to make more money by not paying more taxes." Privately, however, Clarke wondered why wealthy oilmen received tax breaks for "depletion allowances" when all businesses used up resources. Such tax breaks made taxpayers partners in drilling but, when a well came in, the owners kept all the profits. Clarke never complained, but he would remember: When it came to lawmaking, every industry had to fend for itself.

Those around Clarke saw that headlines didn't flap him. If the Soviets' detonating a nuclear bomb two weeks before his son was born hadn't worried this Christian, nothing would. As he and the crew strung wire, Soviet communists walled off East Berlin while Chinese communists banished U.S. ally President Chaing Kai-shek to Taiwan. The war had destroyed the Nazis only to clear a way for the communists.

Alarmists went wild. Wisconsin Senator Joe McCarthy began a witch hunt, first ruining many Hollywood careers by alleging that the film industry supported a communist takeover, then outing 205 so-called communists within the United States government. President Truman denied McCarthy's claim, then showed Moscow who had the superior firepower by detonating the world's deadliest doomsday machine, the hydrogen bomb. Insanity seemed to be prevailing and in the middle of it, from backwoods North Carolina, emerged an unlikely young evangelist whose strange cadence attracted thousands to church revivals. Clarke admired Billy Graham not because he was a fellow Baptist but because Graham didn't let the world dictate his destiny. Graham stood up to the world, and as a result, hundreds of thousands found true meaning, true freedom and a true passion for living.

Pressure continued to mount on telephone's razor-thin margins when President Truman nearly doubled the minimum wage from 40 cents an hour to 75 cents. Even with the increase, Bastrop and Monroe Bell telephone workers still walked out. Clarke was astounded to learn that Southern Bell had 44,000 non-supervisory workers. President Hal Dumas cried to the press, "We have failed by about $20,000,000 annually to make up through increased telephone rates the wage increases already granted in the last ten years."[122] By late May 1951, 32 of Bastrop's 38 operators went on strike.

Southern Bell's losses, if true, gave Clarke no comfort and proved that bigger is not better. If Bell couldn't turn a profit with its giant economies of scale, nobody could. Clarke suspected what the unions suspected, that management used creative accounting to resist pay increases while soliciting rate increases. Clarke knew the nuts-and-bolts costs of telephones and with the customer density Bell enjoyed, the company was surely turning a healthy profit. More troubling to Clarke, Bell would eventually pay workers top wages and hike his cost for experienced labor.

Young Mr. Williams digested the information but obsessed about none of it. He felt that agility and adaptability started with clear thought, and workers noticed his confident manner. Unlike Plain Dealing Telephone's previous owner who worried himself to death, the worse the situation appeared to Clarke, the more he

---

[122] *Morehouse Enterprise*, Bastrop, La., April 10, 1951, p 2.

laughed. His employees knew he wasn't crazy; it was just that, still in his twenties, he'd already seen disasters work themselves out. Clarke had experienced an invasive government, a redundant Army, and every possible type of customer complaint. Older than his years and steeped in scripture, Clarke Williams could see farther down the road than most. Indeed, Clarke encouraged his employees so much they feared he and Mary Kathryn might go home to Oak Ridge.

Their concerns were justified. Just as Clarke and Roy finished the new automated system in Plain Dealing, midnight tornadoes plowed up the outskirts of Oak Ridge on Sunday, March 26, 1950. No one was injured but Mrs. Gussie Kennedy rode her house up and down across the yard, Buck Kennedy's house was completely destroyed, Jim Gregory watched his roof tear away, and when the J. D. Reese family tried to run to a stronger shelter, halfway there they watched the entire building lift from its foundation and disappear into the sky.

Clarke and Mary Kathryn used the disaster to justify an extended trip back home to repair the lines just paid for by subscribers' loans. They moved back to Oak Ridge the second week in May 1950, finding home festooned with rose gardens and fragrant magnolia blossoms. Townspeople, all smiles over the new long distance dialup system, had no idea how dangerously close Oak Ridge Telephone was to defaulting on its customer loans. To keep expenses down, Clarke kept doing the work himself, zipping between Oak Ridge and Marion and Choudrant. As 1950 ended, he concluded that Oak Ridge was automated enough to allow him to oversee the same build out in Marion, prompting him to finalize the purchase of Marion Telephone from Mr. Stephenson on September 30, 1950.

Clarke's faith grew as setbacks continued. The Marion upgrade started in the worst winter storm to hit north Louisiana in fifty years. In February 1951, snow piled up as temperatures dropped below zero. Limbs heavy with ice snapped telephone lines. With emergency services and law enforcement dependent on telephone communications, Clarke found himself back in freezing winds trying to scale ice-clad poles. All four systems needed replacement wire, insulators, and a few poles. With no change in subscriber numbers, the various phone systems absorbed repair costs. Bizarre weather followed Clarke into June when more lines were destroyed by a massive hailstorm, one that reduced 300 acres of area cotton "to sticks."[123] Adding to expenses, crews worked overtime, making Joe Sidney Carter nervous about the companies' razor-thin margins. Often, Clarke did not pay himself as Joe Sidney Carter and Roy Lee tried to keep credit lines open. Clarke felt guilty taking borrowed money for personal expenses. Mary Kathryn reminded him they had a child.

With Oak Ridge automated and Marion, Choudrant, and Plain Dealing coming along, Clarke decided with his father to base operations in more centrally-located Marion. Giant spools of wire, insulators, poles, telephones, thousands of parts, and the only repair truck filled the yard and office at Marion. Since an addition was necessary for the new dialup system, he and Will worked a new headquarters building into the budget. They also agreed with Roy Lee to pull all four telephone systems under one umbrella. They called themselves *United Telephone Company*. Clarke leveraged the solid sound of "United Telephone" in recruiting the best help.

Keeping up with technology was both crucial and expensive. Kellogg Switchboard & Supply, Stromberg-Carlson, and *Western Electric* competed fiercely in building faster relay systems. Clarke found if he waited a little longer to order new systems, he could upgrade on less money by ordering last year's model, a strategy as he balanced between necessity and return on investment.

Try as he might to gain equilibrium, the balance sheets for the four telephone companies remained abysmally red. He hated the thought but admitted he was in the same quandary his father had faced: Clarke had to take outside jobs to keep food on the table. At the same time, Will mentioned that Kittie Williams, the cousin who had raised him in Iuka, was penniless after the death of her husband. She had no place to go. Clarke and Will moved Kittie Hubbard to Marion into Will and Marie's home. Clarke was amused the Mississippi Williamses thought the

---

[123] *Morehouse Enterprise*, Bastrop, La., June 19, 1951, front page.

Louisiana Williamses were doing far better than they really were.

In the spring of 1951, Mary Kathryn announced she was pregnant again. She would deliver sometime in December in the middle of Clarke Junior's first real Christmas. As in Plain Dealing, her obstetrician and delivery room were forty minutes away in Monroe. She had to give herself and Clarke an hour's lead-time once contractions started. She prayed the child wouldn't come on Christmas Day.

The week before Christmas, on December 18, 1951, Mary Kathryn reported contractions. Clarke rushed her to Monroe and waited. And waited. The false alarm embarrassed her. As Christmas Day neared with no signs of labor, Mary Kathryn busied herself with decorating and cooking, insisting that everyone come to her house. Marie and Ola Mae arrived, fussing around the kitchen, cleaning up and cooking. On Christmas Eve, precisely as she feared, the pains started again. She wrestled with whether to alarm Clarke but, when he came home, he noticed right off.

"We'd better go," he said.

"No," Mary Kathryn snapped. "I'm not about to go over there for another false alarm. And I don't want to be in the hospital tomorrow. I want to be here with you so we can watch Clarke Junior." She cried, "I don't want to miss his first real Christmas!"

She envisioned her 2-year-old wide-eyed in Christmas lights and laughter. She wanted to watch him tackle their meager little pine, naked but for a string of lights and some shiny tinsel. She wanted to relive the innocence of Christmas through his eyes, to savor this important moment with Clarke. But contractions kept intruding, closer together and more painful. She told herself she might be days from delivery. More than anything, she dreaded troubling so many on the biggest holiday of the year.

This time the labor was real. Her water broke just as both families arrived. Clarke knew it was too late for a race to the hospital. Mary Kathryn endured quick scolding glances from Ola Mae, who was careening between joy and fright. Though both Ola Mae and Marie had been born at home, they knew labor could go wrong quickly. Reading their worried faces, Clarke ran next door to summon Dr. E. L. Maddry, who pretended he was overjoyed to leave his noisy house on Christmas Eve night. Clarke grimaced that the obstetrician he had paid was enjoying Christmas while the old country doctor did the work.

Dr. Maddry didn't have to wait long. As church bells faintly peeled across town, Mary Kathryn shrieked at 1:00 on Christmas morning, giving birth in her own bed to a baby girl. Ola Mae and Marie assisted the good doctor while Clarke paced outside trying not to worry, holding Clarke Junior fast asleep on his shoulder. Will and Roy talked on, doing their best to bring some normalcy to the night. Then Ola Mae said, "It's a girl, Clarke!"

Tucking Clarke Junior in, he ran into his bedroom. Mary Kathryn smiled weakly, tired and soaked with perspiration. They bounced names around and Clarke asked, "What do you think about 'Annette'? It's a good name, a pretty name."

Mary Kathryn replied, "What about *Marie* for a middle name, after your mother?"

Clarke thought but decided against it. "No, we'd have another Marie Williams and might get our wires crossed if she helps as an operator." Mary Kathryn nodded. They named their healthy baby girl Annette Williams.

The Christmas story was little Clarke's miracle. Though his sister wasn't born in a stable, an emergency delivery at home on Christmas Day came close. He would always parallel his mother Mary with Mother Mary, since both delivered on the same magical night. The brother soon learned, however, that seldom were tiny sisters the same as angels. Annette cried a lot and was loud and smelly and nothing like Jesus. Worst of all, doting grandmothers now put him down to dote over the baby.

Clarke McRae was in heaven. Never more in love with her husband, Mary Kathryn still worried about the mounting pressure on him. He never let on but she knew they were dancing close to the edge of insolvency.

Mary Kathryn Williams: "Every time we had a child, he had to go out and get another job. Because with just 75 or 80 telephones, we just could not make it. At one time he was going to work at a carbon plant in Swartz at 4:00 in the morning as an electrician. He'd come home about 2 to 2:30 in the afternoon and would clear up what telephone trouble we had. And then at night, he would go over to one of the gins and keep books. So he worked really hard all his life."[124]

For Clarke McRae, the fourth mouth cleared up what he had to do. He could no longer wait for new dialups to turn a livable profit in towns that were not growing. Young people were graduating and moving to cities where they found jobs, excitement, and Bell Telephone. Clarke cast about for odd jobs, driving tractors, buses, and harvesters. Around electricity all his life, he honed that skill at the Columbian Carbon Plant a half hour west for the steady income and family medical coverage.

In the fall during around-the-clock cotton ginning, gin owner Charles Roth hired him to keep books from 6:00 p.m. until midnight, weighing in raw cotton from the fields, writing seed checks, and keeping inventory. Up at 4:00 a.m., Clarke operated on four hours of sleep during harvest to meet his own payroll. The Internal Revenue Service deemed taxes mandatory and profit irrelevant.

Through Joe Sidney, farmers, and ginners, Clarke met Monroe agri-businessman Nelson D. Abell, who had introduced Dixie Liquid Fertilizer, a water-soluble fertilizer for row crops. Traditionally, cotton, soybean, corn, and sugar cane farmers slung dry granular fertilizer over crops and waited for rains to soak in the nutrients. No rain, and the fertilizer sat inert; heavy rains, and the granules washed away. Abell injected nitrogen, phosphate, and potash in a liquid form alongside root systems. Feeding was instant but the business was equipment-heavy with

---

[124] *Louisiana Lifetimes*, December 9, 1996, Television production of Century Telephone, Inc.

20-ton on-site tanks. Tractors pulled smaller tanks with steel knives set row-widths apart. As the tractor pulled, the knives hydraulically sank into the ground, injecting fertilizer inches from root systems. Both Abell and Clarke considered liquid fertilizer the wave of the future, but the product had nothing to do with telephones and Clarke couldn't invest in anything else, least of all his time.

Abell saw in Clarke a positive, innovative salesman. The young Oak Ridge telephone man was unpretentious and humble, exactly the kind of man skeptical farmers would believe. Abell offered to consolidate Clarke's three jobs into manager of newly-formed Ouachita Fertilizer. The position brought more money than Clarke had ever seen but meant Will and Roy would have to take up the slack at United Telephone.

> Clarke McRae Williams: "Of course, I was complimented by the fact that I was able to get all these jobs and had a great relationship with all of them. But we didn't have enough money to pay the operators and live and it just took extra jobs to get it. That was the reason I had to expand in order to get enough business that we could have a living."[125]

Expanding the family business was a problem but expanding the family was not. In January 1954, Mary Kathryn discovered she was pregnant with their third child. Remembering all too well the painful Christmas two years before, she found an obstetrician in Rayville, twenty minutes south, at the Ball and Ellington Clinic. As soon as contractions began on September 20, she and Clarke wasted no time getting there. She quickly delivered their third child. Clarke was ecstatic when the nurse brought him a beautiful baby girl. He and Mary Kathryn named her Carolyn.

"What about 'Lee' as a middle name, after my family?" Mary Kathryn ventured.

---

[125] Clarke Williams, Sr. interview, *KNOE Special Report* with Jamie Patrick, KNOE TV8 News, ©1992 Noe Enterprises, Inc.

"Hmm, 'Carolyn Lee Williams.' I guess so if you want."

Mary Kathryn reconsidered, "No, that would leave Annette as the only one without a middle name."

With two children ages five and three and now a newborn, Clarke realized he had duplicated his parents' family of a son and two daughters. But Clarke considered family members both born and collected: All of Oak Ridge was his extended family. Joe Sidney Carter was mentor and financier, and Joe Sidney Junior was like a brother. The two boys spent many hot and cold days together keeping Oak Ridge Telephone operating. Younger Joe admired Clarke for accomplishing much on scant resources and for keeping his cool no matter what. He watched Clarke's faith in God and in others remain strong.

As he listened spellbound to Clarke describe check flights in B-25s, crisscrossing the nation overhead and viewing life from the clouds, Joe Junior noticed that Clarke bore no bitterness for the Army's not letting him fly. When the Army Air Corps became the United States Air Force in 1947, Joe Junior joined up and became a pilot, as much for Clarke as for himself. At each base, Joe stayed in touch with his hero. He was stationed once at Fairchild Air Base in Spokane, Washington, a mere hundred miles east of Moses Lake where Clarke had served in the 482nd Fighter Squadron. They compared notes on military life but Clarke was more gratified when Joe began asking about married life. He knew Joe had left behind a sweetheart in Carroll Ann Smith, and one day Joe Sidney asked, "Clarke, will you be my best man?" He accepted and stood with Lieutenant Joe Sidney Carter at Oak Ridge Baptist on December 30, 1954. He and Mary Kathryn gave the newlyweds a big sendoff, urging them not to like Washington State too much and to come home soon.

Clarke noticed his father looking sallow and a little unresponsive on trips to Marion to check on the new headquarters. In Will Clarke's sixth decade of hard work, his overseeing the project while maintaining the Marion system took its toll. William Clarke collapsed with a stroke that rendered him mostly paralyzed. He slowly regained his ability to write but never spoke another word. When awake, Will sat for hours in his wheelchair watching United Telephone headquarters come up from the ground, a heartbreaking scene every time Clarke dropped by. Just as heartbreaking was seeing his mother go it alone while he bounced between Oak Ridge, Marion, and Ouachita Fertilizer.

On February 1, 1956, Clarke officially opened the fertilizer company with Nelson Abell as owner and A. V. Frost as production superintendent. "It's like handling so much water," Clarke explained in an advance story in the *Monroe News-Star*. "Of course, that fact doesn't take away from its effectiveness as a fertilizer."[126]

Clarke explained to farmers the various organic building blocks of nitrogen, phosphate, and potash. He found the same skepticism for the new idea as he had years earlier for telephones because liquid fertilizer, like telephones, was almost too simple. That's when he discovered that people often overlooked opportunity for that reason. Fortunately for Abell, many tried the liquid fertilizer solely because they trusted Clarke.

Building Ouachita Fertilizer made more good connections for Clarke through the Monroe Area Development Corporation and president Walter Koch. MAIDCO helped procure financing and a prime north Monroe location near large plantations. Clarke observed how a group of strangers had come together to help the new venture and noticed how quickly the strangers became visionaries building their community.

Mary Kathryn connected, too, juggling three children, a switchboard, and several social groups. She helped form the Caddoan Club, a civic and book club tackling subjects from gardening to the Constitution to capitalism to child rearing. As president, she oversaw speakers, fundraisers, dinners, and the Oak Ridge Christmas light competition.

Little Clarke became socially driven as well, leading neighborhood kids on bicycle adventures. When he turned 8, he joined the Cub Scouts of Oak Ridge with friends Andy Barham, Mack Barham, Robert Barham, Larry Barr, Edwin Conger, Vern Deal, and Donny Sharbano. Busy Clarke McRae shared responsibilities as sponsor, scoutmaster, and den father, as he

---

[126] *Monroe News-Star*, Monroe, Louisiana, January 19, 1956, p 3.

juggled the Oak Ridge Lions Club and its charitable fundraisers. Adding to that membership, he attained Junior Deacon in the Brookfield Masonic Lodge, Number 161 F. and A. M.

Clarke's frenetic pace halted suddenly on Tuesday, October 15, 1957. That day Will Clarke's long journey from Iuka, Mississippi, to West Texas, to Louisiana towns Monroe, Oak Ridge, Oak Grove, and Marion finally came to an end. The last time father and son shook rough, calloused hands, Clarke could tell Will was pulling away. Will Clarke scribbled a final note to him and Marie: *"Take the proceeds from my life insurance and invest all the money in the phone company."* He added for Marie, *"Give Clarke the money. You can't go wrong."* Will's final act was to fund Clarke's future.

The son realized that he owed more than his life to Will. It was Will who had started at Cumberland Telephone at the dawn of the Twentieth Century. It was Will who swung from poles in the dry winds of West Texas and fell in love with an operator's voice. It was Will who challenged that girl to meet him in Fort Worth. It was Will who studied Louisiana phone systems while at Southern Bell. And finally it was Will who bought fledgling Oak Ridge Telephone amid economic chaos, jumping from employee to owner. To Clarke, his father was nothing short of a genius. Very few took risks and, while Will had never made it to the top, the father had smoothed out a path as best he could for his son. Will had inspired him not just to take a job but to build something he could call his own. Even with thin profits, a man building his own company would always find the venture worth the risk. In the final summation of Will's life, his son realized he had taught him the most important human need of all, real freedom. Whether or not he achieved wealth, he could be free.

Many times he had heard Will explain his lack of worry with quotations from the "Sermon on the Mount."

Consider the lilies of the field, how they toil not.
Neither do they spin, yet Solomon in all his glory

Clarke McRae Williams came from a family of trailblazers.

His great-great grandfather, Ruben Holman Boone, explored farther west than famous cousin Daniel Boone. He homesteaded in north Mississippi.

Ruben Holman Boone

Clarke Williams' father, William Clarke Williams, began as a lineman for Cumberland Telephone in Iuka, Mississippi. At the same time, his mother Marie Hill became a bilingual operator for San Angelo Phone in Mertzon, Texas. The two met on the phone. When Will moved to Monroe, Louisiana, in 1921, he telegrammed Marie, IT'S NOW OR NEVER. MEET ME IN FT. WORTH. They married the next day.

Clarke McRae Williams (next to his father) was born February 6, 1922. Kittie Marie was born in 1926 and Mary Lee in 1927.

After the 1929 Stock Market Crash, Clarke's parents bought Oak Ridge Telephone for $500 and moved to the cotton town to ride out the Depression.

Clarke, 4, and dog Sweetie Clarke began West Monroe Central Grammar in 1928.

Oak Ridge High School Class of 1939. This is the entire graduating class. (Front to back) Nellwyn Grier, Clarke, Jack Norman, Arthur Bernard Carroll, Douglas Wathan, Reverend Wynne

J. A. RAINBOLT, Principal

C L A S S . . . 1 9 4 1

Clarke paid for college and a car by driving students. Northeast Louisiana University 60 years later would award him an Honorary Doctorate of Arts.

Clarke joined the U.S. Army Air Corps after Pearl Harbor. Though he built and repaired B-25s, the Army denied his requests to be a pilot and kept him stateside while his buddies fought in Europe. He would one day own a fleet of planes.

Clarke met Mary Kathryn Lee while on furlough in Oak Grove, Louisiana. Theirs was love at first sight that lasted a lifetime, though Mary Kathryn worried about incurring more debt to float Century Telephone. They married in Oak Grove on July 21, 1946.

Mary Kathryn's parents were Ola Mae and entrepreneur Roy Lee. Roy became Century Telephone's second investor behind Joe Sidney Carter of Oak Ridge.

Clarke's parents "gave" the failing Oak Ridge Telephone Company to him and Mary Kathryn as a wedding present. The company was a haphazard jumble of wire strewn across barns, trees and fence posts. The bank turned him down but, as he prayed, an investor appeared out of nowhere.

1. Clarke Williams' early management team for Central, later "Century," Telephone: Buddy Payne, left, and Seth Arnold.

2. Century's early board, anchored by financial genius Walter Frank, far right. Behind Clarke Williams, left to right, are Seth Arnold, Mark Maurer, Marvin Hill and Ken Conrad.

3. Clarke brought the Williams family back to Mississippi by buying Mound Bayou Telephone from the Huddlestons in Bolivar County.

4. Clarke joined every organization, befriended everybody, and eventually lead the Independent Telephone Pioneer Association. When others were ready to sell their phone companies, they called Clarke. With him at the 1956 New Orleans convention are (LtoR) Mary Kathryn; sister Mary Lee Williams Wasson; mother Marie Hill; and, across the table, Etta Stripling.

Clarke remained a private pilot most of his life. He and Walter Frank flew to see owners immediately when a phone exchange came up for sale, closing many deals within 3 hours. Occasionally, he took his mother Marie for good luck.

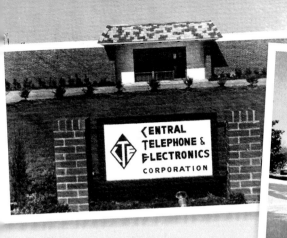

Central Telephone & Electronics was first headquartered in small Marion, Louisiana, site of Clarke's first acquisition. (Top right) Century's first major headquarters was in Monroe's Atkins mansion overlooking the Ouachita River.

Clarke Williams moved to the equity markets in 1968, first trading on the Over the Counter exchange with the ticker symbol "CTE." (Left) CTE's first annual report.

In 1978, Century Telephone began trading on the New York Stock Exchange with its current symbol "CTL." Prior to trading on the exchange, Clarke and Mary Kathryn Williams had never owned a share of stock, but they much preferred paying investors instead of paying interest.

All-American family business.

1. Left to right, Clarke McRae Williams, Jr., Annette Williams and Carolyn Williams.
2. Williams family portrait 1961.
3. Father and son before Clarke Junior's tour of duty in Vietnam.
4. Annette wins Farm Bureau Queen.
5 & 6. Carolyn is presented at the Debutant Ball and serves
as Riverfield High School cheerleader.

Clark Williams, Jr. keeping the family name going at Century

In 1930, when William Clark Williams bought the Oak ... Telephone ...

... Clark, Jr. watched ... grow as his father ... ather, George L. ... of 15 companies ... of operations to ... Mississippi and ... death of Lee, ... incorporate a ... April 30, 1968 ... terprises, Inc. ... York Stock

... work for the ... rs and during ... grew up. Then, ... formation of ... was drafted ... ombat medic. ... on me," said ... ces overseas. ... to me point ... going to be ... your own

... days later, ... d his father

I'd go climb ... one pole."

Clark, Jr. "It was always his feeling that whatever I was going to do with my life should be my decision. But it's all I ever wanted to do. My grandfather did it; my father did it; I've never thought of doing anything else. I guess I have wire in my arms instead of veins."

At first Clark, Jr. divided his days between business management classes at NLU and "absorbing management through osmosis" in the Century offices. It wasn't until 1973 that he assumed "any degree of responsibility" when he was named Secretary of the Corporation. In 1978 he was elected Vice President ... to the Board ... Senior Vice-P ... Operations.

Of his seem ... vancement Clar ... a totally d ... organization ... today. We ha ... structure and ... few people we ... of hat ... 1980 ...

Starting as a lineman when he was 12, Clarke McRae Williams, Jr. survived Vietnam to become president of his father's $100 million company. Among the first to recognize cellular potential, Clarke Junior made Century into a leader of the mobile phone business, making him a favorite of Wall Street analysts. He developed Hodgkin's Disease, a result of Agent Orange, and in 1989, a stroke forced his premature retirement. Clarke Williams, Jr. died in 1994 at age 44, having grown Century to $250 million in gross revenue. At his death, revenues had doubled again. In the last photograph, Clarke Junior is recounting his life to son Clarke McRae "Trey" Williams, III, at an exhibit at Century's annual shareholder's meeting.

Williams Family 1986

All in the family. Attorney Harvey
Perry married Carolyn Williams and
soon his brother-in-law Clarke Junior
asked him to join Century Telephone
as Chief Legal Counsel.

50th Wedding Anniversary, July 1996.

Opening Legacy Aviation at the Monroe Airport, one of
Clarke Williams' most enduring dreams. Carolyn Williams Perry
organized many events for her parents and Century Telephone.

Clarke and Mary Kathryn fulfill another lifelong dream by being baptized in the River Jordan in Israel.

The last family portrait, celebrating Mr. & Mrs. Williams' 50th Wedding Anniversary (Left to right) Clarke "Trey" Williams, III, Vicki Williams (Clarke Junior died two years earlier), Carolyn Williams Perry, Mary Kathryn, Clarke, Annette Williams Carroll, Annette's son Daniel Ogg, and Carolyn's son Jonathan Perry. Seated are Mary Kathryn Perry Edwards and Molly Williams.

The 2002 Dedication of The Clarke M. Williams Memorial Garden at CenturyLink world headquarters in Monroe, Louisiana.

Heat fails to deter crowd

By 10 a.m. June 20 the sweltering Louisiana heat had already taken its toll on the gathering crowd. But it did not stop the flow of vehicles making their way down the dusty road to Century's new corporate complex building site. Approximately 150 people watched with anticipation as Century's senior officers and contractors from Lincoln Builders and Island Construction broke the hard packed ground.

The mayor of Monroe, Bob Powell, and other city officials along with state representative Jerry Huckaby braved the heat to participate in the event.

Century's corporate staff will move into its new home in Monroe by the end of 1992.

"This company began in this area and we are happy to be building here." Clark

Glen F. Post, III and Clarke M. Williams share their excitement over Century's new home.

of our corporate employees in one complex."

"We are committed to helping build the area economically as in the other

Operating Officer, says. "We proud to be a part of this community and we appreci the patience of our employ as we make the transition

New chapter begins with opening of CTE headquarters

• Headquarters is symbol of successful present and anchor for Century's family atmosphere.

By RICK KENNEDY
The Citizen

It was a warm and sunny Sunday afternoon, a perfect day for a special moment, and as Glen Post, III turned to introduce Clarke Williams, Sr. to the crowd, one could sense that the special moment had arrived.

"This is the first time that we've had all of our people under one roof. The family is home, and I would like to thank you for welcoming us home," said Williams, Sr. to the crowd of 500-600 gathered in front of Century Telephone's new 165,000 sq. foot complex.

It was 25 years ago that Williams first incorporated Central Telephone and Electronics to be publicly traded. Back then it served approximately 75 residents.

"This new building alone

• Visitors find new facili impressive and feel it c showcase growth north Monroe.

By RICK KENNEDY
The Citizen

All those who came throu the doors at Century Tel phone's big open house a ribbon-cutting for its new $ million facility last Sund generally came away with t same feeling.

"Wow!"

Monroe Councilman Ly Miller, district 1, said "Th is an amazing building, a it is by far the most impre sive new facility I've seen the city for some time. We a very fortunate to have C here, and this can be a re landmark for the city.

"I have several friends w work here, and now I can s why they are so happy to g work everyday. If I work in a place like this, I would pretty happy, too," he said.
Rhonda Huddox, a Monr resident who had previous

CENTURY OPEN HOUSE — Chairman of the Board and company founder Clarke Williams, Sr. (right center), with a helping hand from Public Service Commissioner Don Owen (left center), cuts the ribbon to mark the grand opening of Century Telephone's new $18 million corporate headquarters on 185 North in Monroe last Sunday. Also on hand were Century President and CEO Glen Post,

Clarke Williams handpicked Glen Post to head up his company and carry on the values and traditions he wanted for CenturyLink and for all present and future employees.

The last CenturyLink Board of Directors on which Mr. Williams served in 2002. (Standing, left to right) Virginia Boulet, C.G. Melville, F. Earl Hogan, Johnny Hebert, Harvey P. Perry, Glen F. Post, III, Calvin Czeschin, James Gardner, and James Reppond. (Seated, left to right) William R. "Bill" Boles, Jr., Bruce Hanks, R. L. Hargrove, and Ernie Butler.

CenturyLink's Technology Center of Excellence

"A man's heart plans his way but the Lord directs his steps."
                                    Proverbs 16:9

"Seek ye first the Kingdom of God…and all good things
shall be added unto you."

                                    Matthew 6:33

was not arrayed as one of these.[127]

The passage was never a license to be idle. As Clarke grew older, he understood Will's use of it to mean that a person should always consider why he is working, that a man should not waste his life in mindless drudgery, and that no amount of fretting ever improved anything. Dramatics prevented clear thought and that created bad decisions. The beauty of the lilies simply existed by the hand of God; the lilies simply *were*, through no effort of their own. In the same way, the beauty of the moment was a person's choice to either revel in or miss altogether. Happiness came in savoring love, smiles, relationships, successes, celebrations, songs, children, holidays, laughter, satisfied customers, and, in short, in giving more than receiving. All these truths Will Clarke had learned in his sixty-three years and taught his son.

Sixty-three is young and, while Will's death came too soon, he had accomplished what Clarke chose to believe was a God-given mission. There was a reason Will had not been the one snatched off that train. His father confided a couple of times that had his leg been one inch farther out, Clarke McRae Williams would never have been born.

Life traveled silently within a thin margin of fate, Will Clarke's a mere inch. Clarke McRae looked himself in the mirror, knowing he was there but for his father's leg resting an inch closer to some faraway bridge. Every decision a person made rippled down to so many others. Success didn't come by drifting; success was the sum total of those decisions offset by something mysterious and unpredictable called *luck*. Together, decisions and luck formed timing. He left the unpredictable to God, knowing that conscious decision-making had far more to do with outcomes, and that decisions required education and effort.

Now he would shoulder the yoke of the Williams family. He hoped to widen those thin margins for his children and their children. With sisters Kittie in Slidell and Mary Lee in Baton Rouge, he would also bear responsibility for Marie as she carried

---

[127] Luke 12:27

on in Marion. Fortunately, he still had Roy Lee and Joe Sidney Carter and a faith that allowed him to dream.

His first decade of business behind him, he now moved like lightning under a full burden. As the undertaker lowered Will Clarke Williams into a grave at Oak Ridge Baptist Cemetery, the son thanked the father a last time for his example. Lives are shaped by an infinite number of forces in an infinite number of ways, which made sense of the Biblical irony, *Lean not unto your own understanding.*

He wondered what his own father must have realized along the way without ever saying so. The power to shape lives, and the world, indeed rested in the hands of parents.

PART III
BUILDING CENTURYLINK

CHAPTER 8

"THE REASON I REMEMBER CLARKE WILLIAMS SO VIVIDLY IS BECAUSE HE STARTED THE MEETING WITH A PRAYER. WE HAD SOME PRETTY TOUGH GUYS IN THERE, [SOME] WHO'D LEAVE WITH YOUR POCKETBOOK IF YOU DIDN'T WATCH IT. I SAID, 'WELL, THERE'S A GOOD GUY.'"
KEN CONRAD, SOLD TO CLARKE WILLIAMS
FIRST MEMBER OF THE CENTURY BOARD OF DIRECTORS

"IT BEGAN TO DAWN ON ME THAT IF I COULD JUST BUY SOMETHING ON CREDIT –I DIDN'T HAVE ANY MONEY– IF I COULD BUY SOMETHING THAT WOULD PAY MY NOTE AND LEAVE ME ABOUT $100 A MONTH LEFT OVER, I WOULD JUMP AT IT."
CLARKE MCRAE WILLIAMS

"IT IS NOT A THING ON THIS EARTH THAT BELONGS TO YOU AND THIS IS THE WAY HE BELIEVED. YOU JUST LOOK AFTER IT FOR THE TIME YOU'RE HERE. YOU'RE THE CARETAKER ONLY AND HE BELIEVED THAT."
GENE ALLEN, PRESIDENT, BANK OF OAK RIDGE

"THE BOARD ACTUALLY BORROWED ONE MILLION DOLLARS AND PUT IN THE COMPANY. HOW MANY COMPANY BOARDS WOULD DO THAT TODAY? WE FIRMLY BELIEVED IN CLARKE WILLIAMS. WE HAD HIS FAITH."
CALVIN CZESCHIN, MEMBER, CENTURY BOARD OF DIRECTORS

Clarke and Mary Kathryn watched with pride as third grader Clarke McRae Williams, Junior, regaled everyone at the 1957 Oak Ridge Elementary School Christmas program with a recitation of Shakespeare's "To be or not to be," though even the most erudite had trouble connecting Christmas to Hamlet.

> *To be, or not to be, that is the question—*
> *Whether 'tis Nobler in the mind to suffer*
> *The Slings and Arrows of outrageous Fortune,*
> *Or to take Arms against a Sea of troubles,*
> *And by opposing, end them? To die, to sleep—*
> *No more; and by a sleep, to say we end*
> *The Heart-ache...*

The child stood firm before a teeming audience of adults and smiling teachers giving an oration of uncanny ability, so much so that Mrs. Annie Reese, in the *Monroe News-Star,* singled out Clarke Junior's reading as "delightful."[128]   Clarke listened, a little shocked to find his 8-year-old Cub Scout such a thespian, and in wonder how he seemed to grasp the words' tragic import. Is it a man's option to suffer the slings and arrows of life in an unfair world and, if too painful, merely take his life and end the sorrow? Everyone has the power, yes, but why consider it? Fear of the unknown, of what's on the other side of death, Clarke smiled, keeps many a man sane. He was comfortable knowing what was on the other side, especially now that Will was there. *If Daddy had only lived one more month,* he thought, *he could have seen his grandson shine.*

No showmen existed among the Williamses, no orators, actors, speechmakers. Clarke wondered who had chosen his son of all sons to deliver such an iconic soliloquy. A fleeting shadow crossed his heart. Superstitious he was not, despite the symbolism of omens and ghosts with which Shakespeare loved to play. And, yet, strong-willed Clarke Junior stood there as Hamlet himself, heir apparent to whatever industry Clarke McRae and Mary Kathryn might assemble. Their future was wrapped up in the boy. Should his sisters join him, and their husbands, so much the better. But Clarke Junior represented the cornerstone on which Clarke McRae Williams would build.

An actual cornerstone had at last been laid on a dial house separate from Mary Kathryn's home. After ten years, she had finally moved Oak Ridge Telephone out of her front parlor. Clarke used the occasion to upgrade yet again with a new technologically advanced dialup system to speed operations still faster. Risk-taking Clarke McRae never entertained the thought of "To be or not to be." Eager he was to advance, to move forward, to see what new and exciting days lay ahead. Trouble seldom fazed him. Yes, life was sometimes unfair and painful, but it was less so if you dwelled on opportunities rather than disappointments. For Hamlet's inability to find happiness, Clarke Williams contrasted an ability to find it everywhere.

---

[128] *Monroe (La.) News-Star*, December 10, 1957, page 2-B

The whole town laughed with the Williamses that Christmas as Mary Kathryn, president of The Caddoan Club, agonized over which Oak Ridge house glowed the brightest with Christmas lights. The vote of club members tied between the outlined and tinseled homes of the Sam Smiths and the Jack Careys, each radiant in reds, greens, blues, and whites. Louisiana Power & Light sponsored the competition, setting aside an electrical appliance for first place, but Mary Kathryn held the deciding vote and split the honor between the two families. She let LP&L figure out how to divide the appliance.

Clarke hugged his softhearted wife. For all his reserved humility, he loved socializing and found humor everywhere, becoming the life of the party at gatherings of the Louisiana Telephone Association and The Telephone Pioneers. He needed the humor because at national conventions, a few smug managers from Bell, AT&T, and *Western Electric* snickered at Clarke's backwoods operation.

"Now, let us get this straight," they would say, stifling a laugh. "We string a mile of wire and get a hundred phones. You string a mile of wire and get one." That's when the hog jowls would ripple in laughter and the men would shake their heads, then get in the dig, "Man, you're crazy. That ain't going to work!"

Clarke would gently smile back and reply, "Tell you what, why don't you attend to your business and I'll attend to mine? I have to. I'm the owner."

Clarke dismissed the ridicule and rarely let the digs take root, unless he was tired or nervous over an approaching loan payment. That's when he surrounded himself, his employees, and their families in prayer. He knew the key was obedience, humility, faith, and the Greater Plan. Clarke ascribed to the belief that a man never stood taller than when he was on his knees. He knew the power of humility. People could sense that strength in Clarke, knowing that for some reason they liked him. Quiet as he was, he accumulated backers at conventions who pushed him into leadership positions, recognizing his genuine depth. He embraced the honors, quietly living the example of humility before raucous conventioneers. His sense of values remained intact, especially away from home. Some noticed.

> Ken Conrad: "They had a meeting in Alexandria [Louisiana] of seventeen independent telephone companies. I was 18. My dad took me with him to introduce me to the business. I got to meet Clarke that day and the reason I remember him so vividly is because he started the meeting with a prayer. We had some pretty tough guys in there at that time and I'm not sure that prayer was comfortable in that room. We had some people in the telephone business who'd leave with your pocketbook if you didn't watch it. I didn't think anybody knew there was a God up there. I was very impressed. I said, 'Well, there's a good guy.' And he spent the rest of his life proving it to me."[129]

The Conrad family, which owned Breaux Bridge Telephone Company next to Bell Telephone in the city of Lafayette, Louisiana, surrounded Bell by buying up five independent exchanges in the heart of Louisiana's Cajun country at the same time Clarke, Joe Sidney Carter, and Roy Lee bought four in the north.

The experience of learning other cultures was eye opening for Clarke. North and South Louisiana were as different as daylight and dark. Hardworking, dour English-speaking and tightly laced Protestants of British descent populated the north, while the southern half enjoyed the song and dance of fun-loving French Catholic Acadians by way of Canada. The north was meat and potatoes, the south, etouffee and gumbo. Many Acadians still spoke an archaic French brogue from the Seventeenth Century. But Clarke spoke the language of acceptance and help, and that, combined with the relationships and goodwill he cultivated in professional groups, dissolved

---

[129] Ken Conrad interview, September 26, 2012, Monroe, Louisiana.

formidable barriers of dialect and culture. Clarke's understated kindness made him welcome everywhere.

When young Ken Conrad's father fell ill, with no other Conrads clamoring to help in the business, Ken began shopping Breaux Bridge Telephone to larger independent networks, primarily General Telephone.   Close friend Marvin Hill, Clarke's sales representative at Stromberg-Carlson, was first to learn of Ken Conrad's plight and imminent sale. Marvin called Clarke, and Clarke immediately drove south.

> Ken Conrad: "Clarke came across as very trustworthy. He'd listen. He wouldn't talk, he'd listen.   Everything   he   drew   from   that conversation, he'd use somewhere else. He had down-to-earth, honest, deep intelligence.   He could analyze and he was right, while I analyzed and was wrong. I'd go to a guy and say, 'I know you want to sell your telephone company to us,' and he'd say, 'No, I don't.' But they wouldn't tell that to Clarke.   He had an uncanny natural foresight."[130]

Ken Conrad sold Breaux Bridge Telephone to Clarke, doubling the size of United Telephone. Clarke hired Ken to continue running the southern part of his holdings. Ken Conrad would serve as the first member of the board of directors for what would become CenturyLink.

The 1950s brought transition and consolidation. Coming out of gruesome war years, America's youth reacted as their grandparents had coming out of World War I. The Rocking 50s paralleled the Roaring 20s as young adults embraced Frank Sinatra and Dean Martin, while teenagers jittered to the rock and roll of Elvis Presley, Jerry Lee Lewis, and other teenie boppers. Their fathers had saved the world from Nazism, and that victory set high expectations higher for what would become the Baby Boomers. The generation grew edgy, idolizing brooding actors James Dean and Montgomery Clift, loners who were trying to

---

[130] Ken Conrad interview, September 26, 2012, Monroe, Louisiana

break free. Men of the war refashioned America into an army-style corporate structure from farms to factories and were horrified when the Soviet Union beat the United States into space with Sputnik. General Patton had warned about the Soviets. Now the Reds had a long-range delivery system for the nuclear warhead they made from stolen American designs. In response, Americans were further embarrassed when a U. S. rocket lifted a few feet from the launchpad then crashed into a fireball. The United States dropped to second place in its own technology.

The war's general, President Eisenhower, resisted another war with old Soviet allies, and the two nuclear superpowers settled into what was called *the Cold War*. In Massachusetts, young, good-looking U.S. Senator John Fitzgerald Kennedy took on the mantle of Clarke's generation. Kennedy frequented Catholic Louisiana, riding in parades, speaking at fundraisers, giving speeches. In 1956 and 1959, he traveled across Conrad territory in Breaux Bridge, from New Orleans to Lafayette, Crowley, Opelousas, and Lake Charles, offering youthful photogenic vigor. Two months after an October 1959 pre-campaign swing, Kennedy would officially announce for the presidency.

Youth rushed toward the future and away from small towns. The children of mom-and-pop telephone businesses who had endured persistent complaints and all night switchboard vigils were determined never to connect another call for as long as they lived. This exodus presented a double-edged opportunity for Clarke Williams. Tired owners began selling exchanges but in markets losing population. Clarke's plan all along, however, had been to synergize technology with coverage and create a network. He was not alone. Principals in General Telephone and Consolidated Telephone saw the same opportunity as thousands of family operations whittled to hundreds of independent exchanges which consolidated quickly to below one hundred independents.

Coastal Breaux Bridge presented tremendous opportunity in the late 1950s as an offshore drilling boom began. Because the petroleum industry provided steady, high-paying jobs, South

Louisiana didn't lose young people. Instead, populations increased as workers poured in from out of state. Clarke offered Ken Conrad the chance to grow.

> Ken Conrad: "When Clarke said something, he meant it. He wasn't a miracle worker—but maybe he was."[131]

Oak Ridge certainly needed a miracle. Unlike the oil boom in Breaux Bridge, the century-old economy of cotton in Oak Ridge created no surge of good jobs. Worse, nearby Monroe drew rural youth like a magnet.

Clarke noticed more vacant houses and storefronts in his hometown . When Mayor Jack Files threw in the towel in June 1959, nobody wanted the office. All but aldermen John S. Barr and C. E. Shepard resigned. For several months, Oak Ridge operated without a city marshal after S. W. "Buck" Kennedy resigned with no successor. Friends goaded Clarke into running for mayor, and with little effort, seventeen years after Will Clarke held the office, Clarke McRae Williams took over as Mayor of Oak Ridge. The election brought new faces W. P. Smith as alderman and J. Leslie Withorne as city marshal, along with a whole new set of problems for Clarke Williams.

Calm in demeanor, Clarke sought out help as economic conditions waivered. Now as a favorite son leader in town, he honed his organizational skills, problem solving, work delegation, and fund raising.

The Bank of Oak Ridge called him, too, offering a directorship. With embarrassed laughter over the 1947 loan denial, the Board of Directors swore in Clarke on October 19, 1961. He would serve for the rest of his life, fortifying the bank's assets with much of his own. Along the way he would launch the careers of many, including future bank president Gene Allen. Possessing a degree in chemistry, not business, Allen learned banking from the ground floor as Clarke rose to become chairman of the board. After Allen took over as president, Clarke was his saving grace with the audit committee.

---

[131] Ken Conrad interview, September 26, 2012, Monroe, Louisiana.

Gene Allen: "I knew they were coming in the next day to audit and always would count the cash in the vault. For some reason the day before, I had set the timer on the vault for the weekend and this was in the middle of the week. So the next morning, Mr. Williams comes in with his committee to do the audit and I can't get the vault open, finally remembering in my nervousness that I had set the time wrong. It seemed suspicious with them coming in and I can't get the vault open. They sat there, all kind of stunned, and Mr. Clarke said, 'Well, that's okay, you know mistakes are made. We'll just come back tomorrow.' He just brushed it aside like it was a routine deal where the others were a bit stunned and shaken. He displayed great respect.

"Years later, we helped many causes and needs. A widow fell on hard times and I told Mr. Clarke, and he said, 'Just get what you need out of my account.' I said, 'Mr. Clarke, I can't do that, you've got to designate a figure for transfer.' He did that a lot, anonymously. I've said it a million times that it's not a person in this world who better emulated the Christian ideal than Mr. Clarke did."[132]

Clarke never forgot the way he felt as he walked away despondent that hot summer day in 1947 with no money to pay for his dial-up system. His embarrassing loan denial after serving his country was never far from his mind, and over the years he impressed on bank employees and committees that any entity could win, simply by exercising kindness.

Gene Allen: "Most banks, if you're poor, they'll charge you three times the rate than for someone

---

[132] Gene Allen interview, September 25, 2012, Oak Ridge, Louisiana.

who's well off. Mr. Clarke's philosophy was, if this poor guy, black or white, comes in and you know he's going to pay you back, Mr. Clarke would say, 'Don't be charging him a high rate just because he's poor.' We did that forever and the bank's never been more solid. It is not a thing on this earth that belongs to you and this is the way he believed. You just kind of look after it for the time you're here. You're the caretaker only and he believed that."[133]

Mayor Clarke McRae Williams' compassion became legendary and his hometown admired him all the more. He may have been mayor and bank director, but he was never above hard work, high up on poles, working lines, stringing wire, and installing phones. He hired crews only out of necessity and exhaustion. In 1956, he and Roy hired construction worker T. E. "Buddy" Payne, after which Clarke and Buddy hit the roads troubleshooting in the company's 1953 Ford truck, ferreting out hums and buzzes during 14-hour days.

The next year, he and Roy hired Bill Newton, Roy and Ola Mae's nephew from Oak Grove. Cousin Bill leveraged his knowledge from construction jobs into leading work crews at Plain Dealing Telephone. Bill moved in with the Lees and stayed two years, helping Clarke maintain his four scattered systems.

Bill Newton: "I had a 1957 Chevy and I thought I would just go over to Plain Dealing and make enough to pay a few payments. But I met my wife there. Clarke would ask us from time to time to come help him with the other phone systems and everybody loved working with him. He nicknamed me 'William Warren.' I don't know why. But he told us time and again if he prospered, we'd prosper. And we did. Employees really felt that and felt he cared. He

---

[133] Gene Allen interview, September 25, 2012, Oak Ridge, Louisiana.

> always made it a point to come out where we were working. He always wanted to know everything about each employee, their wives, their kids, all that. He listened to them and remembered everything. He's the reason we got and retained such good employees. They weren't working for a phone company, they were working for Clarke.
>
> "We were working in Choudrant one day and my hook failed while I was on top of a pole. I fell about twenty feet and hit hard. I just sat there a moment. Clarke came running over, 'William Warren, you alright?' I said, 'Yeah, Clarke. It ain't the fall that hurt, it was that sudden stop.' We just laughed."[134]

As the decade of the 1950s turned the corner into the 1960s, Clarke's reputation as a giving employer, boss, manager, and mentor spread farther. Many eager men showed up asking for jobs. A handsome, smiling 18-year-old named Jimmy Don Reppond caught Clarke in Marion one day. Jimmy knew Will and Marie quite well, but he waited until he saw Clarke to ask, "Mr. Williams, I'd like very much to come work for y'all."

"Mr. Williams is my dad," Clarke replied, "Just call me Clarke." The teenager was polite but acted like a superficial dandy.

> Clarke McRae Williams: "Jim Reppond came to see me at my office in Marion one day. He was a nice looking young fellow with a pleasing personality, but he spent half his time combing his hair. Jim said he wanted some kind of executive job. He was such a nice fellow, I thought I would give him an opportunity. I sent him off to Choudrant, Louisiana, to work with the

---

[134] Bill Newton interview, October 23, 2012, Ash Flat, Arkansas.

construction crew in the middle of a long, hot summer. I figured he'd last two days."[135]

Jim Reppond: "I went to work in Marion on April 1, 1960. Clarke also hired a boy named Glen Keith at the same time and planned to keep one of us full time, whichever one proved his worth. That first day I dug thirteen anchor holes. Glen dug nine. I was the one who stayed.

"There were only about seven employees, total, including billing, collection, and he hired some consultants. I loved my job. It wasn't long before I was climbing poles and doing jobs on my own. Clarke wanted me to learn the whole plant operation. He hired a Bell employee to teach us at night in Marion. He had GTE's Fred Esswein teach us at Plain Dealing. We'd drive over after work and back that night. That's how motivating Clarke was. I wound up as repairman in Marion, Spencer, Oak Ridge, Junction City and Dodge City, and as he bought other companies, he'd send me to help them.

"When I got married on June 2, 1963, I asked Clarke to be my best man. I told him I didn't want to choose between friends and said he'd do as good as anybody. But I was the one who was really honored.

"When we linemen worked in the hot sun and freezing rain, we had a habit of using foul language when we mashed our fingers or dropped tools. Clarke heard me cuss once when I hit my finger. He smiled and said, 'Jimmy Don, you know what you're supposed to do when you hit your hand like that? You're supposed to sing a hymn.' From then on, nearly every time I saw him I'd say, 'I'm singing hymns.' If he came

---

[135] Clarke Williams quote, *Centuryian* commemorative booklet, March 1981, page 19.

around the worksite, I'd start singing, *Amazing Grace* or *Old Rugged Cross* or something. But you know, that's something else that's fascinated me about him. If I go somewhere where nobody's ever seen me and I spend a few hours with them, they will soon be telling me dirty jokes and cussing. But when Mr. Williams went, they never did that. It's like somebody called ahead of time and told them, 'He's a very nice man, a very righteous man, y'all be nice to him!' That brings great respect."[136]

Beginning work with Clarke on April Fool's Day was the luckiest day of Jim Reppond's life. He would develop into one of Clarke Williams' closest friends and confidants, as well as a ranking leader of Century Telephone. His first supervisor was Buddy Payne, who used pages from Clarke's playbook to groom linemen into managers. Among those joining Reppond were Charlie Payne, Sam Williams, Henry Moore, Curtis Gay, and Jeff Hopkins. The Marion crews called Clarke's mother "Miss 'Rie," and between her and Etta Stripling, they kept the boys hopping out of the office and into the field. At the back door, "Rie" posted a sign that the linemen saw every day:

IF YOU DO IT RIGHT THE FIRST TIME, YOU WON'T HAVE TO GO BACK.

Jim Reppond: "In 1963, Clarke entrusted me to move to Salem, Arkansas, to manage Liberty Telephone and Communications. Mr. and Mrs. Roy Lee moved to nearby Hardy, Arkansas. I worked with Billy Joe French, Harlin Hames, Jack Carmon and Bill Newton. Clarke left it up

---

[136] Jim Reppond recollections letter, August 28, 2010, in possession of Carolyn Williams Perry; *Centuryian* commemorative booklet, March 1981, page 19; Jim Reppond telephone interview, January 29, 2013, Monroe, Louisiana

to us five young men to run the northern Arkansas exchanges and we did well.

"The previous owner in Salem was practically forced to sell because he serviced the town but didn't spend any extra money to go out in the rural area. I told Mr. Williams I could build a telephone line out there for $50,000 and pick up 200 customers. I studied at engineering seminars for building, sizing cable wire, some electronics, et cetera, and picked up several reference books. By 1965, Clarke pretty much turned me loose. I'd come up with customers and a plan and he'd get the money."[137]

Clarke McRae Williams: "Jim became a valuable employee, especially when Mr. Lee and I bought the Salem exchange in north Arkansas. The day we bought it, all the employees left except a lady in the office. The man who knew where everything was left in the middle of the night. We had an exchange with absolutely no personnel. Fortunately, Jim Reppond and Bill Newton went up and ran it. It took both of them to do the job."[138]

Billy Joe French: "I showed Mr. Williams the small plant in Hardy, Arkansas. He was very, very mindful of his customers. He was very concerned about how they were being treated and what kind of service they were getting. That's one of the things I noticed about him in every meeting I was in. When Mr. Williams talked to employees, it was all about the customer. It may

---

[137] Jim Reppond recollections letter, August 28, 2010, in possession of Carolyn Williams Perry; Jim Reppond telephone interview, January 29, 2013, Monroe, Louisiana.
[138] Clarke Williams quote, *Centuryian* commemorative booklet, March 1981, page 19.

not be the topic, but it was always mentioned. When he had a customer who was unhappy, it bothered him. He did everything he could to make the customer happy."[139]

Harlin Hames: "Clarke Williams truly believed everybody was part of the company. If you were janitor, I guarantee you he felt your job was just as important as the vice president. When I came in for the interview, I was making at the time $3.25 an hour, which was good pay. At the end of the interview, he said, 'Harlin, I want to offer you a job, but starting a new company, I can just pay you a dollar and a half an hour. But I'll make a commitment to you today that, if you stay with me, and the company does good, I promise you you'll do good.' And true to his word, at the end I was the regional vice president and retired at 55. So he did do exactly what he said he'd do. Best move I ever made in my life."

LH: When he offered you less than half what you were making, what made you trust him?

HH: "He was exceptionally nice. He would get your trust. The way he told you things, you just knew what he told you was true. Obviously we didn't know the company would wind up being anything like it ended up being. But I knew as the company grew that if I did my job, I would grow in the company and it worked out great."[140]

Jack Carmon: "In 1964, Izard County [Arkansas] had 1,057 telephones. Mr. Williams had great vision. He had a Ford station wagon and we drove down a dozer path around to where they were clearing land for, some said, a subdivision at Horseshoe Bend. These guys

---

[139] Billy Joe French interview, October 23, 2012, Ash Flat, Arkansas.
[140] Harlin Hames interview, October 23, 2012, Ash Flat, Arkansas.

cutting brush said, 'This is where there's going to be a restaurant and an 18-hole golf course.' I said, 'Mr. Williams, this is not going to happen.' He said, 'Yes, it is. I can see it. It's going to happen.' And today it's there, the largest town in Izard County with an 18-hole golf course, an airport, nice hotel and restaurants and a state highway through it. He said then, 'I can see this as a development and people retiring and moving here.' There were 1,057 telephones in that county then and now there's probably 15,000 or 20,000 telephones there. Mr. Williams could see that. He saw far in the future."[141]

He also saw designs to improve work and infrastructure. In Oak Ridge, he customized a truck for constructing phone lines. He welded onto the truck a small derrick that lifted up to set heavy poles in the ground, saving backs and injury. Jim Reppond was the first to use it.

Jim Reppond: "It worked fine. When we laid cable in Myrtle, Mississippi, he designed the plow and it worked really good, too. Anytime there was a problem at Oak Ridge, which was nearly every day, he'd call me anytime night or day. And he'd usually go with me, hold a spotlight or throw me something up a pole. He used to take a preacher, Dr. Greene, who'd sit in the middle smoking a nasty pipe and I'd almost gag. Clarke smoked a cigar. But he did a lot of work anytime of the day or night."[142]

No one in telephones could see with any clarity how the race to gobble up independent companies would shake out. In 1956, sixty years after Alexander Graham Bell's patents expired, Congress, the Federal Communications Commission, and the

---

[141] Jack Carmon interview, October 23, 2012, Ash Flat, Arkansas.
[142] Jim Reppond telephone interview, January 29, 2013, Monroe, Louisiana.

Department of Justice accused Bell Telephone and parent AT&T of intentionally shutting out other companies to monopolize the industry. Regulators slapped a moratorium on Bell against all further acquisitions. With the dragon held back, independent telephone companies began bidding wars for smaller independents. General Telephone and Consolidated Telephone emerged as winners. Nearly frozen out for lack of substantial backing, little United-Marion-Plain Dealing-Oak Ridge-Northern Arkansas Telephone couldn't compete. All Clarke Williams had to go on was literally a wing and a prayer, a faith in himself, and a faith in others. Because he had never had money, United's value vested in him and in the trust he placed in others. His value was intrinsic because he genuinely liked people and never deviated from treating them right no matter whose economic interest it served. He was David in a sea of Goliaths looming bigger by the day. But his faith elevated to meet the challenge. He believed God designed impossible odds specifically to demonstrate an awesome power outside the realm of reason. Clarke believed like all Davids that one insignificant but well-placed stone could change the world.

That stone was his unstoppable personal magnetism. His devotion to tomorrow drew him ever forward and people sensed he would not be denied. They latched onto this quality and tried to learn it, knowing that as long as Clarke Williams was around they could laugh, learn, and profit.

Though Clarke and Roy searched for contiguous exchanges they could quilt together geographically, they considered all opportunities. Given enough jigsaw pieces, Clarke knew his network would come together. And to start, his late father had given him the money for the next acquisition. Marie obeyed Will's dying wish and gave his life insurance money to Clarke. Combining that money with his experience in creative financing, Clarke bought Junction City Telephone in southern Arkansas, just above Marion.

> Clarke McRae Williams: "It began to dawn on
> me that if I could just buy something on credit –I
> didn't have any money– if I could buy something

that would pay my note and leave me about $100 a month left over, I would jump at it, just to live on. At this point, I already have Oak Ridge, Marion and Choudrant stabilized. Any new product, if I could just make the payments of the note to buy them and have about $100 left over after all that, well I was to the good. So I continued along that path."[143]

Urged by his entrepreneurial father-in-law to act when opportunities appeared, Clarke jumped when he heard an exchange was for sale. He called the owners immediately and rushed to meet them. Clarke was adept at face-to-face negotiations because he enjoyed making friends, instantly finding common ground, and making the deal as good for them as for himself. His optimism, too, was infectious. He was fun to be around. As his unusually kindhearted reputation grew, stories of his sincerity preceded him in a way that put him above much larger and vastly more capitalized competitors. When blue-suited city slickers came off arrogant and pushy, the David of the telephone industry won every time.

Clarke was adept at turning advantages to his favor in nearly every situation. Traveling hundreds of miles of gravel and dirt roads gave him the excuse he needed to finally realize a boyhood dream. Never once forgetting the feel of aircraft controls from B-25 days, he easily took to flying, passed all tests, and snagged his private license. He and Roy rented planes at Selman Field in Monroe and within four hours could arrive anywhere within a five-hundred-mile radius. Two- and three-day road trips collapsed into a one-day air trip. When Clarke told a phone company owner he could be there in three hours, he was looking at him in three hours.

Where safety was concerned, however, Clarke recognized his limitations as a pilot. To get to a Las Vegas convention, he hired a pilot and a twin-engine King Air to carry his crew 1,000

---

[143] Clarke Williams, Sr. interview, *Louisiana Legends with Gus Weill*, © 1999 Louisiana Television Education Authority

miles west. Because he was not the pilot-in-command, however, did not mean he couldn't be navigator.

> Rector Hopgood: "Clarke was very flexible but if he told you to do something a certain way, you did it that way. He was meticulous like that. I was already at the Vegas convention but Clarke insisted I go back with them. Somewhere over Arizona, Clarke patted the pilot on the shoulder and said, 'The women are hungry. We need to find a place to eat.' The pilot said, 'We're at 15,000 feet.' Clarke looked out the window and said, 'How about right down there? Go check that out.' The pilot said, 'Buckle up!' and he went into a dive. We landed at this little country airport. An old Ford sat out front of the office and Clarke asked the lady, 'Any good restaurants around here?' She directed us to a Mexican place, gave us the keys and we had people in that old beat up car sitting on top of each other, laughing up a storm. The Mexican restaurant was actually good but I worried a little about the flight back."[144]

As Clarke's flying experience grew, the company literally took off. Clarke, Roy, and Joe Sidney's properties grew in size and distance to the point that Mary Kathryn and Marie barely kept up with billing. Clarke and Roy agreed they needed more than mere secretarial and accounting help. They needed an expert who could not just assemble numbers but could understand them and talk to lending institutions.

Clarke's friend in Ouachita Fertilizer, Nelson Abell, had introduced him to financial whiz and Certified Public Accountant Walter Frank. Frank taught accounting at Clarke's alma mater, Northeast Louisiana State College. He was known locally as a genius accounting analyst, financier, and

---

[144] Rector Hopgood interview, February 5, 2013, Monroe, Louisiana

entrepreneur. The chain-smoking, hard-living Frank seemed the antithesis of Clarke McRae Williams but they got along famously. Frank never slept, propelled each day by capitalizing on the next opportunity. During Clarke's stint managing Ouachita Fertilizer, every Monday morning at 7:00 a.m. Walter Frank reported the numbers from the week before.

While Clarke and Roy had scant funds to afford such talent, something in Clarke's plea for help affected the bookish, unsentimental Frank. Walter Frank saw potential, liked both Clarke and Roy, and agreed to shift much of his focus from his own accounting firm, Frank & Hoover, to help streamline United Telephone's bookkeeping.

> Clarke McRae Williams: "I had to continue to grow to stay in the telephone business and hire technicians to take care of it. After technicians, we required people in accounting. I had some very good friends who helped us, Walter Frank, John Luffey, Bill Hoover. And of course it took money to have those type of professionals in the business."[145]

> Walter Frank: "Money, they didn't have. It was unbelievable. The Marion-Oak Ridge Telephone Company by the late 1950s only had $15,000 in *gross* receipts. That was not the money Clarke was making, that was all the money he was taking in from *all* operations. Eventually, by bidding their insurance, I saved him and Roy enough money to buy a Cessna 172 airplane, which multiplied the number of people they could meet. Clarke was not instrument rated which meant he could only legally fly when he could see. On one trip when the weather turned bad, he turned off the instruments so the FAA couldn't track him because he wasn't supposed to be there. On

---

[145] Clarke Williams, Sr. interview, *Louisiana Lifetimes*, December 9, 1996, Television production of Century Telephone, Inc.

another trip, we flew into Oak Ridge one night, the grass strip was not lighted and Clarke landed that plane anyway. How, I'll never know.
LH: You must have trusted him completely.
WF: "No, I was young and didn't have any sense."[146]

Walter Frank began spending time in Marion organizing United Telephone's bookkeeping. Helping him were two of his protégés from Northeast College, Carolyn Garrett and R. L. Hargrove. Often there from 5:00 in the morning until nearly midnight, the trio spent weeks in the small town, clattering away on calculators to organize Marie's handwritten ledgers dating back twenty years. Clarke camped there with them, dragging little daughter Carolyn with him to Marion for kindergarten.

Carolyn Garrett, CPA: "Walter Frank was the brains behind everything. Clarke Williams was the nicest person you would ever meet in your life but very low key. If he was in a room with a lot of people, I'll bet half the people wouldn't know he was there because he wasn't outspoken. You had all these arrogant men in the room but Mr. Williams listened to what everybody said. Mr. Williams was very sharp because he was paying attention to what was going on. So he could take his knowledge of whatever was going on and then with Walter Frank being so brilliant on the accounting end, you couldn't beat the combination of these two people. If you sat across the room and talked with Mr. Williams, you knew when you left the room how honest he was. He never said, 'I'm this religious' or 'I'm this honest,' you just knew when you left that room."[147]

---

[146] Walter Frank interview, October 18, 2012, Dallas, Texas
[147] Carolyn Garrett interview, October 19, 2012, Monroe, Louisiana.

> R. L. Hargrove, CPA: "Clarke was a man's man, always fair. He was someone you really wanted to be friends with. He was a God-loving man. When we'd go out of town, he'd find a place where he could go to church and worship, even on the road. Walter smoked Salem cigarettes hanging out of his mouth like a cigar. In my first accounting class, Walter walked in looking like he was sixteen years old with that cigarette hanging out of his mouth. I said, 'Boy, does your mama know you smoke?' Then he walked up to the chalkboard and wrote, *Walter Frank, Your Instructor.* The first 9-week grading period needless to say I didn't have a very good grade but after that, I went to work for him part-time."[148]

Walter Frank recognized value in both people and projects. His quick mind assimilated figures on the spot and he could project what an exchange was worth. A couple of days more, he could generate a detailed report and find financing. With numbers in hand, he knew exactly what loan officers and committees would ask.

> Walter Frank: "Clarke would look at a company and ask me, 'What can I pay for it?' I didn't look at the financials of the company or billings or receipts. I didn't care what their books looked like. I looked at density. I wanted a map of [population] density, what the potential was for that area. I wrote in the [purchase offer] agreement up front that once we set a value, we would go before the state's public service commissions to see if we could get the rates increased. We went before the commissions [promising better service] and I would get those

[148] R. L. Hargrove interview, September 26, 2012, West Monroe, Louisiana.

dollars and use those dollars the best way. I eliminated the regulatory lag."[149]

Jim Reppond, SVP Ops: "Just about everything we bought was in bad shape. That's why they were for sale. The public service commissions were forcing owners to rebuild and they didn't have the money, or they had bad public relations. The first twenty years, we just got by. I'd go meet with the public service commissioners sometimes and would just almost beg them to give us another chance. And they always did."[150]

Walter Frank: "Also, we couldn't afford lawyers and engineers so we did a lot of that work ourselves. I wrote all the contracts. Some coworkers kept insisting we were going to get sued because, me not being a lawyer, I didn't know what I was doing. We never got sued. But when we bought the large Olive Branch [Mississippi] exchange, for the first time we hired a law firm to draw up the contracts. Well, we got sued."[151]

Walter Frank learned the telephone business inside out, becoming adept at valuing every aspect from plant and material to personnel. He even quantified a value for Clarke, to determine whether the founder and president was worth keeping.

Walter Frank: "At one point, we were paying six dollars an hour, which was a good wage at the time. Some executives naturally were paid more and, since it was Clarke's company, he was at the very top making forty-two dollars an hour. I told him, 'After looking over the numbers, I found

---

[149] Walter Frank interview, October 18, 2012, Dallas, Texas.
[150] Jim Reppond telephone interview, January 29, 2013, Monroe, Louisiana.
[151] Walter Frank interview Part 2 of 2, October 18, 2012, Dallas, Texas.

somebody we cannot afford.' Clarke said, 'Who?' I said, 'You.' I told him, 'You come in here every day and you go back in the equipment room and test the lines.' He said, 'But I like doing that.' I told him, 'You might like to but we can't afford a $42-an-hour central office technician.' He stopped doing that and focused more on the company."[152]

As Clarke, Roy, and Walter bought more companies, more company owners sought them out when they decided to sell. The three men fine-tuned a system that balanced fundamental value with potential rate hikes as a means to upgrade.

Carolyn Garrett, CPA: "As a general rule, nobody had money in the 1960s [to invest]. Back in the '60s, income of telephone companies was generated by losses. If you didn't make money, you got a rate increase. The secret back then was *not* to make a lot of money and get a rate increase. The public service commission determined the amount of money you made.
LH: So the more you showed a loss, the more likely you'd get rate increases?
CG: Absolutely."[153]

The loss game forced utilities to pour more money into infrastructure as increases went into effect. If an increase in rates pooled on the balance sheet or, heaven forbid, grew to a windfall, company managers got into trouble. Only two- to three-percent profit was allowed because enriching a monopoly reflected badly on elected officials. When United Telephone financed acquisitions, the team did a high-wire act between showing enough profit to get financing and not too much to lose rate increases. Since Clarke required strict accounting, United Telephone remained stressed for cash flow as economies of

---

[152] Walter Frank interview, October 18, 2012, Dallas, Texas.
[153] Carolyn Garrett interview, October 19, 2012, Monroe, Louisiana.

scale took years to catch up. This accounting equilibrium caused Walter to seek, continually and creatively, new avenues of funding as an avalanche of small exchanges went on the market. Once families made the decision to sell, they were ready to sell right then, which is why Clarke didn't dally. Bankers and financiers grew interested in the little phone company that could. They became fascinated with the financing genius of Walter Frank, the deal-closing savvy of Clarke Williams, and the business expertise of Roy Lee. Small doors opened bigger doors.

As their acquisitions burgeoned, Clarke attempted to streamline and standardize plants and equipment. After repeatedly trying to find a master technician to operate crews out of Central Office equipment headquarters, he found Fred Esswein, a technical genius who had worked at General Telephone. Fred traveled from his Springhill home in rural northwest Louisiana all over Clarke's territory.

> Clarke McRae Williams: "Fred not only went out to repair something but if a piece of equipment was entirely out of order, he could fashion a device that could do the job until the company could afford to replace it. Fred offered to work with us anytime we needed him. He would come in at 5:00 in the morning and work all night if necessary. Many times he spent all day and all night with our company."[154]

On May 22, 1965, United Telephone's forward momentum stalled when Roy Lee collapsed and died of a heart attack at his home in Hardy, Arkansas. Clarke lost both father-in-law and advisor. He eulogized of Roy, "Once given a chance to think something through, he could always figure out a way to establish

---

[154] Clarke Williams quote, *Centuryian* commemorative booklet, March 1981, page 19.

a plan. He was a difficult individual to deter once he formulated an idea."[155]

With Roy's organizational skill gone, Clarke and Walter agreed United Telephone had outgrown casual decision-making and needed a more corporate structure with trusted advisors. Since Clarke excelled at convincing people, Walter suggested they bypass more debt and offer equity instead. Investors wanted someone with vision and Clarke not only had that, he had integrity. He and Walter would give investors the opportunity to ride up the value of United Telephone's expansion while using their interest-free money to fuel acquisitions. Clarke and Walter agreed they could stomach the tremendous accountability, a certain loss of control, and the inherent risk, but Clarke had been numb to risk for years as debt snowballed. He never once considered that his efforts would not pay off for those who trusted him, knowing as long as he kept sight of what God intended, he would never fail, especially among unbelievers.

Clarke felt a deep personal mission to take care of those who had faith and inspire those who had none. He accepted people at whatever stage he found them, stepping forward with kindness just when someone needed it most. This attracted people to him, but his accepting money from strangers was different. Clarke was humbled by their belief and trust in him and stayed on his knees praying for perfect stewardship. Investors weren't just buying a phone company, they were buying Clarke's remarkable faith and confidence.

> Walter Frank: "Going public was a necessity. With the companies we were buying, we couldn't make money fast enough to service the debt. I wrote the prospectus that investors who could invest $50,000 could be on the board. We met with an underwriter in Las Vegas, very nice, but he said we weren't big enough. Clarke invited

---

[155] Clarke Williams quote, *Centuryian* commemorative booklet, March 1981, page 12.

Admiral Barham to invest $50,000 and be on the board. He was a fine fellow."[156]

As investors invested, acquirers acquired sometimes for cash but mostly for stock swaps, which meant merging some owners onto the board. Clarke gave owners the opportunity to remain involved in the telephone industry. He never feared their countermanding his ideas; he was assembling a considerable brain trust. He respected their history: They had grown up in the telephone business, as he had, had worked in it from childhood, as he had, loved it, and brought to the table a wealth of ideas and vision.

Clarke's vision expanded through every aspect of the industry, including construction. He could conceive a project and from inception manipulate a mental diagram as if he were sitting at a drafting table. In brother-in-law Seth Arnold, to his good fortune, he found a construction whiz. Seth, who had married Mary Kathryn's little sister Maxie four years after Clarke married Mary Kathryn, began working for Clarke out of high school.

> Clarke McRae Williams: "Seth took the construction crews to Mound Bayou, Mississippi, to install a new system. Walter and I drove over there and drew up a design for a total one-party system on the back of a paper sack. Seth took the paper sack and built a beautiful system."[157]

Seth rose to coordinate construction crews in Louisiana, Arkansas, and Mississippi. With Ken Conrad running what became Clarke's South Louisiana Division, Clarke promoted Seth to manage the North Louisiana Division, including south Arkansas and east Texas. By letting others grow in their jobs, letting them problem-solve along the way, Clarke empowered

---

[156] Walter Frank interview, October 18, 2012, Dallas, Texas.
[157] Clarke Williams quote, *Centuryian* commemorative booklet, March 1981, page 18.

everyone from the bottom up. He felt the best ideas often came from those seldom acknowledged. Everybody had a part in his great dream and he wanted a part in theirs, and, for that, employees loved the lanky Mr. Williams. He sincerely listened. As far as Clarke was concerned, anyone at any time could come up with a million dollar idea and he wanted to be standing there when it happened. The *little company that could* from Oak Ridge began running circles around the Bell dinosaur.

Clarke swelled with pride in the fall of 1967 when Clarke Junior entered Louisiana Tech in business administration. No one was surprised when he ran for class president. Clarke was overjoyed that his son began willingly to plot a path that led to running the Williams family enterprise. As Clarke Junior finished his first year, Clarke Senior—he abhorred "Senior" and never used it—officially formed a holding company on April 30, 1968, to hold the shares of the fifteen different exchanges he, Walter, Roy, and Joe Sidney had acquired over twenty odd years. With 10,000 access lines across three states, Clarke named the new company "Central Telephone and Electronics" with himself as president and CEO. He and Walter set Central's initial public offering at one million shares with ticker symbol CTL.

They sought out corporate attorney Roy Liuzza of Hudson, Potts, and Bernstein to draw up articles of incorporation and hired politically connected Monroe attorney William "Billy" Boles as chief counsel. Boles was a master at navigating the conflicting rules and regulations of public equities. He would help take Central a giant step higher and to do so, he brought with him budding attorney Chuck Ryan.

> Chuck Ryan: "Billy Boles was instrumental not only because of his financial assistance but also because whatever the company did in buying, expanding, enlarging, or raising rates always required consent of the Public Service Commission as a 'supervised intrastate telephone operation.' The small companies we might acquire were all subject to the five

commissioners' jurisdiction and Billy Boles very skillfully negotiated with them, especially with New Orleans Commissioner Matt Knight. We had many filings. Of course it got to the point very quickly where it became an *interstate* operation rather than an *intrastate* operation. So they got the idea early on that they needed to form a holding company to own the stock in all these companies being acquired."[158]

Though few in Louisiana had heard of Central Telephone, Clarke Williams' reputation in business circles rose. He became the object of consideration by several managerial and advisory boards. In addition to winning Mayor of Oak Ridge every four years and taking the lead directorship in Bank of Oak Ridge, he also helped his alma mater, Northeast Louisiana State College, negotiate more funding from Governor John McKeithen. He joined the boards of Louisiana College in Pineville and Riverfield Academy in Rayville, and continued to help lead Boy Scout councils, an interest he started when Clarke Junior was a Cub Scout. He united with many civic and professional groups also, mainly the Louisiana Telephone Association.

As they sought and acquired far-flung exchanges, Clarke and Walter recognized that Marion was too out of the way as a headquarters. Since he and Walter spent more time flying from Selman Field, they moved Central Telephone operations into a hangar next to Monroe's Fleeman Aviation. Clarke now literally lived at the airport and loved every minute of it. He soon upgraded from the relatively slow-flying Cessna to a six-seat Beechcraft Bonanza that could cruise nearly 200 miles per hour. The faster plane meant they could be anywhere in a seven-state area within three hours and land at the smallest airfields. Sellers were impressed by the plane but more impressed that Clarke had dropped everything to come see them.

Clarke couldn't get enough of flying and looked for reasons to fly his sleek airplane. When Clarke and Mary Kathryn

---

[158] Chuck Ryan telephone interview, February 5, 2013, with Harvey Perry.

decided on an ambitious flight to exotic Acapulco, he computed a flight path and determined he could take the whole family plus luggage. Flying over the rugged mountain wilderness of northern Mexico, an ominous feeling came over him as he realized he had made a grave mistake.

> Annette Williams Carroll: "We took several trips when we were young, one to Acapulco. The Bonanza was very small. Either Carolyn or Clarke were in the very back with the luggage. We had a grand time but Daddy said later, 'I cannot believe that there I was flying over all those mountains. It was me and my family. If we'd gone down, that would have been it. There I was flying, thinking about all that.' It really scared him so we never flew anywhere as a family again."[159]

Despite how the Army had sat on him, Clarke always knew he would make a great pilot. He paid attention to minute details of wind, aerodynamics, weather, and the plane. More than anything, he kept his wits in dicey situations, maintaining the same calm, even-keeled approach as he did in everything. When things went awry in the cockpit, he never panicked.

> Annette Williams Carroll: "Once, on a flight before the Acapulco trip, I looked up and Mother was at the controls while Daddy was standing up in the plane, stomping with everything he had on the floor. The landing gear was not going down. We kept asking, 'What is it?!' and they said, 'Oh, nothing.' After a while, he cranked something and we landed. He always remained calm or he

---

[159] Annette Williams Carroll interview, January 30, 2013, Monroe, Louisiana.

would have had some hysterical people in there."[160]

For fun, Clarke once grabbed an elderly friend sitting in front of an Oak Ridge store and said, "Come on! I want you to come fly with me in my airplane."

The elderly gentlemen cried, "No, sir, Mr. Williams! If that thing starts falling, everything I grabbed would be falling, too."

> Annette Williams Carroll: "Daddy must have told that story a hundred times, laughing. He was trying to create an opportunity for people to do something that they never would. I was never scared to fly with him or do anything with him."[161]

As acquisitions became more distant, Clarke sought a still faster airplane. He trained, passed the tests, received a multi-engine license, and bought a twin-engine Beechcraft Baron. With two 260-horsepower Continental engines, the Baron cruised upwards to 236 miles per hour. He swooped in to Junction City, Arkansas, one afternoon to pick up Bill "William Warren" Newton and Harlin Hames.

> Bill Newton: "He had dropped us off weeks before in the Bonanza, and on the plane he told me, 'William Warren, if we have a problem, I can light this thing in a strawberry patch.' When he showed up in the new twin to pick us up, he put me in the front seat with him, took off, we got airborne, leveled off, then Clarke said, 'Take the controls.' He reached down and got a big manual from between the seats and said, 'I need to learn how to fly this thing.' I said, 'Clarke, you mean

---

[160] Annette Williams Carroll interview, January 30, 2013, Monroe, Louisiana.

[161] Annette Williams Carroll interview, January 30, 2013, Monroe, Louisiana.

to tell me you bought a twin-engine airplane and don't know how to fly it?!' He started laughing. I said, 'Them strawberry patch landings are over with!'

"Later, we flew to a grass strip at Breaux Bridge but a truck was stuck on it, making the landing area pretty short. He was letting [veteran] pilot Dalton Potts fly and Potts said, 'No problem.' Dalton shot past the truck but realized the grass was real wet. He applied brakes and the plane seemed to get faster. I knew we were in trouble when we passed Ken Conrad, on the ground waiting for us, and saw the look on Ken's face. We were headed straight for a big pecan tree. Before we hit the tree, Dalton stomped the left brake and pushed the right engine to full power. The plane twisted 180 degrees and started back down the runway. There was no talking during all this. Clarke got out of the plane and I noticed his imprints in the dash. He asked me, 'William Warren, you alright?' Dalton got out like nothing happened, said, 'If I'd had time, I would have told y'all what I was going to do.' I pulled Clarke to the side –they were going to New Orleans– and told him not to worry about picking me up later, that I'd find another way back to Plain Dealing. He said, 'No, you're going back with us.' When they came back, Clarke was flying the plane."[162]

Everyone in the company knew Clarke loved to fly but few knew he paid for the planes out of his own pocket.

Carolyn Garrett, CPA: "Walter Frank had Mr. Williams set up another company, United Antenna, to purchase the planes. Walter thought the expense of the planes was a cost that CenturyTel [former Central Telephone] did not

---

[162] Bill Newton interview, October 23, 2012, Ash Flat, Arkansas.

need, since they were trying to put CenturyTel
stock on the American Stock Exchange. The cost
of United Antenna that Mr. Williams was paying
into was greater than his salary at CenturyTel. I
used to tell him that he had to pay CenturyTel to
work for them!

"Mr. Williams did not want any expense which
was personal deducted from the companies nor
did he want it to show up that he owed any of the
companies money at the end of the year."[163]

The cost of private aviation in time and money did not deter
Clarke. He read voraciously everything about aviation including
fights for major airports, especially the legendary fight between
Dallas and Fort Worth. In 1964, the Federal Aviation
Administration warned the two cities to unite or lose funding for
airport improvements. Love Field in Dallas by the mid-1960s
controlled 49 percent of Texas air travel while Fort Worth
dropped to one percent. Though the Kennedy assassination was
fresh on everyone's mind, Dallas won the air war, became a
major airline hub, and began attracting corporations from around
the world. Clarke perked up when the cities finally agreed to an
airport equidistant from each other in the independent telephone
land between Grand Prairie and Grapevine.

Chuck Ryan: "Mr. Williams envisioned that the
long distance telephone business generated by
serving such a big airport would be lucrative. A
company came up for sale there and a widow
named Mrs. Mathilda Larnard owned the stock.
We flew out, got a car, drove to Grapevine,
knocked on her screen door, and she was one of
these wonderful Texas ladies who had so many
beautiful mannerisms about her, so genteel and
so nice. We sat at her kitchen table and drank
coffee. Mr. Williams had a very persuasive way

---

[163] Carolyn Garrett interview, October 19, 2012, Monroe, Louisiana.

about him, talking with her about her late husband, her family, the area around Grapevine, etc., in a genuine air that exuded respectability. He exuded confidence in what he was talking about, that he was a man who was honorable and trustworthy. We all knew that about him but he was able to project that to perfect strangers. That was one of the most persuasive mannerisms about him. He didn't have to try to do it, it just came naturally to him. The Grapevine negotiation was a typical experience with Clarke. "Well, they got down to business and he explained the limitations facing small telephone companies and benefits she would gain as part of a larger organization. She understood that and how he would give stock in return for the stock of her company. They talked about the dollars involved, the value. I'd taken my yellow legal pad out, listened to their negotiations and as they hammered out the deal, I made notes. They reached a deal so I wrote down the substance of the agreement. They both looked at it, read it, but they didn't sign anything. They didn't initial anything. They just had their respective words of honor that this is what they were going to do. When the agreement was finalized, Mrs. Larnard became a board member of Central Telephone. At the time it didn't seem significant but Mrs. Larnard became a very active board member with good ideas and thoughts that benefitted the company."[164]

Harvey Perry: "Mrs. Larnard was 60 years old or so. She had a background in banking, she was a golfer and a pilot. You didn't have that many

---

[164] Chuck Ryan telephone interview, February 5, 2013, with Harvey Perry.

women serving on corporate boards of directors at that time."[165]

Flying to the small airstrip before it became giant Dallas-Fort Worth airport proved visionary indeed. Central Telephone profited for years from construction of the mammoth airport and more as tumbleweed gave way to international flights.

For Clarke and Walter, acquisitions were usually complete by the time sellers watched them land the twin Baron. Finer points were sewn up sometimes within minutes. But financing remained the obstacle that required every creative move Walter could dream up.

> Walter Frank: "Ernie Butler from Stephens Incorporated in Little Rock came to see us. Stephens had underwritten Allied Telephone [later AllTel] but felt they paid too much for the Tulsa telephone exchange so Stephens dropped them as a client. They were looking for another telephone company by August 1970 and agreed to take us public [Central originally offered stock in 1968]. We had an analyst named Jon Jacoby who convinced Jack Stephens to take us on. They took us public about the same time they took a little country department store public called Walmart [October 1, 1970].
>
> "We were acquiring smaller exchanges because we didn't have any money for big deals but we were acquiring. Clarke could negotiate very well if he had the guidelines, which is where I came in."[166]

At first somewhat concerned whether he could sell a million shares in a fledgling telephone company of now thirty-one different exchanges, Clarke was ecstatic when he delivered the last stock certificate to Fred Huenefeld in early February 1969.

---

[165] Harvey Perry in Chuck Ryan telephone interview, February 5, 2013.
[166] Walter Frank interview, October 18, 2012, Dallas, Texas.

At one-dollar a share, Central Telephone and Electronics now had a million dollars interest-free. Walter had been right and the financials he authored clinched the sales.

> Clarke McRae Williams: "We began to realize that there's a lot of problems in financing even in a family-operated system. You need a lot of net worth. My net worth was very marginal. It appeared the best thing to do was to go public. We needed to raise funds so we made a best-efforts project to sell one million dollars of stock at one dollar a share throughout the state of Louisiana only. That was very successful. A million dollars looked like all the money in the world. In fact, with a million dollars, it looked like you could do any kind of project that you needed to do."[167]

> Mary Kathryn Williams: "As far as the stock was concerned, I was just a little in awe because I'd never been in on anything that sold stock. We'd never bought any stock before. But he was so enthused about it that I said, 'Well, he must be doing it just right' because he nearly was always right about what he did and what he decided to do. Because every decision he made that had anything to do with the family or a lot of people such as customers and employees, he always prayed very hard about it. So I figured that whatever he decided was going to be all right."[168]

---

[167] Clarke Williams, Sr. interview, *Louisiana Lifetimes*, December 9, 1996, Television production of Century Telephone, Inc.
[168] Mary Kathryn Williams interview, *Louisiana Lifetimes*, December 9, 1996, Television production of Century Telephone, Inc.

> Clarke McRae Williams: "This meant it would no longer be my company. I was privileged to be the head of it but it became a public company."[169]

The relationship between Clarke and Walter Frank flourished professionally and personally. Each admired the other for his abilities and genuinely enjoyed each other's company even though their private lifestyles were as diametrically opposed as any two could be. Lamenting Walter's hard drinking, chain-smoking, and fervent atheism, Clarke worked to make his own life an example for good. Without speaking words, he urged Walter and all men to consider their eternal soul. Walter never reciprocated with welcoming signals to Clarke. He considered religion abhorrent and Clarke knew proselytizing would only push him farther away.

> Walter Frank: "He'd have been in trouble. One time he did try to send me a document on religion, thinking I needed to be a better guy, more religious. But I can't blame him. Clarke was a fine fellow. He lived his religion. You won't find anyone to tell you otherwise."[170]

> Carolyn Williams Perry, daughter: "I knew there were people who would question Daddy, 'How can you, a fine Christian man, associate with somebody the likes of Walter Frank and his morals?' And Daddy would say, 'What I do with Walter Frank is involved between eight and five. What Walter Frank does after 5 o'clock is none of my business.'"[171]
>
> "Walter would work all day and night and not go to sleep. Then all of a sudden he would disappear.

---

[169] Clarke Williams, Sr. interview, *KNOE Special Report* with Jamie Patrick, KNOE TV8 News, ©1992 Noe Enterprises, Inc.

[170] Walter Frank interview Part 2 of 2, October 18, 2012, Dallas, Texas.

[171] Carolyn Williams Perry during Bruce Hanks interview, February 5, 2013, Monroe, Louisiana.

> I could see Daddy worrying about Walter. I'd say, 'Daddy, do we need to check on him? What if he's dead somewhere?' He'd say, 'No, he's just recharging his batteries. Once he's taken care of that, he'll surface.' But I know he worried about him."[172]

> Chuck Ryan: "Walter would always appear on the scene with a travel suitcase always on the go. Nobody knew exactly where he lived or with whom he lived; that was his business. For some lawsuit, Walter had to give a deposition, was sworn to tell truth, gave his name, and the next question was, 'Where do you live?' It took about 8 or 10 pages to get that answer! He had wives and girlfriends, but Walter always maintained good relations with ex-wives. He made some of them business partners."[173]

Just as he worried about Walter, Clarke Williams also increasingly worried about his son. "Little Clarke," as family called him, made a concerted effort to establish his own identity as he pushed and shoved from out of the shadow of a beloved father. He drank, partied, collected speeding tickets, and had a few scrapes that caused embarrassment and worry for Clarke and Mary Kathryn. As much as Clarke was mild-mannered and quiet, Little Clarke was rowdy and outspoken and not above college-boy mischief.

> Annette Williams Carroll: "We were fearful for Little Clarke. He wrecked three or four vehicles and he went to Tech and from Tech he would go

---

[172] Carolyn Williams Perry during Walter Frank interview, October 18, 2012, Dallas, Texas.
[173] Chuck Ryan telephone interview, February 5, 2013, with Harvey Perry.

for a weekend to Mexico, to Nuevo Laredo or wherever. He was a wild child."[174]

Two years into college, Clarke Junior's revelry stopped. He opened a letter from the United States government giving him an all-expense-paid trip to Vietnam. Many of his friends had been drafted and some came limping back from the tropical hell. Their stories weren't good. Nobody had heard of Vietnam when suddenly, every night since Kennedy, the *CBS Evening News with Walter Cronkite* increasingly showed bombings, assaults, air strikes, raids, and villages burning on the other side of the world.

On this side of the world, war protests, marches, and draft card burnings took the other half of news coverage as President Lyndon Johnson escalated the war in 1965 with no clear objectives or deadline. As the body count grew, so did the country's disenchantment. College campuses became war zones. In February 1968, America's "most trusted man" in annual surveys, CBS News anchor Walter Cronkite, flew to Vietnam to see for himself. He came back, ashen, reporting to American viewers, *It is increasingly clear to this reporter that the only rational way out will be to negotiate, not as victors, but as an honorable people who lived up to their pledge to defend democracy, and did the best they could.*[175] Cronkite rarely editorialized but grimly implied the mighty United States had found a war it would not win. When President Johnson heard Cronkite's assessment, he lamented, "If I've lost Cronkite, I've lost Middle America." In a matter of weeks, Johnson conceded he would not seek reelection.

Vietnam turned out as only the beginning. After the unsolved evil of the Kennedy assassination, America began ripping at the seams as disenchanted baby-boomers voyaged into the murk of dissent and drugs. Blacks marched en masse demanding Civil Rights. The "Sexual Revolution" formed a

---

[174] Annette Williams Carroll interview, January 30, 2013, Monroe, Louisiana.

[175] "Who, What, When, Where, Why: Report from Vietnam by Walter Cronkite,". CBS Evening News. February 27, 1968.

fourth front attacking America's most sacred institution with the advent of the birth control pill. Divorce skyrocketed. Birth rates plummeted. In twenty short years, victorious Lady Liberty was unrecognizable. Two months after Cronkite's revelation, Civil Rights leader Martin Luther King was killed and in two more months the one presidential candidate who promised to halt the war, Senator Robert Kennedy, was also assassinated. Young Palestinian Sirhan Sirhan killed Kennedy as he left to clinch the Democratic nomination. As a result, Richard Nixon finally clinched the presidency. He promptly ratcheted up the Vietnam War in a vain attempt to win it.

Clarke Junior had just turned nineteen. He appealed to Clarke, "Dad, Vietnam is a bad place. I don't want to go. You've got to do something or find some way to get me out of this. Can't you call Senator Long or Allen Ellender or Governor McKeithen or somebody? Ellender opposes the war. I am your only son."

Clarke Senior pulled back, mildly repulsed. He, too, had been an only son but had volunteered willingly to defend his country under the same threat of death as every other soldier. His son's obvious fright bordered on cowardice, the one emotion a father never wants to see in a son.

"Son," Clarke Senior began, "the Army instills discipline. The Army will do you good."

Clarke McRae Williams Junior mustered into the United States Army on June 8, 1969. The day he boarded a military transport, Brown University graduating seniors humiliated Secretary of State Henry Kissinger by turning their backs on him in protest as he began his commencement address. At the Monroe airport, when green-clad Clarke Junior shook hands *goodbye* with his father, Clarke felt the handshake of a soldier. But his eyes saw in his son's eyes the futility of going off to a foreign country that wasn't worth winning.

Clarke wrestled with his decision. Perhaps he could have garnered an *only son* exception, but Clarke Junior needed discipline and what the Army inadvertently taught Clarke in World War II had proved invaluable. Unbeknownst to any involved, that day would set into motion a catastrophic derailment in the plans of Clarke, Mary Kathryn, and what would become CenturyLink.

In Vietnam, Private Clarke McRae Williams, Junior, trained as a medic, courageously attending wounded soldiers in the heat of battle. When he had time to think, he whiffed a vaguely familiar scent. Many jungle battlefields were sprayed with defoliant, the same chemical used on cotton back home. Chemical companies Dow and Monsanto nicknamed it "2, 4-D." The Army needed a way to flush out guerrilla insurgents in Vietnam's tropical overgrowth and 2, 4-D worked perfectly –in concentrations a hundred times the legal limit in the United States.

The Army also used the defoliant to destroy crops, forcing communist farmers to American-controlled cities. Operation Ranch Hand eventually sprayed over 20 million gallons of defoliant across 25 million acres. Because the military shipped the defoliant in orange-striped barrels, GI's nicknamed it "Agent Orange."

As Clarke Junior flew toward Vietnam, he passed another Oak Ridgan coming back from the war. Clarke admired his old friend, Rear Admiral Eugene A. Barham, retired now from the United States Navy. He admired Gene's ability to outlast the often-nonsensical military Clarke had experienced. In twenty years, as Clarke built a sizable telecommunications business, Gene built a distinguished naval career spanning World War II, Korea, and Vietnam.

What the admiral told Clarke about Vietnam was not what he wanted to hear. Barham's views about Vietnam paralleled exactly those of Clarke Junior. The decorated admiral made no bones about his disgust for how military leaders were prolonging the war and he fearlessly said so at a Daughters of the American Revolution luncheon where Mary Kathryn was presenting Annette. Though a heavy message for such an occasion, Admiral Barham did not mince words. "Neither hawks nor doves understand why or what role the war in Vietnam is playing," he stated. "Limited war presents a very serious and unrecognized challenge to our democracy today."[176]

While Admiral Barham's views shook friends in hinting that the communists might be winning Vietnam, Clarke saw Gene's return as a great opportunity and asked him to join his board just as it renamed the company *Century Telephone Enterprises*. The board had discovered that an obscure company had used the name *Central Telephone* longer.

> Clarke McRae Williams: "'Central Telephone,' we thought was a great name and we threw in 'Electronics' because technology was coming fast and furious. But as we began considering going on the New York Stock Exchange, the name Central Telephone and Electronics was also so close to General Telephone and Electronics that it was not acceptable so we had to change the name. We had one small exchange in Mississippi and the name of the company was Century Telephone. About ten of our people got into a room and we hashed over the various names that we might could come up with and it just seemed that 'Century' sounded better and we adopted the name Century Telephone Enterprises. The telephone industry was about a century old, and there was a Buck Rogers era when I was a boy, futuristic, and 'century' just seemed to tie in with growth and the future. And we just really liked the name."[177]

Changing the name from *Central* to *Century* also allowed frugal Clarke to keep the distinctive diamond-shaped CTE logos across letterhead, cards, and company headquarters. He was proud to see the new name hoisted into place and wondered why

---

[176] *Monroe News-Star*, "Admiral Barham Speaker for Patriotic Luncheon," Feb 25, 1969, p1-B.
[177] Clarke Williams, Sr. interview, *Louisiana Lifetimes*, December 9, 1996, Television production of Century Telephone, Inc.

he hadn't thought of it before. *Central* was far more pedestrian. *Century* represented a hundred years of strength and stability over generations.

As Century Telephone Enterprises became the new face of a quarter century's steady growth, Clarke was doubly proud to have the Admiral aboard. Brass shining and multi-colored bars across his chest, Barham was impressive in Navy blues. Board members quickly found the Admiral demanding military-type respect. He let Clarke know he preferred not only to serve as a board member, but he fairly demanded to be named Executive Vice President. Clarke acquiesced and in so doing took on a formidable partner who speedily forged his own chain of command. Exactly as an admiral would, he stepped on deck, commanding attention, respect, and ultimately control.

> C. G. Melville, Century Board member: "In the late 1960s and early '70s, men wore long hair. Mine wasn't down to my shoulders but I was in my early 30s and had a lot of hair. The Admiral says to me, 'You know what? I think I ought to take you and hold you down and give you a haircut.' I said, 'What?' He said, 'You should wear your hair shorter than that. That looks horrible.' I said, 'Admiral, this is the way people wear their hair.' He said, 'I don't care. I think it's horrible. You ought to get a haircut.' I said, 'I'll think about it.' I didn't want to get into an argument with the man. He was a lot older and, of course, being a flag officer he thought he was in charge of everybody."[178]

> Jim Reppond, Senior VP: "I was working 70 or 80 hours a week, working late, and the Admiral stopped by the office on a Saturday night at 9 o'clock to go to the bathroom. He said, 'What are you still doing here?' I said, 'I'm trying to keep

---

[178] C. G. Melville telephone interview, February 8, 2014, New Orleans, Louisiana.

up.' He said, 'Well, anybody can't get their work done between eight and five, five days a week, then the company doesn't need them.' I wasn't real crazy about that statement. He sent Bill Smith down to my office one day to ask if I would go down to [remote south Louisiana community] Greensburg and be the manager down there. I wrote my resignation letter and disappeared a few days. Then I told my wife, 'I'm going to be here when he's gone.' I stayed.

"In September 1971, Admiral Barham made a play for taking the company over. He wanted Mr. Williams to be chairman of the board and not be involved with the company. He talked Mark Mauer into it and he talked Walter Frank into it. They came to me and said, 'The Admiral is fixing to make a play for Clarke's job,' and they said, 'You'd be better off if you backed the Admiral.' I told them, 'No, indeed.'"[179]

When Clarke realized the attempted coup, he was deeply hurt. A friend had coveted his hard work and, cloaked in the admiralty of the United States Navy, had ignobly tried to wrestle it out of the hands of a boyhood friend. He thought Gene would avoid his eye but he didn't. Defiant, the Admiral gazed at him with the hard, studied look of a man whose soul had long since galvanized against war and death, fighting the enemy on one hand while fighting bureaucracy on the other. The long fight had desensitized him so that he trusted no one. Even destruction of a close friendship was collateral damage once control became the objective. Under the guise of whipping Century into a military-style machine to accelerate growth, Barham in essence attempted a corporate coup d'état, a takeover. Had he succeeded, Clarke Williams would have been forced to resign.

Instead, defiant under the Admiral's threatening glare, the board voted against Barham. Admiral Barham was instead asked to resign and did on December 1, 1971.

---

[179] Jim Reppond telephone interview, January 29, 2013, Monroe, Louisiana.

Jim Reppond: "Mr. Williams never said a word to me about it, whether it hurt him or not but everyone knew it did."[180]

As always, Clarke internalized the pain. He had never before experienced such a betrayal. Aside from infrequent personnel problems of personality clashes and nonperformance, and a few challenges from competitors, no one had ever deliberately tried to cause problems in his life, certainly never tried to shake his business from him. Barham's attempt was astonishing. Clarke steadied himself in scripture. The Old and New Testaments abounded with stories of betrayals, how they started and how they ended. And they never ended well for the betrayer, while obedient men of God survived and flourished.

Clarke was careful to watch that he didn't betray his upbringing. *Remember who you are and where you came from*, Will Clarke would say. Clarke fancied himself as everybody's kid brother who became, over the years, everybody's favorite older brother. Admiral Barham shattered that quaint notion. Clarke again thanked God for preparing him early in life. Rather than remain disillusioned, Clarke took the treachery as confirmation of the volatile, dangerous combination of money and power. Money alone changed relationships, but ambitious power on top of it created monsters, turning friends into thieves. Judas to Christ and Brutus to Caesar, history was full of betrayals.

Weighing his measured response, a song came to him on the radio. He first heard the haunting melody of Simon & Garfunkel's "Bridge Over Troubled Water" about the time Admiral Barham had come home. If he had put the two events together sooner, the song would have been a warning. He smiled. It didn't matter. He had always known the Bridge for when troubled water came. It had sustained and delivered him safely many times. God had protected his paths in such a way that, on that bridge, he had hardly noticed angry threats below.

---

[180] Jim Reppond telephone interview, January 29, 2013, Monroe, Louisiana.

The swirling threatened to drown, and people always complained of *drowning* in work and trouble. Drowning in debt most of his life, he knew the threat, knew its face, had always known that with one slip, he could lose everything, but he also knew to keep his eye on the prize. Only material wealth burned away to nothing. Spiritual wealth was Christ walking on a stormy sea, bridging trouble for a boatload of frightened men. The Apostle Peter had had the guts to defy reason and step out of the boat, implying that mortal man did have supernatural power if he simply believed. But the moment Peter glanced away from Christ and let the raging waves shake him, he sank. Even then a loving hand with a firm grip reached down and lifted him. That was true, unconditional friendship, a hand in a storm. When Clarke could find no human hand to grab, he was completely confident he rested in the palm of his Heavenly Father. Tomorrow would always present an unknown, but troubled water would threaten only those without faith.

Unfortunately, the Admiral would be the first of many trials. The little telephone company that Clarke once operated from his bicycle was now worth millions. Clarke was bewildered to find many wanted their hands on it, no matter what they had to do to get it.

> C. G. Melville, Century Board member: "Two guys came on our board as part of acquisitions, one from Mississippi and one from Indiana. We had to kick one off because he gave Clarke such a hard time, telling Clarke how to run the business. The other tried to lead a shareholder revolt against Clarke. We endured know-it-alls, alcoholics, and attempted thieves. One officer was asked to resign because he was muscling gifts out of vendors, boats, shotguns, landscaping. It was incredible. Clarke was more than generous by giving him severance pay he didn't deserve.
> "Clarke was such a great and a goodhearted man. He could not believe that anybody could do

anything wrong. He was not naïve, he was just the type individual who said, 'This man looks like a good, good decent man and that's what he is, a good decent man.' But we all have skeletons in our closet and some of those skeletons popped out when they were associated with Clarke because he could be taken advantage of. The bottom line is he gave everybody a chance and most were good people."[181]

Clarke forgave numbers-only Walter Frank for siding with the Admiral. He had to. Century Telephone was in motion with moving parts across five states while competitors furiously sought the same properties. Most were small until a Goliath appeared that took Clarke's breath away. Far up in the cool north of Wisconsin, a city exchange came up for sale. La Crosse Telephone Corporation of Wisconsin was the combined size of all the access lines he, Roy, and Walter had spent twenty-five years assembling. But La Crosse might as well have been on another planet for the differences Clarke, Walter, and Billy Boles found: Northern versus Southern hospitality, urban versus country, and union versus non-union.

Walter and Billy Boles rifled through La Crosse's financials and easily found why it was for sale. For starters, La Crosse management had incurred $7,500,000 in short-term debt at an astounding interest rate of 145 percent of bank prime. La Crosse Telephone had also been increasingly held hostage by the local International Brotherhood of Electrical Workers, a powerful union demanding higher pay and greater benefits, and, despite the company's crippling debt, adding employee positions and shortening hours.

Walter ran the numbers and found a way to structure the purchase. He found Century could refinance the short-term debt with $4,500,000 from a first mortgage using eight-and-one-eighth percent bonds combined with $3 million from cumulative preferred eight-and-one-eighth percent stock, sold on the power

---

[181] C. G. Melville telephone interview, February 8, 2014, New Orleans, Louisiana.

of Century's string of successes. Clarke and his team then renegotiated La Crosse's bank loans, reducing quarterly principal payments from $400,000 to $200,000. The bigger independents took notice. They had been circling for a fire sale but the gentlemen from Louisiana offered La Crosse owners an honorable exit and promised to keep every employee. By beating the competition with compassion, Clarke and the board pulled the trigger and doubled the size of Century Telephone. Clarke was euphoric. His company was now the tenth largest independent telephone company in the United States.

The euphoria was short-lived. Employees, union leaders, newspaper editors, and the town itself quickly expressed resentment at a small southern company's taking them over. The acquisition seemed to be viewed as the Civil War in reverse. In no time, when Century hired a worker who would not join the union, local IBEW labor leaders called a strike.

> Nolan Moulet, CTL accountant: "It was not a pretty strike, it was a rough strike because the people in La Crosse at that time, and the whole state, was pro-union. And here's a small little company down in Louisiana had acquired them. They didn't know what to do. During the strike, a magazine ran an article on Mr. Williams that said, *The man who acquired it is this Southern gentleman from Louisiana trying to acquire this 'big' telephone company and does he know what he's jumped into?*
>
> "Someone in the strike group cut six inches out of an 1,800-pair cable coming from the switching system. In 1973, there was no color-coded wire so someone had to sit there and tap every wire to reconnect each switch to each house. After the strike, I was working out of the La Crosse accounting office and was also a standby operator. The first phone call, I answered, 'Hello, this is your operator,' and the person on the other end started screaming, 'You can't fool

me with that accent!' I didn't think I had an accent but the chief operator came by and told me, 'Nolan, you're not going to work out.' He sent me back to accounting."[182]

Around that time, in the summer of 1972, a friend of Clarke's who was more like a brother, Arthur B. "Pod-nah" Carroll, mustered out of the United States Air Force. Clarke had always been a little envious; when he and Pod volunteered for the Army Air Corps during the war, the Army grounded Clarke but made Pod a pilot. Pod lived the dream, flying missions over Europe. Colonel Carroll wound up making a career of the Air Force from fighter pilot to reconnaissance pilot to operations officer in Korea. In Vietnam he commanded missile combat crews. His last assignment was top-secret at Strategic Air Command, watching for threats from the Soviet Union. Colonel Carroll ascended to Operations Director of one of SAC's Intercontinental Ballistic Missile wings.

At a particularly tight time for Century Telephone, with Pod miles away at Strategic Air Command, Clarke needed help. The Colonel sent his boyhood friend a blank check. "Write whatever you need," the letter to Clarke had said. Pod's investment was a Godsend and just in the nick of time. By then, Clarke saw that God's rescues would nearly always arrive right at the last minute. He was eternally grateful for Pod's help, and when the returning hero moved back to Oak Ridge with wife Peggy, Arthur Junior, Gay, George, and Dawn, Clarke offered him a key position. Century board member Loy K. Heard had resigned after three years and Clarke also needed a Vice President of Personnel. The Colonel accepted.

To Clarke's dismay, Pod echoed the sentiments of Admiral Barham. Arthur told him he had stuck it out in the military for thirty years to attain "full-bird colonel" only to be disgusted with how top brass were conducting Vietnam. Negotiators at the Paris Peace Talks enjoyed champagne while young men were

---

[182] Nolan Moulet interview, February 5, 2013, Monroe Louisiana.

dying. Now two decorated veterans had confirmed what Clarke Junior sensed from the beginning.

When Little Clarke did return from Vietnam, Clarke detected a change. His son nodded his head, confirming everything Colonel Carroll was saying. Clarke had worried about what his son might encounter in the combat zone, but now, between the Admiral and the Colonel, he worried more about the long-term mental effects of Vietnam.

As Little Clarke resumed college studies at Northeast Louisiana University, Colonel Carroll flew to La Crosse where IBEW members were in full strike. The Colonel assumed command and reassigned nonunion personnel to cover the jobs. Used to hostility but new to the assignment, the Colonel negotiated with the union far longer than normal.

> Jim Reppond: "Mr. Williams never had any dealings with unions, especially northern unions, and union members could be quite cruel. They were doing things to employees like sticking them with pins, spraying deer scent on them, that kind of stuff—one of the rare times I ever saw Clarke Williams get really mad. Colonel Carroll was in charge of the union deal and on the first one, the union won. We conceded and gave them what they wanted. In 1977, four years later, Colonel Carroll dealt pretty hard with them and it broke the union. It was also the people he hired, the replacement workers and all of the Century employees who went up there that kept everything going while the strike was on."[183]

> Carolyn Garrett, CPA: "Century booked half the rooms in a hotel then transferred in employees from other locations to work at La Crosse on two-week turnarounds. They started to hire local employees and train them. By the time the union got an injunction to keep Century from

---

[183] Jim Reppond telephone interview, January 29, 2013, Monroe, Louisiana.

transferring employees from other states, Century had filled all the positions with local people. Since the new people didn't have an axe to grind, most did better jobs than the strikers, productivity increased, and profitability returned to what had been a troubled company. The union folks just priced themselves and psyched themselves out of the market."[184]

Union leaders had underestimated the "little Southern company." As it turned out, many in La Crosse didn't agree with union tactics. They emerged from silence to applaud Century's policies. While Clarke kept his word to keep everyone employed, many of the more belligerent union members chose to leave. Clarke kept pay and benefit levels in line with previous union contracts and, in some instances, increased them. His benevolence had the effect of diffusing the union's arguments and power. Even staunchly pro-union members realized that the little company from Louisiana had become the best blessing they ever had. Instead of their having to fight for every concession, Century Telephone automatically gave them a better work environment, better hours, better training, better equipment, and in short, a better life. While not all was perfect, at least the rank and file no longer had to endure contract-renewal episodes of pitting friend against friend, threatening strikes, threatening scabs, shouts, yells, arguments, pickets, sabotage, and hurt feelings that never healed. This Mr. Clarke Williams from Monroe, Louisiana, was truly a gentle man and a giving leader. He was unusual, different, and Godly.

Just as La Crosse learned what compassionate leadership meant, Clarke's southern-bred team also learned that northerners could be nice, too. A string of northern acquisitions stacked up and everyone found, amid great changes, that Clarke Williams was the rock.

---

[184] Carolyn Garrett interview, October 19, 2012, Monroe, Louisiana.

Calvin Czeschin, CTL director: "In Lorraine, Ohio, we had a board meeting just after finishing negotiations with the union. In the first round the union always wanted to prove themselves. We'd gotten over a pretty nasty terror with that so Clarke invited a group of management to dinner with us the first night. In the room was the board with spouses, the local management with spouses and corporate officers with spouses, probably fifty people. After dinner, Clarke quietly stood up and said, 'I want to tell you about a few of these people.' From no notes, he introduced every person in that room and told what every person in that room did, and usually told whom their children were and where they went to school. My wife Sissy and I have talked about it several times because you just can't do that unless you like the people you're working with, unless you really know the people. Clarke was very unusual in that the first time you saw him each day, he'd shake your hand. It just makes an impression on everybody. I know there were ten people in management who walked out of that dinner shaking their heads, saying, 'How did he do it?! He knew our children and knew what our children were doing. Amazing.' Clarke Williams was just a gentleman of the first magnitude."[185]

Stewart Ewing, EVP, CFO: "He could work a room faster than anybody I've ever seen, speak to everyone in the room and really make everyone feel special. He could really touch everyone and basically be ready to go before the rest of us barely started. He wanted to build a company that had genuine family values, one that he could feel good about. What he was doing

---

[185] Calvin Czeschin interview, October 23, 2012, Mountain Home, Arkansas.

> was helping people have quality jobs and decent
> benefits. He treated all employees the same, too,
> everyone with respect."[186]

> David Cole, Comptroller: "Mr. Williams never
> looked at employees as employees. He saw them
> as people with families."[187]

Clarke enjoyed people, meeting, talking, learning about and remembering them, but he never shared his own pain. His nerves may have seemed like steel to the board and to the financial group, but he internalized much of his stress during very dark financial times in the 1970s when the entire country was struggling. After the 1960s ripped many families apart, the nation sank deeper with the tragedy of Watergate. Richard Milhous Nixon, a man who consistently topped the list of the most admired men in America, became the first president ever to resign. Bicentennial celebrations in 1976 came none too soon as Americans tried desperately to forget the long nightmare.

The Bicentennial Year also brought a presidential election. Out of nowhere, a peanut farmer from Georgia burst on the scene with a toothy grin and a charming, soft Southern drawl. Once the Washington outsider Governor Jimmy Carter took office, the country finally moved on.

President Carter's honeymoon proved short. Arab oil embargoes, skyrocketing gas prices and post-Vietnam inflation caused the Carter administration to institute a tight monetary policy, one so severe that it throttled the economy and rocketed interest rates to double digits. That spelled disaster for Century Telephone, leveraged to the hilt.

> Harvey Perry, SVP Senior Counsel: "The
> finances of the company at that point were pretty
> rocky during the late '70s. Walter Frank and

---

[186] Stewart Ewing interview, February 3, 2013, Monroe, Louisiana.
[187] David Cole interview, February 3, 2013, Monroe, Louisiana.

Billy Boles kept the company afloat financially."[188]

Ken Cole: "There was a time that Century almost went out there because financially, we weren't going to make it. But Walter was able to procure a big loan out of New York to tide us over. The figure was astronomical but I'm sure Mr. Williams was going to repay that debt personally if he had to, no question. He felt personally on the line for everything."[189]

Bruce Hanks, Financial Officer: "I never saw Mr. Williams show any nerves on things like that. He may have had them when he went home, but he never showed them to us. I always had faith in the business because I always had faith in him."[190]

Calvin Czeschin: "The board actually borrowed a note one time to keep the numbers in sync where they wouldn't be blown out by the bank. We went through one quarter that way. The board actually borrowed one million dollars and put in the company. How many company boards would do that today? That's because we firmly believed in Clarke Williams. We had his faith."[191]

With interest payments doubling, all Clarke Williams had was faith. He had a negative net worth but his network of strategic acquisitions was still young and developing. Many new systems were coming on line. Many rate cases remained before

---

[188] Harvey Perry as part of Ken Cole interview, February 5, 2013, Monroe, Louisiana.
[189] Ken Cole interview, February 5, 2013, Monroe, Louisiana.
[190] Bruce Hanks interview, February 5, 2013, Monroe, Louisiana.
[191] Calvin Czeschin interview, October 23, 2012, Mountain Home, Arkansas.

public service commissions, most of which Century won. And Clarke's people were growing and developing.

Century Telephone was on a roll even if it was rolling across thin ice. Clarke never stopped looking up for power and comfort. As long as everything he was doing aligned with His will, nothing could stop him. On his knees, Clarke felt that the growth of Century had to be His will for the many thousands of employees and their families who were now riding on his decisions.

The burden was heavy but his greatest longed-for prayer was about to be answered. As Clarke believed in the Son of God, he also believed he shared a common bond of fatherhood with the Almighty. Now the time had come for him to trust his son. Clarke Junior through the 1970s steadily rose through the ranks, proving to others he was more than just the boss's son.

He had much to prove.

What Clarke Junior faced ahead would take the prayers of everyone at Century. He took the reins at the very point when Century Telephone would either blaze higher or go down in flames. And the one route to success that Clarke Junior chose would take every ounce of faith Clarke Williams had.

CHAPTER 9

*"SO MANY TIMES, CHILDREN DO THINGS JUST TO PLEASE THEIR
PARENTS. I DIDN'T WANT CLARKE TO COME INTO THE BUSINESS ON THE
PREMISE THAT IT WAS EXPECTED OF HIM."*

CLARKE MCRAE WILLIAMS

*"MY DAD NEVER ASKED ME TO COME INTO THE BUSINESS. IT WAS
ALWAYS HIS FEELING THAT WHATEVER I WAS GOING TO DO WITH MY
LIFE SHOULD BE MY DECISION."*

CLARKE WILLIAMS, JR.

*"HE ONLY GOT MAD AT ME TWICE AND NEVER RAISED HIS VOICE.
WHATEVER HE TOLD ME I TOOK IT TO HEART BECAUSE AS I GOT OLDER,
I LOVED AND RESPECTED HIM ENOUGH THAT I KNEW THAT WHATEVER
HE TOLD ME, IT WAS FOR MY OWN GOOD."*

CAROLYN WILLIAMS PERRY

*"THERE WERE TIMES WHEN HE DIDN'T NECESSARILY LET FACTS AND
FIGURES GET IN THE WAY OF WHAT HIS OBJECTIVE WAS BECAUSE HE
KNEW WHAT THE ULTIMATE OUTCOME WAS GOING TO BE."*

HARVEY PERRY, GENERAL COUNSEL AND SON-IN-LAW

*"HE'D SAY, 'GLEN, DON'T FORGET NOW. IF YOU WANT TO GET
SOMETHING DONE, YOU MEET FACE-TO-FACE WITH PEOPLE. YOU GO SEE
THEM.'"*

GLEN POST, PRESIDENT, CENTURYLINK

*"MY PROBLEM WAS TRYING TO BALANCE ENOUGH BUSINESS TO TAKE
CARE OF THE PEOPLE WHO IT TOOK TO RUN IT. SO I HAD TO CONTINUE
TO GROW. MANY A TIME WHEN I THOUGHT I WAS ABOUT THE RIGHT
SIZE, EXPENSES WOULD INCREASE AND I'D HAVE TO GET MORE
REVENUE SO I'D BUY SOMETHING ELSE."*

CLARKE MCRAE WILLIAMS

Oak Ridge, Louisiana, surrounded the Williams family with an uncomplicated Americanism befitting Norman Rockwell. The village bustled in the cotton comeback after World War II; however, wartime advances in mechanization lessened the need for hands and gave farm children an excuse to bolt for the cities.

But not the Williams family.

Carolyn Williams Perry: "We loved Oak Ridge and Mother was very active in the PTA and all the little functions we would have at school. We would have little miniature brides and grooms, the little miniature weddings, Halloween carnivals, Easter parades. Everybody knew everybody, and I used to walk downtown to a store owned by T. L. and Florence Smith. Saturdays, all the farm help would get their checks. You could not walk down the sidewalks in Oak Ridge on Saturday because it was so lined up with people shopping. It was the ideal place to grow up."[192]

Annette Williams Carroll: "We were very much protected because Oak Ridge was such a close-knit community. All these families looked out for everybody's children. We had aunts and uncles we were not related to but they were an 'aunt' out of respect and as a term of endearment."[193]

Though Clarke was torn between Monroe and Oak Ridge, he and Mary Kathryn Williams had no intention of leaving Oak Ridge. It was a part of them, it fed their souls, and with Clarke's continuous travel, Oak Ridge was a refuge of simplicity. In 1964 and past ready to move from her rambling white clapboard house, Mary Kathryn caught Clarke between trips and lobbied for a new brick residence on a slab. Clarke's life was one construction project after another, but until Mary Kathryn insisted, he had given little thought to a new headquarters for the family. He liked the tall white bay-windowed house on Railroad Avenue.

Mary Kathryn prevailed. In 1965, Clarke turned 43, Mary Kathryn, 36, Clarke Junior, 16, Annette, 14, and Carolyn, 11, as they started a new life together in a modern, one-story red brick

---

[192] Carolyn Williams Perry interview, Sept. 15, 2012, Baton Rouge, Louisiana.
[193] Annette Williams Carroll interview, Jan. 30, 2013, Monroe, Louisiana.

home twice the size of the old one. With white columns supporting a long verandah and dark shutters, the stately Williams home fit into Oak Ridge's antebellum flavor, firmly Southern but, like its owners, understated. Clarke grinned to himself that the façade evoked a sturdiness that masked the truth. His whole financial life had been shaky from the moment the Bank of Oak Ridge denied his first loan. Some might have called his method a pyramid scheme, acquiring, borrowing, mortgaging, and acquiring more, but after twenty years of priming the pump, cash was beginning to flow. He couldn't enjoy his wife's idyllic world just yet but someday he would.

The red bricks and verandah presided over an acre lawn that would soon contain Clarke's favorite hobby, a vegetable garden. He kept the clapboard house next door as both rental property and reminder. Some nights in his new house, in his new bedroom, in his new bed, as notes and payrolls came due on Century's razor-thin cash flow, he lay awake, occasionally considering bankruptcy. He would slide to his knees to lay his troubles down. If he tried to figure it out on his own, God might let him and he would fail for certain. No, the Almighty had carried his family this far. If he stayed the course and did not succumb to fear, he, his family, and his employees and their families would all find a safe and secure home. That vision sustained him. He kept his head clear and filled with positive ideas, looking for every opportunity to laugh and make others laugh. His children's laughter sustained him most of all.

> Carolyn Williams Perry: "Daddy was fun. He liked to play jokes. I was asking all the time where Mother was, and he would say, 'Well, she went to see the chickens and the hogs ate her. You want to speak to the hogs?' That was among the first things I remember, his great sense of humor."[194]

---

[194] Carolyn Williams Perry interview, Sept. 15, 2012, Baton Rouge, Louisiana.

Annette Williams Carroll: "I was the middle child so when we would travel, they always put me in the middle because my little sister and my older brother were always picking at each other. They'd start scrapping and there I was sitting in the middle and when they got a spanking, I did too! Daddy had a firm hand but later on he sat us down and just talked to us and made us feel about the size of a cigarette paper by the time he finished pointing out the things we'd done and about how badly *he* felt. That would make us feel awful. Just talking to us in his kind, gentle way was discipline in itself. Mother would often tell us, 'You just wait until your daddy gets home.' Bless his heart, Daddy worked hard all day, then he had to come home and spank us. I know he didn't want to because he wanted to come home and play with us."[195]

Clarke and Mary Kathryn felt strongly about discipline: They believed that wayward adults sprang from wayward children. *Spare the rod and spoil the child,* admonished scripture, but these parents could not bring themselves to carry out severe punishment. The same empathetic way Clarke dealt with strangers was the way he looked into the little faces waiting at home. Little Clarke, Annette, and Carolyn developed a deep bond with their father. The most egregious act they could commit was disappointing him.

If any of the three pushed the envelope, Clarke Junior led the way. Some of the more genteel circles around Oak Ridge labeled the rambunctious boy a *hellion.* When he was nine, he rode his bicycle too close to a Missouri Pacific railroad crossing just as Oak Ridge dowager Miss Rose Boozman drove over it. Crossing over the tracks, her large gleaming Buick tilted up, obscuring her view, and she hit Clarke Junior. After a moment

---

[195] Annette Williams Carroll interview, Jan. 30, 2013, Monroe, Louisiana.

of sheer fright for both, Clarke Junior trotted away laughing and the 90-year-old drove on in palpitations.

> Annette Williams Carroll: "Little Clarke could boss me a lot more than Carolyn. We'd be watching TV and he'd say, 'Carolyn, go get me a sandwich.' She'd say, 'Get it yourself!' Then he would say, 'Annette, go get me a sandwich.' And I'd say, 'Okay.' So he called on me more. Carolyn and Clarke were a lot alike. They were both out there, energetic, doing. I would sit back and watch to see if things went well and then I would do it. I didn't want to be the first one to make the mistake."[196]

Daughters Annette and Carolyn fell under the tutelage of their mother, as tradition dictated, dressing up in white and pink and attending an endless schedule of teas, socials, receptions, and church and charity meetings. Though Mary Kathryn had had a taste of society in the farm town of Oak Grove, nothing compared to the Old South propriety of Oak Ridge. In some circles, the caste system was alive and well as the older ladies tried to recreate the genteel, pre-Civil War ways their grandmothers had described to them. Three generations later, the bar of romanticism for something lost was quite high. Their handbook, *Gone with the Wind* by Margaret Mitchell of Atlanta, lay on coffee tables or next to prized cookbooks, but most preferred David Selznick's Technicolor motion picture spectacle to Mitchell's actual truth. Mitchell made no bones about her dislike for her own heroine and her feelings about the smashup of an affluent, superficial, and arrogant civilization. In southern towns from Texas to Virginia, however, moonlight and magnolias yet prevailed.

As part of this glamorized world, girls were expected to learn, first, their pre-determined place in it and, second, the precepts of everything proper. Under the sharp eyes of

---

[196] Annette Williams Carroll interview, Jan. 30, 2013, Monroe, Louisiana.

dowagers wary of crude men and worldly ways, Annette and Carolyn grew up in a bubble, encouraged seldom to think beyond home. True, their mother had worked and their grandmothers had worked, but in the society of Oak Ridge, Mary Kathryn was determined to bring up her daughters at a higher level and leave the work to men. While middle child Annette may have toed the line and remained cautious, little sister Carolyn joined Clarke Junior in trying the patience of their parents.

> Carolyn Williams Perry: "One time I skipped Methodist Youth Fellowship with three girlfriends, and it looked like we had been kidnapped from Oak Ridge. I drove us to Mer Rouge to see some boys and that didn't turn out very well. When I got back, Daddy threw my keys in the back yard. I know now as a parent he was scared to death but he never raised his voice. There was a certain tone and a certain look and if you got that tone and that look, you knew you had done wrong. The last thing I wanted to do was to disappoint him.
>
> "Later, we were at my grandmother's in Plain Dealing when a guy came to pick me up for a date. I had on a little shirt that maybe showed two inches of skin. I was walking out the door and Daddy said, 'Mary Kathryn, are you going to let her walk out of this house half naked?' I didn't know what to do. Mother said, 'Well, Clarke, we don't have anything else for her to wear.' Thank goodness my date drove up.
>
> "He got angry at me only two times. He didn't really get mad, he would warn me, 'Carolyn,' and calling my name sternly was hurtful because it felt like to me that we were not related. I would tell mother, 'I'd rather him take away everything I have than to treat me cold.' But he never had to raise his voice. As I grew up, he would just say,

'Now, you listen to me. I'm going to tell you this.' Whatever he told me I took it to heart because as I got older, I loved him enough and I respected him enough that I knew that whatever he told me, it was for my own good."[197]

Big brother was expected to work alongside Big Clarke. To Clarke's pleasant surprise, the boy enjoyed the outdoor work stumbling behind his father, amazed that his dad worked high up where birds flew. Little Clarke soon worked on his reluctant father until Clarke let him shinny up a pole while dad braced below. Clarke grinned. It was in the boy's blood, this telephone business. Clarke Junior proved he came from a long line of pole-climbing Williams men, scampering up poles with a youthful vigor all the crewmen envied.

Clarke Senior took a pair of Will Clarke's old linemen spikes to a local welder and had them cut to fit his son's adolescent legs. After that, for Clarke Junior there was no turning back or coming down.

> Clarke Williams, Jr.: "Most of my friends were farmers, so when they'd be out on their tractors— I didn't have a tractor to drive—I'd go climb a pole."[198]

Like his dad, Clarke Junior loved working in the fresh air. He enjoyed the vistas from forty feet up, and he loved the camaraderie of the people who worked for his father. The summer before Little Clarke turned 12, in 1961, Clarke Senior asked Roy Lee if his grandson could spend summers with him working in Hardy, Arkansas. That's where Billy Joe French, one of Century's best crew chiefs, presided over hundreds of miles of wire across hilly Ozark country.

---

[197] Carolyn Williams Perry interview, Sept. 15, 2012, Baton Rouge, Louisiana.

[198] Clarke McRae Williams, Jr, "Clarke Williams, Jr. keeping the family name going at Century," *Monroe News-Star*, Feb. 1983.

Billy Joe French: "Mr. Williams asked if Little Clarke could ride with me and if maybe I could teach him a few things about installing telephones, maintaining phones, and make him work a little bit and keep him from getting hurt. We rode together that first summer and bonded. Of course, he was a kid and wanted to stop at every community grocery store to get a soda pop or sandwich. I'd say, 'We don't have time. We've got a bunch of stuff we got to get done today.' But he would never eat breakfast, was always hungry, so I'd stop and, of course, he never had any spending money. He liked potted meat and Vienna sausage and I'd buy it for him. Of course, he wanted to play a little. And I'd sing songs to him and we would talk and we would argue but most of the time I would not stop. He'd get mad and would sit over there in the truck with a yellow pad and start writing. I'd say, 'What are you writing?' He'd say, 'Well, I'm taking down all the names that, when I get to be boss of the phone company, I'm going to fire.' So I'd say, 'Let me see that.' And he would have my name on top! Well, if I did something good during that day, he might move my name to the bottom. I'm not sure he ever took my name off the list."[199]

Little Clarke might be the boss's son but he showed up for work every day, with or without his yellow pad. He enjoyed hanging with the roughnecks, their swaggering and boasting, and even their good-natured ribbing over Little Clarke's supposed life of privilege. At first, the teasing had annoyed him, and his yellow list grew considerably. But over time he realized they were doing him a favor by not treating him special, that laughing at him meant that they liked him.

---

[199] Billy Joe French interview, Oct. 23, 2012, Ash Flat, Arkansas.

Billy French knew Clarke Junior was growing up when he put away the yellow pad, but when he fell into the teenage trap of cigarettes, French and Roy Lee worried that the boy was growing up too fast.

> Billy Joe French: "Us old boys were bad to smoke, and Mr. Lee smoked. The last summer he rode with me, Little Clarke started bumming cigarettes from me and others and got into his grandpa's cigarettes. Little Clarke didn't like my brand. He liked Mr. Lee's menthols. Mr. Lee was very concerned, 'Is Little Clarke smoking? I know he's getting into my cigarettes.' I tried to discourage the boy from smoking, talked to him about how bad smoking was. That's when everybody was learning how bad cigarettes were. I told him I needed to quit. But when you're young and healthy you don't think anything is ever going to happen to you."[200]

Clarke Junior was barely fourteen in 1964 when U.S. Surgeon General Dr. Luther Terry announced that smoking was a killer, issued the federal government's first report linking lung cancer and heart disease, and placed warning labels on cigarette packs. The warning only confirmed what many suspected, given male deaths in their 50s and 60s while women, most of whom did not smoke, lived twenty years longer.

By this time, Clarke Junior began keeping his own hours, much to the chagrin of his parents. He was 15 when Clarke piled the family into the plane for the trip to Acapulco. The plan was to take off before daybreak, but Little Clarke changed that.

> Carolyn Williams Perry: "The night before, Daddy said we were going to get up at 4 or 5 o'clock in the morning. I woke up and all the lights were on and mother was on the couch

---

[200] Billy Joe French interview, Oct. 23, 2012, Ash Flat, Arkansas.

crying. Nobody had seen Little Clarke. Daddy and several men were out looking for him. They found he had bottomed out his car on a railroad track on some dirt road so we were more than two hours late leaving on that long journey. But it was just Clarke being a boy. He was a character."[201]

In 1967, Clarke Junior graduated Oak Ridge High School and entered Louisiana Tech's business curriculum. But when the Army draft lottery was announced, Clarke drew number six. The dreaded draft notice arrived, and at 19 years old, under protest, Clarke Junior shipped out.

Carolyn Williams Perry: "Daddy kept saying to Clarke, 'You really need to get into the service. This will straighten you up.' And mother kept saying, 'No, no, he can't go.' I remember Little Clarke saying, 'If you can do anything, Daddy, get me out of this service.' But I think Daddy had taken a lot of Clarke's running around and shenanigans until he had had enough. So Daddy said, 'Son, the Army will be good for you.'"[202]

Clarke Junior barely finished finals before boarding a transport. *The Army will be good for you,* Clarke had said, and those words rang in both men's ears.

After boot camp, Clarke Junior arrived as a medic to a colossal operation after a troop buildup of one million American soldiers. North Vietnam's army numbered just over half that but was supported with weapons, materiel, and intelligence from communist countries. The year before, 80,000 North Vietnamese had attacked thirty-six provincial capitals in South Vietnam on the very day Hanoi had asked for a cease-fire to celebrate the Tet Lunar New Year. The Tet Offensive surprised

---

[201] Carolyn Williams Perry interview, Sept. 15, 2012, Baton Rouge, Louisiana.
[202] Carolyn Williams Perry interview, Sept. 15, 2012, Baton Rouge, Louisiana.

the U.S. Army and shocked the United States with massive bloodshed, costing the two sides over 45,000 dead and 61,000 wounded. Between news accounts and letters home, many fathers who had tasted swift combat in World War II found themselves torn between patriotic duty and a growing fear that either no one was in charge in Vietnam or the U. S. had lost its way.

Clarke Junior saw the malaise first hand in troop movements that seemed pointless and erratic. In high grass battlefields, Huey helicopters at his back, shooting and explosions only yards in front, he continuously patched up, sutured, and wrapped open wounds on young men. On quieter days, villagers called him to deliver babies. Like every other clean-cut American boy, he wrestled with the mind games, yanked as he was between two extremes: mothers giving birth and soldiers inflicting death.

Large green Army C-123 planes and some helicopters continually crisscrossed the sky, spraying clouds that soon left trees and bushes naked and Vietcong guerrillas exposed. GIs did not know that Monsanto chemists had warned government officials years before that overheating the defoliant in a hot tropical sun created a deadly dioxin molecule with long-term adverse health effects, sometimes dormant for years.

The Army granted Clarke Junior leave in the summer of 1970 and flew him to Hawaii for rest and relaxation. Clarke loaded up the Williams family, grandmothers included, and flew everyone out to meet him. For a week, the seven Williamses scampered along sandy beaches, enjoyed luaus under Hawaiian starlight, and took in the fiftieth state. They were surprised to find the paradise a hotspot for tourists with the success of CBS Television's *Hawaii 5-O*. The show's catchphrase, *Book 'em, Danno*, rang from every street corner.

Clarke Junior asked about the business, including acquisitions and certain crew members. Senior asked how the son was finding Army life, offering his own stories of frustrations in the service and making jokes at the Army's expense. But the Williams tour turned solemn as the family climbed on deck of the *USS Arizona* Memorial in Pearl Harbor.

The crowd stood eerily quiet as the lone tour guide recounted the last hour of the doomed ship. He talked of the 1,102 sailors the U. S. still considers on active duty, their bodies trapped below tourists' feet. A simple plaque read:

> *To the Memory of the Gallant Men Here Entombed*
> *and their shipmates who gave their lives in action*
> *on 7 December 1941, on the U.S.S. Arizona*

The father and son stood in silence. Pearl Harbor had been the reason Clarke had joined the Great War twenty-nine years before; now he looked at his son, fresh from a different battlefield. In a year of scant correspondence and few phone calls, Clarke Junior had changed. He was less mischievous and more serious. He enjoyed a laugh and genuinely appreciated his family's coming to see him, but he was calm and subdued. Father and son now understood each other without speaking.

The day Clarke Junior left Honolulu Airport to return to Vietnam, the family stood with him, admiring the sharp figure he cut in his khaki uniform. Clarke Senior fought back the tears everyone else let go, touched his son, and said a quick prayer. They hugged, and within minutes the family watched his plane sail into the sky.

> Carolyn Williams Perry: "The day Clarke Junior left to go back, I remember we all stood in a circle and held hands and Daddy prayed. And honestly, I don't know how he did that, how he got through it, knowing his son was going back to Vietnam."[203]

Back in the jungle under heavy enemy attack, for Clarke Junior, Hawaii lingered more as a dream. The noise of battle, screams, yells, gunfire, Huey helicopters, and defoliant shocked Clarke Junior back to reality. As he pulled together gaping wounds, chest cavities red with blood, bones protruding, the

---

[203] Carolyn Williams Perry interview, Sept. 15, 2012, Baton Rouge, Louisiana.

madness hovered around him. He worked tirelessly, performing beyond the call and saving many lives. For his efforts, Clarke McRae Williams Junior was awarded the Army Commendation Medal and the Bronze Star. But a year in the surreal disarray of Vietnam was all Clarke Junior could endure. When his chance for discharge came up in February 1971, he jumped at it.

> Annette Williams Carroll: "When he came back from Vietnam, he talked a lot about being a medic. I asked him, 'You think you might go to school and be a doctor now since you have all this knowledge?' He said, 'No, it would take too long.' He just wanted to jump back into work."[204]

> Clarke Williams, Jr.: "Vietnam had a settling effect on me. The Army brought home to me point blank that if you're going to be anything, it's going to be on your own shoulders."[205]

Clarke and Mary Kathryn were overjoyed their son returned in one piece and decorated. He seemed to have brought back allergies and sinus trouble, though, but most people in the humid South suffered that. Clarke closely watched his son for signs that perhaps his ambitions had changed. Above all, he was careful not to take for granted that his son would follow in his footsteps.

> Clarke McRae Williams: "So many times, children do things just to please their parents in an attempt to make their parents proud of them. I didn't want Clarke to come into the business on

[204] Annette Williams Carroll interview, Jan. 30, 2013, Monroe, Louisiana.
[205] Clarke McRae Williams, Jr., *Monroe News-Star*, Feb. 1983.

the premise that it was expected of him. A forced or coerced situation is rarely a good one."[206]

During two weeks of Junior's re-acclimating to Oak Ridge, father and son debriefed about military experiences, changes in the telephone business, and what lay ahead for them.

> Clarke McRae Williams: "We had a long talk about it. I didn't overly encourage him because I wanted him to be sure it was what he wanted to do and for the timing to be right. Too often today, people exist in a state of frustration because they don't like the work they are doing. I think I'd be terribly unhappy to work at a job every day that I didn't like."[207]

> Carolyn Williams Perry: "When Clarke said he wanted to come in, Daddy said, 'Fine. You put together a plan of how you want to see this company go forward.'"[208]

While there were no guarantees Clarke Junior would enter the management of Century Telephone, that's what he did on March 1, 1971, hardly twenty days after shedding his uniform. Mostly to learn the management side from the trenches up, but partly to keep from serving directly under his father, he began his career far down the ladder as an assistant to the Executive Vice President. Both Clarkes knew that the father-son dynamic was difficult in any family business, especially one growing rapidly.

Finishing school at Northeast Louisiana University, Clarke Junior gratefully joined Century's inner circle, coupling his

---

[206] Clarke McRae Williams, Sr., "The Third Generation Begins," *Centuryian*, March 1981, p. 22.
[207] Clarke McRae Williams, Sr., "The Third Generation Begins," *Centuryian*, March 1981, p. 22.
[208] Carolyn Williams Perry interview, Sept. 15, 2012, Baton Rouge, Louisiana.

summertime experiences as a lineman with learning what poles, wires, and equipment cost. Anxious to stand out and separate himself from his father's worshiped image, Clarke Junior spoke up often. He had definite convictions. He had seen enough of wartime and death, he felt, to know who he was, and he wasn't shy about saying so. Indeed, in his last semester at NLU, when an accounting professor insisted he show up for class every day, Clarke explained that he was working full time and as long as he passed the exams, should graduate. But the professor thought otherwise and would have flunked him except that Clarke resigned the class. He never went back, lacking a single credit hour to graduate.

In 1973, he took over for his mother as Secretary of the Corporation, recording every company detail as he listened to board members. Clarke Junior ramped up his on-the-job education hastily through the 1970s, and at each level Clarke Senior waved him forward when he was confident the son could handle the task. Clarke Junior enjoyed the work environment and the people, and specifically appreciated, most of the time, his father's silently guiding hand. Clarke Junior knew he was far more gregarious and outgoing than his father and often felt his father's gaze of restraint. The son found that public speaking and jousting with the board came far more easily for him than it had for his reserved father.

As Century Telephone grew through the 1970s, the Williams family expanded with it. Clarke Junior married Marilyn Carso, Annette married Danny Ogg, and, in the summer of 1976, youngest daughter Carolyn, at 21, brought home a young bankruptcy attorney named Harvey Parnell Perry. Harvey was of the Morehouse Parish Perrys whose fabled plantation straddled the Ouachita and Morehouse Parish line and gave its name to Perryville, site of a major transmission station along the Southern Natural Gas pipeline. Harvey's namesake, grandfather Harvey Parnell, had been governor of Arkansas. But it wasn't family history that bothered Harvey as he met the Williamses, it was his own. Harvey was ten years older than Carolyn and divorced with three children.

The couple feared their relationship might be a hard sell as they pulled up to the hilarity of swimmers, water skiers, boats and bar-be-que at the Williams family camp on Lake D'Arbonne, the one get-away indulgence Clarke had allowed himself.

> Harvey Perry: "Our fears proved unfounded. What I remember most is that they were all so receptive of me. I told Carolyn I'd balk if I had a 21-year-old daughter who brought a 31-year-old man home to meet the family, and with three children? I told her that was the only time I ever questioned her daddy's judgment. He didn't discourage it but rather encouraged the relationship. They were really good to me and my children from day one."[209]

Clarke and Mary Kathryn embraced the Perrys, hosting them for every major holiday. The first Christmas Carolyn and Harvey dated, Harvey bought son Parnell a model train with every intention of assembling tracks and train on Christmas morning for Parnell to enjoy. But his potential father-in-law, the ever-improving Clarke Williams, wanted better for a boy who might become his step-grandson. Clarke bought plywood and green outdoor carpet and built a city around the train. Harvey's three children fell in love with the Williamses.

Carolyn Williams married Harvey Perry on September 9, 1978, in Clarke and Mary Kathryn's white lattice gazebo in their backyard, surrounded by family, friends, and the flower gardens Clarke had designed. In childhood and now in marriage, Carolyn remained surrounded by her father's love and handiwork. She had no qualms about leaving home to become a stepmom to three children. She knew that she was not leaving at all, that her loving, simple folks gladly shared with children they considered their own. They embraced Harvey, as much a son as Clarke Junior. After six more years of Harvey's handling

---

[209] Harvey Perry interview, Sept. 15, 2012, Baton Rouge, Louisiana.

Chapter 11 bankruptcy cases, in 1984 Clarke Junior asked Harvey to come aboard as General Counsel of Century Telephone.

On his knees in the early morning, Clarke thanked God with the deepest gratitude for everything working out so beautifully, for the next generation's voluntarily stepping up to take on the difficult yoke of leadership. With Clarke Junior rising through the executive ranks, Carolyn advised the company on charitable endeavors while sister Annette offered vacation relief in the office.

> Annette Williams Carroll: "I worked summers for Daddy when his secretary went on vacation, because in college I minored in Office Administration. He was really easy to work for. Twice I showed him new techniques on writing letters and how business correspondence had changed. They changed office policy because of me."[210]

Tragedy struck Clarke and the entire village of Oak Ridge on Saturday, September 18, 1976, when the town awoke at midnight to a plane crash. Clarke and Mary Kathryn didn't hear it, but hardly a half-mile from their house, out of the darkness single-engine Piper Cherokee N3918W flew in low for a landing. The aircraft lined up with the lighted grass airstrip on the John Rolfe Windsor place along Louisiana Highway 137. The very first pilot with whom Clarke had flown, Erle McKoin Barham, was at the controls of his aircraft. Friends called him "Niney," a nickname his older sister gave him at birth because he was a "teeniney baby."

Niney had flown four friends —Joe Sidney Carter, Junior; former L.S.U. football MVP Abner Wimberly; James McLendon; and Duke Barr—to Baton Rouge where they had joined 68,057 fans to watch the L.S.U. Tiger football team trounce Oregon State's Beavers 28-11. After the game, the five

---

[210] Annette Williams Carroll interview, Jan. 30, 2013, Monroe, Louisiana.

flew an hour-and-a-half back to north Louisiana on a moonless night. About a quarter past midnight, as he'd done many times before, Barham circled the field several hundred feet above and keyed his radio microphone to activate the runway lights. Everyone watched as the long yellow rectangle lighted up out of pure black. Monroe tower reported unlimited visibility and calm winds with no reports of fog under the canopy of stars.

Niney leveled off on a glide path approach between the dotted lines marking the runway. As he neared, the lights commenced to undulate as if some were dimming and, sure enough, he flew into a thick layer of ground fog. Blinded by the reflected whiteout from the Cherokee's intense landing light, Niney Barham and Joe Carter, also a pilot, lost sight of the runway lights 200 yards forward, losing depth perception. Barham made the snap decision to circle back for another approach. He shoved the throttle forward to regain altitude, the engine's torque yawing the plane left in the white fog. As best as Clarke could figure the next day, having flown into and out of the field many times, when Niney powered back up, turned left, and came out of the blinding fog, it was too late. A huge, tall gum tree suddenly came out of the dark in front of them.

Clarke envisioned the catastrophe as he stood on the ground in bright sunlight under the plane's glide path, trying to figure out why Niney banked so steeply left, forgetting the tree line. "Ground fog," surmised Randy Brooks of the Federal Aviation Administration and Frank Shretter of the National Transportation Safety Board as they sifted through debris. Facing the end of the runway, Clarke gazed to his left where a shredded treetop stood like a silent giant that had slapped the plane out of the sky. It spoke volumes. Like all good pilots, Clarke put himself in the pilot's seat to understand and rehearse. When the fully loaded plane struggled to climb in a left bank, the landing light burned through the fog just as the giant tree loomed. Niney could not jerk the ailerons fast enough and the tree sheered off the left wing, spinning the Cherokee like a cartwheel toward the ground. The five men braced, hearing the engine at full-throttle grind in protest. Tail and wings flew off the Cherokee on impact, but the fuselage remained remarkably intact as it rolled, coming to rest upside down. The screech and bang of wrecking was over in six seconds.

Sitting in the very back, John Duke Barr swayed suspended by a seat belt, stunned and upside down but regaining his bearings. In the dark, he heard moaning and smelled airplane fuel mixed with the sickening smell of blood. He knew the plane could burst into flames at any second. He knocked open the back door next to his seat, fell out onto the ground, hobbled to the other side of the fuselage, pried open the door, and began pulling the others out into the foggy dark. All appeared unconscious except big Abner Wimberly, who writhed in pain. Barr hoped somebody had heard them, but not a single car came driving by on Highway 137. Looking straight up, the stars overhead he had watched during the flight still twinkled as if nothing had happened. In the gloom, Barr began running through tall cotton toward feeble streetlights in Oak Ridge. At the first house, he banged on the door, and a call to sheriffs and ambulances rallied emergency personnel in twenty minutes from as far away as Rayville.

That Monday, Oak Ridge doubled in size. Cars lined streets and roadways. All four funerals took place the same day, three at the Methodist Church and one at the Baptist. Clarke served as pallbearer for Niney Barham and Joe Sidney Junior, remembering that Niney had given him the flying bug and that he had stood next to Joe as best man. The loss of his friends and the loss of their potential sickened him.

All except Niney Barham were in their mid-40s. Barham was 60, a flight instructor rated to fly by instruments, a man who had worked for American Airlines. Niney was proud of his three sons, Edwards, Thomas, and Robert. Edwards and Robert would serve as state senators, while Robert would become Secretary of Louisiana's Department of Wildlife and Fisheries. Abner Wimberly had played for the Green Bay Packers, served as assistant L.S.U. football coach for six years, and developed Wimberly Oil Company. James McLendon, an Oak Ridge civic leader, had served in Korea. Carter had maintained his father's vast acreage after Joe Sidney Senior died.

Clarke had talked to each of them just the week before. The loss reminded him of how much he would lose if he kept his driving preoccupation with business and travel. He was nurturing Clarke Junior and building a team at Century, but his long intensity had overshadowed so much. He saw Mary Kathryn, Annette, and Carolyn with renewed eyes and vowed to find more time for them. Four men who were alive Saturday were dead Monday, proving money, schedules and success didn't mean a thing compared to relationships.

The crash affected Mary Kathryn, too. Clarke had flown N3918W and had bought a Cherokee just like it, the one in which he had flown the family to Mexico. "Please don't take any chances like that, Clarke," she begged. He thought better than to recite his safety record since both knew that, at 150 miles per hour, flying could turn dangerous in the blink of an eye. Clarke the pilot continually rehearsed dangerous scenarios but never worried about them. As his flight systems became more sophisticated and Century Telephone grew larger, Clarke eventually hired experienced pilots. But there were no guarantees. The Barham plane had two experienced pilots in the front seats. On the ground and in the air, Clarke had trusted God this far and would continue to do so. Who knew how much his friends' deaths were accidental and how much may have had some purpose? That was God's affair, and to dwell further was pointless. His friends would have urged him forward in faith. Of that, he was certain.

Not long after the crash, a tall, lanky young man with jet black hair, packing accounting and master's degrees in business administration from Louisiana Tech, showed up for an interview with crusty old Walter Frank. He was an unlikely aspiring corporate executive who hailed from the small lumbermill town of Farmerville, Louisiana. Glen Fleming Post, III, loved to hunt and fish and had been a standout in basketball and football. He had to be. His father was locally famous basketball coach Glen Post, Jr., who demanded the best of his son, on the court and off. Walter Frank hired him and let him stay close to home by placing him in the Marion accounting office.

Glen Post: "The first month I was at Century about killed me. I wasn't used to sitting behind a desk, being an outdoors person. The office I was in had no windows. I met Mr. Williams when he came to Marion. He came around my little desk, shook hands, and talked with me. He had a unique ability to make people feel special. He had a lot of charisma. I remember the first trip we went with him on the plane to Hershey, Pennsylvania, to a U.S. Telephone Association event. It was the first trip [wife] Cynthia went on with me. I was young and didn't know what I was doing, where I was going really, and he made us feel so comfortable and welcome. When we came back, I told Cynthia, 'I want to be like that man.'"[211]

Clarke latched on to the Farmerville boy's unassuming manner, so much like his own. While Glen balanced his life with hunting and fishing, on the job the young man was all business. In fact, in the interview with Walter and later, as Clarke got to know him, the twenty-something made no bones of his intention to move up, remembering later, "I told them I didn't want to be an accountant all my life. They hired me anyway."[212]

Glen told them he wanted to grow with a growing company. The young man wanted more than a job; he wanted a challenge. He wanted a life he could build. Both ambitious and honest, he had already set career goals. Clarke saw in Glen a younger version of himself, a man happy only when helping others; further, he recognized in the younger man his own sentiment that truly successful people always enlisted and returned the help of others. Glen was not the type to climb across the backs of others. His quiet, unobtrusive, but deep religious beliefs were a plus,

---

[211] Glen Post interview, Sept. 25, 2012, Monroe, Louisiana; and *Louisiana Business Journal*, Vol. 2, No. 2, Spring 1996, p. 15.
[212] Glen Post, *Louisiana Business Journal*, Vol. 2, No. 2, Spring 1996, p. 14.

too. Instead of proselyting, he lived by example at a simpler, happier level, letting coworkers know he was there for them day or night.

Just as Clarke was observing him, Glen was watching, too. The younger man began to take notes about this unusual founder of an unusual company. The two recognized each other striving to live lives beyond reproach, resisting the temptation to be all things to all people. They fought to change the world rather than be changed. Clarke and Glen behaved the same everywhere to everyone, unwavering and dependable. With little life experience, Glen sensed he was lucky to have found such a gifted, guided leader.

While Clarke Williams never had bad days, Century Telephone did. As Clarke bought more exchanges, cash flow challenged Walter and Glen. Unless plant and equipment were beyond repair, like a kid in a candy store Clarke bought the exchange.

> Harvey Perry: "Mr. Williams wanted to buy everything he looked at but from time to time he passed, knowing his objective. Sometimes he didn't necessarily let facts and figures get in the way of what that objective was because he knew the ultimate outcome. He would drive our chief financial officers crazy sometimes because we'd look at an acquisition and, to them, everything had to work out on paper. For Mr. Williams, everything had to work out in terms of what his ultimate objective was, which was to acquire that company, clean it up, refurbish it, and make money. It was up to them to make it work once he decided what he was going to do."[213]

> Billy Boles, Sr., attorney and banker: "When Clarke wanted to buy an exchange and first wanted to borrow money, I asked him how many

---

[213] Harvey Perry interview, Sept. 15, 2012, Baton Rouge, Louisiana.

stations he had. I wrote it down, divided it, and it came to $125 per station. I thought, 'We can't get hurt on that,' so I told him we'd lend the money. That shocked Clarke and he said, 'You're the first banker I've seen who loaned money on a telephone company.' It began a great relationship."[214]

Carolyn Williams Perry: "Johnny Hebert, a main shareholder, had some money to invest and asked Daddy, 'What do you think about me putting this money in Century?' Daddy said, 'I can't promise you that what you're doing won't be a mistake. I don't think it is. I think you're going to see a good return on your money if you invest with us.' Johnny wound up being one of the biggest stockholders and sat on the board for several years."[215]

Clarke Williams, Sr.: "My problem was trying to balance enough business to take care of the people who it took to run it. So I had to continue to grow. Many a time when I thought I was the right size, expenses increased and I'd have to get more revenue so I'd buy something else.[216]
"One time we went to see a banker to borrow money for expansion. The old banker began telling us why we might not get the loan and how he had been in banking for 40 years, etc. I asked the gentleman how many banks he had ever seen go broke during that time? He said, 'None.' I then asked how many telephone companies he

[214] Billy Boles, Sr. interview, *Louisiana Lifetimes*, Dec. 9, 1996, television production of Century Telephone, Inc.
[215] Carolyn Williams Perry interview, Sept. 15, 2012, Baton Rouge, Louisiana.
[216] Clarke Williams, Sr. interview, *Louisiana Lifetimes*, Dec. 9, 1996, television production of Century Telephone, Inc.

had seen go broke? He said, 'How much did you say you needed?'"[217]

Annette Williams Carroll: "Anytime Daddy had a new business venture or acquisition in mind, Mother would say, 'Oh, no! That's another debt.' And he would say, 'Well, it's a sure thing then. If you're against it, then I know it's going to work.' And they'd laugh about it."[218]

Mary Kathryn's fears were well founded. As interest rates skyrocketed to an unprecedented 21 percent prime, Century's financial situation turned desperate, as local rates were often much higher. As balance sheets bled, in 1978 Clarke Junior stepped into a slot as vice president and sparred with accountants over how to head off catastrophe.

Overleveraged as rates shot to new heights, Clarke and Clarke Junior admitted their problem and the only solution: They had to sell every bit of ownership they could to survive and keep their jobs. The two went on road shows, hawking Century to financial analysts across the nation, bargaining with over 110,000 access lines and expanding rapidly through mid-America. Satisfied with healthy revenue growth, analysts on Wall Street embraced the Louisiana telecom. On Tuesday, October 24, 1978, Clarke McRae Williams, son of a telephone pioneer from Iuka, Mississippi, and an operator from Mertzon, Texas, stood at the podium of the New York Stock Exchange and gaveled the open. He bought the first share of Century Telephone "CTL" to trade on the Big Board. Back home, he stuffed the certificate into an envelope on which he wrote: *Never sell this unless it is absolutely necessary.*

Clarke McRae Williams: "We went to New York, signed all the papers and did everything

---

[217] Clarke Williams, Sr., *The Farmerville (Louisiana) Gazette*, June 28, 1979, front page.
[218] Annette Williams Carroll interview, *Louisiana Lifetimes*, Dec. 9, 1996, television production of Century Telephone, Inc.

necessary to get on the New York Stock Exchange. We were honored to be presented to the Exchange and I was privileged to buy the very first share of stock that came across the ticker on Century Telephone Enterprises, 'CTL.'"[219]

Mary Kathryn Williams: "When we came back, he was so enthusiastic and he said, 'We have finally done it. We are on the way now. It's one of the most thrilling things I ever had happen to me.' He was really almost walking on air."[220]

Clarke Junior witnessed from the front row as small-town Century jockeyed alongside AT&T. Accounting would never be simple again; thousands of shareholders would demand every intimate company detail, information competitors would also see.

Clarke walked away from the glitzy, noisy floor of the New York Stock Exchange and within hours was standing amid softly swaying pine trees near Downsville in north central Louisiana. He was leading a group of men surveying 1,142 acres for the Ouachita Valley Council of the Boy Scouts of America. Clarke had worked tirelessly for more than a year heading up a committee that raised an astounding $1,472,890. He broke up the task into six committees, from new gifts to auditing, appointing John Lolley, John Mullens, Warren White, Derwood Cann, Ron Doughty, and Gary Thomas. Clarke's handpicked committees gently encouraged major north Louisiana businesses to give.

"I feel that scouts who are involved with the program are better citizens," he told the press. "I never achieved the rank of Eagle Scout in my own scouting days, but my son, Clarke Junior,

---

[219] Clarke Williams, Sr. interview, *Louisiana Lifetimes*, Dec. 9, 1996, television production of Century Telephone, Inc.
[220] Mary Kathryn Williams interview, *Louisiana Lifetimes*, Dec. 9, 1996, television production of Century Telephone, Inc.

did."[221] A grateful Ouachita Valley Boy Scout Council chose Clarke for its Silver Beaver Award. He served as president of the group from 1979 to 1980, rotating off just in time to become president of the Board of Directors of the Northeast Louisiana University Alumni Foundation, where he served through 1981. He also served on the boards of two banks, the Louisiana Telephone Association, the Trustees of Louisiana (Baptist) College in Alexandria, the Salvation Army, and the Lions, all while rising to a 32nd Degree Mason and Shriner.

High-ranking officials in Washington, D. C., began seeking out Clarke for guidance and expertise. After President Ronald Reagan renewed conservatism and settled down the financial markets following President Carter's term, famed astronaut and United States Senator John Glenn rendezvoused with Clarke in Baton Rouge. Clarke was an unabashed fan of the iconic astronaut, the *face of the Space Age.* Clarke liked Glenn's sincere humility and encouraged him to run for president. Glenn in turn was happy to see that another mild-mannered nice guy could win, too. "I sincerely thank you for your generous contribution to my Presidential Exploratory Committee," Senator Glenn wrote to Clarke. "Annie and I enjoyed sharing the evening with you last week."[222]

Assuming the presidency of Century Telephone likewise required hundreds of small steps. In 1980, Clarke recommended Clarke Junior as a director to the Century Board of Directors, which elected him unanimously, appointing him to the Executive Committee. Late that year, as 20 percent-plus interest rates threatened Century's existence, Clarke and the board decided to shake down and reorganize in an attempt to stabilize. On November 18, 1980, in an all-encompassing restructure, the Board elected Clarke Junior as Senior Vice President of Corporate Operations. He had just turned 31.

---

[221] Jennie Jo Siscoe, "Homefolks," *Richland Journal*, Rayville, Louisiana, April 9, 1984, p. 2A.

[222] U.S. Senator John Glenn letter, dated Nov.18, 1982, in possession of Carolyn Williams Perry.

Senator Robert Barham, boyhood friend: "Clarke Junior developed a wonderful personality growing up. He never met a person he didn't enjoy coming to know and becoming a friend with. As we grew up, that was his biggest attribute. He was such a vibrant person and always a friend to everyone he met. Also, if he was in charge, it was going to be done his way. It's fun to be around someone who wants everyone who's involved in something to enjoy what they're doing but has a clear idea of what he wants accomplished. So people naturally gravitated to Clarke because he had such a winning personality."[223]

George Campbell, president, Region's Bank: "Businesses go through different cycles. Clarke came along at the absolute perfect time for Century Telephone. He was an entrepreneur but he was an entrepreneur with a vision. Unlike a lot of entrepreneurs, Clarke, in order to accomplish the goals he had for his company, he had to bring in some special expertise and one of his greatest accomplishments was seeking out and bringing in the kind of technical help and quality of people that he brought to Century. Many of those people have stayed involved with Century over the years and were responsible for its continued success."[224]

Clarke Senior masterfully eased Clarke Junior into the role, letting go of the reins slowly. Century Telephone had hopscotched from Oak Ridge to Marion to Plain Dealing to

---

[223] Senator Robert Barham interview, *Louisiana Lifetimes*, Dec. 9, 1996, television production of Century Telephone, Inc.
[224] George Campbell interview, *Louisiana Lifetimes*, Dec. 9, 1996, television production of Century Telephone, Inc.

Arkansas to Wisconsin in a manner akin to two partners playing cards: Clarke Senior would set up the acquisition and Walter Frank would push it through. The partnership worked beautifully because of complimentary personalities. But as Clarke Junior grew up in the business, he credited the genius of Walter Frank but noticed after reorganization that Walter continued to make high-level decisions without consulting anyone. Genius Walter, of all people, knew the requisite accountability of a public company, but he had enjoyed free rein for so long, he couldn't slow his momentum. When confronted, Walter, after building Century for over twenty years, did not like being questioned or second-guessed. Heated arguments broke out between him and the incoming regime, namely Clarke Junior. Finally, when Clarke Junior discovered that ancillary vendors to the company were owned by Walter Frank but without disclosure, Clarke Junior demanded Walter's resignation. The departure shook Century to its foundation.

> C. G. Melville, board member: "Clarke [Senior] called me and was really upset about Walter's departure. He depended on Walter so much. He called me and all the other directors to tell us that we were going to have to let Walter go. He said, 'Walter is going in a different direction.' He didn't go into detail, I didn't ask but I assumed that Walter had run amuck. I said, 'Well, what are we going to do?' because I thought Walter was such a strong part of the organization. He said, 'C. G., we've got some people who've come along now who will be able to do just as good a job if not better.' When he told me that, I was relieved. I said, 'Let's do it. If that's what you want to do, that's fine with me.' I felt that Clarke was an astute enough businessman that he knew what he could and couldn't do. He replaced Walter with R. L. Hargrove, a fine guy who did

the company well for all the years he was with us."[225]

Glen Post: "Walter was an amazing guy. He had a photographic memory. He could remember page so-and-so, section 3, of this loan agreement that was 200 pages long. But he thought that we couldn't make it without him. He told somebody he didn't think we'd make it. He patted me on the back, gave me some compliments, but he did not think we would make it."[226]

With Walter Frank's departure, Century Telephone flowed into a river of change sweeping the whole country. On Tuesday November 4, 1980, former movie star and California Governor Ronald Wilson Reagan upended President Jimmy Carter's reelection, winning nearly 51 percent of the popular vote to Carter's 41 percent. But most telling was Reagan's landslide electoral victory ten times over the sitting president, 489 to Carter's 49. President-elect Reagan promised an immediate buildup of the United States military to resolve the Cold War once and for all. He slashed taxes to stimulate growth and eased monetary policy to bring down interest rates. Century's financial group, bankers, shareholders, financiers, and directors breathed a sigh of relief. As interest rates dropped, they began refinancing Century's immense debt.

Two weeks after Reagan won the presidency, Century Telephone's transformation began. To make Clarke Junior the Senior Vice President for Corporate Operations, the board peeled power away from Colonel Arthur Carroll and William Smith, senior vice presidents in charge of telephone operations and commercial operations, respectively.

---

[225] C. G. Melville telephone interview, Feb. 8, 2014.
[226] Glen Post interview, Aug. 14, 2013, Monroe, Louisiana.

"There was not a single person left," Clarke Junior told Wall Street analysts later, "except for my father and I."[227] While that may have been an oversimplification, Century's deep housecleaning created a paradigm shift for the company. New ideas came with new people.

Century's general legal counsel for seven years, J. J. Dixon, left. Monroe attorney Billy Boles bridged the gap before recommending his son, William Junior, fresh out of law school, as Century's chief attorney.

> Bill Boles, Jr., corporate attorney: "We talked to Clarke, Clarke Jr., R. L. Hargrove, Colonel Carroll, Glen Post, and Bill Smith, who ran the various departments. Dad said, 'J.J. is leaving and Bill Junior is now going to be handling y'all's account. Is that okay?' I was just months out of law school. All I'd handled was a court foreclosure, a divorce, and a couple of real-estate loan closings. Dad said to me, 'Whatever they tell you, tell them you can do it. We'll figure out how to get it done.' It was typical dad. So I went over there and Mr. Williams said, 'Young William, you think you can handle this?' I said, 'Can do, Mr. Williams.' But I was terrified. The first thing we did was a $15 million loan from Teachers Insurance in New York, which I though was all the money in the world. I was handling Century's first unsecured deal and I went up there and studied every document in the vault for weeks. I said, 'Glen, tell me we'll be able to pay this money back!' He said, 'We'll be fine.' They gave us a check for $15,000,000 and R. L. and I walked around the corner and deposited the check immediately in Farmers Guaranty Bank. I was shaking."[228]

---

[227] Clarke Williams, Jr., Oct. 5, 1987, *Telephone News*, Phillips Publishing Inc., Potomac, Maryland.
[228] Williams Boles, Jr., interview, Feb. 5, 2013, Monroe, Louisiana.

As Clarke Junior learned the ropes with a fresh, young team, he felt health problems start to crop up. Through the 1970s, Clarke Junior found sinus infections, persistent coughs, and bouts of bronchitis increasingly severe. By 1979, the lymph nodes in his neck stayed swollen, night sweats came frequently, and it took his body longer to fight infection. When he agreed to medical testing, the doctors discovered he had Hodgkin's Lymphoma, a cancer in his lymph nodes caused by errant white blood cells. Because doctors also found cancer in his spleen, Clarke was entering Stage 3 of the cancer, serious but treatable.

> Carolyn Williams Perry: "The Hodgkin's disease was scary. It took the doctors a while to diagnose it because Clarke thought he had bronchitis or something. He went to the medical center where they were on the breaking edge of treatment for Hodgkin's disease so he was able to get the treatment. They removed his spleen and Clarke did great."[229]

Doctors stopped the Hodgkin's with a series of radiation treatments and diagnosed Clarke Junior cancer free. He had beat it, but his body didn't feel the same after the radiation. On track to run the company, Clarke Junior remained quiet so that he would not alarm the board, investors, and shareholders. Clarke Senior saw his son's miraculous improvement as an answer to prayer, and Junior had to agree.

Starting in 1977, Vietnam veterans began showing up at veterans hospitals with Hodgkin's, and the trail eventually led back to Agent Orange. Clarke Senior agonized over his part in having pushed his son to Vietnam. He had come back wounded after all.

The doctors told Clarke Junior that while his liver would for the most part filter his blood, it would never compensate for the

---

[229] Carolyn Williams Perry interview, Sept. 15, 2012, Baton Rouge, Louisiana.

missing spleen 100 percent and that his immune system would thus be compromised. By 1980, data from World War II veterans who had had their spleens removed showed those veterans died from pneumonia at five times the rate of the general population and suffered significantly higher rates of heart disease, especially hardening of the arteries. When Clarke Junior had heard enough warnings about how his life would change, he shut out the doctors and threw himself wholly into Century Telephone.

With reorganization, solid financing, diving interest rates, and climbing revenues, Century's stock rose dramatically. *The Wall Street Journal* reported that the revenues of little independents were trending up, while returns for giant AT&T were declining. They were about to decline even more. In 1974, the U. S. Justice Department had filed suit, *United States vs. AT&T*, calling Ma Bell's hand once and for all. *Western Electric's* immense capitalization not only produced cutting-edge technology that kept AT&T ahead technologically, *Western Electric's* huge "monopoly profits," as determined by the Federal Communications Commission, were also subsidizing AT&T's networks in direct violation of U.S. Antitrust laws. If AT&T kept artificially low rates, it could strangle neighboring independents out of their profits.

For six years, Clarke and Clarke Junior watched events unfold, anticipating as Century surged ahead. To appease regulators, AT&T lawyers made the radical offer to break up the Bell System completely in a move to keep control of high-profit *Western Electric*. On January 8, 1982, U. S. District Judge Harold Greene took AT&T's offer and with a bang of the gavel shattered the world's largest corporation into seven Regional Bell Operating Companies. But Greene had his own shock in store for AT&T: He split control of *Western Electric*, spinning off half of Bell Labs, all the Bell trademark and the Yellow Pages to the seven so called "Baby Bells."

Century's directors celebrated. One-hundred-year-old American Telephone & Telegraph had at last been humbled. For independents, the gold rush was on. Without cowering to the giant, they could now compete in every area, especially in the lucrative long distance market. But the two Clarkes saw before nearly everyone else something completely different on the horizon. The timing of the Bell breakup was not mere chance. Far more important than old ways of communicating, now into view came *personal computers* and with them *the Internet*. The Internet would need connectivity, and telephone systems offered the only networks.

Starting in the United States, the Internet would change life as everyone knew it. Interconnectivity was made possible by a juggernaut revolution in science as the electronic world turned from analog signaling—the use of electromagnetic waves and pulses—to something called *digital*, the conversion of analog information streamlined into "bits" using the binary system of 0's and 1's. Alexander Graham Bell had converted voice sound waves into electrical pulses across metal wire. Now, a century later, high speed computing could convert the electrical analog pulses into lightning-fast digital codes that could transmit far more efficiently using far less energy. The breakthrough led the way for another revolution called *cellular*.

Clarke had witnessed rapid changes but nothing like this. He and Clarke Junior saw that telephones would soon come off the walls and out of houses and move to, of all places, everyone's automobiles and perhaps even into their pockets. The concept was so science fiction that few comprehended it and fewer still believed it.

Clarke Senior believed. His dream and that of every person who'd climbed poles in the dead of winter was finally coming true: Thousands of miles of wires, poles, and insulators would finally turn obsolete. Car radio-telephones had been around since the 1960s but only for the rich. During the 1970s, some bigger farmers around Oak Ridge and Morehouse Parish had begun installing the large cumbersome radiophones and transmitters in vehicles at high monthly fees. Calls required a mobile operator to dial the number and the vehicle had to be in close proximity to widely-spaced mobile phone towers. With limited frequencies, in most areas only three customers could make calls at the same time. Near urban areas, customers often waited thirty minutes before they could make a mobile call and by then many were out of range.

Clarke Senior had never considered jumping Century into the mobile telephone business because infrastructure was cost prohibitive. Radio towers and telephones required a great deal of electrical power to transmit and receive. But he had been aware of the coming portable trend as far back as 1972, when Amos Joel of Bell Laboratories developed the concept of a cellular switching system, a series of transmission towers unlike radio towers. Instead of transmitting circular omnidirectional beams, cellular towers radiated focused, directional beams relatively short distances.

Three horizontal antennae forming a triangle topped each cellular tower. Each antenna would beam in one direction. The three together created hexagon-shaped coverage, and an array of such towers puzzled together provided coverage in the design of a honeycomb, thus called *cells*. To minimize interference with the towers next to it, each tower in the series would use a different frequency. By building out a series of cellular towers, a mobile *cell* telephone could automatically hopscotch, not from one tower to the next, but to the next tower using the same frequency. As more towers rose closer together, especially along roadways, the telephone itself would use less energy to communicate with the tower, substantially prolonging battery life and range. Joel's concept was brilliant but a decade in advance.

Clarke felt that in this cataclysmic shift the Lord was presenting the time for a long-awaited change. Communication was shifting from ground wires to airwaves, from analog to digital, and ultimately from desks and kitchens to cars and pockets, all as Ma Bell was fracturing into twenty-two independent telephone companies.

Amid the excitement balanced with thoughtful prayer, Clarke recommended to Century's Board of Directors that Clarke McRae Williams, Junior, replace him as president and chief operating officer. Board members had anticipated the request for some time and voted unanimously for the new king.

On February 23, 1983, Clarke Junior assumed the mantel his father had carried for nearly forty years. He was 33.

> Clarke McRae Williams: "In comparing myself to Clarke, Jr., I see a resemblance in our line of thinking. There is difficulty at times because I am constantly aware that Clarke Jr. is an executive officer and my son. I think I tend to be more critical of him than I am of anyone else. He has good business perception and it is instinctive of me to try to prevent him from making an error when actually he seldom needs help. He has a natural ingredient to communicate with people on any facet or level of business. In his present capacity, everything is falling into place. It is very rewarding to work with him and I am pleased and proud of his involvement in telephony."[230]

> Clarke Williams, Jr.: "My dad never asked me to come into the business. It was always his feeling that whatever I was going to do with my life should be my decision. But it's all I ever wanted to do. My grandfather did it; my father did it; I've never thought of doing anything else. I guess I have wire in my arms instead of veins."[231]

Clarke Junior's sense of humor and cleverness set the tone for his administration. He would need all the wits he could muster because Century encountered rapids, both external and internal, right off the bat. In a shock to management, to the board, and to the founder, a senior vice president suddenly

---

[230] Clarke McRae Williams, Sr., "The Third Generation Begins," *Centuryian*, March 1981, p. 22
[231] Clarke McRae Williams, Jr, "Clarke Williams, Jr., keeping the family name going at Century," *Monroe News-Star*, Feb. 1983.

demanded out of right field a $100,000 bonus. He had been Clarke's lifelong friend.

> Jim Reppond, SVP Operations: "This person approached Mr. Williams and said, 'Clarke, you promised me if I resolved the union issue in La Crosse, you would give me a $100,000 bonus. Well, it is ten years later and I would like to have my bonus.' Mr. Williams told him that it was news to him."[232]

Both Clarkes called in Chief Financial Officer Glen Post. Post had never heard a single word or promise about a bonus, certainly not such a large sum as $100,000, for settling La Crosse. Such an agreement would have required board approval.

Though there was no basis for the $100,000 demand, rather than engage in lawsuits and publicly embarrass the company, Clarke told a roomful of stunned directors, "I just want to get this over with."[233] Some vehemently protested, saying the demand bordered on extortion. In the end, the board did recognize that the senior V.P. had made a significant contribution toward resolving the strike in LaCrosse, gave him a check, and promptly showed him the door.

> Jim Reppond, SVP Operations: "He just saw the opportunity to milk Mr. Williams any way he could. When he left, he kept coming back with long distance plans, where you aggregate all of your traffic with some other company to get your minute rate down with AT&T. He called me on several different occasions trying to get me to help him get his foot back in the door at Century."[234]

---

[232] Jim Reppond telephone interview, Jan. 29, 2013, Monroe, Louisiana.
[233] Recollection of Jim Reppond, telephone interview, Jan. 29, 2013, Monroe, Louisiana.
[234] Jim Reppond telephone interview, Jan. 29, 2013, Monroe, Louisiana.

Burned again by a friend, Clarke prayed sorrowfully for the soul of the latest Judas. Thirty pieces of silver had meant more than a lifetime of friendship. Clarke knew that his old friend's personality had changed over the years and suspected that financial trouble had played a role in his betrayal. Though Clarke and Mary Kathryn hardly lived like royalty in Oak Ridge, he now saw how imagined wealth made them a target. Money was a powerful wedge, as the Bible repeatedly warned. But when the former friend audaciously began showing up at Clarke's church, sitting behind him, and touching him for still more money, Clarke's son-in-law Harvey Perry sent a cease-and-desist letter.

Harvey, the board, and close lawmen knew that pressing a friend for money was bad enough, but a man crossed a serious line when he used church to threaten and intimidate. The Judas questioned Clarke's Christianity, but Clarke knew that was the façade of someone hurting. Clarke continued to behave politely and never stopped praying.

He advised his son not to take the lesson to heart, but to keep balance when conducting business with friends. The father insisted the son not push people away because two of his father's friendships had soured. Clarke reminded Clarke Junior, Glen, and other young people at the office that no one should live his life in distrust and that everything eventually works out, if not in this life then certainly in the next.

Clarke Junior had precious little time to ponder betrayal. He was now leading a young reorganized team into uncharted and choppy waters. With the AT&T dragon slain, a Pandora's box of powerful independent telephone companies furiously attacked for the spoils. By summer 1983, GTE Chairman Theodore Brophy was licking his chops over the breakup of AT&T. "We are the great beneficiary," he told reporters. "We can sell equipment to Bell. We can offer equipment to Bell customers."[235] GTE President Thomas Vanderslice added that

---

[235] "GTE licks chops over AT&T breakup," *Monroe News-Star World*, June 26, 1983, p. 10E.

AT&T's divestiture presented so many opportunities that "it would be an insurmountable problem to try to take advantage of all of them."[236]

Clarke Junior couldn't agree more. Now the foe was no longer AT&T but rather all the bigger independents who emerged from the first round of consolidations. To meet them, Clarke Junior reshuffled and reassigned his management team again. Glen Post became Senior Vice President of Financial Operations and Controller; Bruce Hanks, V.P., Revenues; Gary Perleberg, V.P., Network Planning; Harlin Hames, V.P., Mid-South Division; Jack Robinson, V.P., Southern Division; Tony Davis, V.P., Internal Audit; Robert Esker, V.P., Special Projects; W. F. Provance, V.P.; Harold LeGrone, V.P.; Ken Cole, V.P., Data Processing; and Marvin Cunningham, Assistant V.P., Financial Operations. Clarke Junior soon added Stewart Ewing as V.P. and Controller, moving Glen Post also up to Treasurer, and Ray Finney, V.P., Human Resources; and he talked his brother-in-law, attorney Harvey Parnell Perry, into joining the team as a vice president and General Counsel. The median age of Clarke Junior's team was 32, half that of his father.

The old man was proud of the new team but gently admonished the men not to underestimate the stamina required to face some high-stakes challenges ahead. This group would be challenged, too, as the Reagan administration tried to lift America out of recession. Cutting taxes and beefing up the military would create jobs across the spectrum, but the president's widely-touted "trickle down" Reaganomics would take time. Both Clarkes and board members were shocked when the most famous Monroe-founded company, Delta Airlines, posted its first loss in 36 years. Discounted fares for hotly contested routes were to blame, and Clarke Junior saw the same could lie ahead for Century. The company had to blaze its own trail. For Clarke Junior, that meant scoring first and fastest in cellular.

In 1981, the Federal Communications Commission divided the United States into 734 geographic markets called *Cellular*

---

[236] Ibid

Market Areas and split the 40 MHz allocation of bandwidth into two 20 MHz channel blocks. Channel Block A went to non-wireline carriers, while Channel Block B went to landline carriers such as Century. Clarke Junior jumped at licenses for B Blocks in the fourteen states where Century operated 200,000 access lines. But because applications flooded the FCC, Congress immediately realized that vetting each applicant for expertise would take years and stop the new technology cold. They passed the Omnibus Budget Reconciliation Act of 1981, adding subsection 309i authorizing the FCC to grant licenses on the basis of random selection or lottery. The FCC would hold back the top 30 markets so that experienced telecommunications competitors would bid for them. The FCC didn't want to risk a flood of non-telephone speculators driving up costs for the consumer. The commission was also directed to favor "underrepresented" groups such as women and minorities "to foster diversity in ownership of mass media."[237]

While the FCC established a lottery mechanism, Clarke Junior and his team researched Century's fourteen states to find customers who could most afford the new but pricy mobile phones. Topping the list was Michigan, where for a dozen years Century had owned and operated the Central, Midwest, and Public Service Telephone companies. With nine million people, eighth most populous state in the country, Michigan families earned above-average 1980 household incomes of $19,200. But the most telling factor for both Clarkes was a very high home ownership rate, 73 percent, the second highest in the nation. The two-peninsular state would be Century's first cellular gold mine. After polling his father, board members, and Glen Post, Clarke Junior launched some major horse-trading with officials of Continental Telecom of Michigan. Clarke picked out five Century exchanges in four states contiguous to Continental's holdings. Both boards agreed to swap Continental's 35,000-customer Michigan exchange for Century's 11,000 customers of

---

[237] *The Communications Act: A Legislative History of the Major Amendments, 1935-1996,* by Max D. Paglin, James R. Hobson, and Joel Rosenbloom; ©1999 Pike & Fischer, Silver Spring, Maryland.

Elberfield Telephone in Indiana, Uniontown Telephone in Kentucky, Century Telephone in Texas, and two exchanges in Missouri. Clarke made up the difference in customers with $12 million in cash. Since no one could predict who would win the licensing lottery, Clarke's team signed partnership agreements with all other Michigan wireline carriers for participation in Flint, Lansing, and Grand Rapids. Part was better than nothing, and with FCC approval, "Century gained 20 percent of the cellular market in Grand Rapids, 17 percent in Lansing, and 15 percent in Flint," Clarke Junior told Wall Street analysts. "With the breakup of the Bell System, we are currently the seventeenth largest exchange telephone holding company in the United States...and the eighth largest non-Bell telephone company."[238] Century had clinched Michigan, grabbing the whole state before GTE and others could turn around. It was Clarke Junior's first big win.

Clarke Senior was proudly thrilled by the way his son had played chess on so large a geographic chessboard, much more complex than when he started. He was also thrilled that his dream was coming true, that finally all those small, insignificant exchanges had become a huge, valuable network. As Clarke Junior took the reins, both were grateful that Clarke Senior had had the foresight to buy all those mom-and-pops at just the point in the 1950s and '60s when their owners wanted out. Yes, for many years Clarke had tiptoed along the edge of bankruptcy, and several times he'd felt that God had stayed his hand from throwing in the towel. Many nights he had spent convincing Mary Kathryn to stay the course and not to worry. He knew he had strained the bonds of their marriage. Now, as his son sailed the company into stormy technological seas, he found himself again worrying that his life's work might be at risk.

> Virginia Boulet, CenturyTel attorney: "I don't think Mr. Williams was convinced that cellular was the wave of the future, that you could drive

---

[238] *Wall Street Transcripts*, "Remarks by Clarke M. Williams, President CTL, to the Financial Analysts of New Orleans, May 9, 1984," published July 2, 1984.

a car 60 miles an hour down the highway while talking and seamlessly hand off the call to another tower. That made no sense to him. And he was not convinced that people were going to need that phone in their pocket all the time. It was at that point when he said, 'You know, it's time we got someone younger in here because this is an age-driven thing. People my age are not that dependent on being in constant communication. But I see it, I see my son-in-law taking his pager to church, for goodness sake! These people need to be in contact.' And that's when he said it was time 'for Clarke Junior to run this company because he does have that vision.'"[239]

Clarke Senior recited more than once that the larger part of wisdom is knowing what you don't know. He had an audience in the younger team who knew their generation's likes better than he, yet they respected the elder Mr. Williams greatly. No one could argue that his ancient lessons of complete faith, vision, and integrity had rendered a monumental result. This was especially true for Glen Post, who had become closer than a brother to Clarke Junior as Clarke Senior mentored them both.

Glen Post: "Mr. Williams was a father figure to me. I told Cynthia, my wife, he was like a second father, a close relationship that grew closer over the years. We communicated well. I learned a lot from him in all kinds of ways, especially his compassion for people and his great generosity and integrity. He was a man of vision and most importantly he had an ability to *inspire people to loyalty*. I had a chance over the years to go to work for other companies, people wanting to hire me, but they were never taken seriously. I never

---

[239] Virginia Boulet interview, Oct. 22, 2012, New Orleans, Louisiana.

thought once of leaving, just never had the desire, and it was because of the man Clarke Williams was. We had the desire to help him be successful because of his genuine view of helping other people."[240]

The timid founder had softly but soundly built the company one block at a time, never pushing himself on anyone, never demanding his way, never so much as raising his voice to make a point. Glen and Clarke Junior learned from the old man that people would strain to hear a near-whisper but discount a loudmouth. Thus, people not only listened to Clarke Senior; they respected, believed, and admired him. The two young men also noticed that when challenges loomed large, the old man did not enter battle fearfully.

> Glen Post: "It's a tough world and when Mr. Williams needed to be tough at times, he could be tough. To make decisions and go forth despite opposition, if he decided he wanted to do something, he'd get after it. He'd fly around and meet individual members of the board of directors and he'd say, 'Glen, don't forget now. If you want to get something done, you meet face-to-face with people, you go see them.' So we'd go around if there were a big decision to make and meet face-to-face with members of the board to explain to them what we were trying to do. Sometimes I felt it was a little too time consuming but he knew what he was doing."[241]

Clarke Junior and Glen learned from the master about face-to-face negotiations as the regulatory world grew more complex. With the breakup of Bell Telephone, the whole game changed, not just for telephones but also for cable television. Clarke Senior, as early as 1968, began picking up an occasional cable

---

[240] Glen Post interview, Sept. 25, 2012, Monroe, Louisiana.
[241] Glen Post interview, Sept. 25, 2012, Monroe, Louisiana.

system that paralleled a Century phone exchange. In those areas, Century pioneered bundling services by combining telephone and cable bills. In 1984, with Bell no longer a threat to monopolize cable TV, the FCC relaxed Section 214 of the Communications Act requiring telecoms to prove that their expansion would serve public interests. Clarke Junior pushed the relaxation of 214, telling *Broadcasting* magazine, "The public interest is disserved by the delays [caused] by the Section 214 application process and by increased costs to operators, the public, and the commission."[242] The National Cable Television Association agreed and did not challenge the FCC's granting phone companies the right to absorb cable systems. Clarke Senior's earlier cable acquisitions over two decades would prove valuable to Clarke Junior as he negotiated with other telecoms in the scramble for cellular licenses.

Century found the battlegrounds in top markets rapidly stacked against them with much bigger money. Exactly as Clarke Junior had feared, large independents were combining with large capital groups to soak up big city cellular franchises. *The New York Times* reported on October 3, 1984:

> *More than 100 companies that applied to build cellular mobile phone systems in 60 of the nation's larger cities negotiated partnerships to avoid licensing lotteries scheduled for Wednesday and October 23. The Government said today that it was canceling Wednesday's lottery for licenses in cities ranked 31 to 60 in size, because competitors in 29 of the 30 cities had forged settlement agreements.*

Century Telephone in Monroe, Louisiana, had grabbed as much area as it could, though still shut out from the big leagues. The Clarkes had to find expertise in cellular systems quickly to immediately upgrade the exchanges they did control. After scouring for talent nationwide, in February 1986 Clarke Junior

---

[242] "Easing Rules for telcos and cable," *Broadcasting*, Mar. 12, 1984, p. 50.

found an expert right under his nose, a boyhood friend whose grandfather put the Williams family into the phone business in the first place. David Earl Hogan, the son of Earl Hogan, whose father had sold Oak Ridge Telephone to William Clarke and Marie Williams, was successfully climbing the ranks of the cellular business in Jackson, Mississippi. Hogan worked at a young company called "Long Distance Discount Services," the forerunner of WorldCom. Before joining LDDS, out of college, David rose through the ranks of IBM's telecommunications division for ten years, landing a corner office in New York City.

> Clarke Williams, Jr., in a video address to analysts: "David came to Oak Ridge when he was in the fifth grade. He and I had a little skirmish and after that we became the best of friends. We both graduated Oak Ridge High; I was in the top 10 out of the nine of us in the graduating class [laughter] but David really was at the top. We both went to Louisiana Tech; he graduated with honors in engineering and went on to get an MBA in business [while Clarke Junior went to Vietnam].
> "After IBM, he spent three years in Jackson where he got heavily involved with this new deal called telecommunications, these ancillary services to the wireline system like cellular, paging, and voice messaging. I asked him to head up our business group and take it in the direction and build it to the success we know it can be."[243]

Clarke convinced David to leave LDDS, convinced Century directors to elect him Senior Vice President in charge of Corporate Marketing, and quickly promoted him to president of the Business Group. David single-handedly took on the responsibility of Century's push into cellular communications,

---

[243] Clarke McRae Williams, Jr., Century Telephone in-house television production, Oct. 1987.

paging, voice messaging, and what Clarke Junior called "the interconnectivity side of the house."

> Earl Hogan, David's father: "When David came back to Monroe and put Century Telephone's cellular business online, he developed that from zero and put all those people on it from ground zero. But he had in mind to do something on his own. Later, he found some partners in Chapel Hill, went to Atlanta to establish a company, and their business was to take cellular businesses from a [startup] franchise, magnify the value, and, five years later, he would benefit by what he did for that company."[244]

Before David Hogan made those intentions known, Clarke Junior threw him into the mix of analysts meetings to explain cellular. For the first time, the team went to Europe where they offered 600,000 shares in private placement to investors in London, Edinburgh, Paris, and Geneva. They came back with $8.4 million.

Clarke Junior found he could be as persuasive as his father but in a different way. Shy Clarke Senior believed in the soft sell. Clarke Junior enjoyed the spotlight, warmed up to analysts with jokes and colloquialisms, and made usually dull meetings into fun events. Consequently, analysts enjoyed the folks from Louisiana and, looking at their impressive numbers, Century's stock prices ticked higher. Clarke Junior installed a jukebox in his office and as soon as the bell on the New York Stock Exchange rang at the close of trading at 3:00 p.m. Central Time, if Century's stock ended *up*, the jukebox blared. Everybody in the Riverside office heard Clarke as he turned many Fridays quite festive. If nothing happened at 3:00, they knew Clarke Junior was on the phone trying to determine why Century stock closed *down*.

---

[244] Earl Hogan interview, Sept. 25, 2012, Oak Ridge, Louisiana.

With both convinced cellular was the new key, David and Clarke Junior quickly filed for cellular licenses in every conceivable market in which Century Telephone Enterprises operated.

> David E. Hogan: "The operating strategy for the business group is twofold. First, in markets where we have a cellular franchise, we will be offering cellular and paging and voice messaging in flexible combinations to our customers. There are certain other very attractive cellular markets where we do not have the franchise where we intend to offer paging and voice messaging."[245]

For two years, David negotiated fractions, portions, partnerships, buyouts, and full licenses in every area Century could get into. As towers and transmitters began going up across the country, many winners of cellular licenses welcomed Century's cash in forging partnerships. The entire cellular system required building all at once, a massively expensive proposition for the players. Rather than winner-take-all in a lottery, the government now favored competitors joining together to share not only the single licenses in each market, but also all costs, risks, and profits. The new technology was no place for the inexperienced.

Many companies such as Allied Telephone in Little Rock sought out Century. Century, AllTel, and Perco Telephone of Perryville, Arkansas, hammered out a partnership in Arkansas in which AllTel controlled the market with 51 percent, Century came in with 29 percent, and Perco with 20 percent. The alliance scared off General Telephone and Southwestern Bell.

> Clarke Williams, Jr.: "After the lottery, we were scattered in twelve states. After [David's] long negotiating nightmare, we ended up unbelievably well. Of 22 metropolitan statistical areas, we've

---

[245] David Hogan, Century Telephone in-house television production, Oct. 1987.

got 13 [as of fall 1987] and pieces of four more."[246]

Clarke Junior had to begin selling off pieces of Century to fund the company's cellular explosion. He eyed the cable TV franchises his father began buying in 1968, which Century had to divest in 1973 when the government changed the rules, then reinvest in 1982 when Congress changed its mind yet again. By fall of 1987, Century Cablevision served 17,000 customers in six states, but while the division turned sizable revenues, "our cablevision properties are showing book losses," Clarke Senior told analysts. "They are not losing cash, but they are not meeting the full cost of depreciation...indicating there would be no contribution to earnings from cable for the next few years."[247]

> Clarke Williams, Jr.: "We started looking at cellular and decided to sell our cable holdings. We put them up for sale in December 1986. We had $12.5 million invested in it. I told the board if we got a $17 million bid, we should take it. The high bid to my surprise was $22 million. That makes 1987 a hit year."[248]

Clarke Senior pulled his son aside. While convinced Century was on the right track and astounded at early successes, the elder Williams feared Century was becoming a runaway train. Clarke Senior was still CEO and Chairman of the Board and knew analysts continually scrutinized the company. What concerned him were not just the tremendous startup costs for cell towers and transmitters, but also the years of lag time for the consumer. People had taken years to warm up to using telephones in the first place. Infrastructure build-out for cellular

---

[246] Clarke McRae Williams, Jr, "Century Telephone: Doing things it didn't think possible," *Telephone News*, Oct. 5, 1987.

[247] Clarke Williams, Sr., *The Wall Street Transcript*, Dec. 29, 1986, pp. 84,118.

[248] Clarke McRae Williams, Jr, "Century Telephone: Doing things it didn't think possible," *Telephone News*, Oct. 5, 1987.

systems might have to happen all at once, but acceptance would never be that quick.

At the dawn of the cellular age, mobile phones cost between $1,300 and $2,000 each, plus installation. Flat monthly access fees hovered around $40, but each call averaged 40 cents a minute, with nighttime rates at 24 cents a minute. "Roaming charges" entered the vernacular and piled up when a mobile phone ventured out of its home area. The steep charges kept many sidelined, waiting for prices to fall. That was the lag, Clarke Senior explained, and in that gap, losses assuredly would pile up. He began hedging with analysts, explaining in industry trade publications:

> Clarke McRae Williams: *We are zealously guarding our cellular rights...to protect our wireline service areas from being diluted by the rapidly growing cellular companies. We think in the future the most profitable business will probably be in the cellular, paging, and voice-messaging segment of the industry. But they will all be dependent on the health of the business community. We have to undergo some losses in the start-up of cellular, but it is our belief that the future is so dynamic in cellular that losses incurred will be rewarded by good earnings in the future.*[249]

On Sunday November 1, 1987, Century entered the world of cellular. With the flip of a switch, cellular service and paging systems began in Monroe with 135 clients. The rollout went so smoothly that only two weeks later, Century Cellunet-Telesystems went online nationwide. As if to remind engineers that technology was not infallible, three days later, on the Sunday before Thanksgiving, a toll switch serving Century's highest concentration of customers in La Crosse, Wisconsin, short-circuited, knocking out long distance service to 23 cities

---

[249] Clarke Williams, Sr., *The Wall Street Transcript*, Dec. 29, 1986, p. 84,118.

in western Wisconsin for nine hours. Frantic students in three area colleges couldn't complete Thanksgiving travel plans. On top of Century's embarrassment, just then another Louisiana enterprise announced it was coming to La Crosse. The New Orleans Saints announced that spring training would start in La Crosse in two months.

Next, a nightmare, even more far-reaching, reared its head, first in accounting, then in the boardroom. Glen Post and the financial team identified patterns of share purchases that showed Century was being targeted by newly-identified *corporate raiders*. New York financier Carl Icahn had successfully conducted a hostile takeover of Trans World Airlines, then stripped away TWA's assets to repay the loan. Thousands of employees lost their jobs. TWA eventually disappeared, while Icahn became very wealthy. In Texas, oilman T. Boone Pickens criticized the management of Gulf Oil Corporation, initiated bidding for a hostile takeover, and failed only when Chevron offered a $13 billion "white knight buyout" of Gulf Oil. Executives worldwide were shocked at the sudden power of wealthy individuals to smash large corporations. Clarke Senior told Wall Street that while Century would never attempt a takeover, he was pulling back from the equity markets.

> Clarke McRae Williams: "While we are interested in telephone acquisitions that are mutually beneficial to both acquired and acquirer, I hasten to add we are not interested in any hostile acquisitions. We expect to meet approximately 85 percent of our budget requirements with internally generated funds. At this time we see little reason for us to go to the market for capital."[250]

Century's financial strength and successful expansion into cellular had drawn the attention of New York millionaire

---

[250] Clarke Williams, Sr., *The Wall Street Transcript*, Dec. 29, 1986, p. 84,118.

investor Mario Gabelli, who specialized in stocks of telecommunications and media and had been admiring Century's steady growth. By the time Post confirmed Gabelli's pattern of stock purchases, the Wall Street wizard had accumulated 14 percent of Century's outstanding shares, far above what Clarke Senior controlled of his own company. An apparent corporate raid was on.

> James Kilpatrick, national columnist: "It is small wonder that financial analyst Mario Gabelli, writing in Barron's, has warm things to say about [independent phone companies expanding on government-backed Rural Electric Association low-interest loans]. He highly recommends Century Telephone Enterprises, and for good reason. Century is certainly enterprising. Over the years, 23 Century affiliates have borrowed $127 million from taxpayers. They still owe $68.6 million."[251]

Despite columnist Kilpatrick's critical view of an R.E.A. program that enabled high-quality communications to remote customers, Gabelli was going public in a rapidly authoritative way. Glen Post, Clarke, Harvey, and Clarke Junior studied how other companies fended off raiders, zeroing in on jam-maker Smucker's in Ohio, a state of stringent anti-takeover laws. Many companies loaded up on massive debt to create a so-called "poison pill," but Clarke Senior resisted that. He had just attained some security after forty years of living with debt. The trio of investment banker George Stephenson, company attorney Virginia Boulet, and specialist counsel Andy Correro of the Jones Walker law firm in New Orleans came up with an ingenious solution. The board would change the voting structure of equity holders from one vote per share to ten votes per "super voting share" for each shareholder of record prior to May 1987. Gabelli had bought most of his shares after 1987.

---

[251] James Kilpatrick, "Lending a hand to poor little phone companies," *Monroe News-Star*, Feb. 4, 1991, p. B1.

Glen Post: "We put the ten vote shares in place because we knew our stock was undervalued (we were in the process of gaining cellular franchises and building out networks) and wanted to help ensure that a short term investor could not accumulate shares and buy the company below our real value. We knew we were a potential target. Mario Gabelli and [investor] Fred Moran began accumulating shares and together owned about 18 percent, but they had not yet held the shares long enough to gain the ten votes. It was at this point that we decided to freeze the ten-vote shares for everyone who had them on that date, but not allow any other investor to gain the super voting rights going forward."[252]

Stewart Ewing: "The ten votes per share was patterned after Smucker's. We were concerned we might have losses from developing wireless. Fortunately, telephone operations performed better than expected and wireless customer acceptance was faster than expected so we never experienced a net consolidated loss. We froze the shares because the stock price increased over a period of years such that the market incorporated the value of our wireless business in the stock price, plus the complexity of tracking the ten-vote shares was difficult and led to possible disputes, such as with Gabelli."[253]

When the board decided to freeze the ten-votes-per-share rule and then abandon the program as Gabelli's shares

---

[252] Glen Post email to Harvey Perry et al, April 13, 2014, forwarded to author.
[253] Stewart Ewing email to Glen Post et al, April 14, 2014, forwarded to author.

approached eligibility, the Wall Street wizard filed a lawsuit charging illegal changes in Century's corporate governance equity rules. A federal judge found that the only shareholder affected was Gabelli and that Gabelli brought on the change himself for attempting a raid. The lawsuit was thrown out.

Long before the Gabelli attempt, Clarke, Clarke Junior, and the board had instituted a liberal Employee Stock Ownership Plan that offered company ownership and better retirement options to those who actually built the company with their own hands. By adopting the ten-for-one rule and grandfathering in ESOP super-voting shares, they permanently concentrated 40 percent of the voting power with employees. To Clarke, ESOP confirmed again that giving always won. He had instituted the ESOP program not for tax purposes but because he genuinely believed that workers climbing poles, stringing wire, helping customers, answering calls, and selling technology had as much to do with building the company as those at headquarters. Now they served as a shield against opportunists.

> Virginia Boulet: "Mr. Williams was not like many other telephone entrepreneurs who tended to hold onto their equity or voting control at all costs. He used the equity of the company to grow it and to reward his management and employees. So, he personally had less voting control over the company than his peers at other companies had. His focus was always on long-term growth of the company, and time-phased voting was crafted just to accomplish that goal. Those were the days of coercive two-tiered takeovers and a get-rich-quick mentality that ruined companies in their path. Changing to time-phased voting was reasonable at the time and fair to all. Over time, with more shareholder protections in laws and SEC regulations, and difficulty interpreting 'beneficial ownership' provisions as fund managers accumulated shares for ever-changing pecuniary interest holders, we

froze and then eliminated time-phased voting."[254]

As lucrative as the board made Century's stock to employees, securities were not an easy sell. Employees well remembered Monday, October 19, 1987, when world stock markets fell like dominoes. With American exchanges last in the 24-hour day, the dominoes fell westward, plummeting the Dow Jones Industrial Average 508 points to 1,738.74, a record 22.61 percent drop. By 1991, investors were barely creeping back into the market. The bulk of Century's investors had stayed because the two Clarkes had convinced analysts of Century's good governance, solid earnings, and remarkable expansion into cellular.

Sharing that belief in the coming cellular boom was David Hogan. He had quietly been assembling a group of cellular and investor friends with whom he could partner to branch out on his own when the time came. Clarke Junior began detecting a distance. After two years of hard work breaking Century into cellular, David felt he was capable of running more than one segment of operations. He wanted to oversee all operations.

> Harvey Perry: "David brought skill sets to CenturyTel that we did not have. He had a background with IBM and paging that qualified him to start our cellular business from the ground up. He also brought in new people that had skill sets we did not have. I think David wanted total responsibility for all operations, Telco, Cellular, and paging. It reached the point that it became more difficult for all of us to work together."[255]

Clarke offered David a better combination of salary and stock, but David yearned to be chief operating officer. Clarke

---

[254] Virginia Boulet email to Stewart Ewing et al, April 14, 2014, forwarded to author.
[255] Harvey Perry email corrections, April 16, 2014, to author.

Junior faced a dilemma, caught between a very talented boyhood friend and Glen Post, who had been learning all operations side-by-side with both Clarkes for ten years.

> Glen Post: "Clarke, Mr. Williams, and the Board appointed me chief operating officer. David, of course, did not like this decision. About a year or so afterwards, after much discussion, Clarke Junior and I decided that due to the disruption David was causing with our management team and some of our business partners, David had to be let go and Mr. Williams agreed. Clarke and I met with David in Clarke's office and Clarke did most of the talking when we told him. I remember Clarke telling David, 'This is tearing my guts out' to do this."[256]

> Bruce Hanks: "I know when Clarke brought David in, he was needed. But when David left, it was painful. Mr. Williams' best friends were the Hogans. I have to say David was Clarke Junior's one best friend, too."[257]

Clarke had considered David a brother. Clarke Senior put a hand on his son's shoulder without saying a word. Now betrayal had happened to both of them, the loss of friendship in the course of business. As David drove away, Clarke Junior felt part of himself leaving, but he allowed no room for sentimental attachment, not when so many minds together agreed that Glen Post had studied and earned his position. David's drive and ambition had been good for the company, but his personal timetable and that of the company never lined up.

Like his father, Clarke had trained himself to shake off disappointment by moving on quickly. He had seen his father

---

[256] Glen Post corrections in email to Harvey Perry, June 28, 2014, forwarded to author.

[257] Bruce Hanks interview, CenturyLink headquarters, Feb. 5, 2013, Monroe, Louisiana.

survive great loss and still emerge stalwart and secure in his faith. Clarke Junior thanked God for sending him to such a father.

Christmas 1987 ushered in headlines across the nation, *"You can soon call from your car."* At over $1,000 per unit, companies blazed the way into cellular by taking car phones from novelty to necessity for executives and key employees. As cellular use doubled and doubled again, prices fell swiftly and private ownership exploded. For Century, revenues began shifting from landlines to towers. Partnership agreements allowed each cellular company to bill roaming charges as customers from other areas drove through. Clarke Junior recognized that just as long distance charges had been the cream of his parents' company, roaming charges would be his. As Century built hundreds of miles of cell towers along interstate corridors, roaming charges created a river of revenue, erasing construction costs in no time. Profitability soared. By early 1989, Century stock tripled from a 1987 Crash low of $12 per share to $36.

While the cellular build-out pushed the company into the red, third quarter results sprang from $589,000 in 1987 to $2.8 million in 1988. From 1987 to 1988, cellular and paging revenues in the first nine months jumped 407 percent from $1.4 million to $7.2 million. Century stock emerged as a darling of Wall Street.

> Bob Fudickar, Investor Relations: "Clarke Williams Junior was thought of on Wall Street as an absolute visionary for the telecommunications industry as a whole. His prowess and charisma on Wall Street was extraordinary. He drew a crowd not only to hear his Southern dialect but to hear his unique approach of describing Century as a unique telecommunications entity."[258]

---

[258] Bob Fudickar quote in *The Centuryan*, Special CWJr Retirement Edition, 1990.

The Clarkes' road show trips talking to analysts and investors around the country had paid off. As stock ticker symbol CTL soared, the board of directors approved a three-for-two stock split in July 1988 and a second three-for-two the following February. The January 1989 edition of *Telephone News* ranked Century Number One in the telephone industry for shareholder return on investment, an enviable 132 percent return in 1988 alone. By the end of 1989, Century's market capitalization would grow to more than one billion dollars, fueling one of the fastest infrastructure expansions in history.

> Clarke Williams, Jr., 1989 Annual Report: "At the end of 1988, there were about 2 million cellular users in the U. S. Some analysts predict that that number could climb to as many as 10 million by 1993. We are positioned as a long-term player in this exciting industry. The results of our strategy are becoming clearer. Truly successful companies build their business on basic principles of conduct that shape their interactions with their various constituencies. We've always had such principles. The vision of our Chairman and Founder Clarke M. Williams was to establish and build a company that operated on a simple yet very powerful foundation—the Golden Rule. Century has operated upon that practice and I believe our success is directly related to our principles."[259]

Clarke Junior and Century were on a roll, expanding quicker than billing could keep up. Even though they had built an identical building alongside Century's headquarters in the old Atkins Mansion on Riverside Drive in Monroe, those offices overlooking the Ouachita River had filled fast. They rented and bought three other buildings scattered across the city. And for the very first time, the Clarkes began entertaining calls from

---

[259] President's Message, 1989 Century Telephone Annual Report.

chambers of commerce in other states asking if Century Telephone would consider headquartering in their cities. Dallas, Little Rock, Atlanta, Memphis, and others came calling.

In 1989, Clarke McRae Williams Senior determined the time had come to turn over full control of Century to his son. The board elected Clarke McRae Williams, Jr., Chief Executive Officer and president. Clarke Senior retained chairmanship of the board. His long dream had finally come true.

> Glen Post: "Clarke Junior had a lot of talent, a lot of ability; he was very smart, but this was not the only thing he wanted to do. He wanted to be out hunting, fishing, and golfing, and lots of other things. He did a lot and he also worked a lot. Clarke Junior was great at delegating and he let me do my job whether it was CFO or COO. He was very good about that. I kept him informed and kept Mr. Williams informed. We all had great relationships. I didn't have any problem with Clarke Junior and he and Mr. Williams got along pretty well. They had some times when they'd do a little head-butting, but Clarke Junior had great respect for his dad. He recognized what he had done."[260]

> Clarke McRae Williams: "The most important accomplishment Clarke made for Century was developing an excellent management team, one that is now recognized by financial analysts throughout the United States as one of the strongest management groups in the telecommunications industry. One of the highly important factors in Century's rise in the stock market was his development of cellular. He did something I think no other telephone company had done. He started a cellular group by bringing

---

[260] Glen Post interview, Sept. 25, 2012, Monroe, Louisiana.

new blood into Century, new sales and marketing
people. That was a rather innovative approach
while most other companies tried to make
cellular fit into their existing structure. Clarke
had the foresight to know that cellular required a
new approach."[261]

With the next generation coming to power, both Clarkes
determined they needed a new consolidated headquarters within
driving distance of Oak Ridge. They shared a favorite place
they'd driven past for years on U.S. Highway 165 north of
Monroe, a pecan orchard on Fish Hatchery Road fronting an
installation of the Louisiana Department of Wildlife and
Fisheries. On the backside was pastoral Bayou Desiard.

Like a park facing the highway, the 26-acre mature pecan
orchard greened up every spring into a vision of serenity and
strength. Father and son envisioned a magnificent headquarters
building crowning the ready-made park. With board approval,
the two Clarkes bought the land and began calculating the size
and cost of a building large enough to consolidate all their
offices and also allow for growth. When outrageous bids came
in, Clarke Senior balked. Suddenly, those offers from Dallas
and Little Rock began looking very good. Aggressive
departments of economic development were offering tax
incentives that covered a major chunk of construction.

"The last thing I want to do is leave Monroe," Clarke Junior
told reporters, "I'm obviously happy here or I wouldn't be here.
But things could be much better. Having Monroe and West
Monroe side-by-side creates waste and duplication. You have
two governments, two mayors, two councils, and two school
boards. When you've got that much duplication, it's hard to get
anything accomplished."[262] Within days, he was criticized for
the comment, a letter writer construing that he favored degrading
the parish school system by consolidating with Monroe's
blighted inner city school system. Louisiana Governor Buddy

---

[261] *The Centuryan*, Special Clarke Williams Jr. Retirement Edition, 1990.
[262] "Century may build new headquarters," *Monroe News-Star*, June 3,
1989.

Roemer swooped in to stem any talk of the company's leaving Louisiana, and for a while, Clarke Junior basked in the attention.

Just at the pinnacle of success, however, popping champagne brought Clarke Junior less joy as summer 1989 progressed. His pride in seeing mobile antennas sprouting from cars and trucks was checked by pressure he felt in his chest as if he couldn't breathe. He wondered about the radiation doctors used on his chest in 1980 to stop his Hodgkin's Disease. He coughed incessantly, preferring to think his problem was bronchitis or sinus drainage, but he admitted he felt an overall weakening. Then, as headaches developed, he hoped he was not developing migraines. Eventually, his hands and arms went numb. He gained substantial weight.

> Carolyn Williams Perry: "He just did not want to take care of himself. Daddy kept saying, 'Son, you've got to lose weight and you need to exercise.' He said that because Clarke had started having problems with his lungs because that's where they radiated so much of his cancer, there behind his breastbone. Doctors said his lungs were coated with a hardened substance that made it extremely hard for him to breathe. Then he would get overweight. This went on for about five years of him just not taking care of himself and Daddy preaching to him. It was hard. I think Daddy knew, especially when the doctors told Clarke, 'If you don't stop and improve your lifestyle, you're not going to be here in five years.' Clarke Junior would go to the hospital, they would drain fluid off his lungs, and he would be right back, going wide open."[263]

On Monday, September 25, 1989, Clarke Junior's doctor checked him into St. Francis Medical Center, where specialists

---

[263] Carolyn Williams Perry interview, Sept. 15, 2012, Baton Rouge, Louisiana.

determined that the heavy doses of radiation to his chest in 1980 had destroyed the Hodgkin's but severely burned arteries in the process. Scar tissue had been forming ever since, particularly in the arteries of his neck and shoulders. He would require extensive arterial bypass surgery immediately, targeting the carotid artery leading to his brain.

Early Thursday morning September 28, Clarke Junior was wheeled into an operating room full of green-clad surgeons and white-clad nurses. Hours were gone in a second, and nurses wheeled him into Intensive Care where they hooked him up to all manner of electronics and tubes. Clarke felt something go seriously wrong, and as he could still string two thoughts together, he realized that his right side was numb, much worse than the numbness that had forced him to the hospital. As he struggled into consciousness from anesthesia and pain killers, he felt ominously that snapping back this time would not be as easy as before. He wanted to hurry up and get back to work. He knew his father sat in his chair, and he hoped the older man didn't fiddle much with either his desk or his projects. Clarke Junior then realized he couldn't even speak.

Doctors reluctantly explained to him that during surgery a clot had formed, broken off, and lodged in his brain, shutting off blood to that section. While on the operating table, Clarke had experienced a full-blown stroke. The new clot-dissolving drugs the doctors administered essentially saved his life. Clarke Junior had a chance, though slim, of regaining the function of his right hand and foot.

Feeling gradually flowed back into his body, except for his right side. His speech slurred, but he was alert and back on the mend. As soon as he was moved from critical condition to serious, visitors began lining up. Glen Post came in and told him he had been praying for him, and with a mind still sharp, Clarke began asking about the status of projects.

Outside, Glen told reporters, "He is doing much better. He is able to move all limbs, but he does have a slight impairment of his right arm and leg. The doctors say the stroke caused no mental impairment. In fact, I discussed business issues with him today, and he is looking forward to returning to the office in a few weeks."[264]

But weeks dragged into months as Clarke Junior desperately tried to rush his rehabilitation. The use of his right side refused to come back. Knowing that the swift train he had set in motion at Century was zooming away without him, he sank into depression. Cancer, radiation and stroke was the thanks he got for serving his country.

> Marta Cole, Clarke Williams' administrative assistant: "When Clarke Junior was in the hospital after his stroke, Mr. Williams was so worried and concerned about his son. He would stay at the hospital and he would come to the office, bring in his clothes, shower, and then he would leave at lunch and go back to the hospital. I mean, that was really taking a toll on him for a while. It was a very sad time and it was a very sad time around the office, too."[265]

At the office, glitches hit Century's cellular projects, paging startups, and voice messaging activations across the country. Clarke Senior, at 67 years old, admittedly a relic, reclaimed the helm of a much larger, faster, and more sophisticated ship. Most reference points he had known were no longer there, Clarke Junior having shifted everything in six years. Century was now a true technological telecommunications giant running at full gallop, just as Clarke Junior liked it. His father and founder did not relish climbing back up the learning curve, a very steep one, and he prayed hourly that God would restore his son's health. Considering his prayer selfish, he added, "Nevertheless, Your will, Lord, not mine." He prayed for strength. Luckily, Clarke Junior's young team surrounded the father.

---

[264] "Century's CEO in serious condition," *Monroe News-Star*, Sept. 30, 1989, p.1.
[265] Marta Cole interview, Oct. 18, 2012, Dallas, Texas.

The board approved one of Clarke Junior's projects and bought large Universal Telephone for $90 million. After months of rehab through Christmas and New Years, Clarke Junior could still visit the office for only short periods, dragging his right foot yet insisting he would soon be back. His doctors told Clarke Senior a different story.

In a few short weeks, everything had changed. The father's ideal world for Century Telephone—his taking the breather for which he had worked so hard for so long, and then, with pride and gratitude, his turning over the reins to his son—that ideal world was suddenly, heartbreakingly gone. "The Lord giveth and the Lord taketh away," he whispered from Job's lament in the Old Testament, "Blessed be the name of the Lord."

He intended to go forward no matter what, with the same guidance and loving Hand from those long days and years when he had groped along in the darkness. He kept Glen Post, Carolyn, Harvey, Annette, and his administrative assistant Marta Cole close to him, talking out his feelings, talking out the scenarios, mostly unpleasant, now that it appeared Clarke Junior would never again be the man he had been.

> Bob Fudickar, CTL Investor Relations: "Clarke Junior went through several rehabs, and the rehabs and Clarke didn't sit well. The mindset wasn't there; he wasn't ready. He went from being so active to being pretty debilitated. So he was really discouraged."[266]

> Carolyn Williams Perry: "Clarke Junior tried to come back. The stroke affected his right side and he could not write. It affected his speech, and he tried to hang with it for about a year, but everyone realized he just had to hang it up."[267]

---

[266] Bob Fudickar telephone interview, March 8, 2014.
[267] Carolyn Williams Perry interview, Sept. 15, 2012, Baton Rouge, Louisiana.

Glen Post: "Everything went back to Mr. Williams' faith. He would say, 'I'm going to get through this. God's going to take care of this.' He didn't say it in those words, but I knew it and he knew it. What hurt him more than anything was that Clarke Junior's personality changed after he had the stroke. The doctors told him it would, that Clarke Junior would be very positive and then fall to the other extreme. Everything bad would come out. Clarke had always been confrontational if he needed to be. He had this Type A personality so his frustrations at being sick and not being involved in the company and trying to figure out all that, those frustrations came out. And a lot of it was targeted toward Mr. Williams. That was harder on Mr. Williams than probably the sickness itself. What killed him was that Clarke Junior changed so much and was so frustrated, even frustrated toward his dad. That really hurt him. And bothered me. It was hard for me to see both go through that."[268]

Clarke McRae Williams now faced the toughest dilemma of his life. How would he break the news to his son that his days at the family business were over? How could he so cruelly add insult to such tragic injury? He could barely bring himself to imagine it. The temptation of many was to ask God *Why, why, why* take a faithful servant this high just to drop him? He saw that question in many sad eyes around him, the need to blame someone for such injustice. But Clarke knew better. As Paul wrote, "Now we see through a glass darkly, but then we will know."[269]

Glen Post: "Mr. Williams never questioned God's hand in anything that happened. He was

---

[268] Glen Post interview, Aug. 14, 2013, Monroe, Louisiana.
[269] 1 Corinthians 13:12

always thankful, accepting that that's just the way things work out sometimes. It was not God's fault in his view."[270]

He needed all the faith, resolve, and prayer he could muster for that day in 1990 when he sat down with his handicapped son in his son's now-former office. Clarke Junior, sullen and sickly, not a little angry at the world, knew what his father was going to say. Both knew the decision could be delayed no longer, even as Clarke Junior held out all hope that rehab would eventually restore him. Both realized that the race for Century's competitors had never stopped. But Century's projects in large degree were on hold. In many ways, the whole ship was drifting. Clarke Senior told his son what his son already knew, that Century had to move on and that, well, he needed him to take disability retirement as president and CEO.

Clarke Junior exploded.

Erupting like a volcano, he hurled forth every venomous thought on his mind. In cruel accusations, months of pent up anger and frustration blazed forth toward the father he loved and would always love, but bitterness took hold and formed terrible words. What exactly was said would die with both men— perhaps begging for more chances, perhaps culpability for the death penalty of Vietnam, perhaps about their widely divergent beliefs on things eternal—whatever Clarke Junior shouted in anger, Marta Cole outside in her office heard through solid "soundproof" doors. When the tide swelled and receded and silence at last prevailed, the door opened abruptly and Clarke Junior came hobbling out, red-faced, angry, and hurt, and he swept out the door. That day was the last anyone would see Clarke Junior at Century Telephone.

Marta peeked in to see if Mr. Williams was all right. The founder looked as though he had aged ten years in a matter of seconds, standing silent for a long time, peering out the window, white, shaken. He was watching Clarke Junior and his dream drive away. Clarke Junior kept driving all the way out to his

---

[270] Glen Post interview, Sept. 25, 2012, Monroe, Louisiana.

hunting ranch near Dallas, Texas. For a while, he did not answer his portable phone, the very device he had helped pioneer. Clarke Senior asked his son-in-law, Harvey Perry, and Century attorney Virginia Boulet to fly out. The company had to continue and everybody had to move on.

> Virginia Boulet: "Mr. Williams said, 'It's clear to me now that, despite the way I would like life to happen, I'm going to have to step back into the company because Clarke needs time with his family. He's got a very short time left on this Earth and he needs to spend that with his family and getting things right with them. So would you go out to his ranch and tell him?' I said, 'You don't want to tell him?' He said, 'You know, my biggest weakness is that if he says to me, 'No, I want to stay,' I wonder if I'll have the strength to tell him 'no,' particularly at this point in his life. I love him so much. But for the sake of the company, he's got to go.' When Harvey and I got there, Clarke Junior looked up at us and said, 'My daddy sent you, didn't he? I need to resign, don't I?' So we hammered out the terms of his resignation and severance. He never objected."[271]

The abrupt turnabout rippled throughout the industry. *Forbes* magazine called to inquire of Clarke Junior's stroke. "It's been a great disappointment," Clarke Senior told the reporter. What business writers and Wall Street really wanted to know was whether Century was for sale, since the elder Williams had already retired once. Wrote *Forbes*:

> *Century has outperformed every other telephone stock in the eight years since the AT&T divestiture, a better than 600% return. It earned*

---

[271] Glen Post interview, Sept. 25, 2012, Monroe, Louisiana.

$37 million, $1.20 per share, on revenues of $280 million in 1991. Analysts are predicting $1.40 for this year.

Williams has traveled to nearly every Century office in the last two months, giving employees his vision of the future. "I want them to know that we are in this for the long haul," he says. "That we are still in growth mode." As tempting a takeover prize as Century might seem (the stock jumped 10% after Centel announced it was for sale), Williams' message is clear: Forget it.[272]

The word was out. Rough waters lay ahead for Clarke Junior's company, and he couldn't stand not being part of it. He began traveling, whiling away weeks at a time with like-minded friends, including his cousin Philip Williams, Bob Fudickar, and Mac Oliver. Sometimes he would take his young son Trey. The men bounced between Clarke's Texas ranch, the Somerset Hunting Club near Newellton, Louisiana, and Clarke Junior's beloved Mexico. He had always had an affinity for its rustic, unruffled, primitive way of life with no clocks, and the feeling that John Wayne might ride up any moment in a cloud of dust. John Wayne, to Clarke and many others, symbolized a man's freedom.

> Philip Williams, cousin: "I never thought much past Saturday night most of my life, but Clarke was a visionary even when we were kids, telling us what he was going to do. I never paid any attention to him, but later those things came true. He could see trends coming when I didn't know what a trend was. He was a very super-intelligent guy and was born to do what he did. He did get bitter when the stroke threw him. He went from being a great speaker to not being able to talk at

---

[272] Christopher Palmeri, "Minding its own business," *Forbes*, Feb. 17, 1992, p.110

all and could barely move. I had to cut up his meat for him and carry his medical supplies everywhere we went. He told me a couple of times, 'I know I'll never see 50.'"[273]

He may have been born to take Century higher, but now he experienced a reversal in fortunes. After years of stressful, hard work that took another toll on his body, Clarke Junior wanted no more complications. If he were to be robbed of a normal, full life, he would fill every minute with what he wanted to do, no holds barred. He wrote his last letter to the employees of Century Telephone.

> *Probably the hardest thing we have to do in life is say goodbye to people we deeply care about. So I am not going to say goodbye, I'm just going to say, 'I'll be seeing you.' For me to say goodbye to the Century Family would be, for me, a fate much worse than death; therefore, I'll leave it in the expectant tense.*
>
> *The decision I made to retire was the most difficult and excruciatingly painful one I ever had to make. The stroke left me with enough impairment that I knew I could not return to the job as the same man I was before. Anything less than 100 percent for me is not satisfactory. My philosophy has always been to try to stay a step ahead of the norm, to cultivate a uniqueness in my approach to life and business.*
>
> *I will desperately miss the informal interaction with you and pray that will continue from those who stepped into my place. I take satisfaction in the fact that it requires three good men to occupy the former position I held.*
>
> *I have loved every minute of my life at Century. There is no greater organization in the*

---

[273] Philip Williams interview, March 7, 2013, Baton Rouge, Louisiana.

world because of the Century "Family." We have all played our part in making Century an enviable industry leader. I'll be in touch with a stock report and tell you 'what I know when I know it.' I'll bum a ride on the airplane when it leaves to go around the country so I may see my many friends as often as possible. Until then, I love each of you and may God's richest blessings be upon you all.[274]

The touching letter resonated with employees to the farthest reaches and especially to his father. But as the patient flitted about the country trying to escape his fate, Clarke Senior grievously lamented his son's apparent "beat-the-clock" self-destructiveness. Clarke Senior understood the behavior, but it added to the stress of running the company. Clarke Junior, in his view, had gone from skillfully leading a major corporation to reverting to the rebel teenager who'd given him and Mary Kathryn fits. Now, his condition serious, his actions were reckless and selfish. He cavalierly discarded even his doctors' advice.

On the hot summer day of June 20, 1991, in a turn of events as cruel as the Hodgkin's he got for serving his country, Clarke Junior was robbed of his rightful place in turning the first silver shovel to break ground in the pecan orchard. He was nowhere around as dignitaries showed up. Century's three-story, state-of-the-art, 160,000 square-foot headquarters would rise there and everyone knew that, even though he and his father had designed the building together, Clarke Junior had been the one to make it happen. Now he was far away, except in spirit.

On site, Clarke Senior, Monroe Mayor Bob Powell, State Representative and former Congressman Jerry Huckaby, financiers, and other dignitaries chipped at the hard packed dirt with silver shovels as if breaking concrete. The blistering sun, cut only by checkerboard shadows amid the pecan trees, seared and hastened the event. Clarke Senior thanked everyone,

---

[274] Clarke Williams, Jr., final letter, *The Centuryan* Special Edition, 1990

thanked employees, and thanked his absent son. Sympathetic faces looked back at him. Handshakes, backslaps, and pictures, and the crowd soon vanished so that all Clarke could hear was the wind rippling across the ryegrass and through the pecans. Behind him in the field that led to the bayou he could see the building rise up, still a dream but real for him. He wished Clarke Junior had been there.

Back at the Riverside headquarters, Clarke Senior regained a sense of his own company while moving forward with Clarke Junior's plans. The board looked at the founder with compassionate eyes, acknowledging that in many ways he had been a father to all of them and to employees. He had brought them all together and enriched their lives in every possible way. It seemed cruel and unfair that he should be father to so many but lose his own son. Though Clarke knew that the turn of events was indeed a travesty, he let each know without uttering a word that dwelling on the unfairness in life was a complete waste of energy.

Besides, God had provided. With no hesitation, after watching the bookish young man grow as close as another son, Clarke recommended that 38-year-old Glen Post replace Clarke Junior as President, in addition to continuing as Chief Operating Officer. The directors heartily agreed. If ever a duplicate of Clarke Williams Senior existed, it was humble and intelligent Glen Post. Kind, thoughtful, reserved, and compassionate with regard to employees, Glen had a great vision and knew the numbers intimately. Appropriately nervous, he stood before them, blinking behind large-rimmed glasses, acknowledging deep gratitude but most thankful that Mr. Williams was still there as a guide.

Glen needed that rock. Despite tremendous pressure, Clarke Senior had never waivered. Mr. Williams felt, knew in his heart, and could see in his mind that his faith was built on bedrock principles. Throughout his life, his resolve grew stronger, to the point that no matter how fierce the storm, he knew he would weather it and be standing come daybreak. He had built his house not on shifting sand but on solid rock, and on that rock stood Century Telephone. The world couldn't get enough drama with its continual strife and turmoil. But his anchor stayed in front of him right there on the desk, an old worn-out Bible he used not as a paperweight but as a guide to know the world, a gift greater than a crystal ball. Human nature in all its folly hadn't changed in 4,000 years and that made Man predictable. That's why Clarke McRae Williams chose the path less traveled. People who failed to read simply continued in their mistakes.

> Marta Cole, Clarke Williams' administrative assistant: "He was like my second daddy. Both were Godly men. Mr. Williams and I talked religion from time to time and then, after Clarke Junior had his stroke, he decided to write a little booklet. *What I Believe and Why,* he titled it. Mr. Williams worked on that little booklet for months and months and constantly he would go home, he would come back, he would have made changes. There were Bible verses in there, then there were things that he said and why he believed that Bible verse and then what he believed to back it up. He wanted to do that for his children because he wanted them to know how he felt, the way he felt. He wanted to get it right."[275]

> Carolyn Williams Perry: "To Daddy, his faith was a daily thing. It was never like, 'Sit down, I want to tell you about this.' We *talked* about it. When I was old enough to teach Sunday school, I went to him because he was so good at writing his lessons. He would get every Bible commentary and he would not let you read just a couple of verses. You had to start back at the chapter before because he felt too many verses were taken out of context. He would make you

---

[275] Marta Cole interview, Oct. 18, 2012, Dallas, Texas.

read the chapter before, the chapter afterward, and about five commentaries. I was teaching from Genesis to Revelation, and he helped me so much. And then with all he had going after he had to replace Clarke, he wrote, *Why I Believe What I Believe.* He made copies and gave one to all of us. He said, 'If you were ever in doubt as to what your daddy always believed, here it is on paper.'"[276]

Young Glen Post was writing, too. His whole adult life, he had watched from the front row as this monumental man created wealth out of few words. Now he watched even closer as Mr. Williams' world seemed to crash down around him. Through great tension and unhappiness in the office, Glen watched him emerge as steadfast and true as in happier times. There was power in that, a great deal of power, and Glen tried to put all of Mr. Williams' lessons, mostly unspoken, into words. Everybody had words of advice, but very few let their lives speak for themselves. As Glen accumulated these observations in a journal as a personal guide, he realized others could benefit as well. He would eventually publish in-house for employees and associates of Century Telephone, "The Unifying Principles."

As the situation with Clarke Junior descended, Clarke Senior retreated into the Word. He prayed fervently for his family, for his Century family, and for the company as a whole to the farthest end of the wires. He could see those linemen working as he had and he prayed for them and their families, people whose faces he likely would never see. And an encouraging answer seemed to come from above. Despite unexpected disappointments, calamities, financial near ruin, and loss of a beloved son, he realized he had lived a life with no regrets. No amount of wealth could buy that, nor could wealth

---

[276] Carolyn Williams Perry interview, Sept. 15, 2012, Baton Rouge, Louisiana.

buy it back. He had done what he was supposed to do. He had been obedient.

As Clarke wrapped his company in prayer, the rest of the Century Telephone team worked feverishly on new and exciting projects. In 1992, the board of directors agreed to buy Central Telephone Company of Ohio for a whopping $135 million. As the former Centel Corporation subsidiary served over 65,000 access lines, the acquisition grew Century by another 20 percent, zooming toward a half million customers.

Clarke recommended that the directors promote President Glen Post to Vice Chairman of the Board and from Chief Operating Officer to Chief Executive Officer, as he was doing the work anyway. Glen was now in the exact position to which Clarke Junior had risen. Clarke Senior was back as Chairman only, exactly as he had been the day of Clarke Junior's stroke three years earlier.

Meanwhile, Clarke Junior assessed his mental acuity as back in full and he wanted to come back. He desperately missed the business, still studied it, and, as a major shareholder of Century, nitpicked recent developments.

> Bob Fudickar: "We, his friends, would make him get out, got him back hunting. We'd go to the Kerrville ranch and Somerset Hunting Club near Newellton. We got him traveling, and he started getting better. He improved dramatically. His sense of humor came back. We questioned why he always sat in the back of the plane and he'd say, 'You never heard of a plane backing into a mountain!' Clarke got a lot better in his mind and felt he could be better off. His attitude improved markedly and he wanted to come back [to Century], not in active management, but he was certainly hoping to get back into an active board position. But it just wasn't to be. Some board members lobbied for him but, in the end, they

decided it best not to let him come back. And
that was tough on him."[277]

The rejection was complete at Christmas 1992 when the
grand building he and his father envisioned together was
finished in their beloved pecan orchard. Clarke Junior had
driven past the construction when he knew no one would be
there and had stood in bittersweet awe, as he knew his father,
Glen, and the board would later do. Century's home rivaled the
best corporate headquarters he'd seen from New York to Los
Angeles.

On a dazzling spring day in April 1993, with hundreds of
employees watching from the pecan grove and television news
cameras rolling videotape, Glen, Clarke Senior, and dignitaries
stood dwarfed before the pink and red granite entrance. People
marveled that the edifice was more beautiful than anyone had
imagined. From the structure's clean lines and breathtaking
atrium to every detail of design, Lincoln Builders and Island
Construction had completed a stunning work of art: Louisiana's
Taj Mahal of telecommunications. Sophisticated business
visitors would have to rethink their ideas about hick town
Monroe.

Everyone   congratulated   Mr.   Williams   on   his
accomplishment, but he waved off the praise. Blue-suited and
wearing a red and blue "Save the Children" necktie, the founder
stood up to the podium and congratulated Century's lifeblood,
its employees, for what their hard work had accomplished.
Orations over, Clarke held oversized Monroe Chamber of
Commerce scissors, slicing six-inch red and gray ribbons to
launch Century's next half-century. As the ribbons fluttered
down to applause, the face Clarke most wanted to see was not
there. Nothing was ever perfect—except the abiding love of the
Father. He felt deeply a kinship to God in a deep yearning for
his son. All the faces were there but one, smiling, clapping,
sharing the moment with him. The click of the scissors cut a

---

[277] Bob Fudickar telephone interview, March 8, 2014.

lifetime of struggle in two and began a whole new era for a whole new generation.

Employees and families trampled the ribbon into the cavernous atrium ablaze in sunlight. With employees looking down from all three floors, clicking shutters reverberated with flashes of dignitaries and the founder. "Mr. Williams!" an employee shouted down to Clarke Senior. "Did you ever think you'd have this many employees?"

The founder chuckled and replied, "I didn't think we'd ever have this many customers!"[278]

The hearty laughter of so many soothed a broken heart. Brutal fate had kept Clarke Junior from occupying the very walnut-paneled office he had designed for himself. Clarke knew his son was disheartened as the company zoomed on without him. Clarke Junior understood without wanting to that the boardroom could not contain two presidents. The directors had all been there when Clarke Junior had amazed and astonished the entire industry; now they feared his mercurial mind.

With so much going on –Clarke Junior's stroke and departure, building a dazzling new headquarters, and him, at 71, performing an encore at Century– Clarke finally could no longer ignore his growing physical weakness. Starting in March, his energy level flagged considerably, but standing at the podium during ribbon cutting ceremonies, Clarke felt an unmistakable sinking. Tests revealed chronic renal deterioration. His situation was so serious that doctors began immediately looking for a kidney donor.

As he weakened further, a university committee at Northeast Louisiana University, now University of Louisiana at Monroe, decided to bestow the university's rare and highest honor on Clarke McRae Williams. At ULM's August 1993 commencement exercises, for only the eighth time in the university's sixty-year history, scholars granted an honorary doctorate to the humble founder of Century Telephone.[279] Robed

---

[278] Recollection of John F. Jones, CenturyLink governmental relations, as told to the author.

[279] "Century chairman to receive honorary degree from NLU," *Monroe News-Star*, Aug. 12, 1993, p. A5.

and tasseled, Clarke received a standing ovation in a triumphant return for a student who had done quite well with only a two-year degree.

Clarke Junior was too weak to attend but knew he had had more to do with Century's recent success than anyone else. He was purposely slipping into the shadows, with the feeling that if his father had insisted, he could have regained a directorship on the board with renewed purpose. But Clarke Senior did not force his will on anyone, not even for his son.

As the elder's medical issues worsened, doctors launched a nationwide search for a kidney donor only to find Clarke's perfect match right under their noses. Sister Mary Lee tested positive as a match and selflessly offered to give her brother one of her kidneys as his Christmas present. The two spent their 1993 holidays recuperating from the transplant. Doctors monitored Clarke's levels until they were certain his body had accepted the organ. Slowly, energy returned and Clarke returned to his desk.

Clarke Junior drew farther distant. Inconsolable after losing all hope for a seat back on the board, his condition deteriorated except for the occasional hopeful but fleeting improvement. During one such time on the first anniversary of Century's ribbon cutting, Clarke Junior bought himself a present, a gleaming new white Chevrolet Camaro convertible. Riding in it with the top down was pure freedom. The wind, the sound of moving through fresh air, the blue sky and green forests splotched with red and pink azaleas, happy yellow daffodils and snowy dogwood, his face turned up to the warm sun, Clarke loved the garden called Earth. He breathed deeply, gasping for air and freedom, freedom he could feel ebbing away. This he must have known, for he suffered another stroke in early May 1994 that left him weaker than ever. Wife Vicki chauffeured him on their drives through the countryside.

On Wednesday, May 11, 1994, they went for a ride to visit friends, dropping by First American Bank to see old friend George Campbell, check their accounts, get some cash, and, as they had many, many times before, talk up the monumental success of Century Telephone. Too weak to go into the bank that day, Clarke Junior asked Vicki to fetch George while he sat in the open car. Campbell's secretary was so sorry, "but he's in a meeting. Can you come back a little later?"

"Sure."

Outside alone, basking in the sun, Clarke looked around the parking lot he'd taken for granted a thousand times, jumping out of his truck to see George and tell a few jokes. Exciting and carefree days they had been. No one ever knows the pinnacle of his life until it is well behind him. That's the only way to know it. And now the memory loomed heartbreakingly inside a body that couldn't move.

Clarke Junior thought it ironic that here he was in the exact same condition as his grandfather Will after Will's stroke. Clarke was nine years old at the time and had felt keenly sorry for his immobile grandfather who could hear but could not speak, dawdling slowly in his wheelchair. Now, 37 years later, a stroke had felled another Williams. His wheelchair was a convertible. It almost didn't make sense that the intense pressures Clarke Senior had endured hadn't given him a stroke. He wished fervently he had paid much closer attention to his father's spiritual teachings in his youth when he thought his father was a fool.

We are all fools, he thought, watching people carelessly walk in and walk out, nodding to the man sitting alone in the convertible, unaware and preoccupied in their own heads. What Clarke could tell them would change their lives and cause them to really live. But they were all in such a hurry, just as he had been, clamoring to get someplace with little thought as to why they were rushing. With hindsight, he now thought like his ponderous, endearing, admired father. The forced time off had caused Clarke Junior to focus only on those few aspects of life that really mattered. As he watched the same rush of which he had been guilty, he realized the rush itself is what sped up everything. It was why life flew by. Now, at the end, he knew that in following their routines, people were not rushing toward something, they were rushing *from* something: themselves. They thought staying busy was a measure of life when it was really an escape from introspection, a *running away from* instead of facing key issues. Collateral damage piled up in broken relationships, lost children, missed potential, addictions, and unrealized dreams.

Clarke had to laugh not at the misfortune of others but at himself. Another irony suddenly struck him. Here he was immobile in a flashy convertible in an anonymous parking lot, when he was Clarke McRae Williams, Junior, one of the world's handful of entrepreneurs who had created cellular communications. One of the few who gave mankind its greatest freedom now sat immobile. Watching the frenzied come and go, his smile dropped as it occurred to him he had only hastened their rush. Constant communication allowed even less planning and forethought as people ricocheted off events and relationships like pinballs.

When Vicki returned empty-handed, Clarke was disappointed. He fought wondering if his friends were deliberately slipping away, not wanting to see him in his condition. If so, he didn't blame them.

"I guess I'll regret that for the rest of my life," George Campbell later told reporters, "that I didn't get to see him on [what turned out to be] the last day."[280]

Thursday morning, May 12, Bob Fudickar's phone rang suddenly at 8:00 a.m.

"Bob," Vicki Williams said breathlessly, "you've got to get over here. Something's happening to Clarke."

> Bob Fudickar: "I lived three blocks from them, saw him daily, and this was one of many calls but this time was different. His breathing was labored, he did not look well, he was uncomfortable, and it was hard for him to talk. But, as usual, Clarke was pretty stubborn. We had rehearsed what to do at least a half dozen times, so his cousin Phillip Williams and I strapped him into the front seat of Vicki's big

---

[280] "Century's Williams dead at 44," *Monroe News-Star*, May 13, 1994, front page.

green BMW. He was in pain, he was moaning, and he was barely holding consciousness. We were telling him, 'Hold on, buddy, we're almost there!' We rushed to St. Francis [Medical Center] while Vicki called ahead on the cellphone. They were particularly busy at the emergency room when we arrived and no wheelchair or gurney was waiting. Vicki ran looking for someone while I pulled Clarke Junior from the car. I had only taken about three steps holding him as the gurney was getting to us, and Clarke took like a last breath, groaned, and he relaxed in my arms. He was gone."[281]

Condolences flooded in from across the country, from employees to fellow members of the United State Telephone Association to hunting friends to Wall Street wizards. Clarke Senior read them or heard them, gratified that his son's short life had touched so many.

Charles Schelke, Smith Barney Shearson, New York: "Clarke was quite a visionary. In the mid-1980s nobody knew the outlook of cellular, that it was going to be hugely popular. Obviously he was taking a big risk paying tens and hundreds of millions of dollars for cellular licenses. He identified trends and acted on them very effectively. In fact, he was the person to talk to to find trends in the industry. But this is also a great personal loss. Clarke made you feel good. He was a very warm human being, and he had a great sense of humor."[282]

Judy McAda, USTA executive director: "If we were all gathered because of something

---

[281] Bob Fudickar telephone interview, March 8, 2014.
[282] "Century's Williams dead at 44," *Monroe News-Star*, May 13, 1994, p. 3A

controversial, by the time he finished one of his jokes we were in a much more conciliatory mode. Clarke was famous for his Cajun jokes. We loved his southern, Louisiana perspective on everything. He was really well thought of on Wall Street."[283]

Glen Post: "He could walk into a room of dead-serious analysts and have the whole room laughing in a matter of minutes."[284]

Mac Oliver, hunting companion: "Clarke was fun and spontaneous but driven. He told all of us on hunting trips, 'If you want to go with me, keep a bag packed. When I say the posse rides at 9:00 a.m., I don't mean 9:02.'"[285]

Bob Fudickar: "Clarke was unbelievably generous and I don't mean in gifts of trips, he was generous with his speech and his actions. Now, he could fuss at you, not feeling well, but everybody who knew him loved him, I can tell you that."[286]

Bill Newton: "Clarke Junior was a God's blessing in disguise. We lost him way too soon."[287]

Services for Clarke McRae Williams, Junior, were held on a date he would have appreciated: May 13, 1994, Friday the 13th. His friends acknowledged he would have found it fitting

---

[283] Ibid
[284] Ibid
[285] Ibid
[286] Bob Fudickar telephone interview, March 8, 2014.
[287] Bill Newton interview, Oct. 23, 2012, Ash Flat, Arkansas.

because not too far back down the road, luck in his health had turned against him, then run out completely.

As Clarke Senior sat on the front pew, Mary Kathryn wept beside him, as did nearly everyone else along the row. He could hear sniffles far back in the church. Everyone considered the loss a tragedy on many levels but mainly because a parent should never bury a child. Hearts froze in the audience as parents shuddered to imagine what would happen to them if they got news their child had died. If funerals, especially this one, had any redeeming reason, it was that the dread reminded parents that each and every moment as their children grew was infinitely, enormously, and irretrievably precious. The mourners' eyes fixed on Clarke Senior, aged many years since the last time they had seen him. Everyone felt the tragedy.

Except Clarke.

Not a tear moistened his eyes. He stared at the gleaming casket, solemnly, turning his eyes to face others only when interrupted. But he would not cry. His lack of emotion did not stem from remembering the harsh words his son had hurled toward him. He knew those words had come from a frustrated prodigal son, not from the optimistic, fun-loving, hardworking Clarke Junior he had had the honor of fathering. No, Clarke Senior simply refused to feel the pain anymore. Through prayer and intense scripture reading, absorbing great wisdom from centuries of human experiences, he long ago knew a man has but two choices in facing adversity: either you let it beat you, or you beat it. Resolutions never came out of pity.

And, yet—and yet his son was in that casket. If success were the measure of a man, the son had accomplished that in six short years. If money were the measure, Clarke Junior had knocked it out of the park. Century's gross revenues when he returned from Vietnam were only $5,691,000. By the time he took over as president, the father handed him control of a $100 million company. When he resigned seven years later, Century's revenues had more than doubled to $250 million, and, now, with his funeral only days before the 1994 shareholders' meeting, those revenues had nearly doubled again to $433,197,000.

Clarke stared, alone in his thoughts. *But money is not the measure.* It will never be the measure, because if money had real power, it could correct all of life's mistakes, regrets, and disappointments, even death. People who sought to escape calamity were certain that with enough money they could be happy. Nothing, however, could be more of a lie; Clarke knew that. He had seen many times how throwing money at an empty heart gave just a moment's pleasure before vanishing. Houses were never big enough; halls never wide enough nor ceilings tall enough. Many a mansion served as a prison. And yet people never stopped chasing money, even praised him for his monetary success, and with some envy. But he'd discovered way back what King Solomon discovered: *Vanity, vanity, all is vanity.*

> Carolyn Williams Perry: "When Clarke Junior died, somebody asked Daddy, 'Clarke, how can you stand it?' Daddy said, 'Well, I cried all my tears the past five years after Clarke had his stroke, knowing his health was declining even worse.' I guess Daddy started preparing himself for that day five years ahead of time."[288]

> Molly Ann Williams, Clarke Junior's daughter: "When Dad died, I remember Granddaddy in the limousine saying, 'You know, it should never be this way. A parent should never bury his child.' He was more worried about Trey and me and how we were handling it and how we were getting through it. He was a very strong man. He was concerned that I was okay even though he was in pain. He would call and check on me."[289]

Hundreds of sad eyes watched as the funeral procession pulled away from Monroe's Parkview Baptist Church en route

---

[288] Carolyn Williams Perry interview, Sept. 15, 2012, Baton Rouge, Louisiana.
[289] Molly Ann Williams interview, Jan. 29, 2013, Monroe, Louisiana.

to Oak Ridge Baptist Cemetery. In abiding by Clarke Junior's final wishes, the line of cars snaked circuitously up Old Bastrop Highway and through downtown Bastrop, winding toward and through Mer Rouge, then back down toward Collinston, and finally through the green fields toward Oak Ridge. Clarke Junior had wanted to make one last run through the calm countryside of his youth; he wanted everyone with him on his last trip to see what he had seen. The cotton fields and oak trees of Oak Ridge were where everything had started. Now he was going home.

Clarke Senior gazed out the window, watching familiar fields go by, seeing nothing but a father and son traveling the same road together long ago. The inquisitive boy had never stopped asking questions. Now, just as Clarke Junior's spirit was absent the body, Clarke Senior's spirit was gone, too. He was not on the pew or in the car, he was back in his garden at home. Clarke Senior never felt more alive as when dirt caked his hands and fingernails. When he had walked the noisy horn-blowing, siren-screaming streets of Manhattan, endured the cacophony of shouts at the New York Stock Exchange, heard news blaring on televisions in every building, all he could think about was his garden. If he couldn't physically be there, he went there in his mind.

Now, amid the mottled stones of departed friends, the memories he surpressed swirled about him and Mary Kathryn. Last rites hushed the huddled crowd. Clarke remembered standing in the same place in 1957 watching his father lowered into the ground. Now, mere feet and a lifetime hence, he was watching his son go. The seasons revolved in order but this was out of order; that's what everyone was thinking. Clarke didn't dwell there. With faith and trust in God, and both his father and his son now in the Father's hands, he worried, fretted, and questioned no more. Certainly he missed them and that clouded his old eyes as he heard Clarke Junior's shrill boyish laughter echo from the back yard. He fought back the tears, comforted in blessed assurance that he would soon see them, touch them, and hug them again.

He knew without a doubt that life is a continuum, an eternal chain linking parent to child to grandchild, all down through time. The circle would be unbroken, in the by and by, Clarke knew that was so. That gave him comfort when the noise left. In his peaceful garden, he was reminded of life's unchanging, undeniable seasons, spring, summer, fall, and winter. Each year brought new problems and promises, but the cycle never changed. Youth's springtime grayed with autumn and a loving embrace was the best anyone could hope for on Earth.

For after the autumn comes the winter.

CHAPTER 10

"I LEARNED A LONG TIME AGO THAT I DID NOT KNOW WHAT I REALLY NEEDED TO KNOW SO I HAD TO TRY TO ENGAGE PEOPLE WHO KNEW WHAT TO DO. IF IT'D BEEN ALL MY FIGURING ON IT, WE PROBABLY WOULDN'T HAVE GOTTEN ANYWHERE."

CLARKE MCRAE WILLIAMS

"HE ALWAYS TALKED TO ME REAL KIND, LIKE A FATHER TO DAUGHTER. HE NEVER SAID HE WAS BUSY, NEVER FELT BAD, AND HE ALWAYS TOOK THE TIME TO LISTEN."

VERETTA HECKARD, HOUSEKEEPER

"HE HAD CONFIDENCE IN ME AND I DIDN'T WANT TO LET HIM DOWN."

RUBY NELL HIGGINS, COOK

"I DON'T ALWAYS ACHIEVE WHAT I'D LIKE TO DO BUT I TRY TO LIVE SO THAT IF THIS IS MY LAST DAY ON EARTH, MY SALVATION WILL BE SECURE WITH THE LORD."

CLARKE MCRAE WILLIAMS

If Clarke McRae Williams learned one truth on his journey, it was that life rarely works out as planned. Sometimes it's better, sometimes it's worse, more often it's neither. That's the nature of living on this planet, of being a son, daughter, student, husband, wife, parent, grandparent, or great-grandparent. Only the seasons are guaranteed, Spring, Summer, Fall, and Winter. Each soul experiences all four in repetition as if practicing year to year for some grand performance. And if a person is lucky enough to survive the traps of rebellious youth, wisdom in old age reverses all thoughts of greatness.

Clarke McRae Williams started his life there, with no thought of celebrity or selfish ambition. Though he chose a path that most found too risky, never at any time did he fear, because scripture taught a childlike faith, which he embraced. Clarke humbly asked for guidance and he got it. Although from beginning to end there was much he did not know, he was smart enough to admit it. His self-effacement attracted people to him, inspiring more loyalty than that of lifelong friends. Others filled in the blanks he did not know. Together, he and those he gathered built a family called a corporation through which thousands of lives would flourish well into the future.

The days after Clarke Junior's death turned into weeks, then into months, and finally into years. Clarke's memory of his son never diminished. He could still see his face, still hear his voice, still smell that young boy asleep in his arms after a summer's evening chasing fireflies in a town as comfortable as a blanket. Clarke Senior got used to the idea that he would someday see his son again, not now but in a little while. As he and Henry Moore tilled his garden in the quiet of Oak Ridge, he pondered what his son was doing on the other side. Was he watching? Was he content? Had Jesus wrapped him in love that passes all understanding?

Clarke Junior pinned the accelerator to the floor right up to the end. His father knew that's what he was doing in the new convertible: He was grabbing all the air and sunshine he could as he zoomed toward an uncertain, mystical portal. Clarke had imagined that portal all his life. Now in his straw hat and rolled up jeans clasped by red and navy suspenders, he joked that he looked like the scarecrow. He loved it, loved the simplicity of hoeing, the *chop chop* of soil, the tilling that wordlessly helped him think and pray through life's many reversals.

There was Henry, more simple and humble than anyone he knew, who chattered on and laughed and hoed. Clarke depended on Henry for much more than correct placement of green beans, tomatoes, squash, and Aloe Vera plants. Most of his life, Clarke had observed the careworn but chuckling black gentleman with leathery hands and bright smile. In him he found a kindred spirit, unpretentious, sincere, genuine, and loving people and God. Clarke envied his uncomplicated life. By the world's standards, Henry was poor and Clarke was rich, but Clarke knew otherwise. The temptation was to trust material wealth but that made material the master and the person a slave. Only in the quiet could a person ever learn who he was. Clarke reminded himself and his Sunday School classes that Christ never owned a thing but He changed the world. How many millionaire capitalists had done that?

Clarke loved Henry for his steadiness and dependability, especially during the years when Clarke Junior changed in both personality and spirit. Clarke rarely allowed those last bitter words from his son, but that voice would surface occasionally, suddenly. *"Dad,"* the son had said of his newfound religion, *"I fear for you. I want to see you in Heaven but you won't be there unless you join my church, the only true church."*

A studied and determined Biblical scholar, Clarke had rocked back on his heels, incredulous at his son. He knew exactly what scripture said, specifically in the New Testament regarding Jesus Christ as the Way, the Truth, and the Life, that no one could go to the Heavenly Father except by Him. That was the case Christ had made, not to encourage exclusivity but rather just the opposite, to let the poor in spirit know they had a direct connection when they chose it. But for one mortal to judge another's eternal destination placed not the accused but the accuser in serious peril. The one judging was foolishly attempting to place himself on a level with God, which was the height of arrogance. And if Scripture said anything at all, it was that God despises arrogance. In Clarke's view, for any person to say another was bound for Hell practically insured that the accuser was headed that direction. No one had exclusivity on Heaven or on God's love, for the simple reason that no one was God but God. The Father would decide and decide alone who entered Heaven.

"I love you, son," was all Clarke could say. *"Nothing will ever change that."*

"I love you, too, Dad," the response came, and Clarke knew his son had meant it. God would overlook an innocent man's brainwashing as He overlooks the temporary lapses all make. What was less likely that God would overlook was a church leader hoodwinking an entire flock with silly talk about having a claim above everybody else. Satan was clearly the force behind separation from the Father and fracturing the church, which meant that a judge of others was the very tool of Hell. No good father ever placed the bar impossibly high, just as the Apostle Paul admonished, "Fathers, provoke not your children to wrath." A thundering, violent God was a figment of Man's

imagination, was actually Man accusing himself for failing. In Clarke's view, any Christian church that felt exclusive entrée to God and Heaven was no different from the Jewish leaders of Christ's day who had turned synagogues into exclusive clubs, barring others and looking down on them.

Clarke Junior knew the truth now.

As Clarke walked the new marbled halls where Clarke Junior should have been, he was comforted knowing that Century, by God's grace, would outlive them all, employees, customers, shareholders, and the founder himself. He smiled. All the lonely days working solo, dangling from poles in freezing sleet and blistering sun, had been worth it. The hundreds of people around him now as he passed office after office, desk after desk, all of them smiling, laughing, glad for a reason to get up that morning, made him whisper prayers of thanksgiving. He was thankful he had caught the secret of loving others in a selfish world. Now each person added to his great dream, and that dream added to everyone else.

Clarke Williams loved people naturally in a way that couldn't be taught but could be learned by people willing to place others first. That's why he stopped spontaneously on business and pleasure trips, whenever the opportunity arose, to see someone, meet someone, or say a kind word to someone who needed it. Encouragement cost nothing and propelled people to greatness, so he gave himself time to give people time, right down to hand signing Christmas cards to thousands of employees.

What was there but encouragement? The power of kindness? He remembered his father's laugh, his jokes, but most of all his encouraging words, and the great quotations he tried to instill in his children. In the peace of his garden, chopping the soil, tilling, raking, the smell reminded him that he, his father, and his son came from clay and that, like them, his body would return to clay. Seedlings sprouted, grew in the sun, produced many seeds, and then died. Their work done, the next generation took over.

Century Telephone was a model of God's plan for putting others first. That bedrock principle would never change, even if the company did, and he prayed fervently that it wouldn't. He prayed for wisdom for those who followed, that they would read the signs, seasons, stars, trends, and never lose sight of their goal on a stormy sea. There were no shortcuts to harvest, and there was no such thing as personal wealth.

> Carolyn Williams Perry: "Daddy never really considered his wealth or what he made belonged to him. He credited God. Whatever he had, it really belonged to The Lord."[290]

> Stacey Goff, CenturyTel attorney: "He didn't care about money, not about making money for himself or building 'a great thing I built.' Anybody in our building would have done anything for Mr. Williams, not because of big checks or fear but because they loved him. Wherever we went, he'd talk to folks about their families, not about business. He literally was the most Christ-like person I ever saw in person. Day in, day out, he was steady. He just cared about other people."[291]

> Gene Allen, banker: "That's the way it is. Mr. Clarke felt that we never really own anything. Even if you've got your name on a title to a house or a car, who does it belong to when you go on? Does anything really belong to you? No, it is not a thing on this Earth that truly belongs to anyone, and this is the way Mr. Clarke believed. Not a thing on this Earth. You just kind of look after it for the time you're here. You're the caretaker. And then when you leave, somebody else assumes responsibility. It's not

---

[290] Carolyn Williams Perry as part of a Gene Allen interview, Sept. 25, 2012, Oak Ridge, Louisiana.
[291] Stacey Goff interview, Feb. 5, 2013, Monroe, Louisiana

your   job   anymore.   And   that's   what   he
thought."[292]

Clarke knew the position of caretaker well. From youth, he
had observed that the more a person focused on himself, the
faster life slipped away. The more he clutched desperately for
things, the less he had. That's why Clarke always insisted in
every transaction, "If this deal is not good for you, I don't want
you to do it." It was that simple. God always worked out the
details, rewarding those who accumulated not wealth but souls.

In the months after Clarke Junior's death, Clarke spent
more time at home in Oak Ridge nurturing his garden and spirit
while juggling the chairmanship. Occasionally, he caught Mary
Kathryn watching him with a slightly worried look on her face.
He would grin back. They had a bond beyond love, a meshing
of souls, so that one could hardly function without the other. He
had remained true to everything from the beginning, above all,
true to himself.

Despite full, complicated days, he still denied no one his
time. Amid his resuming control of Century, family cook and
housekeeper Ruby Nell Higgins had to put her mother in long-
term care and needed daily transportation. But Ruby Nell was
46 and had never driven a car. Henry drove her most places. She
asked Mr. Clarke, who was running a billion dollar corporation,
to teach her to drive. He did more than that. He bought her a
blue Ford Crown Victoria and started teaching her on the streets
of Oak Ridge.

> Ruby Nell Higgins, cook, housekeeper: "Mr. and
> Mrs. Williams helped me raise my two kids. My
> mom took sick and I needed to go back and forth
> so, at 46, I decided I wanted to learn how to drive.
> Evenings, Sundays, weekends, whenever we had
> time, he would take me down Avenue Road and
> let me drive. One time [alone, getting ready for
> a lesson], I hit his traveling bus and dented my

---

[292] Gene Allen interview, Sept. 25, 2012, Oak Ridge, Louisiana.

blue Crown Victoria. I had to go in and tell him and, without looking up from his breakfast, he smiled and said, 'You and Mary Kathryn goin' to break me.' Mary Kathryn had just run into a pole in her car. He was so soft spoken, and he said, 'That's okay, I'll take care of it.' He just eased my fears. Whatever you did, he calmed you down with his calming voice. He never got excited. I had never tried to drive a car, and when I got my license he had me drive him to Century in Monroe. I didn't let on that I was nervous, and when we got there, he said, 'Okay,' and gave me the keys and said, 'Go home.' I said, 'I got to go by myself?' He just grinned. It was good, because he had the confidence in me and I didn't want to let him down."[293]

Clarke and Mary Kathryn would later build Ruby Nell a house. He did the same for housekeeper Veretta Heckard and sent her daughter to college based on the daughter's college entrance interview with Clarke when she was in the third grade.

Veretta Heckard, housekeeper: "I was cleaning up Mr. Clarke's office in 1992 [before working at the Williams house] and I heard my little girl Nedra talking to somebody. I asked my coworker, 'Who's Nedra talking to?' She said, 'Mr. Williams.' I said, 'Who's Mr. Williams?' 'He's the founder of the company.' I said, 'Oh, Lord.' I peeked in and this little man in a black suit was sitting there talking to my third grader like she was an adult. They talked 30 minutes and after that my daughter said, 'Mama, I met Mr. Williams and he said when I get out of the twelfth grade, he would help me go to college.' Soon after, I went to work full time for the family. He'd look out his bay window and drink

---

his coffee and just talk to me, talk to me real kind, like a father to a daughter. He never said he was too busy, never felt bad or whatever, he always took the time to listen. He was always there to fix everything!"[294]

Fixing everything invariably involved money. He gave tens of thousands to various churches, charities, individuals, almost anyone who sought him out for help. Money was the one thing that didn't mean much to him. It meant a lot to others, he found, which made Man even more predictable, sharing the twin germs of excellence and failure as the stopwatch ticked. Clarke was glad he had been quiet and listened to that still, small voice. Anyone could hear it at any time, he told everyone who asked, it just took faith and sincerity.

The year after Clarke Junior died, Tennessee friend and fellow independent owner W. S. "Babe" Howard was sued by kinfolk impatient to cash out of the family business. A Chicago holding company had offered $25 million, but Babe pleaded that a better deal was ahead. He couldn't gather money fast enough to please the relatives and called Clarke. The Chicago group had identified Howard's Millington Telephone, in a Naval Air Station town bordering Memphis, as a lucrative communications plum. Clarke sent Century analysts to conduct due diligence, then loaned the $25 million, which enabled Howard to keep a significant interest in a thirteen-county franchise of BellSouth Mobility. Years later when Babe sold the franchise, he paid off Clarke's loan and pocketed the balance of the $48 million sale price. Clarke had kept him solvent and made him a millionaire. Babe Howard went on to fund many charities in Millington and built the town's baseball stadium.

Clarke saw the lesson of Babe repeat continually: people unwilling to wait for investments to mature. Dollar signs seemed to make people take aberrant, often destructive action for quick gratification. Too much money led to hedonism followed by paranoia that the money might be lost. Too little

---

[294] Veretta Heckard interview, Jan. 30, 2013, Monroe, Louisiana.

money led to weariness and lost hope. Both extremes made people crazy. It was Clarke's experience that a person who knew only consumption was himself consumed. The world taught that money solved all problems when it actually magnified them. He reminded himself that few had had the benefit he had of a Counselor in whom he trusted, someone he followed in blind faith, an act the world called folly. As far as Clarke could figure, the joke was on the sophisticated who struggled in darkness to "find meaning" or "find themselves," chasing their own tails all over Earth trying to find happiness from the outside.

The straw-hatted Johnny Appleseed of Oak Ridge considered these truths as he puttered and pondered amid fragrances of magnolia, sweet olive, roses, and rosemary. Life was sweet and abundant if a person had enough sense to ask God for that abundance and then obey His plan to get there. Abundance came when the gardener learned to use disappointments for what they were: fertilizer. The lesson was simple. Floating in God's river was far easier than swimming upstream against it.

Century's river had become a torrent as Clarke wearied of the whitewater of business. He was not melancholy about finishing his journey, knowing the hands into which he was placing the company were true and the Hands into which he was crawling were eternal. Under Glen Post, Century blossomed into unbelievable abundance. By 1996, the company passed the half-million landline customer mark and served 100,000 more with long distance. In 1997, after extensive due diligence and focused resources, Clarke and Glen more than doubled the size of Century with the $2.2 billion acquisition of Pacific Telecom's 660,000 access lines in twelve states. Wall Street applauded but company accountants sweated, as Century had gained nearly a billion dollars in long-term debt.

Also in 1997, Century launched into the commercial and home security market by buying Delta Security Alarm's 4,000 residential and industrial customers in Louisiana, Arkansas, and Mississippi. The board added Century Protection Systems the next year and, while at it, paid $221 million for Ameritech's directory publishing division plus nineteen Wisconsin exchanges serving 89,000 customers. The board then announced an astonishing 50-percent dividend in the form of a three-for-two stock split, the fourth such split in ten years. Wall Street applauded again, and Century exploded again in market capitalization, a vast abundance Clarke had never imagined.

In 1999, the board repeated the same stock split. Standard & Poor's admitted Century Telephone to the S&P 500 Index. At the May annual meeting, shareholders voted to change the name to *CenturyTel, Incorporated,* and, as the 21st Century roared in, Clarke hired the company's first female Chief Operating Officer, Karen Puckett.

> Karen Puckett, EVP, COO: "Century was far and away the most ethical company I ever saw. Mr. Williams knew intuitively what to do even when the numbers didn't show it. He didn't let the numbers drive him totally where many in the company would. And competition was tightening. You had wireless substitutions going on, and you had cable companies throwing out voice services. So we had this large decline in our major product line called 'voice.' And the voice product line might have a 65- to 75-percent margin. We were trying to transition into 'HSI,' High Speed Internet, that approximated a 25- to 30-percent margin. So you have margin compression going on [making less money with rising costs]. In a competitive world, you have to market, have to have a market plan, go by it, and identify the addressable markets that you're going to penetrate. We had to start running our business more from a marketplace standpoint than just a pure financial standpoint."[295]

> Harvey Perry: "Mr. Williams was watching the

---

[295] Karen Puckett interview, Feb. 3, 2013, Monroe, Louisiana.

industry he knew in major transition, which had to be difficult for him. To put things in perspective, we once got $150 from our customer and another $500 from the government or other subsidy funds [per Rural Electric Authority mandate to serve remote areas]. What Karen is describing is a transition to getting a substantial portion of the revenue from the customer. Eventually, rather than getting two lines, customers would drop the landline because they were using cellphones and the next generation wouldn't get a landline at all. That's why the cable companies were able to give the voice service away. Mr. Williams saw that competition coming before others did. He was a big proponent of us finding other sources of revenue."[296]

In need of a major course correction, Glen Post steadied himself in the same way his mentor did. They both embraced technological advances with the assurance they would make the shift by not forgetting long-range goals or people. They believed the company was not just numbers but was a living, growing family of individuals who had their own dreams and aspirations. Nothing propelled Century toward success as directly as or more forcefully than all those individual dreams and aspirations focused in one direction. Clarke had spent his whole life listening to those dreams, shaking hands, and talking to everyone from the new hire up, because he knew that within each individual lay the answers both for that person and for the whole company.

Clarke McRae Williams: "I emphasize listening to the people who make up the bulk of our company. The people who are actually out in the weather and meeting our customers and are

---

[296] Harvey Perry as part of the Karen Puckett interview, Feb. 3, 2013, Monroe, Louisiana.

actually working on our facilities should be able to have an input in management. I listen to what these people have to say and try to glean from a consensus of how well the company is doing its job. Sometimes you may be sitting up dumb and happy thinking everything is going well when really there are serious problems beneath the surface that need to be recognized. I listen to what the members of our company are saying and try to sift all this out, and hopefully come up with answers to what the company really needs."[297]

Glen Post: "First of all, you have to live it by example. People have to see it lived. You have to earn that respect from people. Once they see it at work, they really do buy into it—once they see it. People really do want to live like that. It's really where they want to be, but just sometimes they have a hard time getting there. If they see other people who abide by these principles, they see the value of it. It makes a big difference in them."[298]

Glen had dreams and boldly expressed them to Mr. Williams from his first day, when he said he did not intend to remain just an accountant. Glen Post came to love Clarke Williams as a father. He appreciated the old gentleman for his tremendously giving spirit. From climbing poles in the 1930s to flying jets in the 1990s, Clarke had not let success change him one iota. His humility was legendary throughout the industry and his reputation unblemished. Clarke's heartfelt appreciation never faltered, and in all those he showered with praise grew a spirit of helpfulness no amount of money could buy.

Clarke felt his winter setting in. Glen prepared himself and CenturyTel for the coming reality. Mr. Williams seemed

---

[297] Clarke Williams, Sr., *The Wall Street Transcript*, Dec. 29, 1986, p. 84,118.
[298] Glen Post interview, June 27, 2013, Monroe, Louisiana.

superhuman but he was not. Glen noticed a marked change in energy after Mr. Williams' kidney transplant the year before Clarke Junior died. The overwhelming double setbacks had inflicted a heavy toll. While Mr. Williams' head remained unbowed as usual, both men knew the truth.

Glen was grateful to both God and Clarke for allowing them twenty years together. All the universities in the world couldn't offer what he had learned about leadership at the feet of Clarke Williams. Glen looked for ways to keep Mr. Williams' principles alive, to save them for those who would never know him, never work with him, never feel his genuine kindness and interest in everyone else. Glen lived in humble gratitude, because by sheer luck and Divine Guidance, the simple accounting job he asked for had led him to the world's best company.

He sat down and reviewed years of notes, teachings, admonitions, observations, and personal guidance from the founder, amazed at how Mr. Williams' trial and error had saved his student decades of learning. The young President of CenturyTel boiled those years down into seven Unifying Principles:

- **Fairness**

  Treat others as we would like to be treated.
  Exercise fairness in all dealings with customers, business associates, and fellow employees.

- **Honesty and Integrity**

  Be truthful and demonstrate integrity in all our dealings.
  Act ethically and do the right thing, even when it's difficult and even if it takes longer.

- **Commitment to Excellence**

  Perform our jobs at the highest level each day.

Focus on serving our customers—
both internal and external.
Produce quality work while
continuously becoming more
efficient and effective for long-term
success.
Commit to winning in our markets
and to being the performance leader
in our industry.

- ## Positive Attitude

  Approach our work with enthusiasm
  and an "anything is possible" spirit.
  Encourage one another to try new
  things even when difficult, as we
  recognize that **excellent outcomes
  often come from having the
  courage to fail.**
  Build and sustain a positive
  atmosphere.
  Promote family and fun while we
  engage in productive and challenging
  work.

- ## Respect

  Recognize and respect each
  employee, each customer, each
  shareholder, and each business
  associate as individuals deserving
  our compassion.
  Build relationships through
  inclusion, collaboration, and
  responsiveness—everyone's input
  and time counts, and every idea can
  have an impact.
  Be responsive to others and keep the
  promises we make to one another.
  Encourage and consider different

perspectives.

- **Faith**

  Maintain confidence in our abilities as individuals to perform our jobs effectively.

  Trust in one another's capabilities, expertise, and experience to deliver our best.

  Have confidence that the strength of our combined, collaborative efforts will lead us to a successful future.

- **Perseverance**

  Carry out our Vision in a manner consistent with our Unifying Principles in spite of obstacles.

  Be creative and innovative as we face challenges and respond to opportunities.

  Be flexible and embrace change. Never give up.

Glen Post: "Mr. Williams wanted people around him who shared some faith. He never told me that but I saw it. In faith, you had his back and he had yours and that's why you were there. I felt if I made mistakes—and I made plenty of them—that he wasn't going to say, 'Boy, you made a mistake. You're in trouble.' He'd say, 'That was OUR decision. We'll do better on the next.' Of course, with him involved, we didn't make too many. But we weren't afraid to go back out. When he delegated something to you, you weren't afraid to go make a decision. Being troubled by it wasn't in his nature."[299]

---

[299] Glen Post interview, Sept. 25, 2012, Monroe, Louisiana.

> Virginia Boulet: "The Unifying Principles, that's
> the roadmap."[300]

Clarke was deeply gratified. Somebody had been listening. As workers placarded the new name *CenturyTel* in brass letters across all its buildings, with the giant corporation emboldened to go forth, Clarke knew the seasons of Century were now behind him. The time had come for him and Mary Kathryn to bow from the stage. Tens of thousands of personalized Christmas cards, service anniversaries, births, and condolences were now impossible. Losing that personal contact troubled Clarke most of all.

The kidney Mary Lee selflessly gave to her brother began to fail. Hemodialysis became a daily necessity, to the point that Clarke installed an expensive dialysis machine in his bedroom. His energy roller-coastered between fatigue and almost normal. He looked up at poles he could no longer climb and smiled that he wouldn't have to climb them anymore. When he approached the stairway to Heaven, he would fly.

> Veretta Heckard, housekeeper: "He came from
> the dialysis all sick and tired but he'd always ask,
> 'How's your family?' He was weak but never
> complained. Mary Kathryn would leave
> instructions to make sure he drank his
> Ensure®. He had no choice but to drink it or I'd
> tell Ms. Williams."[301]

Strength and joy were renewed in his season of grandfatherhood, a time Clarke enjoyed, when an old man could be a kid again, with no repercussions for ice cream cones, late night cookies, or giggles past bedtime. Clarke and Mary Kathryn had enjoyed two waves of grandchildren, starting with the first set in the mid-1970s when Molly Ann was born to Clarke Junior and wife Marilyn, and Daniel and Damian Ogg to Annette and husband Danny. The second set came in the early

---

[300] Virginia Boulet interview, Nov. 22, 2012, New Orleans, Louisiana.
[301] Veretta Heckard interview, January 30, 2013, Monroe, Louisiana

1980s with Mary Kathryn and Jonathan born to Carolyn and Harvey, and Trey born to Clarke Junior and second wife Vicki.

At last the old patriarch could lay down his duties as a titan of the telephone industry, wean Century's management from his daily presence, and settle into his greatest, most joyful role of all. His job now was to do just the opposite of how he had parented Clarke Junior, Annette, and Carolyn. Now he wholeheartedly embraced the job of spoiling, sparingly, yes, but he delighted in constructive coddling just the same.

> Mary Kathryn Perry Edwards: "Granddaddy left work at work. When he was at home, he was all there. When we were small we would go see him and Mimi [Mary Kathryn], and the minute we walked in the door, Granddaddy would say, 'We need to go find what the squirrel has brought you!' So we'd go hunting in the trees and usually it was candy, orange slices, or a candy bar in a Century cup and a letter for each of us grandkids with our names on them. The letters were really scribbly like they came from the squirrel but later we knew Granddaddy did it. He took the time to do all that, him and his phantom squirrel."[302]

> Molly Ann Williams: "Granddaddy was the rock of the family. He was the one you turned to. He was the go-to guy for lots. He would always tell us as we left, 'Remember who you are and where you came from.' Occasionally, he'd ask us grandkids, 'Are you suffering adequately?' You had to suffer to have a good time, he thought, to know what a good time was."[303]

> Jonathan Michael Perry: "We [the Perrys] drove every Sunday morning the thirty minutes to Oak

---

[302] Mary Kathryn Perry Edwards interview, Jan. 29, 2013, Monroe, Louisiana.
[303] Molly Ann Williams interview, Jan. 29, 2013, Monroe, Louisiana.

Ridge Baptist Church. Then we'd eat dinner with Granddaddy and Mimi. Granddaddy would always ask, 'Son'—he never called us grandsons by name, it was always 'son'—so he said, 'Son, what did you learn in church today?' He did that every single Sunday so you knew you had to listen, you couldn't goof off. We'd talk about it on the way home and talk about it eating lunch. I remember that and also that Mimi cried singing every hymn."[304]

Trey Williams: "When we got together as a family, we would spend a lot of time together, especially at Lake D'Arbonne. It was no going out on a Saturday and coming back on a Sunday. Sometimes we'd go out to the lake and spend a week or two out there. Same thing at Christmas. Our Christmases weren't going out to Granddaddy and Mimi's on Christmas Eve, opening our presents and going home. We'd go there when school got out, on the 18th or 19th, and we'd stay through New Years. We'd turn the big room into a pallet room and all the kids would camp out on couches and air mattresses. Granddaddy just always wanted us to get together and have fun for an extended period. Every summer he piled all six grandkids into his bus and we traveled for a week or ten days."[305]

Daniel Ogg: "During the day, Granddaddy would busy himself with small jobs. When he was working outside, whether it was dragging a water hose across the yard, remaking a fishing pole, cutting a line, or setting a trap for a varmint, he

---

[304] Jonathan Michael Perry interview, Jan. 29, 2013, Monroe, Louisiana.
[305] Clarke McRae "Trey" Williams, III, interview, Feb.14, 2013, Baton Rouge, Louisiana

was whistling! He couldn't carry a tune when singing but when he whistled, he was great."[306]

Damian Ogg: "Whenever Granddaddy sent us on a mission, he would always tell us that after we get there and do what needed to be done, to turn our hats around so we would know to head home. That expression originally was for Henry who needed some assistance in directions, but Granddaddy carried the expression over to all his grandchildren."[307]

All was not fun and games and a few mistakes came expensively. Clarke turned everything into teaching lessons because, while he enjoyed fun and inspired fun in the youngsters, having fun did not negate acknowledging responsibility. Since all six of Clarke and Mary Kathryn's grandchildren lived in cities, when they came to sedate, stately Oak Ridge, they let loose. The one-street quaint town offered a certain charm to a child's eye, one of slow pace and lax rules. And since everyone in town loved and admired Clarke and Mary Kathryn, they heartily accepted the Williams grandchildren.

Molly Ann Williams: "Oak Ridge was our playground. One time we went over to the cotton gin and it was full of cotton. Daniel had a fascination with fireworks and he had these little firecrackers. We were popping firecrackers and jumping in the cotton like we'd done before and we came home. The whole family is there all in the living room when the door bell rings. The cotton had caught fire and the whole bale burned up! So Granddaddy had to deal with his grandchildren burning up a lot of cotton, which

---

[306] Daniel Ogg email, "Tales of Granddaddy," April 1, 2014, in author's possession.
[307] Damian Ogg email, "Tales of Granddaddy," April 1, 2014, in author's possession.

he had to pay for. He was embarrassed and also furious with us but he didn't come down hard on us, which is unusual because I'd be very unhappy if my children did that. Granddaddy was such an amazing person. He was not just our grandfather; he was a parent. He was strong but gentle and so loving to all of us. He was never scary. My dad was loud and scary, but Granddaddy never raised his voice. Because he was so gentle and loving in all matters, it hurt us grandchildren more if we disappointed him than the few times he scolded us."[308]

Jonathan Perry: "Trey and I lived with Granddaddy and Mimi during the summers while we worked for Granddaddy. They had the maximum DirectTV. Trey and I fell asleep one night watching TV and I woke up about 3:00 or 4:00 in the morning and on that channel was a Cinemax [X-rated] show. I switched it off. Granddaddy was up all hours of the night and I was glad he didn't come through our room and see that. But the next morning at breakfast, he was reading the paper, Mimi was in there, and without looking up he said, 'Boys, I know what y'all were watching last night.' DirectTV would tell you the most recently viewed shows. I tried to explain but [with Mary Kathryn present] he held up his hand and said, 'That's all. Don't talk about it anymore. You don't watch those kinds of programs in this house.' By the afternoon, he had every movie channel cut out. He cut everything down to basic cable. One Christmas, we kids were watching 'The Nutty Professor' with Eddie Murphy, and Granddaddy walks in when Murphy is passing gas. 'What are y'all

---

[308] Molly Ann Williams interview, Jan. 29, 2013, Monroe, Louisiana.

watching? How in the world can you sing Christmas carols one night and watch that filth the next is beyond me. Turn it off.'"[309]

Mary Kathryn Perry Edwards: "When I was a sophomore in high school, Granddaddy took much of the family to see [Evangelist] Billy Graham in Atlanta. We sat in the stands through the service but after Billy Graham delivered the message, the Christian rock group 'DC Talk,' came on stage singing heavy metal Christian rock songs. After one minute of the loud music, Granddaddy said, 'Okay, it's time to go! You don't sing Christian music that way. Hymns are for personal reflection, quietly.'"[310]

The generation gap proved miles wide but never so wide that Clarke's love for his grandchildren couldn't bridge it. The younger Williams children would remember the glow and warmth of their simple home in simple Oak Ridge for the rest of their days, and Clarke knew it at the time. As in most of his life, Clarke possessed the ability to live in the moment yet never take his eye off the future, and when his grandchildren filled his house with merriment and mischief, he knew decades before they would realize it that he had attempted to teach them the meaning of unconditional love. There existed so much quality of life in the world that had nothing to do with business, status, or money, and he desperately wanted to pass that knowledge on to his grandchildren. Unconditional love, as he'd seen time and again, was the purest form of Christian faith. It was selfless and the only hope anyone would ever have of making sense of a selfish, crazy world. That's why Clarke found it easier and preferable to put himself last and others first.

---

[309] Jonathan Michael Perry interview, Jan. 29, 2013, Monroe, Louisiana.
[310] Mary Kathryn Perry Edwards interview, Jan. 29, 2013, Monroe, Louisiana.

Annette Williams Carroll: "When we would fish, Daddy always enjoyed making everyone comfortable, from baiting the hook to taking the fish off the hook, to placing the fish in the well. Only when everyone was set and waiting for a bobbing cork, did he sit to rest. Even when he was ill, he was always thinking that the guys at the office needed him there. Always working, whether it was home, office, or garden, he never resented interruptions. *He never resented anything someone asked him to do.*"[311]

Don Carroll, son-in-law: "He was personable, a great conversationalist. I immediately felt at ease when I met him in August 1983 while dating Annette. It was his way to provide good feelings and comfort to his guests, friends and traveling companions, always. He had a skill of nurturing things—a company, a project, his organic garden, stray animals.

"After one Christmas dinner, he asked Mrs. Mary Kathryn to package up some cakes and pies and said, 'Don, come go with me.' We drove East from Oak Ridge toward Boeuf River and turned North on a small parish road coming to a neat little home where an elderly black lady in her 90's lived. She greeted, 'Come in, Mr. Clarke.' They talked about her family and his, a pleasant and interesting conversation. He had presented the gifts and in addition gave her some one-hundred-dollar bills to 'tide her over.' This was an humble act coming from an humble man. He abundantly repeated acts of kindness many times with people in need."[312]

---

[311] Annette Williams Carroll email, "Tales of Granddaddy," April 1, 2014, in author's possession.
[312] Don Carroll remembrances of Clarke Williams, Aug. 2014, in author's possession.

More than any other leader in the Bible, Clarke Williams identified most with Moses, an humble, easy-going man, shy and quiet because he stuttered, who faced a moral dilemma while in the court of Egypt's Pharaoh, world leader of the day. Moses was Pharaoh's adopted son, favored for his humility, while Pharaoh's real son was arrogant. The day came when Moses, a Hebrew, could no longer turn a blind eye to the brutal treatment of Hebrew slaves. Would he float along in the wealth and luxury to which he had become accustomed? Or would he be man enough to subjugate his desires and take a stand to face injustice head-on and fight for those who couldn't? When Pharaoh passed the kingdom to his son, God turned Moses from a stuttering, privileged young man into a dynamic leader who defied the new egotistical Pharaoh. In the name of God, Moses demanded an end to 400 years of slavery.

Arrogant Pharaoh II had always resented Moses but now dared the Hebrew God to just try taking away his slaves. God showered down ten plagues on the Egyptians, pestilence, locusts, raining fire and ice, turning the Nile River to blood, and finally bringing death to Pharaoh's son. Pharaoh capitulated. What Clarke got out of that was, once Moses threw over his own natural desire for ease and comfort, he willingly succumbed to God's omniscient Will, became supernaturally empowered, *and changed the world.* Under real threat of annihilation, Moses as a man could not know with any certainty how events would unfold, but he channeled all his faith, heart, and mind outside himself, trusting that whatever God wrought was best for generations to come.

Like a moth to flame, however, humiliated Pharaoh defied God again. Once Moses led the Israelites away, Pharaoh led his troops to recapture them, trapping them at the Red Sea. Jammed like mice with nowhere to go, the Israelites cowered under an exultant Pharaoh, proving, in his mind, that no God existed. That's when Moses lifted a plain wooden staff, prayed to his God, and suddenly an entire ocean split itself down to the seabed. God made a way through what had been absolutely impossible. Shocked, Pharaoh held his troops back as Israel scampered away between towering walls of water. But he knew his soldiers were watching to see if he would be humiliated again. Despite astonishing supernatural power staring him in the face, Pharaoh ordered all his horsemen and chariots to pursue. They mindlessly obeyed a mad leader. As the horsemen gained on the Israelites, God closed the sea over them, drowning every soldier and horse. Pharaoh had lost his son, his slaves, his respect, and now his army. The nation of Egypt would never recover its former greatness.

And Pharaoh never touched Moses once.

Quiet Clarke Williams from little Oak Ridge got it. Arrogance loses, not in the beginning but always in the end—always—because the arrogant repel people. They wind up alone and forgotten. Clarke spent most of his life walking dark canyons between walls of debt, leading all types of people in one direction, believers, non-believers, Godly, ungodly, through stretches of impossibility. But his humble spirit attracted people, and they all helped him pull in the direction for which he privately prayed. To many, he seemed Pollyannaish, but he repeatedly proved the smart money wrong.

Like Moses, never once did Clarke entertain running for cover. If Moses could raise a simple stick and part an ocean out of faith, and if Christ could take five loaves and two fishes and feed 5,000, Clarke's humble obedience could take a simple phone company of seventy-five and turn it into three million. Had he turned back when cornered, nothing miraculous would have ever happened, many employees' families would never have been lifted out of economic bondage. Never considering how their benefactor's faith had divided and conquered adversity, Century's employees would raise children, educate them, buy houses, cars, and land, and take vacations. They might never know Clarke Williams or how God used him, but they would know a bright path had opened for them where none existed. Clarke smiled in his anonymity, glad his name was not on a building or plaque. "To God be the glory," he had often said, telling his managers the same thing Christ had told his disciples: If you wanted to be the greatest, all you had to do was be the least. Simple.

Reporters clamored for an easy truth, the "key" to his success. As a magnificent story of accomplishment, the sage of CenturyTel drew seekers out of the woodwork. The truth he shared was so simple that it was hard for nearly everyone to understand.

> Clarke McRae Williams: "Today CenturyTel is a publicly held corporation by thousands of people throughout the United States. I feel truly honored to be in the position of the chairman of the corporation. But we've got so many young people who are running the company who are doing a great job. We were written up in *The New York Times* recently who said Century is one of the best-managed small telephone companies in the United States. Well, I took a lot of pride in that, in that our people are doing it. It's not me. I learned a long time ago that I did not know what I really needed to know, so I had to try to engage people who knew what to do. If it'd been all my figuring on it, we probably wouldn't have gotten anywhere. It really belongs to other people who have brought Century to where it is. And I just have a really great pleasure in seeing the young management that we have here now. We have Glen Post as our president and he's doing a great job. As you know, for about seven years, our son Clarke Junior was the president, and he brought us along and did a great job and had us moving really well. And when he was disabled, Glen has taken over, has never missed a beat and is doing a great job. The article in *The New York Times* just makes me feel great to know that we have been recognized as a company that is doing a great job."[313]

---

[313] Clarke Williams, Sr., interview, *KNOE Special Report* with Jamie Patrick, KNOE TV8 News, ©1992 Noe Enterprises, Inc.

One of Louisiana's premiere authors and interviewers, a mentor to President Bill Clinton's campaign manager James Carville, and a legend and raconteur in his own right, Gus Weill, host of Public Broadcasting's *Louisiana Legends,* was among the last to interview Clarke. As he listened for the key to Century's monumental success, Weill was amazed by the founder's simplistic message.

> Gus Weill: *Do you feel the American Dream is still out there?*
> Clarke Williams: "Oh, yes, definitely. I feel there's an opportunity for <u>anyone</u> who wants to achieve a certain goal. You ask yourself what do you like to do? What might a young person do to get started today? If they know what they really like and concentrate on that, I don't see anything to stop them. If I had it to do all over again, I don't know of anything I could really change much. Every morning there's something new that comes up in the field of technology that makes something a little bit better, a little bit nicer and *gives you an opportunity* to have something to sell the customer that you didn't have before.
>
> *Are you still interested?*
> "Oh, yeah. I still love to see an installer putting in a telephone. Many times I'd like to be there myself.
>
> *What should a man or woman possess to be successful, to fulfill his or her dreams?*
> "I could answer that a couple of different of ways, but, first, he or she should be a person of **integrity** and **honesty**. He or she should be a person who **cares** about the person with whom they are dealing or the customer they expect to have. Not last, but maybe should've been first, is my own personal belief in the blessings that **God**

has given me, not anything I've done. I live to the best of my ability to uphold those teachings and I think that goes in business as well as the church."[314]

Despite Clarke's avoidance of praise, national recognition magnified CenturyTel's value to analysts and shareholders and, once again, made the company a target. As the century clock rolled over from 1999 to 2000, Glen's management team renewed gobbling up access lines, not in retreat from cellular but to shoot toward locking the market for broadband Internet services. The Internet had begun spreading exponentially toward the suburbs. Clarke Junior's masterful wireless campaign had made CenturyTel millions, but profit margins shrank as roaming charges died away and phones plans became cheaper. Clarke's team determined the next boom would be personal Internet access. They decided to put CenturyTel's entire wireless business up for sale and concentrate on wirelines. A just-perfected carrier technology called *fiber optics* would vastly speed up data rates by quadrupling the use of a single frequency. Internet usage would explode.

That interested Clarke, even if technology came too rapidly. He looked around the executive suite. No one in upper management had been born when he upgraded Oak Ridge Telephone with dialup. Fiber was this generation's dialup. He had lived to watch the telephone grow from novelty to necessity, from one in every sixth house to six in one house. Americans did a lot of talking now, and yet with so much communication, it seemed there less understanding. Oak Ridge had been more than a community, it had been a large family with face-to-face interaction. Now, neighbors hardly knew each other. Clarke shrugged. He had no answers for the paradox. His job was to bring people together in the hope of mutual agreement, advancement, patching things up, or merely hearing each other's voice.

---

[314] Clarke Williams, Sr. interview, *Louisiana Legends with Gus Weill*, © 1999 Louisiana Television Education Authority.

To that end, CenturyTel snatched up an additional quarter million access lines in Wisconsin to become that state's second largest provider, first purchasing from Verizon, for $195 million, 133,000 lines in 77 exchanges, then another 70,000 in 42 exchanges. Glen Post and the board also approved the $170 million purchase-partnership with Telephone USA of Wisconsin, LLC, to buy 35 more exchanges with 62,650 lines.

For a while, CenturyTel's buying spree renewed Clarke's strength as he battled failing kidneys and frequent dialysis. Then, in February 2001, he felt his body weakening again, and he asked his and Mary Kathryn's personal estate attorney, John Blackman, to draw up his final will.

> John Blackman: "Clarke Williams was a *gentle* man. How he did everything he did, I'll never know. Some leaders are able to not get down into the weeds but are good enough to study things and get an overall perspective and vision that nobody else can see. They just have this uncanny ability. Clarke was the guy who came up with the ideas and told his management, 'We're going to be here in three or four years. We're going to be doing this.' Sometimes people would raise their eyebrows and say, 'Do what?' Despite being hardworking, he was still the greatest gentleman you ever met and that stands out. People recognized they could trust him. Some would sell for a lesser price just to sell to Clarke Williams. This man was different because he always considered others first."[315]

As GTE exited landlines, CenturyLink bought GTE's Missouri operations of 127,000 access lines. But when CenturyTel next grabbed GTE's 230,500 access lines in Arkansas, pushing CenturyTel over the three-million customer

---

[315] John Blackman interview, June 25, 2014, Baton Rouge, Louisiana.

mark and making Arkansas its second largest state, it awakened a rival.

Such major dominance in Arkansas gave pause to competitor Joe T. Ford, chairman and chief executive of Little Rock's Alltel Corporation, the sixth largest wireless carrier in the United States with over six million customers. Ford and his son Scott had always been able and friendly rivals in the acquisition game. Indeed, Alltel was one of many bidding on CenturyTel's auction of its wireless operations. Apparently, Ford couldn't understand the strategy of CenturyTel's chopping off its substantial cellular system in favor of reaching back for more wireline phones. Reading CenturyTel's public financials in Securities and Exchange Commission filings, Ford saw CenturyTel's glaring $3 billion debt. To the Fords, selling new wireless systems at the dawn of a new wireless age meant one thing: CenturyTel could be in trouble.

The Fords decided CenturyTel's management appeared to have lost its way in the malaise of Clarke Junior's death and Clarke McRae's pulling back from the company. In a show of bravado, starting in summer 2001, Ford and son Scott, president of Alltel, began a relentless, hostile campaign to take over CenturyTel. They publicly insisted on meeting with Century's board essentially to demand the merger of CenturyTel into Alltel. On July 26, the board of directors considered the Fords' unwelcomed entreaties but each director knew that the Arkansans' style was perfectly opposite to that of humble Mr. Williams. If he negotiated a deal correctly, however, Clarke stood to become immensely wealthy by selling out to the Fords and finally embracing a life of ease.

Clarke Williams never even considered it.

The chairman rejected personal gain in favor of keeping Century's thousands of workers employed. He would never abandon them or Monroe or Louisiana. The board unanimously rejected Alltel's presumptuous push. Heartbreaking to Clarke most of all, Joe and Scott Ford's father-and-son life mirrored the life he had dreamed of with Clarke Junior. Clarke felt he understood Joe and was happy that he was living out the dream of having his son succeed him. But their bully approach was too much, too foreign to the way he and Clarke Junior had done business. Clarke took to his knees, not for himself, but for them.

In August, angered by Century's rejection, the Fords crushed any possibility of friendship by going around Clarke and Glen and appealing exclusively to Century's thousands of shareholders with a $6.1 billion takeover bid. The Fords offered a 40 percent premium on Century's stock price. The battle was on, pitting shareholders against the interests of employees and their families. When the Fords didn't get their way, they solicited shareholders personally and took the fight public, attacking through the press to force Clarke, Glen, and the board to accept Alltel's offer.

The New York Times headlined on August 15, 2001:

Alltel in Hostile $6.1 Billion Bid for Phone Rival

The Alltel Corporation, the large telecommunications company, made an unsolicited $6.1 billion takeover bid yesterday for CenturyTel Inc., a smaller rival that provides phone services in rural areas, suburbs, and small towns.

The hostile offer by Alltel, which would also assume $3 billion in debt, represents the company's latest move to capture more market share at a time when valuations for telecommunications companies are considerably lower than they have been in the recent past.

...The unsolicited bid for CenturyTel, based in Monroe, La., was made in a letter sent yesterday to the company's vice chairman and president, Glen F. Post, III. The offer, for either $43 a share in cash or 0.6934 of an Alltel share for each CenturyTel share, represents a 40 percent premium to CenturyTel's closing price of $30.62, which was up 15 cents. Shares of Alltel rose 51 cents, to $61.06.

... *"CenturyTel's board has determined that the company is not for sale,"* [a CenturyTel] *statement added.*

Alltel officials said that even if CenturyTel formally rejected their offer, they would continue to pursue a takeover by taking the bid directly to shareholders. In the letter to Mr. Post, Alltel's president and chief operating officer, Scott T. Ford, wrote about the benefits of the merger of the two companies and then said, "Under these circumstances, we believe that your stockholders would agree with this assessment and enthusiastically support the merger."

After noting that 7 of CenturyTel's top 10 institutional shareholders have also invested in Alltel, he added, "In light of the significance of this offer to the CenturyTel and the Alltel stockholders, we are publicly releasing the text of this letter."

Alltel hired Merrill Lynch and Stephens Inc. to advise it on the offer. Alltel is motivated to acquire CenturyTel as a way to shore up its position in the United States' telecommunications market, which has had its share of bad financial news in recent months. A combined company would have one of the largest shares of rural subscribers, with about 7.2 million wireless customers and more than $10 billion in revenue.

Taking over CenturyTel would give Alltel strong footholds in northern Louisiana, Mississippi, Michigan, and Wisconsin. Most of Alltel's business is concentrated on the Eastern Seaboard and in Kansas, Nebraska, and the Southwest. There is no overlap in the two companies' wireless businesses.

CenturyTel has not been immune to the bad financial news coming out of the sector. On Aug.

4, the company reported slightly lower second-quarter earnings, despite a 22.6 percent revenue rise, and cut its full-year revenue forecast because of continued weakness in the economy.

But some Alltel officials suggested yesterday that CenturyTel's results were a result of poor management practices. CenturyTel officials did not return calls seeking comment.

Alltel fared slightly better. Its second-quarter profits fell but met analysts' estimates as wireless revenue rose 9 percent and it added more subscribers than expected. [316]

Clarke and Glen were disheartened that *The New York Times,* which recently praised CenturyTel as one of the best managed in the country, was now letting the Fords publicly call them poor managers. They found the Fords' audacity unconscionable.

"Our management practices couldn't be very poor," Clarke told Glen of the hypocritical statement, "or the Fords wouldn't have wanted what we've built or be so insistent to buy us out. We don't want them, they want us." Clarke, Glen, and the board rejected the Fords' reprehensible tactics of pitting financial needs of shareholders against those of employees. To Clarke, the fight was another Goliath threatening David. The trouble with Goliaths, as Scripture taught, is they presume David is alone and vulnerable. Clarke knew righteous men had an invisible Protector.

> Harvey Perry: "Mr. Williams probably knew he wasn't going to live much longer and, had the company sold, he would have made several million dollars not just from the sale of stock but from a golden parachute agreement. Had we agreed to sell to Alltel—and theirs was not a bad offer—and if Mr. Williams had supported it, we

---

[316] Jayson Blair, *The New York Times,* Aug. 15, 2001.

would have sold. Frankly, all of us would have been very well off financially, but he was more concerned about our employees and consolidation. Our new [headquarters] building would've been shut down. We had 800 to 1,000 people working here. It would have had a terrible impact on Monroe, and regional offices would've shut down. I know all of that played into Mr. Williams' decision not to do it."[317]

Karen Puckett, COO: "It was unethical. They were nasty. This was the first 'bear hug' in telecommunications history. We were already in the midst of selling our wireless operations because we saw wireless margins going down [as cellphones and plans became cheaper]. We were positioning ourselves to be a broadband rural provider, but they said, 'We want all of you.' And we said, 'Well, all of us isn't for sale.' So a few days later we were presenting at an analyst meeting in San Francisco [on a roadshow that would lead to Wall Street], everything went well, and Glen and I are packing when I looked over at the television in my room because I heard 'CenturyTel' and saw Scott Ford talking about a hostile takeover of CenturyTel. It was like having an out-of-body experience. *'Did they just say a hostile takeover of CenturyTel?'* That's how we found out! I think they knew we were in San Francisco away from our employee base, and you can imagine how disruptive that was for our employees. So we were selling our wireless and had no wireline deals or replacement revenue streams on the table. Out of the sky, Verizon put up their systems for sale in Arkansas, Kentucky, and Missouri. We bid on just Arkansas and

---

[317] Harvey Perry as part of the Karen Puckett interview, Feb. 3, 2013, Monroe, Louisiana.

Missouri because Kentucky had problems, union and otherwise. Even though the Fords were consolidating wireless, Alltel bid against us for landlines. So we're in a hostile with them and they were bidding against us to make us weaker, frankly, so we wouldn't get a replacement revenue source."[318]

Harvey Perry: "Mr. Williams was sick and it was right at the end of his life. We had a meeting and he said, 'I'm not going to be here so it's your company now. But if it was me, I wouldn't merge, not with Alltel.'"[319]

Tired of the struggle, mystified at how intelligent men let money blind them, causing the betrayal of friends, Clarke felt sick having reached the end with vultures circling. He had spent a God-directed life building something beautiful, helpful, idealistic, optimistic, and life-giving, leading thousands to be their best in the most righteous ways. The Fords portrayed their actions as in the interests of shareholders, but Clarke saw through that justification. Everything Clarke acquired, he made sure to tell the sellers, *If this isn't a good deal for you, then I don't want to do it.* And he meant it. He never dreamed of trying to snatch something from an unwilling owner.

Under fire, Clarke never retaliated, never sought revenge, and instead prayed for those who made themselves enemies. Historically, all those who lined up against him suffered the curse of momentary gain but eventual loss. Through his life, Clarke had watched the slow regression of loyalty and kindness, muddled under the pressure of overwhelming money. He recognized a degrading of morals through popular media and Madison Avenue's convincing people what's right is wrong and what's wrong is right. And it seemed people were more easily

---

[318] Karen Puckett interview, Feb. 3, 2013, Monroe, Louisiana.

[319] Harvey Perry as part of the Karen Puckett interview, Feb. 3, 2013, Monroe, Louisiana.

hoodwinked than ever. Clarke's experience had been that a man who fools others mostly fools himself.

The drama continued with the Fords writing private letters to Glen Post while simultaneously giving them to the press. Further outrageous, Scott Ford hosted a conference call with analysts and investors on Wednesday, August 15, 2001, to discuss why CenturyTel should be forced to negotiate. Alltel posted the call on its website.

CenturyTel's lawyers had no choice but to call Alltel's hand: They filed suit in federal court on Friday, August 17, 2001, alleging false statements, unfair promotion of Alltel's unsolicited bid, and interference with CenturyTel's plans to auction its wireless division. The board sought injunctive relief and damages. The lawsuit gave the Fords private time to consider standing down. With no word, on Tuesday, August 21, CenturyTel notified the Securities and Exchange Commission of the Fords' "false and fraudulent" statements meant to influence both share price and to affect operations, a serious charge.

The Fords barreled ahead, releasing to the press, "Alltel would like to sit down with CenturyTel management and discuss Alltel's proposal for a friendly merger of our two companies. We think it would be much more productive to negotiate than litigate."[320] Scott Ford gathered purported comments from CenturyTel's major shareholders, sprinkling them throughout condescending letters that he continued to send, at the same time, both to the press and to Glen, often on newswires before they reached Glen's office.

> *August 27, 2001*
> *Glen Post*
> *CenturyTel, Monroe, LA*
> *Dear Glen:*
> *...Many of your largest shareholders have already publicly pointed out the merits of our bid, calling the Alltel-CenturyTel merger 'a very powerful combination' and making it clear that*

---

[320] *CNN Money*, "CenturyTel sues Alltel," Aug. 21, 2001, retrieved at http://money.cnn.com/2001/08/21/deals/centurytel/.

CenturyTel's management 'should be sitting down at the table' to talk with Alltel. Financial analysts who know and understand our industry also strongly favor Alltel's offer. They have called our proposed merger 'an excellent geographic and strategic fit,' 'an excellent match,' and 'the best course of action.' They have described the offer as 'an attractive bid' and 'quite generous.' Like us, they are confident that Alltel's offer has real value and benefits for your shareholders.

In contrast, we believe that your publicly-stated business strategy faces serious obstacles in achieving anything comparable to the value of Alltel's offer....

Your wireless business is sub-scale and, over the past eighteen months, has consistently underperformed its regional cellular peers, including Alltel... Alltel is confident that its proven management team...could improve performance...

...We continue to be mystified by your refusal to discuss our offer. Your continued refusal should raise critical questions for your shareholders:

- *Are you practicing good corporate governance by ignoring your own shareholders' suggestions that you discuss our offer with us?*
- *How and when, precisely, do you expect to create and deliver value to the CenturyTel shareholders comparable to the value of Alltel's offer today, particularly in light of the potential tax and value leakage that could result from the sale of your wireless business?*

- *How confident are you in your ability to improve your wireline business' performance and why has there been no evidence of this improvement to date?*
- *How confident are you in your ability to acquire and integrate additional wireline businesses at prices and in a manner that will enhance value for CenturyTel's shareholders?*

...We urge you to meet with us without further delay...and we would urge you to use this time productively —by negotiating rather than litigating.

Very truly yours,
Scott T. Ford[321]

Clarke shook his head. There it was again. Under the guise of "increasing shareholder value," pompous Goliath was talking down to David, as if somebody from a small town was stupid for refusing to talk to a big city know-it-all. The slicker was really a wolf, a corporate raider, hungry for the deal and publicity. Clarke had seen that personality many times before.

The Associated Press checked out Ford's claims by polling some of CenturyTel's large investors. "I don't think this letter is going to rattle CenturyTel," responded Paul Wright, a vice president of Loomis Sayles & Company that owned 621,000 shares of CTL. He added, "If Alltel would bump their per-share bid into the $50s, CenturyTel's board would be pressured."[322]

"This clearly has a battle-of-personalities feel to it," explained David Katz, chief investment officer of Matrix Asset Advisors, Inc., which owned 364,000 CTL shares. But Katz echoed that CenturyTel's board should "engage in a constructive dialogue" with Alltel.[323]

---

[321] Ford letter submitted to *Arkansas Business*, published Aug. 28, 2001, http://www.arkansasbusiness.com/article/60831/scott-ford-again-urges-centurytel-to-consider-merger; CNN Money, Aug. 28, 2001, http://money.cnn.com/2001/08/28/deals/alltel/

[322] AP-"Alltell pushes rival to begin takeover talks," *Milwaukee Journal Sentinel*, Aug. 29, 2001, p. 40.

[323] Ibid

August 28, 2001
PERSONAL AND CONFIDENTIAL
Mr. Scott T. Ford
ALLTEL Corporation, Little Rock, AR 72202
Dear Scott:
 I received your letter, which was faxed to me as you were releasing it to the press. Your letter does nothing more than urge us to reconsider the same proposal that our Board unanimously determined, after careful consideration, was not in the best interests of CenturyTel. There is no reason to reconsider that decision.
 While we also believe that your letter is clearly misleading, we have no intention of engaging in your public letter writing campaign.
 We are fully aware of our responsibilities to our shareholders and other constituencies, and we will continue to respect those obligations as we pursue our growth strategies.
     Sincerely, Glen Post[324]

The last straw came, as far as Clarke was concerned, when Scott Ford told Reuters, "We didn't meet a single shareholder, save one or two, who said it was about price. Everyone else said it was about a board in a small town."[325]

Of all the unmitigated gall. How arrogant. Scott Ford could not accept that the founder of a great company might be a hayseed from Oak Ridge and the president from Farmerville, two of the smallest towns in America. But Ford also unwittingly had called the vast majority of his own customers "small town" hicks. Almost all Americans can trace their roots to a small town and are sensitive to putdowns by the high-and-mighty. Arkansas

---

[324] Glen Post letter faxed to Scott Ford and released by CenturyTel, Aug. 29, 2001.
[325] (Reuters) Tom Johnson, "Alltel Renews Pressure on CenturyTel," *BBC Enorth*, Aug. 29, 2001,
http://english.enorth.com.cn/system/2001/08/29/000128192.shtml.

is a state of communities, beautiful, quaint, and full of hard working citizens who, if they read Ford's comments, must have cringed in righteous anger.

Jeffry Bartash opined for CBS.Marketwatch.com in Washington:

> "All [Alltel has] done so far is alienate CenturyTel executives who've accused Alltel of improperly disclosing sensitive information and using the media to browbeat them into merger discussions. A wall of anti-takeover provisions protects CenturyTel and much of its voting stock is concentrated in the hands of employees or longtime shareholders. The company's board, meanwhile, doesn't have to discuss the offer until its next meeting in 2002. Unless Little Rock, Ark.-based Alltel sharply boosts its initial offer—about $43 a share—few analysts expect CenturyTel to reconsider."[326]

Bartash was right, but before anyone could escalate the three-week war of words, an epic disaster silenced both sides. On Tuesday, September 11, 2001, two jetliners plowed into the World Trade Center in Manhattan, a third jet exploded into the Pentagon, and a fourth dove into the ground near Shanksville, Pennsylvania. Three thousand innocent people were killed. All commerce, trading, delivery systems, airlines, and normal living virtually halted for days as millions worldwide watched television, trying to make sense out of why nineteen brainwashed Al-Qaeda terrorists had killed so many.

Clarke froze as he watched both towers telescope into a heap of dust. He visualized those scampering down a hundred flights trying to get to safety, passing doomed firefighters on the way up. The morning had started with a clear blue sky, a tinge of fall in the air. Then without warning....

---

[326] Jeffry Bartash, "CenturyTel ignores Alltel plea for talks," *CBS Marketwatch*, Aug. 28, 2001,
http://www.marketwatch.com/story/centurytel-ignores-alltel-plea-for-talks.

Clarke prayed for them, their families, and even their killers. He was not the least bit surprised at how Satan operated, filling simple minds with jealously and hate, then attacking the innocent. It mattered not whether a person believed in God or evil or nothing at all; the World Trade Center's destruction was real. He felt much as he had on that ill-fated Sunday afternoon before Christmas 1941, that day when over 3,600 young Americans were killed or wounded at Pearl Harbor, a paradise turned into a flaming hell. But, as Japanese leaders soon discovered, they had awakened a sleeping giant.

Back then, Clarke had felt uncomfortable matching hate for hate, and sixty years later he still felt uncomfortable with the evil of war. He had seen too much of Man angry with others, with governments, with fathers, with religions, and all of the anger boiled down to one common denominator: Man was inherently angry with himself. Failures and shortcomings were the bane of existence, and everyone had them. But Christ had taught Clarke that those perceptions were mirages kept alive by self-doubt, a waste of energy that short-circuited potential. In short, Clarke never dwelled on failures because those who did ultimately blamed everyone else.

He knew that, studied it, learned it, and taught it. The difference by 9-11 was that his body was failing. He now faced the ultimate betrayal, locked in a 79-year-old body racked with pain and a barely operable renal system. Some days he thought it almost preferable to die suddenly like those on 9-11 rather than to live the lingering death of old age. Yet he never complained, only forewarning others what to anticipate.

> Clarke McRae Williams: "I don't always achieve what I'd like to do but I try to live so that if this is my last day on earth, my salvation will be secure with the Lord."[327]

> Carolyn Williams Perry: "Starting sometime in 2000, Daddy was weakening and he came to our

---

[327] Jennie Jo Siscoe, "Homefolks," *Richland Journal*, Rayville, Louisiana, April 9, 1984, p. 2A.

house on Deborah Drive. We had to take a blanket to him because he was so cold. He said, 'My kidney is failing.' He wound up having to go to dialysis every other day."[328]

His condition worsened, forcing him to stop going to the office. He called Glen for updates. All the sadness of 9-11, the funerals, the bagpipes, the memorials, reminded everyone of life's hourly value. He was proud that Louisiana gave the first new fire truck to New York City that Christmas. But by Spring 2002, with green leaves and blossoms, it was time to get on with life. Clarke wished he could get up. Bedridden, on February 6, he welcomed the Williams clan on the occasion of his 80th birthday, reminded he shared the birthday with President Ronald Reagan.

> Carolyn Williams Perry: "We all went over, including Aunt Mary Lee and Uncle Bill, and sat around his bed letting him open each card and gift. He was happy but somber. He was taking dialysis three times a week and he practically had no energy or strength. He had willed himself that strength early in dialysis so he could go to the office for a few hours, but he finally just stopped going altogether. Mike Simmons, who also worked for CenturyLink in the mailroom, would come to Mother and Daddy's around 5:00 a.m. three times a week to drive Daddy to dialysis. He was very faithful to Daddy and we appreciated it."[329]

> "When Daddy told me he did not have long to live, he called me and my sister into his room and said, 'I don't have much longer to live and your mom and I are fine with it. But I want you girls

---

[328] Carolyn Williams Perry as part of Veretta Heckard interview, Jan. 30, 2013, Monroe, Louisiana.
[329] Carolyn Williams Perry email to author, March 25, 2014.

to be fine with it.' And of course, I was not. I told him, 'No, I was not going to do that.' And he said, 'Carolyn, now when I tell you something, you have always believed it. And I want you to believe this.' I said, 'Now, that's not right and we're going to take care of this.' He looked at me and said, 'Now Carolyn, have I ever told you anything that was not true?' I said, 'No sir.' He said, 'You and your sister need to go pray about this. Because like I said, for your mother and me, it is fine.'

"He always said, 'When I do die, it is a win-win situation. If I don't die, I'm here with y'all and if I do die, I'm with my Lord.' So he said, 'You need to think about that. And whenever you keep thinking you cannot live without me, you need to think about that.'"[330]

Absolutely no one wanted to think about that. They were encouraged when he was upright and walking. A month later, the Fords finally conceded warfare wasn't worth it. After Mario Gabelli, CenturyTel directors had already placed much of the voting strength with employees so the Fords had no choice but to give up. They wound up the high bidders for CenturyTel's wireless operations. On March 19, 2002, the board approved selling the wireless division to Alltel for $1.65 Billion. It was the last vote Clarke Williams would cast. Joe Ford would soon call to apologize.

Glen Post: "I really don't think the Fords understood how sick Mr. Williams really was. Joe Ford called me and apologized. He said he didn't know he was gravely ill and if he had he would not have moved forward with their takeover process. Although he was known to be

---

[330] Carolyn Williams Perry as part of Veretta Heckard interview, Jan. 30, 2013, Monroe, Louisiana.

a pretty ruthless man in business, I think he was sincere."[331]

Five days later at North Monroe Hospital, one mile from CenturyTel headquarters, CenturyTel Chief Operating Officer Karen Puckett gave birth to a son, Kyle, prematurely, on March 24. She had kept her pregnancy hidden through the Alltel battle for fear management would lose focus worrying about her. Perhaps the stress had taken its toll, so she stayed close to the hospital nursery with Kyle. He would soon have a neighbor.

> Carolyn Williams Perry: "I dropped by at the house in Oak Ridge to see how Daddy was feeling and Mother met me at the door frightened and said Daddy was losing blood and needed to see Dr. David Raines. She was exhausted. David said he needed to be hospitalized immediately to stop the bleeding. The next day we were told he needed surgery to survive and that he might not make it, even with surgery."[332]

Doctors with grim faces assured Clarke that he needed surgery even this late in the game. He called Glen. It was the day Glen had been dreading for a long time. Mr. Williams wanted Glen to bring the papers to his bedside so that he could relinquish chairmanship of CenturyTel and sign over all power to the young president. "I may not make it out of surgery," the old man said. Glen brought over the papers, Clarke scribbled blue ink across a few lines, and with less than one penny's worth of ink, the keys to a $4 billion and growing company transferred. Clarke McRae Williams no longer controlled his life's work. After 56 years, it was over. Mary Kathryn softly wept. Clarke's gray eyes looked into Glen's and both felt the load shift. Clarke was relieved that Century would outlive him.

---

[331] Glen Post email to author, June 24, 2014.
[332] Carolyn Williams Perry email to author, March 25, 2014.

> Jonathan Michael Perry: "The nurse came in and told Granddaddy, 'Okay, Mr. Williams, we need your jewelry.' He said, 'Don't have any.' She said, 'What do you call that wedding ring?' Granddaddy said, 'You're not taking my wedding ring off. You can cut it off if something goes wrong or you can let my finger fall off, but I'm not taking this ring off and giving it to you.'"[333]

Longtime family friend Dr. Larry Barr performed the surgery without a hitch. Clarke spent one night in the Intensive Care Unit on a ventilator but was strong enough by noon the next day to be taken off. "I have my Clarke back," Mary Kathryn said. Back for how long, Clarke thought, was anybody's guess, but privately he was content to lay down the old clay temple formed by the Sculptor in 1922. He was confident the spirit that powered the clay had been used for good.

Clarke had served on the board of North Monroe Hospital for years and now was his own customer, as was Kyle Puckett. Karen was thankful. "I'd see Kyle, then swing around and see Mr. Williams, because he was there for quite some time."[334] Clarke was less than a mile from his office, an office now quiet and still, phone messages on the desk never to be returned.

God's choreography was not lost on Clarke as Karen bounced between a new life and an old warrior, one entering the game, the other exiting. Clarke didn't mind. The exit was only a portal to the next game. Like the Apostle Paul, he had run the good race, he had fought the good fight. And he still had a sense of humor.

> Jonathan Michael Perry: "Granddaddy was in ICU and Trey and I were visiting when the nurse came in and said to Granddaddy, 'Your wife brought you some new pajamas.' When she offered to help him change into his pajamas,

---

[333] Jonathan Michael Perry interview, Jan. 29, 2013, Monroe, Louisiana.
[334] Karen Puckett interview, Feb. 3, 2013, Monroe, Louisiana.

Granddaddy said, 'There's no need for you to have to do that. I've got two strapping grandsons that can change my pajamas.' Trey and I freaked out. He looked at us and said, 'What's wrong with you boys? Get to shucking!' He would ask me, 'How's school going? Are you struggling with anything?' I told him I was having a hard time with economics. 'Son,' he said, 'economics is the easiest thing you can learn. Go to the store, get a brand new red apple for five cents, shine it up to be the best looking apple you've ever seen and sell it for 25 cents. That, son, is simple economics.'"[335]

Winding down like a grandfather clock didn't prevent Clarke from catching opportunities to improve the lives of others. When his cheerful nurse bounced around the room checking IVs, resetting machines, and checking Clarke's heart rate, blood pressure, and medicine, he interviewed her. He found that she had four children at home and had to drop out of her college nursing program to hold down enough jobs to stay afloat.

"How serious are you about nursing?" he asked.

"It's what I've always wanted to do," she replied, smiling but never missing a beat as she fluffed his pillow and smoothed the sheets. Clarke thought a moment because he knew she probably wouldn't believe him but he blurted anyway, "Then, I'm going to put you through school. I mean it. It will all be paid for. Go enroll."[336]

Shocked, she began crying tears of joy. Something in his voice and in his spirit told her this man would not let her down. He would do exactly what he said. She hugged him and left in a dither. He could hear shouts and laughter reverberate down the hall.

---

[335] Jonathan Michael Perry interview, Jan. 29, 2013, Monroe, Louisiana.
[336] Carolyn Williams Perry recount as part of Jonathan Perry interview, Jan. 29, 2013, Monroe, Louisiana.

Carolyn Williams Perry: "Mother stayed at my house and we sat with Daddy for the next seven weeks, right by his side, and watched him gradually decline. *Through all of this he was never mad, ungrateful, or unappreciative.* He would tell every nurse, every doctor, 'Thank you,' when they would leave the room. Toward the end, he kept saying he just wanted to go home. I just thought he was talking about Oak Ridge. I realized he was referring to Heaven. The last words I said to him were to rest well, have a good night, that I loved him and would do my best to be able to take him home. The morning of June 5, we got up to get ready to leave for the hospital when the phone rang...."[337]

Clarke McRae Williams, son of parents who met on the phone, climber of poles, bicycler of bills, mechanic of B-25s, acquirer of purpose, and lover of all people, enjoyed the kaleidoscope of his life not for accomplishments but for how those successes created opportunities for others. He remembered his dad's weatherbeaten face and his mother's weeping when they had nothing to eat and his sadness for her. In this way, he was part of all families.

He remembered a 16-year-old girl, high-spirited and confident in her red lipstick and in love with the lanky boy who had a telephone company. She had cast her lot with his, answering calls at all hours, depending solely on his faith in himself. He remembered a baby boy born in Shreveport because that's where they happened to be and that boy's development from little cowboy boots to standing tall on Wall Street. The son saw things the father never dreamed, a world of no wires tacked on barns and fence posts.

He remembered two little girls, giggles and curls and falling asleep in his lap, carried on his shoulders through cold rain and

---

[337] Carolyn Williams Perry email to author, March 25, 2014.

hot summers. Everything had its seasons. Nothing stayed the same and wistful came the memories. But change brought growth, he knew that, believed that, taught that, because growth was life. He knew beyond a shadow of a doubt that the irrepressible race of time on this Earth would give way to the new world where the more time a soul had, the more time a soul would have.

Clarke McRae Williams had no qualms about passing through seasons, and as twilight approached he saw the horizon clearly. He knew many people there, people he had heard all his life, faceless voices on wires but as friendly and helpful as could be. Everyone was on a journey, mostly alone, and he thanked his God for walking with him, showing him the way when the way was cloudy. And it was always cloudy.

The spontaneity in life, the not knowing, the unseen, the murky vision, the uncharted territory, the fears had strengthened his faith. He knew now that *is* life. His parents found each other across a wire and now he existed and his children existed and his grandchildren existed. He realized that he, his entire family, his descendants and all the families of CenturyTel, owed their lives to the simple human need to communicate, to share, to not be alone.

At daybreak, the moment a sunbeam streaked from the east, light streamed into Clarke's room in increasing intensity until everything seemed white. He felt himself relax just as he had as a child falling asleep in Marie's arms, completely and wonderfully, embracing all remembrance of laughter, delight, friends, Mary Kathryn, and the little faces of Clarke Junior, Annette, and Carolyn. He remembered how they had frolicked so carefree and happy, knowing more as children about living than any adult ever would. He would see them again on a green hill under an azure sky.

He felt his hands release.

The next sound came with the rustle of angels' wings as one of his favorite refrains echoed softly:

Turn your eyes upon Jesus
Look full in his wonderful face.

And the things of Earth
Will grow strangely dim.
In the light of his
Glory and grace.

E P I L O G U E

Surely goodness and mercy shall follow me all the days of my life
and I shall dwell in the House of the Lord forever.
Psalms 23:6

Clarke McRae Williams believed in the Light. He believed in eternity in the sense that it was a real place where souls who knew each other would live as they had in the physical world, would talk, share, love, and praise the Heavenly Father in music and euphoria unknown on Earth. He believed in the Next World and knew his race on the ground led to and prepared him for the Next Chapter, one that would forever be free of pain.

Clarke McRae Williams believed that death in the sense of physical death was merely a threshold to the Next Chapter. Everything physical, he knew, would pass like dust in the wind. When he looked into the eyes of the young men and women in the office, many of whom he handpicked, he saw their lives, their dreams, their families, their children, and their futures. In both a spiritual and a physical sense, he knew his life threaded through theirs and he would in some small way live through them forever.

Clarke McRae Williams, son of Oak Ridge, Monroe, Iuka, and Mertzon, had spread his wings across a nation, first out of necessity, then out of a sense of obligation to his fellow Man. He felt a deep thankfulness for first having listened intently to what others ignored and for then acting on guidance others never saw. He let God lead.

If anything baffled the young man from Oak Ridge, it was why others never took the time to find answers so readily available to them. He had figured out early that the world dealt in physical pleasures and that those pleasures deceived even the most intelligent. No one knew it all and everyone shared the same temptations of ease with little thought to things spiritual. Life would have been comical had it not been so tragic in its repetition of the same mistakes, mistakes no amount of money could overcome. F. Scott Fitzgerald had been right.

And so we beat on, boats against the current,
borne back ceaselessly into the past.

Except for Clarke McRae Williams. He was the lone standout, the trailblazer, the ultimate friend.

He had learned the secret of self-denial. If Moses parted the Red Sea, so could he. He had plugged into a supernatural power by the simplest means: He prayed. Then he listened.

The great juggernaut from the mind of Clarke Williams became a real force in the real world. His dream had transformed into such a game changer for so many millions that five months after he died, *Business Week* ranked CenturyTel as America's top United States-based telecommunications company and Number 16 out of the world's top 100 information technology companies. The *Business Week* criteria included revenues, sales growth, profitability, and stock appreciation. The business that Clarke McRae Williams had created came out on the very top.

Glen Post replaced Mr. Williams as Chairman of the Board, presiding over a boardroom entirely configured by the founder. As Clarke McRae had ingeniously replicated himself through each life, nearly all of the members spoke as if he were still in the room. Following the Williams blueprint came relatively easy. Each personality acted with the same humility of Mr. Williams, weighing each decision thoughtfully for what it would mean to all concerned. No hostile takeovers, zero-sum games, bickering, or infighting would ever occur. The great ship would sail ponderously through still waters and leave the drama to others.

As the Post regime began in totality, CenturyTel returned to its roots as one of the nation's leading pure-play rural local exchange carriers. If anything, Glen Post accelerated the acquisition tempo of his mentor, starting with the buyout in Alabama of Verizon's 300,000 access lines. Post and company would let others battle it out for wireless networks, where margins were dropping, while CenturyTel would quietly build Internet networks and server farms. Post quickly absorbed more

Verizon access lines—another 354,000—in Missouri, upping CenturyTel's national total to 2.5 million across 22 states.

To move digital information faster over expanding bandwidths, the board aggressively sought fiber optic networks. In June 2003, Century bought Digital Teleport, a 5,700-mile fiber network covering Missouri, Arkansas, Illinois, Iowa, Kansas, Texas, Nebraska, Oklahoma, and Tennessee. That December, Level 3 Communications sold to CenturyTel the Midwest Fiber Optic Network, the backbone of a number of carriers including CenturyTel across Arkansas, Missouri, and Illinois.

With cash flows significantly improved, in 2004 the board increased equity values with a $400-million buyback of CenturyTel shares and bought another $13 million shares in 2005. In June, with the buyout of KMC Telecom Holdings, Century again extended its fiber optic network across sixteen markets in eleven states from Wisconsin to Ohio to Alabama, Texas, and Kansas. In 2007, CenturyTel absorbed Madison River Communications, another 165,000 access lines and a 2,400-mile fiber network in Georgia and North Carolina. When the momentum seemed it could be no better, an opportunity suddenly appeared that overshadowed all previous acquisitions combined.

In 1899, Cleyson Brown had formed Brown Telephone Company in Abilene, Kansas, tracking much the same life as Will Clarke, Clarke McRae, and Clarke Junior, that is, acquiring to expand and survive. By 1991, the world knew Brown's company as Sprint. In December 2004, Sprint merged with cellphone network provider Nextel, spinning off the landline Local Telecommunications Division. The new company on May 17, 2006, launched on the New York Stock Exchange as "Embarq Corporation," serving eighteen states from Nevada to Florida and North Carolina to Ohio.

Serving as Embarq's president was a career military man who had served as President Bill Clinton's vice chairman of the Joints Chiefs of Staff. Admiral William A. Owens had honed his leadership skills watching the Soviets from aboard nuclear submarines moving silently beneath the North Pole. His crews stayed on the edge, prepared at any moment for nuclear warfare. In 1990, Owens commanded the U.S. Sixth Fleet alongside General Norman Schwarzkopf during Operation Desert Storm, then served as advisor to Secretary of Defense and future vice president Dick Cheney.

By the time Admiral Owens rose to the Joint Chiefs at the Pentagon, however, he knew that with the demise of the Soviet Union, the Cold War was over. He urged his colleagues from the Navy, Army, Air Force, and Marines to end tug-of-war battles over billions of taxpayer dollars. Owens himself saved millions by voluntarily slashing his own submarine force by nearly half from 120 to 70. Adamant that turf battles were crippling the U.S. military and putting American soldiers in peril unnecessarily, he published his findings in an alarming book, *Lifting the Fog of War*.

Owens retired from the military and focused in the private sector on information-sharing and telecommunications companies. In 2000, as CEO of Nortel Corporation, a vendor of CenturyTel, Owens met Clarke Williams as Mr. Williams privately battled failing health.

> Admiral Bill Owens: "I had been around the world a lot and when you met Clarke Williams, it was a memorable time because you knew this was a man of substance and he was a gentleman. He was businesslike, pleasant, welcoming, and I immediately found that my relationship with him was quick and certain in a way that rarely happens."[338]

By 2008, Owens took the helm of Embarq as CEO. The two-year-old landline company was struggling. Owens recognized that Embarq either needed to acquire expertise or be acquired.

---

[338] Admiral William Owens video interview, May 28, 2014, CenturyLink headquarters, Monroe, Louisiana

Admiral Bill Owens: "Embarq was about a $7 billion company and CenturyTel was a $2 billion company at the time. We knew we needed to find strong leadership. Embarq had been the stepchild of Sprint for a long time and Embarq leadership had been good but had been uninspired and forgotten about inside Sprint. There was a lot of discussion about whether CenturyTel would be able to do it. Would they be able to run a $10 billion-a-year business? Will they be able to understand it and will we be able to do this as an integrated company? And we shareholders were now entrusting those shares and a huge amount of money to this little group, this little management team in Monroe, Louisiana. Where is Monroe? The big part of that discussion was my recollection of Clarke Williams and the knowledge of what the management team was at Century. It was more than just the dollars and cents. It was an agreement that we were going to pass ourselves over to the Clarke Williams management team lead by Glen Post."[339]

In October 2008, CenturyTel agreed to acquire Embarq Corporation for approximately $5.8 billion in stock, roughly three times the business worth of CenturyTel at the time based on the October 24, 2008, closing price of CenturyTel's common stock. Post and board also agreed to assume Embarq's approximately $5.8 billion of debt. They consummated the deal the following July in a tax-free, stock-for-stock transaction.

Admiral Owens joined forces with Glen Post in leading a merger that created one of the largest telecommunications companies in the United States. The board decided that Century's newest evolution required a new name as well, and *CenturyLink* launched July 1, 2009, with Post as President and CEO and Admiral Owens as Chairman of the Board.

[339] Admiral William Owens video interview, May 28, 2014, CenturyLink headquarters, Monroe, Louisiana

CenturyLink was now the largest independent telecommunications provider in the United States and the fourth largest landline telecom.

> Admiral Bill Owens: "What you rarely find and what you always seek is a culture and a sustenance of business that goes beyond profit and loss. What is it that really matters? In a lot of ways, the 40,000 employees of this great company meet Clarke Williams through the continuance of a management team that was nurtured by him and I think they don't even know how much they have been affected by this great guy who came along, founded a telecom business, and made it something more than just a business. The companies that don't have culture have no idea what it is and the companies that do have culture sometimes take it for granted. Beyond loving the man, we should do everything we can to nurture the culture of him taking turkeys to people in the local community at Thanksgiving who are not well-to-do. It's about the smiles and the way he treated the people at CenturyLink and the fairness in business that he represented that went beyond, 'What's it going to do to my numbers this quarter? What's it going to do to my business in the long run?' He was about the long run. He was about being a good man in the long run and built a great team around him that was about a business that was for the long run."[340]

Coming over from Embarq to serve on the CenturyLink board with Admiral Owens was former veteran Congressman and two-time presidential candidate Richard Gephardt. Gephardt, like Owens, had met Clarke Williams only once. In

---

[340] Admiral William Owens video interview, May 28, 2014, CenturyLink headquarters, Monroe, Louisiana

Gephardt's run for the Democratic presidential nomination in 1988, Clarke and Mary Kathryn Williams joined Gephardt at a reception in Baton Rouge. Though the congressman met thousands along the campaign trail, self-effacing Clarke Williams made an indelible mark.

> Richard Gephardt: "I remember he was a really respected business leader in Louisiana and the south, one who achieved tremendous things from a standing start. He was a self-made person and Century was a self-made company. What's always fascinated me about our country is we have people like that who make something out of nothing. They're just entrepreneurs and take risks and get out on the perimeter and make things happen in technologies that are brand-new and nobody knows much about. That kind of risk-taking and entrepreneurship is really the secret to America. We are the land of opportunity but it takes people like Clarke Williams to create that opportunity."[341]

The combination of Post, Owens, Gephardt, and the handpicked board of Clarke Williams blazed ahead like David tackling Goliath. Another impossible opportunity had presented itself, this one bringing full circle the good-natured scoffing Mr. Williams had endured from Bell Telephone managers a half century earlier.

On April 22, 2010, the company agreed to acquire Ma Bell's western "Baby Bell" located in Denver, Colorado. "Qwest" had been the gigantic merger of U.S. West and Southern Pacific Telecom, and on April 1, 2011, CenturyLink pleasantly surprised Wall Street by acquiring Qwest in a tax-free, stock-for-stock transaction. The little Louisiana phone company that had struggled for decades in the shadow of giant Bell had absorbed a large piece of the giant.

---

[341] Richard Gephardt video interview, May 28, 2014, CenturyLink headquarters, Monroe, Louisiana

Post and company were on a roll. Ninety days later, on July 15, CenturyLink gobbled up Savvis, Incorporated, a global leader in the newly-coined "cloud" infrastructure and "hosted IT solutions." Cloud computing, the sharing of resources similar to sharing electricity on the grid of a utility company, was in its infancy. Savvis made CenturyLink an instant global player in an exploding market, allowing the company to accelerate managed hosting and cloud services to business customers.

The acquisitions of Embarq, Qwest, and Savvis in only two years made CenturyLink a national, industry-leading telecommunications leader providing broadband, voice, and wireless services to business and consumers nationwide. The multiplied company further created entertainment services under the CenturyLink©, Prism™ TV, and DIRECTV brands. With an advanced fiber optic network linking several data centers, CenturyLink sped information, voice, and managed services to government as well as business. The company crossed the ocean for the first time.

Pro-forma combined revenues in 2011 topped $18 billion. With a 210,000-route-mile fiber network, a burgeoning customer base, and nearly 50,000 employees, based solely on access lines CenturyLink became the third largest telecommunications provider, now behind only AT&T and Verizon.

In 2013, CenturyLink acquired AppFog, Incorporated, and Tier 3, Incorporated, to enhance its platform-as-a-service and infrastructure-as-a-service offerings. AppFog provided a reliable, scalable, and fast platform for developing proprietary applications, "apps," in the cloud. Tier 3 provided a public, multi-tenant cloud platform with a roadmap for development already in place. With the Tier 3 acquisition, CenturyLink opened its Cloud Development Center in the shadow of Microsoft Corporation in Seattle. Despite the huge presence of Microsoft, CenturyLink clinched the naming rights of the Seattle Seahawks' home stadium.

Back in Louisiana on March 4, 2013, Glen Post, Louisiana Governor Bobby Jindal, Monroe Mayor Jamie Mayo, and Ouachita Parish Police Jury Vice President Walt Caldwell broke ground for a 250,000-square foot expansion of CenturyLink headquarters. The new $50-million "Technology Center of Excellence" promised to create a new Silicon Valley in north Louisiana, pushing Century's annual payroll over $200 million by 2016. The brainchild of Clarke McRae Williams was now Louisiana's largest private employer.

Glen Post and the board proposed to teach excellence beyond technology, software, hardware, apps, and program development. They wanted to teach beyond the balance sheet into the largely uncharted territory of leadership training, which they saw as more significant for a business than its numbers. They recognized that in a world of corporate raiders, bottom lines, and shareholder pressure, clinging to the simple truths of Clarke Williams would be difficult.

> Admiral Bill Owens: "You look at the great business schools today—Stanford, Harvard, Wharton, and China's Cheung Kong Graduate School of Business—and you find that there is no effort, no classes, no discussions in general about the culture of a great man or building a culture. We talk about building brands, we talk about building marketing schemes, how you financially engineer a company, about business failures and the lessons we learn from those case studies, but there are no classes about what good leadership means because many companies don't have a great person around which to celebrate."[342]

> Richard Gephardt: "Business schools teach finance, marketing, accounting, all the things you need to know but they don't spend any time on human leadership. The best characteristic of a great leader is someone who reaches out to their colleagues, their employees and really engages them to help them make the company a success.

---

[342] Admiral William Owens video interview, May 28, 2014, CenturyLink headquarters, Monroe, Louisiana

A bad leader is one who thinks they have all the answers. They know everything about everything and they don't want to hear from anybody else. They want to tell people what to do and how to do it and then check to see that they did it. That's a bad leader. A good leader like Clarke Williams is someone who goes out to his or her employees and says, 'I don't know how to do this. You're doing it everyday. How do we improve it? Give me ideas, help me help us make this company a success.' And when you do that, people will walk through walls for you."[343]

Clarke McRae Williams would have been proud. Finally, people were beginning to see that the Golden Rule works.

Richard Gephardt: "I would argue that the only way to survive in today's cutthroat world—in my view, I think in Clarke Williams' view and in Glen Post's view—is that the best way to earn a good profit is to treat everybody, all of your stakeholders, in the right way, the way you would like to be treated. If you do that, nine times out of ten you get a tremendous positive reaction from all those stakeholders whether they're customers or whether they're your employees. When you think about it, a company is not just the CEO and top leaders, it's every employee you have out there in the country and you've got to count on them to treat the customers right. If you don't treat them right, they're not going to treat the customers right. Then you don't have a successful company. If you run a company in a cutthroat fashion where everybody is kicked in the head and treated poorly, you're going to have an unsuccessful company at the end of the day.

---

[343] Richard Gephardt video interview, May 28, 2014, CenturyLink headquarters, Monroe, Louisiana

That's what Clarke Williams understood and the Golden Rule is what has persisted in the culture of this company since the day he started it."[344]

In the summer of 2014, the nation's top independent telephone conference, the Independent Telecommunications Pioneer Association, inducted Clarke McRae Williams into the Independent Telephone Hall of Fame, honoring him as a pioneer for having withstood the continual start-up pressures in the same arena with giant AT&T. I.T.P.A. engraved his plaque:

It was Williams' vision and leadership as president, CEO and later chairman of the board—combined with the seven Unifying Principles he instituted as the company's foundation (Fairness, Honesty and Integrity, Commitment to Excellence, Positive Attitude, Respect, Faith, and Perseverance)—which propelled the company's growth to its current status.

Memories and condolences flooded CenturyTel headquarters after Mr. Williams died in 2002. Many felt they had lost a brother, a mentor, a guiding torch, and all felt they had lost a kind and gentle friend. Humble and quiet, as it turned out, had won the race. And even in death, Clarke Williams continued to inspire others. Friend of the family and employee Mike Gibbens sat down and penned a poetic tribute.

THE FINAL POLE
A Tribute to the Life of Clarke M. Williams

At last, the lineman puts down his belt
First the father, now the son.
For there are no more poles to climb
The Lord came by and said, "Well Done."

We see his life as an open book
Standards set for all to see.

---

[344] Richard Gephardt video interview, May 28, 2014, CenturyLink headquarters, Monroe, Louisiana

Someone will carry his banner again
His vision lives for you and me.

A gracious man, this worthy soul
Brought honor to our company's name.
His Unifying Principles shaped our lives
We'll always try to do the same.

We gather 'round this fallen man
His goals shall forever be,
The vision that makes our every day
A step toward the victory.

For there are many poles to climb
In the rolling fields on Heaven's shore.
Someday, I'm sure you'll find him there
Tirelessly climbing, just as before.

In one of his last public appearances, Clarke McRae Williams looked out across the new sun-filled atrium of Century's mammoth red granite headquarters. For three flights of stairs up and on every balcony, hundreds of smiling employees stood shoulder-to-shoulder in rapt attention to honor the man who had created their livelihoods out of nothing. What they couldn't see was the great physical pain he was suffering. His renal system was shutting down, and he felt the vigor of life ebbing away for a final time. Now he drew energy from the multitude of smiles looking back at him.

> *Many times I have been asked, "Did you have this 'vision' that you would have this particular company or think the company would grow to this size?" I can tell you as I told them, "Never in my wildest dreams did I think we would have a company of this size." And one million customers, I never thought of that at all. The full impact of having a million customers hit me today. Back in 1930, we think we had 75*

customers—we might have had to count some twice every once in a while to get 75.

My father gave me Oak Ridge Telephone Company because he sent my two sisters, Kittie and Mary Lee, off to LSU and educated them and he could not do that for me so he just gave me that little telephone company, which I appreciate deeply. [Thunderous laughter]

In 1953, we decided that we really had to get larger in this business and we heard about an R.E.A. [Rural Electric Authority] *telephone lending program so I applied for it. It was supposed to help the small telephone companies who wanted to expand to improve their service. All you had to do was just make a loan through R.E.A. and they would send you the money. Well, I made a loan and a fellow from Little Rock, Arkansas, drove down to see me and said, "Fellow, I tell you, you are a small telephone company with only 270 customers. You're so small we cannot even lend you money. You have to have about 500 customers to make a loan." Well, that set me off. I felt like I needed to do that so I had to scatter around kind of like a chicken has to get outside the fence every once in a while to scratch for a living. I had to find another couple- or three-hundred customers so we could even make a loan.*

By 1967, we had grown to 9,300 "stations." We counted telephones in those days as stations. If you had three telephones, that was three stations, so even though we might have had a thousand stations, we only had 700 customers really. But in 1967, we decided we would go to the telephone convention in Las Vegas with these 9,000 stations and this little book we prepared, "Central Telephone and Electronics Corporation." *And we put the word "prospectus"* *on it. We didn't even know what prospectus meant but it sounded good! So we put prospectus on it and we met a big fellow out there with Kidder-Peabody. He was very kind to give us an audience and to look through our book. When he saw that we had 9,000 stations and had revenues of $863,000, he said, "Well, y'all have really done well but when you get up to about 25 to 30,000 stations, come talk to us and maybe we can do something for you." So we figured we had to make another step. To make a long story short, we have continued to try to grow and to improve the service that we had and to continue in the growth in the field of telephony.*

My main point in speaking this morning is to say this happened only because of these people you see around the balcony and throughout the auditorium here today. People like them throughout the Century system, they have made this company what it is. Without them, we just would not be where we are. They are a dedicated, loyal, loving group of people. They are community-minded. I wish you could see them during the Christmas season and at other times of the year the charitable works that they do for the community, for the families that they help. I am overwhelmed with the quality of people that Century has. It is just my great pleasure to be here, and as Ernie Butler said a while ago, "A million customers just blows my mind!" It blows my mind, too.

I want to thank all of you. You deserve the credit and I want to give you a hand.

With resounding applause, Clarke McRae Williams bowed from the stage, fading forever from Century Telephone. But his unmistakable presence remains.

If friendships are the measure of a man, no one could count all the ones he nurtured. If accomplishments are the measure, he proved that without even making it a goal. But if, however, character is the true measure of a man, Clarke McRae Williams walked beyond the sunset with the dignity reserved for a true child of God.

I want to thank all of you.
You deserve the credit.

INDEX

N